D1564234

THE NEW MIDDLE AGES

BONNIE WHEELER, *Series Editor*

The New Middle Ages is a series dedicated to transdisciplinary studies of medieval cultures, with particular emphasis on recuperating women's history and on feminist and gender analyses. This peer-reviewed series includes both scholarly monographs and essay collections.

PUBLISHED BY PALGRAVE:

Encountering Medieval Textiles and Dress: Objects, Texts, Images
edited by Désirée G. Koslin and Janet Snyder

Eleanor of Aquitaine: Lord and Lady
edited by Bonnie Wheeler and John Carmi Parsons

Isabel La Católica, Queen of Castile: Critical Essays
edited by David A. Boruchoff

Homoeroticism and Chivalry: Discourses of Male Same-Sex Desire in the Fourteenth Century
by Richard Zeikowitz

Portraits of Medieval Women: Family, Marriage, and Politics in England 1225–1350
by Linda E. Mitchell

Eloquent Virgins: From Thecla to Joan of Arc
by Maud Burnett McInerney

The Persistence of Medievalism: Narrative Adventures in Contemporary Culture
by Angela Jane Weisl

Capetian Women
edited by Kathleen Nolan

Joan of Arc and Spirituality
edited by Ann W. Astell and Bonnie Wheeler

The Texture of Society: Medieval Women in the Southern Low Countries
edited by Ellen E. Kittell and Mary A. Suydam

Charlemagne's Mustache: And Other Cultural Clusters of a Dark Age
by Paul Edward Dutton

Troubled Vision: Gender, Sexuality, and Sight in Medieval Text and Image
edited by Emma Campbell and Robert Mills

Queering Medieval Genres
by Tison Pugh

Sacred Place in Early Medieval Neoplatonism
by L. Michael Harrington

The Middle Ages at Work
edited by Kellie Robertson and Michael Uebel

Chaucer's Jobs
by David R. Carlson

Medievalism and Orientalism: Three Essays on Literature, Architecture and Cultural Identity
by John M. Ganim

Queer Love in the Middle Ages
by Anna Klosowska Roberts

Performing Women: Sex, Gender and the Medieval Iberian Lyric
by Denise K. Filios

Necessary Conjunctions: The Social Self in Medieval England
by David Gary Shaw

Visual Culture and the German Middle Ages
edited by Kathryn Starkey and Horst Wenzel

Medieval Paradigms: Essays in Honor of Jeremy duQuesnay Adams, Volumes 1 and 2
edited by Stephanie Hayes-Healy

False Fables and Exemplary Truth: Poetics and Reception of a Medieval Mode
by Elizabeth Allen

Ecstatic Transformation
by Michael Uebel

Sacred and Secular in Medieval and Early Modern Cultures
edited by Lawrence Besserman

Tolkein's Modern Middle Ages
edited by Jane Chance and Alfred Siewers

Representing Righteous Heathens in Late Medieval England
by Frank Grady

Byzantine Dress
by Jennifer Ball

The Laborer's Two Bodies
by Kellie Robertson

The Dogaressa of Venice, 1200–1500: Wife and Icon
by Holly S. Hurlburt

Logic, Theology, and Poetry in Boethius, Abelard, and Alan of Lille: Words in the Absence of Things
by Eileen Sweeney

The Theology of Work: Peter Damian and the Medieval Religious Renewal Movement
by Patricia Ranft

On the Purification of Women: Churching in Northern France, 1100–1500
by Paula Rieder

Writers of the Reign of Henry II: Twelve Essays
edited by Ruth Kennedy and Simon Meecham-Jones

Lonesome Words: The Vocal Poetics of the Old English Lament and the African-American Blues Song
by M.C. McGeachy

WRITERS OF THE REIGN OF HENRY II

TWELVE ESSAYS

Edited by

Ruth Kennedy

and

Simon Meecham-Jones

WRITERS OF THE REIGN OF HENRY II

First published in 2006 by
PALGRAVE MACMILLAN™
175 Fifth Avenue, New York, N.Y. 10010 and
Houndmills, Basingstoke, Hampshire, England RG21 6XS
Companies and representatives throughout the world.

PALGRAVE MACMILLAN is the global academic imprint of the Palgrave Macmillan division of St. Martin's Press, LLC and of Palgrave Macmillan Ltd. Macmillan® is a registered trademark in the United States, United Kingdom and other countries. Palgrave is a registered trademark in the European Union and other countries.

ISBN-13: 978–1–4039–6644–5
ISBN-10: 1–4039–6644–3

Library of Congress Cataloging-in-Publication Data

    Writers of the reign of Henry II : twelve essays / edited by
Ruth Kennedy and Simon Meecham-Jones.
        p.cm.—(The new Middle Ages)
    Largely the proceedings of the summer symposia of 2000 and 2001 of
the London Old and Middle English Research Seminar.
    Includes bibliographical references.
    ISBN 1–4039–6644–3 (alk. paper)
    1. Great Britain—History—Henry II, 1154–1189. 2. Henry II, King of
England, 1133–1189—Relations with authors. 3. Great Britain—Court
and courtiers—History—To 1500. 4. Historiography—Great Britain—
History—To 1500. 5. Great Britain—Intellectual life—1066-485.
6. British literature—History and criticism. I. Kennedy, Ruth, Dr.
II. Meecham-Jones, Simon, Dr. III. New Middle Ages (Palgrave Macmillan
(Firm))

DA206.W75 2006
942.03′1072—dc22   2005054608

A catalogue record for this book is available from the British Library.

Design by Newgen Imaging Systems (P) Ltd., Chennai, India.

First edition: May 2006

10 9 8 7 6 5 4 3 2 1

Printed in the United States of America.

CONTENTS

ACKNOWLEDGMENTS

Lomers is the London Old and Middle English Research Seminar, a sociable forum which brings together medievalists from the separate colleges of the Federal University of London but also reaches out to other parishes. These essays constitute the first volume of the forthcoming Lomers International Series. They are largely the proceedings of the Lomers summer symposia of 2000 and 2001 which were initiated by a plaintive statement in one seminar from Emeritus Professor W. A. Davenport: "What I *really* want to know is about the court of Eleanor and Henry and whether or not it had influence on the literature." We have had much pleasure in attempting to help him out, and this volume is a tribute to Tony Davenport and the enormous influence and constant support he has been in the University of London, to Lomers, and to younger colleagues like ourselves. Great thanks are also due to the Institute of English Studies in the School of Advanced Studies at Senate House, London, the teams and finance of which enable Lomers to exist; particular thanks here are due to Warwick Gould, Michael Baron, Joanne Grubb, Francesca Bettocchi, and Gina Vitello, and to Julia Boffey, past chair of Lomers, for her continued unstinting advice and encouragement. We would also like to thank our editor, Bonnie Wheeler, and the extremely helpful anonymous reader, together with all those who have worked on this book at Palgrave Macmillan. Finally, it gives us great pleasure to offer personal thanks and tributes to Rosamund Allen, Christopher Bright, Rosalind Field, Robert Hampson, Patricia Harris-Gillies, Jennifer Neville, Jane Page, Nan Robertson, Ian Short, and Carole Zabbal, for invaluable input and support.

Ruth Kennedy

In addition to thanking those listed above, I would like to append a few more names. It was my good luck to be able to draw on the advice and experience of Maldwyn Mills, David Dumville, Neil Cartlidge, and Judith Weiss, and on the practical assistance of Trinity Hall, Cambridge. Mike Rampey provided a patient and informed audience at a crucial stage in the book's development, while the supportive curiosity of a number of undergraduates provided a spur to its completion. I owe a particular debt to my mother, to my colleague Laura Wright, and to Colin and Betty Davies, for their unfailing interest and encouragement at every stage. Much of the work for this book was done during the Cambridge English Faculty's brief exile in the cramped but convivial surroundings of 27 Trumpington Street; many thanks to Claire Daunton for making facilities available, and to Mary Griffin, Vicky Aldred, Margaret Harrison, and Heidi Hume for their invaluable assistance. My involvement with twelfth-century literature began as an undergraduate, but I owe the roots of my interest to my parents, who took me to so many castles—Pembroke, Coity, Manorbier—as a child. Though he will not now read it, I hope that this volume, with its conviction of the crucial interrelationship of literature, philosophy, politics, and the visual arts, is one that my father would have enjoyed.

Simon Meecham-Jones

INTRODUCTION

Simon Meecham-Jones

> Eight feet of ground is now enough for me
> Whom many kingdoms failed to satisfy
>
> This scanty tomb doth now suffice
> For whom the earth was not enough.

When the adherents of the humiliated King Henry II set up a memorial to their leader in Fontevrault Abbey, they chose for his epitaph to adapt lines written barely a decade before,[1] from Walter of Châtillon's account of the burial of the most illustrious of warriors, Alexander the Great (see p. 21, below). If the choice flattered the extent of Henry's martial achievements, it reflected accurately both the ambition of the man they buried, and the implicit recognition by the Plantagenet elite of the paramount importance of the written text as a potent weapon in the establishment of political and moral authority.

Henry of Anjou ascended a throne in a kingdom in which the structures of aristocratic loyalty had been unsettled by the extended civil disturbance resulting from the hostilities between the supporters of King Stephen and Henry's mother, the Empress Matilda. The challenge that defined the nature of his reign was the establishment beyond question of three legitimacies no longer under immediate challenge by force of arms—the legitimacy of his family claims to the throne, the legitimacy of the Norman governance over a people predominantly alien in their language and many of their traditions, and the legitimacy of England's attempts to extend its sway in claiming new territories in Ireland, Wales, and Scotland.

The central achievement of Henry's reign was to accomplish an identification of his dynastic and political interests with the perceived concerns of an emerging English political consciousness.[2] Whether composing history, or shaping new patterns of mythology in philosophical and poetic works, the writers associated with Henry's court, and those active beyond royal circles, were, willingly or unwillingly, actors in this drama of self-aggrandizement, complicit in an exercise in the cult of personality which was to prove enduringly successful. After his death, the imagery of Henry's successes was ever-present as a stick to castigate his successors—not least his son John. Despite the attractions of a spectacular falling-out of church and state, the contentions of Henry's reign did not seem engaging to the ideo-logical reimagining of English history effected in the Tudor period or worthy of being revisited in a Shakespearean history play—an honor which King John was lucky, or unfortunate, enough to have received. Despite the turbulence of the reign, and the revolts of his sons, Henry's reputation as a wise (if quick-tempered) constitutional and legal reformer, a consolidator of the institutions of kingship and, for these reasons, one of the most respected and successful of English medieval monarchs, has remained all but unscathed by changes in historiographical fashion. Henry is remarkable among pre-Tudor English monarchs in setting the terms for his judgment by posterity, and posterity has been content to take him at something close to his own valuation, or to the projection of Henry promoted by his associates.

This projection was not effected primarily through the writing of praise-poetry or hagiographical family history, but through the fostering of a broad range of literature, technically accomplished and often classically informed, without precedent in English cultural history. Reflecting on the slow development of English court-literature, Lee Patterson draws atten-tion to the singularity of the achievement of Henry's court:

> The development of a court poetry—a poetry, that is, specifically of the court and not merely a "courtly" poetry expressive of aristocratic values in general—is a relatively late phenomenon in England. To be sure, the twelfth-century court of Henry II supported a highly developed literary culture that included vernacular writers such as Benoît de Sainte-Maure, the author of the *Roman d'Eneas*, Wace, probably Marie de France, and perhaps even the young Chrétien de Troyes—not to speak of a large number of Latin writers. But not only was this an exclusively French-speaking court but also one that stands in lonely eminence in relation to the next century and a half.[3]

Nor should this Henrician flowering be understood as a random collection of texts, associated by chance contemporaneity. The comparison with the practice of other English medieval monarchs makes the attribution of the profusion of literature during Henry's reign to mere chance seem implau-sible. Composed at a time when the institution of monarchy was engaged in an ambitious project in the self-definition of the powerful, the literature of the reign of Henry II must also be recognized as bearing witness to the ethical and artistic demands of composition in an atmosphere in which the polemical and propagandizing potency of literature was recognized by writers and patrons within the Anglo-Norman ruling elite.

In part, this heightened awareness can be explained as a symptom of the shifting status of the oral and written record in medieval culture, as a new class of literate administrators altered the relationship of society to written culture. In the words of Brian Stock, "Medieval society after the eleventh century was increasingly oriented towards the scribe, the written word, the literary text, and the document."[4] Stock draws on the work of Prou and Duby to stress the centrality of the second half of the twelfth century as the moment in which the importance of "oral-aural culture"[5] was supplanted by the authority of the written word:

> The change to administrative activity involving scribes took place between the eleventh and thirteenth centuries with the Norman kingdom, as Haskins emphasized, acting as a bridge. The contrast can be seen by comparing the diplomas of Robert the Pious or Henry I with those of Louis VI. The twelfth century emerges as "the period in which diplomatic script attained its apogee" (M. Prou, *Manuel de Paleographie Latine et Française* [Paris: A. Picard, 1892], p. 110). Of course one cannot judge the literary output of a whole nation by the activity of the royal chancery. But in the countryside the picture is not so different. After the brief Carolingian renaissance, written records declined sharply in quantity and quality. From the tenth to the early twelfth century "social relations were once again founded on spoken words, acts and ceremonies rather than on written documents. . .The rights and duties of each individual were laid down and maintained with some flexibility by custom and ancient usage" [Georges Duby, *Rural Economy and Country Life in the Medieval West*, trans. Cynthia Postan (Columbia: University of South Carolina Press, 1968), p. 61].

As written culture asserted its indispensability at the heart of medieval power-structures,[6] this new recognition exerted its influence on the nature of the literature produced. In the writings of Gerald of Wales or Peter of Blois we see a new pride in the status of their vocation as creators of a lasting written record, an awareness of their perceived importance, or self-importance, which animates their texts with the courage to be innovative in their choice of subjects and literary form, outspoken in their expression of judgment. The "altered social psychology"[7] that Stock posits as the consequence of the supplanting of oral and memory-based structures with those dependent on written records finds its voice in a bolder and increasingly creative psychology manifested in the texts produced within such a society.

The extent to which this awareness of a new status for written material was recognized, at least implicitly, or was actively promoted by the governing elite lies at the heart of any understanding of the texts, and text-types, composed during Henry's reign. Evidence for the direct involvement of Henry himself, or of his queen, Eleanor of Aquitaine, in the active patronage of writers remains elusive. Haskins seemed beguiled by the unfamiliar vision of the English monarchy involving itself in the commissioning of artistic pursuits and certainly overstated the likelihood of royal involvement.[8] In the early 1970s, Dronke was indulgent to the possibility of royal interest, without committing himself as to its probability,[9] while the recent evaluation by Broadhurst demonstrates the scant proof of royal interest in the promotion of vernacular literature on which the myth of court patronage has been constructed. Her bracing conclusions, that "there is certainly no evidence that she [Eleanor of Aquitaine] commissioned this text [Benoît's *Roman de Troie*]. Nor can we connect Thebes or Eneas to her with any confidence"[10] and that "every supposed connection between Eleanor herself and the Tristan legend is without foundation"[11] are valuable correctives to the post-hoc mythologizing of the aesthetic priorities of Henry and his Queen which had shaped Haskins' thinking. Nonetheless, the absence of compelling evidence proves no more than that—that no evidence *survives* of any interest, encouragement, or commissioning which *may* or *may not* have occurred. Furthermore, although it seems natural to think of the royal court as the hub of cultural production and experimentation, it is clear that it was far from being the only such center. Certainly the appropriation of words by Walter of Châtillon to the glory of Henry demonstrates the sensitivity of at least some in the king's closest circles to the self-aggrandizing potential of contemporary literature. The consolidation of the institution of monarchy was a crucial element in the embedding of an arriviste Anglo-Norman ruling class into the controlling traditions of English social organization.[12] Despite the consolidation of local powerbases through a combination of force and strategic marriages to high-born Saxon women, mirroring Henry I's marriage to Maud, the power and prestige of this class remained inextricably bound to the fortunes and reputation of the king. Whether texts that magnified and sustained Anglo-Norman rule were commissioned by the king and queen themselves, or by their aristocratic adherents, modifies scarcely, if at all, the role of the texts within the ideological construction of Plantagenet legitimacy. Writing the reign of Henry II was to prove a task achieved, consciously and unconsciously, by the efforts of an impressive variety of writers, drawn from many corners of Henry's extensive domains.

In the first essay of this volume, John Gillingham casts a skeptical eye over claims that Henry himself played any role in encouraging the writing of history. The troubled family history both of Henry's ancestors and of his descendants rendered the textual preservation of dynastic history a delicate, if not potentially self-incriminating, task. Rather, the values of the regime were promoted, less conspicuously and perhaps less consciously, through the development of genres less clearly marked for their ideological purpose—in legal and technical writings such as the great legal text known as "Glanvill." In the next chapter, Elisabeth van Houts examines the writings of three contemporary historians in Normandy to demonstrate the different uses of the authoritative languages of Latin and French in works designed to bolster the legitimacy of the ruling dynasty. If Henry appears to have been unengaged by the writing of histories, van Houts argues for the evidence of active patronage by Henry's mother, the Empress Matilda, in the writing of the history of the dynasty. Her essay also illuminates the continuing closeness of the links that bound the king to his ancestral lands, causing him to configure himself through the assertion of a manifold identity, not content to be merely English, but still anxious to claim an unchallenged French or trans-channel legitimacy.

The role of writing as a means to disguise or to reform the vices of the contemporary world was an abiding concern for the Henrician intellectual elite—evidenced in the profusion of texts about Becket, the much-copied didactic epistles of Peter of Blois, and in the satirical textual reshaping of their own time by Walter Map and Walter of Châtillon. But such disguising of the world in itself does not change the world, though it may mask the reader's perception of the world's imperfections. In this way, a gap was created between a fallen temporality existing outside textual space, and an imagined textual world, or world within a text, which was capable of some measure of perfection. With the revival of the study of Platonic and late classical neo-Platonic texts in the scholastic centers of learning in the twelfth century came also a renewed sense of the implications of Plato's characterization of the poet as the teller of lies, necessarily unable to present anything but a distorted simulacrum of the eternal verities. The texts through which the nature of Henry's reign might be said to have been expressed repeatedly prove to be structured through the opaque configuration of ideas of identity—authorial identity, "national," and racial identity—and the ways in which such ideas were occluded, by the crystallization of tropes of exile. In particular, these texts construct a sense of exclusion—which is expressed through the writer's recognition of the unbridgeable distance that seemed necessarily to exile the author from the models of virtue and heroism constructable within their own texts.

These ideas of identity were to be expressed differently in the diverse media and traditions offered by the multiple linguistic possibilities of twelfth-century Britain. Central to the contradictions that made governing the Angevin monarchy so fraught was the multilingual state of twelfth-century England, and the complexity of the politics of language in England. Curiously, none of the major surviving authors of the reign choose to demonstrate this in their texts. Though we may presume that many or most of the most prominent authors were multilingual to a greater or lesser extent, it is striking that, for each, their work survives in a single linguistic tradition—for example, Walter Map's Latin texts survive, while his authorship of romance texts in French remains conjectural. Only Marie de France addresses the language question directly, with her assurances that her *Lais* and *Fables* are designed to render into "Romance" texts that existed in Latin and English—a claim that the loss of her presumed sources has rendered obscure.

In twelfth-century Britain, to choose to write in any particular language was, inescapably, to make an ideological statement about the purposes of the text and the author's relationship to the structures of power. Often, it was a gesture through which writers articulated an embracing or rejection of their linguistic and racial "identities," and their promotion or reservation from the assimilated and "Angevin" identity modeled and embodied in Henry's exercise of kingship.

For the authors writing in the learned language of Latin, the act of composition required them to come to write through the experience of a double exile—exiled by language, race, and class from the mass of the population around them, while, as writers, exiled from an unmediated immersion in the particularities of day-to-day life by the self-consciousness of the inherited literary traditions they practiced. This painful experience of exile is figured in contrasting ways in the output of Peter of Blois and Walter of Châtillon—expressed more urbanely and evasively by Peter, and with a disordering vehemence in the Latin satirical poems of Walter. Both writers experienced both real and figurative exile—both were French-born, Peter certainly (and Walter possibly) holding positions of authority at the English court, and, as poets writing in Latin, condemned to write more than a thousand years after the zenith of the traditions they sought to emulate. Neil Cartlidge's essay on the writings of Peter of Blois examines the ways in which this most polished of littérateurs used familiar elements drawn from the material of his literary predecessors as a means of commenting, obliquely, on his own times, while both creating, and obscuring, his own textual presence. In Cartlidge's account, Peter's writing adapts elements of the dialogic and *disputatio* forms as a means of expressing the irreconcilable distance between the capability of textual expression and the presumed existence of an objective "truth." Peter uses this highlighting of distance as a means of occluding the particularity of his narrative voice, thereby achieving a measure of "self-protection" from the claims of the text.

In the poetry of Walter of Châtillon, we see the construction of a contrary strategy to withstand the oppressive and potentially silencing prestige accorded to the writings of the esteemed classical masters. Simon Meecham-Jones's essay appraises the dexterity and extreme self-consciousness with which Walter adapts and mischievously distorts phrases and images from the Classical tradition (in particular Virgil and Horace) and from the Vulgate, both to claim kinship with the civilized tradition embodied in literature, and to show in contrast the corruption of his own time. Walter of Châtillon uses the learned language to mark out his independence from the loyalties of kingdom and race. Nonetheless, the gesture of doing so through the use of a register of Latin that was classically inspired but grammatically clearly marked as post-Classical underlines Walter's self-diagnosed awareness of his status as an intellectual exile, an awareness which fires the molten ferocity of his satirical assaults on the politically and ecclesiastically powerful. Armed with authority drawn from the valorized texts that he both reverences and creatively mishandles, Walter of Châtillon asserts his exile as a combative gesture of dissociation from the fallen concerns of the temporal sphere. The textual tradition becomes an alternative locus within which the poet can find sanctuary, not bound by the courtesies and obligations of the merely physical life.

In Walter's lyrics, the inability of the writer to close the perceived chasm between the text and a truth that exists outside and independent of the text is experienced as a tragic frustration. Elsewhere, in the literatures of the time, this frustration is embodied as a bafflement which, though it may prove tragic, can appear comic. The simultaneously liberating and threatening linguistic and cultural diversity represented at Henry's court and throughout his kingdom, and the problematic relationship between that diversity and the ability of literature to render it without distortion, finds literary embodiment in the idiosyncratic prodigality of the writings of Walter Map and Gerald de Barri (or Giraldus Cambrensis). Tony Davenport's essay explores the ways in which these two ebulliently gifted writers articulated their sense of their alienation from the centers of political and cultural power at Henry's court, as biographical circumstance is mapped on to the psychological estrangement that characterizes the practice of literature. This eloquent sense of exclusion is made concrete, with each writer struggling to represent the world as he saw it through satirical fantasy, historical reminiscence, theological exegesis, even through topographical writing. In Walter Map's work, the writer's sense of the inexplicable injustice of the world around him, in which virtue is rarely rewarded, and the will of God is ever expected but far less often witnessed, results in a conflation of high and popular literary styles and a restless experimentation with literary form, to the extent that he escapes classification as a writer of any school or style. Walter Map shows mastery in many different forms but does not deign to be the master of any one, and his achievement, in consciously eluding the audience's understanding, was, anticipating Freud by seven-hundred years, to demonstrate the baffling otherness of literary consciousness, exiled in a world full of unsympathetic phenomena which must remain outside its comprehension. Curiously, Walter's writings often seem to reject the desubjectivizing practices Stock diagnoses in the shift from oral to written modes:

> In societies functioning orally the advent of the written word can disrupt previous patterns of thought and action, often permanently. Above all it transforms man's conception of himself in society. When written models for conducting human affairs make their appearance, a new sort of relationship is set up between the guidelines and realities of behavior: the presentation of the self is less of a subjectively determined performance and more of an objectified pattern within articulated norms.[13]

Map's writing is both energized and troubled by a sense of the arbitrariness of those "articulated norms," reflecting perhaps an unconscious sense of loss for the greater freedom of the evanescent oral mode, as the means of expression take on more permanent, public, and commodifiable forms.

Both Walter Map and Gerald, in didactic mode, cast themselves as teachers through their writing, though for both the role proves problematic. Whereas Map's texts seem finally to prove the impossibility of teaching anything, Gerald's writing—as a historian, as a polemicist, as a collector of marvels—radiates his certainty that literature can serve the dissemination of knowledge, even if the persistent disappointments and eventual failure of his ecclesiastical career might suggest a conclusion not dissimilar to that of Walter Map. Gerald's tenacious attempts to claim the position he believed he deserved within the hierarchies of social power and intellectual authority of Henrician England created a testimony of remarkable vividness, if not consistent objectivity.

Gerald's writings are most remarkable for the honesty with which they witness the Anglo-Norman emplacement of a social elite defined not merely by language, but also by race. In Gerald, the trope of double exile was embodied in his frequent allusions to his mixed race and divided loyalties—recognized by the court elite as "Cambrensis," the Welshman, and by the Welsh as an alien in their midst. Gerald was not alone in experiencing these conflicted loyalties but he recognizes difference, and the inevitable consequences of difference, with a perception that seems to have escaped his contemporaries. In his descriptions of Wales and Ireland, Gerald demonstrates the distinctiveness of these societies—their apparent

alterity, viewed from an English court perspective. The resistance to assimilation of these two societies is established through a description of their
practices and priorities, which constructs cultural difference in explicitly
racial rather than social terms. Gerald's perspective, as an outsider instinc-
tively drawn to record a culture he can observe but can never be within, is
tempered with a sympathy deepened by his certainty that the cultures he
described would soon be subjugated fully, and his certainty that such a
conclusion must be desirable. If the *Expugnatio Hiberniae* is unabashed in its
denunciation of Irish customs, Gerald's *Journey through Wales* expresses a
more complex and elegiac portrait. In the voyeuristic poignancy of its
depiction, Gerald's writing achieves a passived fascination not unlike the
withdrawn pathos of many of the black-and-white nineteenth-century
photographs of Sitting Bull and other defeated Native American leaders,
whose resemblances had to be preserved to prime the imaginations of a
triumphant modernity.

The status of English as a language of low prestige, unsuitable for court
use or for legal proceedings, raises great difficulties in assessing the quantity
and range of composition of texts in English at this time. That Henry's was
apparently "an exclusively French-speaking court"[14] renders unsurprising
the failure to develop a courtly lyric tradition in English, to match that
found in Latin and French. If the tradition of literature in English in
Henry's reign seems embryonic, what was written is of a different nature to
much of the French and Latin literature of its time in being not literature *of*
the court or *from* the court. The perceived difference in authority between
the different languages determined the adoption of particular literary forms
within each language, and that in turn appears to have influenced the prob-
abilities of a text's survival. Perhaps the English language itself, or the less-
authoritative modes of literature it was associated with, was regarded as
being more suitable for "oral-aural culture" than for preservation in
monastic libraries, but the lost transmission of popular English traditions
makes it impossible to determine to what extent, if at all, they were
considered worthy of written status in the twelfth century. Though it is
possible, perhaps even likely, that some of the medieval Romance material
in English that survives in fourteenth-century, or later, recensions may preserve material written in earlier generations, the nonsurvival of such
sources from the twelfth century provides eloquent testimony as to the low
valuation in which such texts had been held. Neil Cartlidge's reattribution
of *The Owl and the Nightingale*, hitherto regarded as the most accomplished
and individual English text of the twelfth century, to a later century has
focused attention on the paucity of vernacular literature that can be safely
attributed to this period.[15]

But the nature of twelfth-century written English is increasingly realized to be problematic in other ways. Long-held notions of Anglo-Norman influence directly precipitating changes in the orthography and morphology of English are increasingly dismissed as manifestations of "The Myth of the Anglo-Norman scribe," while Maroldt and Bailey's bold characterization of Middle English as the product of Creolization has failed to find favor with historical linguists and Creolists alike.[16] In their essays, Mary Swan and Elaine Treharne draw attention to the problematic classification of written English in this period. Both argue for the recognition of a class of texts written in "late Old English," a category of English that they distinguish from the developing patterns of Middle English. Many of the sources for this category of late Old English preserve material of an official or semi-official nature: chronicles, ecclesiastical regulations, grants, and charters. The survival of such documents would seem to undermine, or at least qualify, the accepted notion that the Norman Conquest led to a radical disjunction in the development of Old English prose as a written medium of accepted cultural status. Mary Swan's essay presents an overview of the audience for prose-texts in English in a society in which Anglo-Norman retained much of its prestige as a language for literature, legal proceedings, and aristocratic culture, and Latin remained the language of authority for the liturgy, theology, and for education. She distinguishes two categories of text—those "which are copies of pre-Conquest Old English works" and a category of texts "shown to be newly composed after the Conquest." Elaine Treharne marks out the evidence of patterns of variability found within written texts both before and after the Conquest, and, in doing so, questions the assumptions of orthographical and morphological consistency and correctness that have so often predetermined judgments of vernacular literature. Her conclusions lead Treharne to question the validity of the generally accepted theory of a significant rupture between the transmission of Old and Middle English written forms, a discontinuity upon which theories such as those of Poussa and Maroldt and Bailey are founded.[17]

Elizabeth Solopova argues that the development of vernacular poetry tells a different tale, displaying significant linguistic change and a conscious forging of new aesthetic models. The debate as to the continuity of the transmission of written Old and Middle English is not merely concerned with the classification of linguistic forms. The establishment of such a continuity would seem to demonstrate the survival of an indigenous Saxon/English cultural establishment, not catastrophically overturned by the Conquest, albeit now under Norman lordship. The survival of such an establishment, and the necessary degree of accommodation to the new authority required to achieve that survival, would certainly suggest that sources written in English need to be read with greater skepticism—as elements in the construction of a history of the negotiation of power.

For writers in French in Henry's reign, the requirements and understanding of diverse audiences—insular and continental, monoglot or multilingual—made the complexities of such a negotiation of cultural power more pressing, and the ambiguities of authorship are often presented with a self-consciousness that offers an interesting contrast to the shift in consciousness Solopova diagnoses in contemporary English poetic practice. For Marie de France, the divinely given faculty of wise speech provides a justification for her writing:

> Qui Deus a duné esciënce
> e de parler bone eloquence
> ne s'en deit taisir ne cèler
> ainz se deit voluntiers mustrer.

> [Anyone who has received from God the gift of knowledge and true eloquence has a duty not to remain silent: rather should one be happy to reveal such talents.][18]

In the prologue to the *Lais* and the epilogue to the *Fables*, Marie highlights the process of translation as a proof of the transferability of wisdom, a wisdom perpetuated by an author self-described as "de France" and by her predecessors writing in English, Latin, and Greek:

> M'entremis de cest livre feire
> E de l'Engleis en romanz treire.
> Esope apel'um cest livre,
> Qu'il translata e fist escrire,
> Del griu en Latin le turna.
> Li reis Alfrez, que mut l'ama,
> Le translata puis en engleis,
> E jeo l'ai rimee en franceis,
> Si cum jeo poi plus proprement.

> [This volume was by me created, / From English to Romance translated. / This book's called Aesop for this reason: / He translated and had it written / In Latin from the Greek, to wit. / King Alfred, who was fond of it, / Translated it to English hence / And I have rhymed it now in French.][19]

In the shifting of fictional designs and archetypes from one language to another, it seems that Marie's verse promotes the idea that narrative is capable of expressing and perpetuating models of shared truth. In her essay, Françoise le Saux demonstrates how Marie deftly plays on this assumption of the ability of fiction to "embody" truth as a means of implanting within her texts a sophisticated, but always implicit, critique of the consequences of unjust lordship. There must always be an inevitable distance of interpretation between universally accepted codes of virtue and their application in specific circumstances, and Marie demonstrates this through the distance between the morals of her tales, and the structures of fictional artifice through which they are constructed. It is not that Marie's *Lais* and *Fables* cannot construct a model of virtuous conduct. Such a model is to be found within each of the texts, but interpretation is dependent on the reader's ability to "gloser la lettre"—to discover through an active and engaged process of reading where that construction of moral truth is to be found.

If the reader fails to interpret acutely, the text might seem to propound a moral view contrary to that envisaged by its author, and an awareness of this ability of literature to figure beyond the author's intentions lies at the heart of Laura Ashe's reading of Thomas's *Tristran*. Ashe argues that Thomas attempts "to break free of ideology, which offers universality and generality, offering instead an inscription of specificity and particularity." The ideology she regards him as seeking to break free from is that which figures the reinterpretation of physical life through the conventions of textual models as a pattern of ordering the universe. So pervasive, in her view, was this blurring of understanding of the different experiences of physical life and textual figuration that the author of the *Tristran* felt obliged to make strenuous (if, probably, unavailing) efforts to discourage his readers from assuming similar spiritual imagery in the suffering of Tristran. Of course, to resist a culturally pervasive premise of the ability of fiction to represent a model of moral universality is itself an ideological construction, albeit an unexpected one for its time. In her stress on Thomas's striving to represent the particularity of the events described, rather than their ability to figure general "truths," Ashe argues that Thomas attempts to de-couple the events of his narrative from their place in a greater spiritually interpreted framework—to separate the temporal from a place in the figuration of the metaphysical.

If the *Tristran* articulates a frustration at the inability of the writer to restrict readers' misprision of his text, it could also be read as a response to prevalent twelfth-century practices of the ideological manipulation of the relationship of textual presentation to historical actuality. Throughout Henry's reign, the ability of texts to invest actions and reputations with the sheen of divine justification or inevitability was energetically pursued. These processes of ideological promotion existed at both the courtly and popular level. In sophisticated court productions like Bertrand de Born's Occitan poems in honor of Henry II's daughter Matilda, the aggrandizement of royal authority could be spiced with a playfully transgressive *apparent* questioning of royal dignity and royal authority, permissible at a smaller provincial court though apparently unthinkable in an English context.[20] Henry's toleration of Bertrand's playful guying of royal authority within the conventions of fiction perhaps shows nothing more than the courtliness of Henry's temperament, a surprising trait which Gillingham proposes as crucial to an understanding of the man.

Maybe, though, Bertrand's reminder of the misleading possibilities of textual self-presentation appealed to a king who recognized the importance of the persuasive symbol in fostering acceptance of his regal authority. If Henry's acceptance of a show of public flogging by the monks of Canterbury in penance for the murder of Becket demonstrated his flair for the politics of gesture, Becket's career (before and after his death) provided an alternative model for the "textualization" of lived experience for ideological purposes. The plethora of texts recounting Becket's career demonstrate the widespread and unquestioning acceptance in clerical and popular culture of the application of "literary" techniques to the analysis of contemporary political events. Metaphor is used to invest accounts of Becket's death with the force of spiritual parable, to the point where the events of the martyrdom became enclosed within a pattern of generic expectations drawn from the experiencing of literary models. It was perhaps in rejection of this pattern of reading that Thomas asserted the specificity of the events he recounted, and Marie masked her observation of contemporary mores within the structures of a universalizing and inherited narrative—to defer the reader's expectation of a microcosm/macrocosm parallelism serving as a backbone for each text. Certainly it was this pervasive recognition of the systemic and sustained co-dependence of textual signification and ideological promotion that fostered the characteristic quality of Henrician literature—its intense self-questioning of literary form. In the writings of Peter of Blois, Thomas, Walter of Châtillon, Wace, Marie de France, or Gerald of Wales, the text is suffused with a critical self-consciousness as the author struggles to find an accommodation between literature as a self-sustaining tradition and the realization that textual signification can never exist as a disinterested witness to ethical and political conflicts but always has an active (and persuasive) role in the initiation and promotion of ideological discourses.

Most crucial, and most lasting, of the discourses fostered in Henrician literature was the forging of a complex and ideologically supple model of an inclusive mediated identity that could contain and sanction the contradictions of Angevin England. Appropriately, a discourse that sought to fashion a hybrid and assimilated identity was articulated primarily in the Latin and French texts of the reign.

In contrast, the chronicles in English display a finely tuned but essentially unproblematic conception of identity within the nation, derived from the relationship of man to the land of England. It is an identification plainly visible in the Peterborough Chronicler's account of the reign of Stephen:

> I ne can ne I mai tellen alle þe wunder ne alle þe pines ðæt hi diden wreccemen on þis land. And ðæt lastede þa xix wintre wile Stephne was king, and æure it was uuerse and uuerse. . .Þa was corn dære and flesc and cæse and butere. For nan ne wæs o þe land. Wreccemen sturuen of hungær. . .War sæ me tilede þe erthe ne bar nan corn, for þe land was al fordon mid suilce dædes, and hi sæden openlice ðæt crist slep, and his halechen. Suilc and mare þanne we cunnen sæin, we þolenden xix wintre for ure sinnes.

> [I have neither the ability nor the power to tell all the horrors nor all the torments they inflicted upon wretched people in this country; and that lasted the nineteen years while Stephen was king, and it was always going from bad to worse. . .Then corn was dear, and meat and butter and cheese, because there was none in the country. Wretched men people died of starvation. . . Wherever cultivation was done, the ground produced no corn, because the land was all ruined by such doings, and they said openly that Christ and his saints were asleep. Such things, too many for us to describe, we suffered nineteen years for our sins.][21]

The chronicles express a sense of the unity of the concerns of the inhabitants of the realm, which binds them into an illusory unity, apparently unaffected by the linguistic and cultural traits of their overlords. In part, the failure of the chronicles to engage in the discourse of identity reflects the ideological marking already present in the act of reading (far less writing) such a text in English—a language without currency beyond England's shores. Rather, the chronicles reassert the certainties of territorial loyalty, a loyalty more readily witnessed through the obedience of the peasantry than through the more contingent loyalty of a literate elite, conscious of the contradictions that underpinned the complex and cumulative structure of loyalty in Henry's kingdom—to Henry as count of Anjou, as duke of Normandy, as *Rex Anglorum* [King of the English]. The contestations of Stephen's reign had demonstrated the frailty of assumed loyalties, highlighting the extent to which the exercise of political imperium rested on (at least notional) doctrines of assent, as well as the deployment of military force. It is not surprising, then, that the following generations of writers in Latin and Anglo-Norman attempted to discover a more nuanced, if also more troubled, reconfiguration of the complex balancing of loyalties derived from class, locality, language, and race that characterizes the literate culture of Angevin England—achieved through the myth of Arthur, and the development of an insular Romance tradition.

In the twelfth century, we see the development of a literary discourse of justification, as the Crown and aristocracy developed an ideology to assert their entitlement to the spoils of battle. When William of Normandy had claimed the English throne, he sought to deflect the threat of civil war and usurpation by granting his most senior knights the right to seize and hold land on the northern and western borders of England. The success of the policy was seen in the swift Norman penetration of the fertile and less-easily defensible lands in Glamorgan, the Vale of Clwyd, and Pembrokeshire, building a circle of castles—such as Manorbier, in which Gerald was raised. The expropriation of land was swift and extensive, so that the Montgomery family, for example, laid claim to the land that was later to become the county of Montgomeryshire, before seizing much of Ceredigion.[22]

Central to the discourse of justification was the assertion of the unity of Britain as a single patrimony, and central to that assertion was an appropriation of "British" tradition, symbolized in the figure of the British king and emperor Arthur. The figure of King Arthur was of central importance to Angevin claims that the throne of England entitled them to the historical sovereignty of Britain, justifying Norman colonial expansion in Wales and in Ireland. In her influential *Britons*, Linda Colley has promoted the theory of the "invention of Britishness" in the eighteenth century,[23] but the roots of a sense of cultural "Britishness," as opposed to a geographically inspired sense of unity, grew from much deeper historical roots, developing ideas that periodically had become marked as politically and ideologically imperative—in the twelfth century, and again in the wars against France, and in the Reformation. Colley makes use of Benedict Anderson's definition of nationhood as "an imagined political community,"[24] and it is hard not to see the representation of Britain in Geoffrey of Monmouth's *Historia* as defining precisely such a concept of nation. Geoffrey reworks the Virgilian image of the physical transference of a community, as Troy is renewed first in Rome and then (at least potentially) in Britain. In this way, the "imagined political community" is shown to be not dependent on, or to derive its nature from, the occupation of a predefined physical location. Rather it expresses a communal state of mind. From the biblical accounts of the Israelites' captivity in Egypt and Babylon, Geoffrey and his readers drew the lesson that the political exercise of nationhood might be interrupted and restored so long as the idea of the "imagined political community" is preserved. In Geoffrey's *Historia*, a concept of British nationhood is established which is defined less by race or culture than through the exercise of faith.

Although the cultural and ideological motives that informed Geoffrey's work have been much debated, there can be no doubt that he reinvigorated ideas of a shared British historical past. Whether or not this was his intention, in doing so Geoffrey created an image of "Britishness" which lent itself to Anglo-Norman appropriation as the justification for the exercise of "national" authority beyond the historical frontiers of the kingdom of England. Geoffrey's depiction of the periodic captivities of the British paradoxically permitted the Norman monarchy to present itself not as an external occupation but as the restoration of a lost unity, recreating the imperium of King Arthur. Gerald's vitriolic antipathy to Geoffrey's work reflects his alarmed recognition of the assimilating force of the myth of Britishness constructed there. In its depiction of the depth of racial difference within the notional bounds of Henry's kingdom, Gerald's work does not merely record, but also, necessarily, presents an ideological construction of identity and loyalty which cuts across Angevin ideologies of the legitimacy of the colonial expansion beyond England—a myth that sought to erase the fundamental qualities of difference that so beguiled Gerald.

Curiously, the reign of Henry was to prove a relatively fallow period in the development of Arthurian discourse in justification of the extension of English power, perhaps because of the limited success of Henry's military adventures in Wales. It seems probable, though, that Henry might have contemplated such an ideological appropriation in his final years. The conflicting loyalties inherent in figurations of Arthur, and his crucial status in resolving the vexed question of Britishness, were rehearsed in the spurious pageantry that marked the abbey of Glastonbury's "discovery" of the deathless Arthur's body in 1190, an act which Carley characterizes as a "turning point in the historicising and anglicizing of Arthur."[25] The project of the appropriation of British mythology was here given an indisputably physical form, in which the British worthy was shown to have reached the end of his journey within an English setting, symbolically under English sway, in a gesture designed to legitimize the new regime. The conscious manipulation of the Arthur myth for English colonial purposes by the Plantagenets afforded by this act of public drama has been noted, for example by Cassard:

> Cette stratégie de captation de la gloire antique de la Bretagne devait contribuer de façon efficace à désarmer psychologiquement les Bretons de l'île. Elle présentait également l'avantage de faire des rois angevins les hériteurs légitimes d'Arthur: dès 1192 on voit Richard d'Angleterre offrir à Tancrede, roi de Sicile, la célèbre épée d'Arthur, Calibur.[26]

The purpose of the ceremony was to bury Arthur's imaginative potency along with the bones claimed to be his. In John Davies' resonant phrase, "Arthur was received into the Valhalla of his enemies."[27] Evidence for

Henry's direct involvement in this act of brazen appropriation is tenuous but suggestive. Padel tactfully notes that:

> It is not clear whether this piece of theatre had been planned with Henry's knowledge: what we do know is that the king had done much to further the abbey's fortunes during the final years of his reign.[28]

Carley, recalling Gerald's testimony that Henry had suggested the dig that providentially discovered Arthur's remains, suggests also that "in the aftermath of the Becket fiasco," Henry might have sought "to have promoted Glastonbury as an alternative site to Canterbury for the origins of English Christianity."[29] The figure of Arthur offered a potential precedent from British mythology not merely for bolstering the Crown's political authority but also its claims to circumscribe the power of the church. British myth offered conveniently imprecise memories of the Celtic Church that could be recalled in defiance of the institutions of the papacy whenever English kings quarreled with the incumbents of St. Peter's seat. In so far as the Normans had supplanted the Saxon aristocracy, Arthur's battles against the invading Saxons were capable of being assimilated within the demands of Norman discourse, providing a precedent for the monarchy's campaigning against native resistance. There were, though, clear dangers in proclaiming the virtues of a pre-Norman (indeed, pre-English) worthy such as Arthur, and his success in resisting colonial aggression, resulting in a curiously carping, and often unheroic, depiction of the figure of Arthur. It was in Latin discourse, rather than Welsh or British tradition, that the myth of Arthur as national redeemer had developed—to serve the ideological neuroses of a usurping cultural tradition, and the Romances display many of the inconsistencies and anxieties inherent in this melting together of ideas from unrelated discourses. In her contribution to this volume, Judith Weiss demonstrates both the inescapable ambiguity of Plantagenet figurations of Arthur, and the extent to which that ambiguity was influenced and supplemented by alternative traditions that identified imperial power with figurations of the Antichrist. Her essay explores the troubling and ambivalent presentation of Arthurian material in medieval romance in this period, reflecting the opposing and potentially incompatible priorities of its audience. Where these romances figure the difficulties of sustaining a simultaneously Norman and English sense of belonging, for Weiss these romances reveal the strains involved in Norman attempts to lay claim to an identity that expressed continuity with native British mythology.

The mythological history of Arthur offered one pattern of assimilating Anglo-Norman interests with the traditions of their subjects, but it was not the only one. In her essay, Rosalind Field suggests a causal link between the insecurity that seemed to threaten the Anglo-Norman rule of the kingdom during the contention of Stephen and Matilda and the development of an insular tradition of romance, written in Anglo-Norman in the second half of the twelfth century. She draws attention to the paradoxical drawing together of parochially English subjects into a tradition she characterizes as "baronial, local and insular" but which nonetheless was composed in a language alien to the majority of the population.

The renewed focus of research energies on Anglo-Norman in recent years has demanded a reevaluation of the always-exaggerated extent of its role in medieval England. William Rothwell's researches have drawn attention to the irregularity of the patterns emerging in the evidence of the penetration of Anglo-Norman into widespread usage in England.[30] Rather, the records reveal a pattern of usage severely circumscribed by geographical spread, and by social class. The Anglo-Norman literature of Henry's reign must be recognized as having been written in a language not understood by the greater part of the country, but which nonetheless sought to express the experience of the most powerful subjects of the English Crown. The use of the Anglo-Norman tongue was in practice simultaneously a reflex choice by the ruling elite and an unambiguous gesture declaring both a class-solidarity amongst the mighty, and a separation from the majority of the population— expressed as a linguistic distance, but encompassing a distance that was both of status and of race. It is the more remarkable, then, that the Anglo-Norman romance tradition should have been so engaged in the creation of an "imagined political community." The insular romance tradition becomes a locus of assimilation, constructing a narrative model of the complex negotiation of loyalties that were central to the processes of nativization through which the twelfth-century aristocracy sought to achieve its embedding within the social fabric of the English realm. Field traces the ways in which the insular genre of Anglo-Norman romance defers the psychological difficulties inherent in ideas of identity and loyalty in a subjected land. Although the choice of stories from the mythical past might seem to limit the political expressiveness of the romance tradition, the created distance from contemporary events permitted the romances to bear witness to a sustained, if oblique, examination of the complex issues of good governance and just kingship, given an extra relevance by the anchoring of the tales within "native" narrative traditions and recognizably English locations.

In doing so, the romances construct, albeit implicitly, a highly sophisticated model of a hybrid identity. The same processes of fusion, nativization, and the inevitable diffraction of ideas of identity can be similarly seen in historical accounts such as *The Song of Dermot and Earl Richard*,[31] though here the incongruities of such attempts at fusion are far more clearly evident. *The Song of Dermot* is an account of the Angevin invasion of Ireland which may have been first written during Henry's reign, and which, in its account of the events that led to Henry's intervention in Ireland, clearly belongs to the genre of "literature of justification."[32] In an account of the attack on Limerick, the poet presents the conduct of Richard FitzGilbert de Clare, sometime earl of Pembroke and his band of "Welsh Normans." Without apparent irony, Meiler FitzHenry, a grandson of King Henry I, exhorts his troops to conquer the Irish in the name of St. David. Meilyr was one of the two sons and four grandsons of the Welsh princess Nesta accompanying de Clare on this expedition. Nesta had once been the mistress of Henry I, and was also the grandmother of Gerald of Wales. Her descendants embody, in their conduct and loyalties, the acceptance of Angevin power and (implicitly) legitimacy, and the consequent partial assimilation of the pre-Norman elite into the skein of Angevin nobility:

> Le fiz Henri, le ber Meiller,
> En haut se prist a hucher.
> Devant ala escrïant:
> "Passez, chevalers! Que alez targant?"
> En l'ewe se mist icil errant;
> Ultre l'aport le cheval blanc.
> "Sein Davi!" escrïad haut e cler,
> Kar il esteit [sun] seignur,
> Suz Dampnedeu le Crëatur,
> E li chevaler par grant duçor
> Sein Davi reclama nuit e jur,
> Que [il] lui fust en aïe
>
> De conquere chevalerie.

[brave Meilyr fitz Henry / shouted aloud; / He rode out in front, shouting: /"Cross over, knights! / Why are you hanging back?" / He plunged straight into the water, / [And his white horse carried him across] / When the knight had reached the other side, / 'Saint David' he shouted, loud and clear / for he was his lord / after the lord God the Creator; / Now the knight very devoutly / called on St David by night and day / to help him / to achieve chivalrous deeds] (lines 3434–47)[33]

If there is something heroically inappropriate, to the point of absurdity, in Meilyr's calling on the famously ascetic patron saint of one beleaguered nation to assist in the subjugation of another, nonetheless the scene is telling in its depiction of the commingling consequences of personal ambition, dynastic speculation, and heroic prowess in promoting a myth of identity which reconciled the oppositions of Meilyr's circumstances.

Meilyr's self-justifying appropriation demonstrates in Ireland, as throughout Henry's domains, the determined fusion of native and learned myths and written traditions to create through an imagined myth of assimilation an attempt to justify the legitimacy of a "political community" that had been created by the exercise of military force. So successful was this enterprise that there is a danger that it has been rendered invisible to later cultural historians. It provides a reminder, also, that the intellectual climate of the Angevin ascendancy was colored by a heightened awareness of the colonial nature of its dominance, an awareness apparently absent from the valuations of those historians and writers of later centuries who traced a spurious inevitability in what must have seemed to contemporary observers a far more insecure exercise of power. The Norman Conquest was a bold gamble which, through chance as much as good generalship, had succeeded first in taking power, and then in holding on to what its warriors (from the king himself to his loyal supporters granted land-rights in the new kingdom) had seized. That which was claimed by conquest must have seemed liable to future conquest, as providence permitted. Anglo-Norman romance is haunted by the unspoken urgency resultant from an unconscious expression of the contingency of this occupation.

The same sense of contingency was expressed also in the choice for Henry's tomb of words from the *Alexandreis*, Walter of Châtillon's account of a great warrior propagating the virtues of a superior culture by force, in a display that mixes bravado with insecurity. In recounting the careers of Arthur and Maximius/Macsen Wledig in the literature of justification, the British tradition provided Henry with examples of a warrior who used the throne of Britain to seize an imperial destiny, but also models against which his achievements might be measured. Though Gerald's testimony as to Henry's imperial ambitions must be treated as unreliable, it seems rash to dismiss the probability that such thoughts were not in Henry's mind.[34] Henry began life frustratingly close to this grandest of prizes—the son of an empress, and styled by his contemporaries Henry FitzEmpress. Henry's whole career, with its dynastic and military intrigues in England and France, Wales and Scotland, and Ireland, makes sense only if we see him engaged in the self-construction of himself in the role of a conquering emperor, secure only in the achievement of conquest. The history of his reign is an imperialist history,[35] as Henry sought to use military might and cultural influence to bind his diverse holdings, and it was this self-projection as the first and most confident monarch to embrace England's destiny as an imperial power that guaranteed him the admiration of British historians throughout the centuries of empire. So successful was his projection of himself in this role that, to surpass his father, Henry's son Richard was obliged to devote his energies to tackling God's foes, in a figuration as the crusader-king. In the careers of Henry and Richard, the pursuit of a self-proclaimed destiny unleashed an ambition resistant to prudence and which can seem close to mounting an assault on truth. The ferocity of this ambition scorches the literature of the reign with a boldness and a consequent structural and ethical anxiety that had no precedent in English texts. If anything binds the grotesque twists of providence found in the Anglo-Norman romances with the incendiary and hallucinatory outspokenness of the lyrics of Walter of Châtillon or the shambling wit of Walter Map, it is an expression of troubled striving derived from a persistent measuring of their own, aspiring, time against the actual and alleged achievements of past traditions. If Walter's lyrics embody an extreme demonstration of the power of the text to claim power and precedence over the physical world, something of this sense, too, was (incongruously) captured by the loyal followers who set up Henry's tomb in Fontevrault. In concluding his account of the remarkable, if hubristic, Alexander, Walter had set his hero's worldly achievements in context with a judgment consistent with Christian notions of humility:

> Magnus in exemplo est. Cui non suffecerat orbis,
> Sufficit exciso defossa marmore terra
> Quinque pedum fabricata domus, qua nobile corpus
> Exigua requiuit humo donec Tholomeus,
> Cui legis Egyptum in partem cessisse, uerendi
> Depositum fati toto uenerabile mundo
> Transtulit ad dictam de nomine principis urbem.[36]

> [Alexander the Great is an example. He for whom the world was not sufficient was satisfied with a five-foot house made of carved marble quarried from the earth, where his noble body rested in a small plot of ground until Ptolomey, to whom, as you read, Egypt was granted as his share, transported the remains of the prince, of awesome fate and venerable throughout the whole world, to the city which was called after his name.]

In its misperception of Walter's lines, Henry's epitaph is both comic and poignant. In a gesture worthy of Henry himself, Alexander's meager five-foot place of rest is surpassed by the eight feet needed to house England's king. It is a gesture of intense competition with the legendary past—a gesture that, in its need to over-reach the past, proves incapable of recognizing the meaning of the imagery it seeks to emulate. The literature of the past was to prove a tougher terrain for Henry's scholars and writers to conquer than the war-fields of colonial expansion.

Notes

1. Heinrich Christensen, *Das Alexanderlied Walters von Chatillon* (Halle: Verlag der Buchhandlung des Waisenhauses, 1905).
2. In doing so, Henry was seeking to build on an emerging phenomenon—Gillingham, for example, traces "a developing sense of Englishness" in the

work of Henry of Huntingdon in the first half of the twelfth century; see John Gillingham, "Henry of Huntingdon and the Twelfth-Century Revival of the English Nation," in *Concepts of National Identity in the Middle Ages*, ed. Simon Forde, Lesley Johnson, and Alan V. Murray, *Leeds Texts and Monographs* n.s. 14 (1995): 75–101.

3. Lee Patterson, *Chaucer and the Subject of History* (Madison, Wis.: University of Wisconsin Press, 1991), p. 49.

4. Brian Stock, *The Implications of Literacy: Written Language and Models of Interpretation in the 11th and 12th Centuries* (Princeton: Princeton University Press, 1983), p. 16.

5. Stock, *Implications of Literacy*, p. 14.

6. "From about 1150, records of all sorts become more plentiful. The information they provide is more precise" (Duby, *Rural Economy*, p. 62). "A group of specialists in administration emerges, whose particular expertise is based on the written word and on reckoning, and who are occupied in registering, counting, valuing and surveying" (Stock, *Implications of Literacy*, p. 14).

7. Stock, *Implications of Literacy*, p. 18.

8. Charles H. Haskins, "Henry II as a Patron of literature," in *Essays in Medieval History presented to Thomas Frederick Tout*, ed. A. G. Little and F. M. Powicke (Manchester: Manchester University Press, 1925), pp. 71–77.

9. Peter Dronke, "Peter of Blois and Poetry at the court of Henry II," *Mediaeval Studies* 28 (1976): 185–235; reprinted in Peter Dronke, *The Medieval Poet and his World*, Storia e letteratura 164 (Rome: Edizioni di storia e letteratura, 1984), 281–339.

10. Karen M. Broadhurst, "Henry II of England and Eleanor of Aquitaine: Patrons of Literature in French?," *Viator* 26 (1996): 53–84, 74.

11. Broadhurst, "Henry II of England and Eleanor of Aquitaine," p. 77.

12. Thus Godman, for example, posits cultural rivalry between the English and French courts as a motive for the patronage of Jean de Hauville's *Architrenius*: "The *Architrenius* is inscribed to Walter of Coutances, leading agent of king Henry II of England and his sons. Patron of literature, ambassador to the court of France, he was acquainted at first hand with the ambitions of the rival monarch. This shrewd servant of the Plantagenet dynasty had every motive for receiving in the spirit of Schadenfreude with which it was intended John's poetic subversion of a work that sought to erect an image of the Capetian superman;" see Peter Godman, *The Silent Masters: Latin Literature and its Censors in the High Middle Ages*, (Princeton, N.J.: Princeton University Press, 2000), pp. 322–23.

13. Stock, *Implications of Literacy*, p. 18.

14. Patterson, *Chaucer and the Subject of History*, p. 49. The evidence of Walter Map suggests that Henry was unable (or unwilling) to speak in English: "linguarum omnium que sunt a mari Gallico usque ad Iordanem habens / scienciam, Latina tantum utens et Gallica" [. . .and had a knowledge of all the tongues used from the French sea to the Jordan, but spoke only Latin and French]; see Walter Map, *De Nugis Curialium (Courtiers' Trifles)* ed.

M. R. James, rev. C. N. L. Brooke, and R. A. B. Mynors (Oxford: Clarendon Press, 1983), pp. 476–77.

15. Neil Cartlidge, *The Owl and the Nightingale: text and translation* (Exeter: University of Exeter Press, 2001).

16. C. J. N. Bailey and K. Maroldt, "The French Lineage of English," in *Langues en Contact-Pidgins-Créoles*, ed. Jürgen M. Meisel, *Tübinger Beiträge zur Linguistik* 75 (1977): 21–53. The theory is revisited by Juliette D'Or: "Langues française et anglaise, et multilinguisme à l'époque d'Henri Plantagenêt," *Cahiers de Civilisation Médiévale* 37 (1994): 61–72. An alternative view is put forward by Thomason and Kaufman: see S. G. Thomason and T. Kaufman, *Language Contact, Creolisation and Genetic Linguistics* (Berkeley, Calif.: University of California Press, 1988).

17. Patricia Poussa, "The Evolution of Early Standard English: The Creolisation Hypothesis," *Studia Anglica Posnaniensia* 14 (1982): 69–85.

18. Marie de France, *Die Lais*, ed. Karl Warnke, Bibliotheca Normannica 3 (Halle: Niemeyer, 1925; repr. Geneva: Slatkine Reprints, 1974), 1. Translation Glyn S. Burgess and Keith Busby, *The Lais of Marie de France* (Harmondsworth: Penguin, 1986), p. 41.

19. *Marie de France: Fables*, ed. and trans. by Harriet Spiegel (Toronto: University of Toronto Press, 1987), pp. 256–9.

20. Bertran de Born, *The Poems of the Troubadour Bertran de Born*, ed. William D. Paden, Tilde A. Sankovitch, and Patricia Harris Stablein (Berkeley, Calif. and London: University of California Press, 1986).

21. *The Peterborough Chronicle: (The Bodleian Manuscript Laud Misc. 636)*, ed. Dorothy Whitelock (Copenhagen: Rosenkilde and Bagger, 1954) orthography normalized; facsimile edition; Dorothy Whitelock (with David C. Douglas and Susie I. Tucker); *The Anglo-Saxon Chronicle: A Revised Translation* (Westport: Greenwood Press, 1986), 199–200.

22. J. F. A. Mason, "Roger de Montgomery and his Sons," *Transactions of the Royal Historical Society*, 5th Series, 13 (1963): 1–28.

23. Linda Colley, *Britons: forging the nation, 1707–1837* (New Haven, Conn., London: Yale University Press, 1992).

24. Benedict Anderson, *Imagined Communities: Reflections on the Origin and Spread of Nationalism* (London: Verso, 1983), p. 14.

25. James P. Carley, "Arthur in English History," interchapter A in *The Arthur of the English: The Arthurian Legend and Medieval English Life and Literature*, ed. W. R. J. Barron (Lampeter: University of Wales Press, 1997), p. 44.

26. J. C. Cassard, "Arthur est vivant! Jalons pour une enquete sur le messianisme royal au moyen age," *Cahiers de Civilisation medievale* 32 (1989): 135–46, 143.

27. John Davies, *The History of Wales* (London: Allen Lane Penguin, 1993), p. 153.

28. Oliver Padel, *Arthur in Medieval Welsh Literature* (Cardiff: University of Wales Press, 2000), p. 43.

29. Carley, "Arthur in English History," in *The Arthur of the English: The Arthurian Legend and Medieval English Life and Literature*, p. 48.

30. For example, in William Rothwell, "Language and Government in Medieval England," *Zeitschrift-fur-Franzosische-Sprache-und-Literatur* 93 (1983): 258–70.

31. The text is untitled in the manuscript. Orpen's edition appeared as *The Song of Dermot and the Earl*, a title closely paralleled by Conlon; see G. H. Orpen, *The Song of Dermot and the Earl* (Oxford: Clarendon Press, 1892); Denis J. Conlon, *The Song of Dermot and Earl Richard FitzGilbert* (*Le chansun de Dermot e li Quens Ricard Fiz Gilbert*), Studien und Dokumente zur Geschichte der romanischen Literaturen 24 (Frankfurt am Main: Lang, 1997). Mullally argues that this title "has given some historians a false sense of the author's purpose;" see Evelyn Mullally, *The Deeds of the Normans in Ireland* (Dublin: Four Courts Press, 2002).

32. The dating of the poem remains problematic. The work purports to be based on the experience of Morice Regan, latimer to Dermot, which might suggest a composition date in the period 1175–1200, but the poem survives in a single manuscript which shows signs of apparent textual revision in the 1220s.

33. Text and translation from Mullally, *Deeds of the Normans*, p. 141. The translation of line 3439 is missing in this edition.

34. Thus Clanchy reminds us of the anachronistic nature of the term "Angevin Empire": "Historians since the nineteenth century have for convenience described these lands as the Angevin Empire. Contemporaries, on the other hand, although they acknowledged that Henry II's dominions stretched from the Northern Ocean (that is, from Scotland) to the Pyrenees, never used the term 'Angevin Empire' because they looked on Henry's lands as the lucky acquisition of a quarrelsome family and not as an institution" (M. T. Clanchy, *England and its Rulers 1066–1272* (Oxford: Blackwell, 1983), pp. 75–76). However Clanchy also repeats, with no note of skepticism, Gerald of Wales's evidence "that Henry told his intimates that one strong man might rule the world" (Clanchy, *England and its Rulers*, p. 94).

35. The issue of colonialism in this period has been an intense focus of historical debate in recent years, particularly in response to the work of Rees Davies; see, for example R. R. Davies, *The First English Empire: Power and Identities in the British Isles, 1093–1343* (Oxford: Oxford University Press, 2000); R. R. Davies, *Domination and Conquest: the experience of Ireland, Scotland, and Wales, 1100–1300* (Cambridge: Cambridge University Press, 1990); John Gillingham, *The English in the Twelfth Century: Imperialism, National Identity and Political Values* (Woodbridge, Suffolk: Boydell and Brewer, 2000); Robert Bartlett, *England under the Norman and Angevin kings, 1075–1225* (Oxford: Clarendon Press, 2000); Ian Short, "*Tam Angli Quam Franci*: Self-Definition in Anglo-Norman England," *Anglo-Norman Studies* XVIII (1995): 153–75.

36. Marvin L. Colker, *Galteri de Castellione Alexandreis* (Padua: In aedibus Antenoreis, 1978), p. 273. Translation from Thomas Jolly, "The Alexandreid of Walter of Châtillon: a translation and commentary" (Ph.D. diss., Tulane University of Louisiana, 1968, pp. 257–8).

CHAPTER 1

THE CULTIVATION OF HISTORY, LEGEND, AND COURTESY AT THE COURT OF HENRY II

John Gillingham

Academics from Bishop Stubbs onward have liked to imagine—and they still do—that Henry II was a highly educated king who appreciated the value of learning and literature. In two lectures delivered in June 1878 Stubbs enumerated an impressive number of scholars and intellectuals who flourished in the second half of the twelfth century and, no matter where they worked, he brought them together under a single heading: Learning and Literature at the Court of Henry II.[1] In doing this Stubbs marked out a path that has been followed many times since. In some ways Henry was a great king. Measured in extent of territories over which he ruled, he was undeniably the greatest king England had as yet seen. When he came to power in the early 1150s he had some claim to be the best-educated prince in the West. Both his father, Geoffrey of Anjou, and his uncle Robert of Gloucester, were well-educated men. Huge hopes were invested in Henry from the moment of his birth in 1133 and a great deal of care taken over his education.[2] Given how well educated, rich, and powerful he was, it was only natural that bookish people should have liked to associate him with the world of books. Thus some parts of the French prose Lancelot cycle name the author as Walter Map and have him writing at King Henry's insistence. The prologue of another thirteenth-century romance, *Guiron le Courtois*, attributes a similar role to a "noble roy Henri d'Angleterre."[3] An early thirteenth-century Provençal poem on falconry by Daude de Pradas refers to "un libre del rei Enric / d'Anclaterra lo pris el ric" [a book of the esteemed and powerful King Henry of England], the most esteemed in the kingdom of England].[4] To this near-contemporary perception has been added the twentieth century's greater appreciation of the role of women at court, with the result that Henry II has been seen as one half of a double act with his wife, Eleanor of Aquitaine—that "forthright lady" as Katharine Hepburn characterized her.[5]

As the work of Rita Lejeune, R. R. Bezzola, and many other scholars demonstrates, Henry's power and his wife's glamour have proved to be a perilous combination, hard to resist.[6] In consequence, virtually every writer who lived and worked somewhere in Britain or France in the later twelfth century has at some stage been drawn into the orbit of Henry and Eleanor, "riche dame de riche rei" [the powerful wife of a powerful king].[7] In twentieth-century imagination their court came to be enveloped in an aura rather like that which would surround the White House-Camelot in the time of John F. and Jackie Kennedy. As Peter Damian-Grint has observed, "Reference to the brilliant spectacle—literary, but also cultural in a wider sense—of the Anglo-Norman court of Henry II is so common among scholars as to have become something of a cliché."[8] A small sample: "At his court was the most dazzling group of literary men the Middle Ages had ever seen" (Galbraith, 1935); "the most important intellectual centre in the West" (Schirmer, 1961); the Angevin and Norman court milieu, especially in the two decades from 1154 to Eleanor's imprisonment in 1173, was "the highpoint of the Renaissance of the twelfth century" (Dronke, 1976); "la cour la plus brillante d'Europe se réunissait autour ce prince; il soutenait l'essor de la culture chevaleresque. . .il entretenait dans sa maison les écrivains les plus talentueux et les plus hardis de son temps" [the most brilliant court in Europe gathered around this prince; he supported the rise of chivalric culture. . .he supported in his household the most talented and the boldest writers of his time] (Duby, 1995); "the most glittering court of the day" (Echard, 1998).[9]

Undoubtedly, a number of remarkably original and creative writers in both French and Latin were in various ways linked to Henry II, and to Eleanor of Aquitaine. After-dinner entertainment at an assembly at which, for example, Marie de France, Gerald de Barri, and Walter Map were all present would no doubt have been stimulating and entertaining—had it ever occurred.[10] No doubt also that many aspiring authors and scholars looked to Henry for support and advancement.[11] In this sense he can indeed be said to have stimulated literature. Some authors would have visited the court, whether the king's court, or the queen's, or the court of one of their sons, when that court came to the region in which they lived. A few of them were not only for a while more closely attached to the royal court—that notoriously most protean of things—but also seem to have composed the works for which they are known while members of it. Among them we can count the Frenchman, Peter of Blois; three

Englishmen—Richard FitzNigel, author of the *Dialogue of the Exchequer*; Roger of Howden; and the unknown author of the treatise on English law known as Glanvill—and two Anglo-Welsh authors, Walter Map and Gerald de Barri.[12]

According to Gerald de Barri (or Giraldus Cambrensis), Henry "never forgot anything he had heard that was worth remembering. Hence he had at his command pretty much the whole outline of history" [historiarum omnium fere promptam noticiam].[13] Ulrich Broich believed that Henry, faced with the problem of how to govern so large and heterogeneous an empire, saw in history the literature most likely to persuade so many different peoples that he was their rightful ruler. The result of this insight, he suggested, was the emergence of "eine regelrechte Schule von Historiographen" [a proper school of historiographers].[14] Bernard Guenée, in an influential survey of medieval historical writing, agreed: "Les Plantagenêts, au XIIe siècle, jouèrent consciemment et massivement de l'histoire pour établir l'illustre origine de leur lignage et justifier leur domination dans les pays qu'ils s'étaient acquis. Et, soucieux de convaincre d'abord leurs chevaliers, ils furent même les premiers à patronner une littérature en langue française" [In the twelfth century, the Plantagenets used history massively and on purpose to establish the illustrious origin of their lineage and to justify their domination over the countries they had acquired. And, as they wanted to convince their knights first, they were the first to commission a literature in the French language].[15] Moreover, Henry II is often represented as a ruler who used Arthurian legends to similar purpose. Peter Johanek, for example, characterizing Henry II as a ruler "der alles nutzte, was die divergenten Glieder seines Reichs enger aneinanderband " [who exploited everything that would knit the disparate elements of his kingdom more closely together], wrote: "Heinrich II. hat auch die Integrationskraft, die den Figur des Königs Arthur in der höfischen Gesellschaft des 12.Jahrhunderts zuzuwachsen begann, in den Dienst der Idee vom angevinischen Grossreich gestellt" [Henry II put the integrative force, which in twelfth-century courtly society began to cling to the figure of King Arthur, to work in the service of the idea of a greater Angevin realm].[16] Similarly, Duby envisaged Henry II as king of England, "se posant désormais en successeur du roi Arthur de la légende" [presenting himself as the successor of the legendary King Arthur].[17] It has recently been argued that Henry's authority over Anjou and the Touraine was bolstered by a claim of descent from King Arthur's seneschal, Kay, to whom, according to Geoffrey of Monmouth, King Arthur had given Anjou.[18] It remains widely accepted that Henry II had a particular interest in history and that this made a contribution to what, undoubtedly, toward the close of the twelfth century, became "a golden age of English historiography."[19] Indeed,

remarkably sweeping claims have been made for Henry's impact on historical writing, particularly in England. According to Diana Tyson, "it was
through Henry's encouragement that historiography in England lost its
purely monastic character to become an instrument of propaganda for
the king."[20]

In this chapter I offer a brief survey of historical writing not only in
England and Normandy during the reign of Henry II, but also in Aquitaine
and Anjou during the same period, in order to argue the following:

1. Although Henry's patronage had a very important impact on
   historical writing in French, he seems to have been curiously uninterested in the history of his own times.
2. He showed little or no interest in historical writing of any sort if it
   was in Latin.
3. During his reign the figure of King Arthur was not regarded as a
   cultural asset specific to the Angevin dynasty.

Finally I draw attention to a curiously overlooked link between Henry's
court and another sort of Latin literature—the literature of courtliness.

I begin with a few comments on a subject in which Henry and Eleanor
did have some interest: historical writing in French. Karen Broadhurst, in
reaching the conclusion that "the demonstrable patronage of vernacular
literature by Henry II and Eleanor of Aquitaine was severely limited,"
allowed only seven texts as implying some kind of association between
Henry and the author, and only two as demonstrably commissioned by the
king.[21] The latter were Wace's *Roman de Rou* and Benoît's *Chronique des
ducs de Normandie*. As verse histories of the dukes of Normandy, there can
be little doubt that they were intended, as Ulrich Broich argued, to
reinforce the legitimacy of Henry's own rule over Normandy.[22] According
to Wace himself, he "spoke in honour of the second Henry, who was born
of the lineage of Rou." He also tells us (assuming, that is, that he wrote the
so-called *Chronique Ascendante*) that he began to write the *Rou* in 1160.[23]
An interest at this time in his ducal ancestors and predecessors fits well with
Henry's presence at the translation in March 1162 of the bodies of dukes
Richard I and Richard II to a more elevated place in the monastic church
of Fécamp. According to Benoît, this was done "Par le buen rei, cil qui fu
fiz / Maheut, la buenne empereriz, / Par le buen rei Henri segunt, / Flor
des princes de tot le munt" [By the good king, who was son of Matilda, the
good empress, by the good king Henry the Second, the flower of all
the princes in the world].[24] It also chimes in nicely with his involvement in
the canonization of his predecessor and ancestral cousin, Edward the
Confessor, in February 1161 and his presence at the translation of Edward's

body at Westminster on October 13, 1163—though at that time Henry would have been responding to a recently completed work, Ailred's *Vita Ædwardi*, rather than sponsoring a new one.[25]

But the history of these two vernacular verse-histories of the Norman dukes is revealing. Wace's history comes to an abrupt and irritated end with a brief account of the battle of Tinchebrai in 1106 and of Duke Robert's imprisonment.[26] As is well known, at some date after 1174, Wace's commission was cancelled and the task assigned instead to Benoît. Scholars have not found it difficult to think of reasons for Henry II's change of mind. Wace was taking his time over the composition. He was not altogether "sound" on the legitimacy of the Norman invasion of England. Worse still, when he at last, after some 10,000 lines of verse on the dukes of the tenth and eleventh centuries, reached the reign of Henry II's grandfather, he seemed to take "the wrong side," supporting Robert Curthose rather than Henry I. It has been said that what Henry II wanted was "a story recounting the events during *his* kingship and the reigns of those who directly preceded him," and that Benoît was expected both "to improve upon the *Rou* and proceed beyond it."[27] But I doubt this. Although Benoît claimed to be keen to tell the story of Henry II's great deeds [hauz faiz], he got nowhere near them.[28] The fact that he started again at the beginning and wrote at even greater length, taking over 45,000 lines to get not much further than Wace had got, suggests that if the king had been interested in a history of his own reign, he had signally failed to make this clear. It is true that Benoît expressed his regret that he had taken so long in plastering and laying down ground color (i.e., in getting as far as the death of William I), that he still hadn't reached the stage of applying more subtle and richly colored paints (i.e., dealing with the reigns of the rulers from William II onwards, no doubt Henry II's *hauz faiz* in particular).[29] Nevertheless, it does seem likely that if Henry II had really wanted a narrative of his grandfather's and his own deeds, he would have been capable of making his wishes clear—especially in the circumstances of Wace's dismissal.

There is, of course, a French narrative of some of the most dramatic events of Henry's reign, Jordan Fantosme's verse history of the 1173–74 war between the English and the Scots, but even though it was very probably intended for recitation at his court, this cannot be used to support the notion that Henry himself was keen to sponsor the writing of recent history. As Matthew Strickland has convincingly argued, its two main political purposes were to promote a reconciliation between Henry II and his son Henry, the Young King, who had led the rebellion of 1173–74, and to praise the loyalty and bravery of the old king's nobles during the war. In pursuing these aims Fantosme was quite prepared to criticize as well as praise Henry II. Here we have a work which Henry II himself may well have listened to, but which, as Broadhurst noted, was not dedicated to him and was certainly not commissioned by him—a product of the culture of the court, but not necessarily to the king's own taste.[30]

Do Latin works associated with Henry II suggest that he was interested in promoting recent or contemporary history? The answer to this question must be no. Excluding Adelard of Bath, whose work on the astrolabe was dedicated to Henry before he took power in Normandy and Anjou in 1151, but including the unknown author of "Glanvill," I count a total of fourteen authors writing in Latin who arguably were in some sense writing for Henry II: Osbert of Clare,[31] Ailred of Rievaulx, Henry of Huntingdon, John of Marmoutier, Stephen of Rouen, Hugh de Claye, Robert of Torigni, Robert of Cricklade,[32] Richard FitzNigel, Walter Map, Peter of Blois, the anonymous author of "*Glanvill*," Gerald de Barri, and Daniel of Beccles.[33] How many works by these fourteen did Henry himself commission? Probably two or three. Peter of Blois claimed that the king commissioned the *Compendium in Job* so that he might learn more about patience, and also asked Peter to put together a collection of his letters.[34] In *De Nugis curialium*, Walter Map implies that "this little book" [hunc libellum], presumably one part of the ragbag, was written at the king's behest.[35] Gerald de Barri claimed that his *Expugnatio Hibernica*—the most clearly historical of all his extraordinary writings—was commissioned by Henry. I doubt this. Gerald says that it was so, but only in a letter addressed to King John in 1209.[36] Gerald's *Conquest of Ireland* itself was written in 1188–89 and in what he wrote in those years he says nothing about a royal commission— a revealing silence since he was clearly very keen to get one. I suspect that the letter was meant to encourage John to support Gerald by suggesting he should follow in his father's footsteps, and that what his father was supposed to have done was remodeled to that end. Indeed this issue, the attempt to encourage a present potential patron to act in the manner a famous predecessor is alleged to have done, is at stake in all patronage attributions made later than the work itself.

Of these fourteen authors, no less than eight—Ailred of Rievaulx, Henry of Huntingdon, John of Marmoutier, Stephen of Rouen, Hugh de Claye, Robert of Torigni, Walter Map, and Gerald de Barri—wrote works with some historical content. At first sight simple arithmetic lends weight to the conventional view. Having compiled a list of works dedicated to Henry, Haskins, noting that it included "much recent history, both in Latin and French," felt that his list "represents not unfairly the tendencies of the king's mind."[37] Nonetheless, a closer look at the history of historical writing in Latin during Henry's reign suggests that the king had no enthusiasm for it. What seems to have happened is that hopeful authors offered him works of history, but their offerings elicited remarkably little response.

It would be surprising if several of them were not as disappointed as in the end Gerald de Barri turned out to be. To the second recension of his *Itinerarium Kambriae*, written in the late 1190s and dedicated to Bishop Hugh of Lincoln, he added a preface in which he referred to both Henry II and Richard I as "principibus parum literatis et multum occupatis." He claimed that in consequence he had wasted his time in dedicating to them his first two major literary works: the *Topographia Hibernica* and the *Vaticinalis Historia* (i.e., the *Expugnatio Hibernica*).[38] Unreliable though Gerald can be, in this case the evidence makes it plain that neither Henry nor Richard was much—if at all—interested in Gerald as author; they both had other work for him to do.[39]

During the second quarter of the twelfth century, historical writing in England had flourished as never before. Soon after Stephen had recognized Henry as his heir, Ailred of Rievaulx offered the young prince an account of his ancestors, the *Genealogia Regum Anglorum*.[40] But after Henry II's accession to the throne we enter a virtually history-free period in England. Henry of Huntingdon finished his history with the coronation of Henry II, and with verses celebrating the young king's accession. Although Henry of Huntingdon announced a continuation of his history with a new book for a new king, it never materialized. It may be that only illness or death—he may have died as early as ca. 1157—prevented Henry of Huntingdon from carrying out his intention.[41] But there is a pattern here. No one continued the Anglo-Saxon Chronicle beyond 1154. The history known today as the *Gesta Stephani* (although in the only extant manuscript its title is *Historia Anglorum*) also comes to a stop with 1154.[42] John of Hexham's *Historia xxv.annum*, a continuation of the work of Symeon of Durham, stops with 1153, although its author was still alive in 1191.[43] Ailred continued into the early 1160s to have high hopes of Henry II, as is plain from his *Vita Ædwardi*. But even if we choose to regard it as in some sense historical hagiography, this work was commissioned not by Edward's successor, but by Ailred's own kinsman, Abbot Laurence of Westminster.

It is clear that after 1154 no one in England wrote anything remotely approaching a king-centered history until Roger of Howden took up the pen nearly twenty years later, in the early 1170s. Roger was a royal clerk and active in royal service for some thirty years, from the early 1170s to 1201, but there is no sign that either his *Gesta Henrici et Ricardi* or his *Chronica* were intended to be presented to or dedicated to the king.[44] Although a government insider, he was not writing an official history in the manner of Otto of Freising's *Gesta Friderici*, or Rigord's and William the Breton's *Gesta Philippi*. Ralph de Diceto, dean of St. Paul's, was the nearest the Angevin court came to having an official historiographer. It is a measure of how attached he felt to Henry II that he chose to begin his

Ymagines Historiarum with the year 1148, the year at which he dated Henry's knighting by King David of Scotland. Conceivably he might have dedicated it to Henry, but he did not start writing up the materials he had collected until 1188 and did not complete his first version until 1190.[45] It was in 1188 that Gerald de Barri dedicated his *Topographia Hibernica* to Henry II. Given the dearth of king-centered historical writing in England between 1154 and the early 1170s and the fact that from then until the later 1180s, Roger of Howden ploughed a lonely furrow, it is clear that the king himself was giving no encouragement whatever to English historical writing. It is tempting to conclude that one of the Henry's achievements was to put a stop to historical writing in England. The only things he did to encourage its revival were not intended to have that effect: to speak the angry words that led to the murder of Thomas Becket, Archbishop of Canterbury, and then, in 1188, to take the cross.[46] It was not until after the fall of Jerusalem in 1187 that the real surge in the volume of historical writing came in England.

In Normandy the pattern of Latin historical writing was very different. Here the accession of Henry II as duke did not bring things to a halt, and whereas in England, history flourished from the later 1180s onwards, here it petered out. A product of the abbey of Bec was Stephen of Rouen's long historical poem *Draco Normannicus*, described by Ulrich Broich as a "politische Tendenzschrift."[47] Probably written in 1169, its tone is anti-Capetian and decidedly favorable to Henry. Stephen may well have wanted Henry to read or listen to it, but in the one surviving copy neither patron nor dedicatee are named. Indeed Leah Shopkow has suggested that Henry may not even have been sent a copy. Conceivably once Henry's sons had done homage to Louis VII in 1169, Stephen's support for Norman autonomy was no longer welcome at court; certainly after the murder of the archbishop, his strongly anti-Becket line must have seemed misplaced.[48] The one significant Norman historian writing in Latin during Henry II's reign was Robert of Torigni. While still a monk at Bec, he added an account of the reign of Henry I to the history of the dukes begun by William of Jumièges and then began to compile the continuation of Sigebert of Gembloux which he recommenced after his election, with—as he noted—Duke Henry's approval, as abbot of Mont-Saint-Michel in 1154. Robert's own attitude toward history writing can be inferred from the letter he sent to Gervase, prior of Saint-Cénery, to try to persuade him to write a history of events in Normandy from 1135 to 1151: "ad augmentum famae tuae proficiet. . .Et quod his omnibus majus est, novi ducis favorem non modicum forsitan acquiret" [It will further the increase of your renown. . .And what is more important than all else, perhaps it will attract the not inconsiderable favor of the new duke].[49] However, Gervase was evidently not persuaded by these arguments, and it was left to Robert to press determinedly on with his self-imposed task of winning both fame and favor. The resulting book was the chronicle of which the Rolls Series editor wrote: "we can see that throughout the work his pen is controlled by a design long cherished though not carried out until 1184 of presenting a copy of his book to the king."[50] Despite Abbot Robert's closeness to King Henry—in 1161 he acted as godfather to his daughter Eleanor,[51] and Henry visited the abbey in 1158 and 1166—it is striking that it seems to have taken until 1184 before the king agreed to accept the gift. After Robert's death in 1186 his chronicle was not continued. Apart from some very scrappy annals, only the annals of Jumièges constitute any sort of continuation of Norman historical writing, and it took the drama of the fall of Jerusalem to revive this after a hiatus in the mid 1180s.[52]

In Henry's other duchy, Aquitaine, only in the Limousin was there was a significant tradition of history writing. Its chief representative in this period was Geoffrey of Vigeois, a monk of the great Benedictine house of St. Martial in Limoges. His history, composed in 1183–84, was, as he put it, written "to the honor of God and in praise of my country." Although he took a fairly positive view of the young Duke Richard, Geoffrey's *patria* [homeland] was not Aquitaine but the Limousin, and he generally had little sympathy for the ambitions of the Poitevin dukes of Aquitaine, especially when those ambitions involved threats to Limousin independence.[53] Nowhere in Aquitaine was there a tradition of history attached to the ducal house, and neither Eleanor nor Henry attempted to create one—although the opportunity may have been there. A Cluniac chronicler, Richard the Poitevin, dedicated the first extant recension of his "hystorias," which he completed in 1153 or a little later, to Abbot Peter of Cluny (who died in 1156). In this recension he referred to the reputation of Angevins as mean and arrogant—presumably a Poitevin view of them.[54] But then, in a continuation going up to 1162, he interpolated—or possibly reinstated—a sentence on the education of young Henry, saying that it had been entrusted to Master Peter of Saintes, "qui in metris eruditus est, super omnes coetaneos suos" [who was accomplished in composition, beyond all his contemporaries], and concluded with a decidedly favorable view of Henry's government of Aquitaine, praising the peace it brought to the region.[55] Moreover, into this recension Richard the Poitevin interpolated a history of Robert Guiscard, a Norman hero, together with some paragraphs on Eleanor's grandfather, Duke Guy-Geoffrey of Aquitaine, comparing him with Guiscard, and then a few sentences on the three Norman kings of England. As Jean-Marie Martin has pointed out, here we have a combination of themes seemingly made for the court of Henry and Eleanor.[56] So far as the surviving evidence goes, however, there seems to have been no

attempt to develop what might have been an embryonic pro-ducal historiography. In any case the third recension (ca. 1171) of the chronicle shows
that Richard's reaction to the murder of Thomas Becket was so fierce that
had any such attempt been made, it would almost certainly have
foundered.[57] Indeed in another text associated with the name of Richard
the Poitevin, De destructione castri Julii, Henry II is treated with great
hostility. He is the king of the north. He had begun well but then went
badly off the rails: "primis annis moderate et pacifice rexit. . .Sed mox ad
ingentia mala progressus, iracundia, crudelitatis, superbiae, tantum in se
odii excitavit, ut merita praedecessorum suorum penitus aboleret." These
are words, borrowed from the Breviarium of Eutropius, that Richard the
Poitevin had already used of the Emperor Domitian, in Christian tradition
one of the first great persecutors of the church.[58]

It is in Anjou itself, where the various versions of the Gesta Consulum
Andegavorum point to the existence of a twelfth-century tradition of history
close to the comital court, at any rate in the time of Henry's father,
Geoffrey Plantagenet, that we have the best evidence revealing that Henry II
saw political advantage to be gained from historical writing in Latin, and it
is significantly early in his reign. A claim already made in the Gesta
Consulum was elaborated in De majoratu et senescalcia Franciae in order to
prove, with all manner of epic circumstantial detail, that the count of
Anjou was the seneschal of France.[59] The evidence suggests that this short
treatise was composed in 1158 when Henry was about to invade Brittany,
presumably to provide the evidence to persuade a worried King Louis VII
that the planned attack was being carried out in his name and by one of his
officers. The author, Hugues de Claye, was a knight attached to Henry's
household, and it seems highly probable that Henry knew what he was up
to.[60] This brief work, only eight pages in Halphen and Poupardin's edition,
survives in just one manuscript. Nonetheless, the story and its message were
known at both Mont-Saint-Michel and Canterbury, so it was presumably
quite widely understood at the time.[61]

Jean de Marmoutier dedicated to Henry II his reworking of the version
of the Gesta Consulum Andegavorum attributed to "Breton d'Amboise,"
with its tale of Fulk the Good's message to the king of France: "rex illiter-
atus est asinus coronatus" [An uneducated king is like an ass with a crown
on its head].[62] Marmoutier added a new prologue claiming that this laudatory narrative of his ancestor's deeds would teach Henry to follow the
good and avoid the bad. Containing, as it does, direct quotations from
Bede's Historia Ecclesiastica, "there could hardly be a more appropriate
blending of Henry II's traditional Angevin and new English cultural
backgrounds."[63] There is, however, no evidence as to how Henry received
this work. Marmoutier's next work was his life of Henry's father, the

Historia Gaufredi ducis. Here too he used English material, this time from the *Historia Anglorum* of Henry of Huntingdon.[64] But Jean dedicated it not to the king, but to Bishop William of Le Mans (bishop 1145–87). It is significant that when he described Count Geoffrey's "most noble" tomb in Le Mans cathedral, he remarked that it was the bishop who had it "nobly constructed"; similarly it was the bishop who provided the revenues to pay the chaplains who were to say prayers at the altar for the repose of Geoffrey's soul. In all this there is no mention of Count Geoffrey's son.[65] This is all the more remarkable given the fact that early in his reign Henry had in fact made just such provision.[66] There is something that Marmoutier was not saying, something that he surely would have said if the *Historia* had been intended for the king. The entries for the years 1152 to 1154 in the annals of St. Aubin at Angers show some enthusiasm for the beginnings of Henry's rule, but this too was never developed into something more substantial.[67] Neither in Aquitaine nor Anjou, apart from the tract on the seneschalship, is there any hint to suggest that Henry II was interested in sponsoring a history of his own or even recent times.

Other pointers in the same direction are books of which no copy survives. Two writers extremely closely linked to the royal court claimed to have written histories of Henry's reign. Peter of Blois says he wrote a work, *De prestigiis fortunae*, in which he extolled the deeds of King Henry II, but no copy of it has ever been found.[68] Richard FitzNigel, author of *The Dialogue of the Exchequer,* says "tempore iuventutis editus de tripartita regni Anglie historia sub illustri Anglorum rege Henrico secundo. . .in secunda vero de insignibus predicti regis gestis que fidem humanam excedunt" [I wrote [a little book] when a young man about the history of England under Henry II under three heads. . . .the second dealt with the King's noble deeds, which are beyond human belief]. Although Richard does not say that the king commissioned it, or that it was dedicated to him, he none the less claimed that the book might well be useful in future times and agreeable to all interested "de regni statu sub predicto principe" [in public affairs under Henry II]. Yet despite the fact that he asked that anyone who came into possession of the book should take care of it, no copy of this has ever been found.[69] Clearly neither of these two books can ever have been circulated as "official histories," and their fate suggests that Henry himself made no effort to publicize them.

In the 1190s the links between the court and history became much closer than they had been during Henry II's reign. Not only were there many more historians writing in the 1190s than in any decade of Henry II's reign, but Richard I became the first king of England since Alfred to set out systematically to mould public opinion by means of the written word, by newsletters and fabrications.[70] If the Plantagenet court ever became "le principal foyer de culture historique en Occident" [the principal centre of historical culture in the West],[71] it was in the 1190s, not before and not after. The author of the *Itinerarium Peregrinorum*, writing in the early 1190s, believed that it was virtually a law of history that the names of rulers should be recorded in history books; indeed he said that some princes insisted on it being done, such was their itch for glory: "Scimus historiae legem interdum deposcere ut nomina principum, qui negotiis gerendis assistunt, singulatim scripto mandentur; quod ipsi etiam quodam pruritu gloriae nonnunquam affectant" [We know that the rules of History demand that from time to time the names of individual princes who had a role in the management of affairs should be recorded in writing. They themselves sometimes aim for this, having a sort of itch for glory].[72] This was evidently not one of Henry II's itches. His role as patron of Wace and Benoît was a very important one. Their work certainly suggests that he was interested in vernacular narratives of his Norman ancestors, but there is nothing to indicate that he, unlike William Longchamp and Richard I in the 1190s, was in the least interested in getting jongleurs to praise him. And so far as historical works in Latin are concerned, whether they were written in England, Normandy, Anjou, or Aquitaine, only in the short tract *De majoratu et senescalcia Franciae* composed ca. 1158 by Hugh de Claye is it possible to suspect the king's sponsorship. During Henry's reign there seem to have been a number of authors—such as Richard FitzNigel, Peter of Blois, Jean de Marmoutier, Gerald de Barri, and Robert of Torigni—who either wanted to or did write history in Latin, but they all got little response or encouragement. Other sorts of books, notably the treatise on English law known as "Glanvill" and the *Dialogue of the Exchequer*, show that, so far as Latin is concerned, it is hard to disagree with Haskins's last word on the subject: "[Henry's] clearest impression on literature is seen in the literature of administration."[73]

Enthusiasts for the notion of a vibrant culture at the court of Henry and Eleanor have often wanted to claim for it something more exciting than treatises on law and accounting, indeed for no less than one of the twelfth century's most celebrated creations, the figure of King Arthur. But it is by no means certain that Henry saw in Arthur a predecessor offering him an imperial mythology to match a Capetian Charlemagne. Even if by the 1150s Wace had turned Arthur into a more courtly and merciful king than Geoffrey of Monmouth's hero had been, in Anglo-Norman circles his was still a name that conjured up the image of a powerful enemy—and this whether or not there really were any Welsh or Bretons who fantasized about his return fighting fit from Avalon.[74] According to the Anglo-Norman *Description of England*:

> Well have the Welsh revenged themselves
> Many of our French they have slain
> Some of our castles they have taken
> Fiercely they threaten us
> Openly they go about saying
> That in the end they will have all,
> By means of Arthur, they will have it back
> They will call it Britain again.[75]

William of Newburgh believed that the Bretons defied Henry II when they gave the name Arthur to his grandson, the posthumous son of Geoffrey of Brittany.[76] The Barnwell chronicler's comment on the disappearance of Arthur of Brittany in 1203 was that it was God's punishment for Breton impudence in taking the name as an augury and boasting that they would kill the English and recover the kingdom.[77] Even if we choose to believe Layamon's assertion that Wace presented his *Roman de Brut* to Eleanor of Aquitaine[78] (or gave her a copy of it, much as Philippe de Thaon gave her a copy of his *Bestiaire*, a work he had previously presented to Henry I's second wife, Adeliza of Louvain), it remains the case that Arthur was still too closely associated with the Welsh and Bretons to be readily exploited as a specifically Plantagenet hero.

It is true that in the earlier romances of Chrétien of Troyes, *Erec et Enide* and *Cligès*, the Britain of King Arthur was delineated as though it were the England of Henry II. It is certainly possible that Chrétien intended King Arthur's empire to be understood as an allusion to Henry II's empire. But there is not the slightest indication that this was at Henry's—or Eleanor's—behest.[79] The argument that the letter in Stephen of Rouen's *Draco Normannicus*, in which Henry II wrote to King Arthur offering to hold Brittany *sub jure tuo*, reflects Henry II's real wishes, his desire to reconcile the Bretons to his rule while simultaneously undermining the claim of the king of France to be his overlord, is a problematic one. Stephen, after all, represents Henry II as smiling to his courtiers before he drafts a reply to King Arthur's ridiculous claims.[80] On balance, the more usual view that the letters were literary jokes seems the more plausible. In one of the poems attributed to the courtier-cleric Peter of Blois, the reader is advised: "If on vain hopes you lean, join the British who dream / of Arthur returning."[81] Moreover, as the editors of *De Nugis Curialium* observed, "Arthur is conspicuous by his absence from Map's pages—so conspicuous that it can hardly be the result of chance. Map presumably had some prejudice against

Arthur."[82] As an Anglo-Welsh clerk he was certainly well placed to know the response likely to be evoked by the name of King Arthur at Henry II's court.

Not until 1188 or 1189, the last year of the reign, do we have a reference to Arthur as in some sense Henry II's predecessor by an author attached to the king's court. In the second edition of his *Topographia Hibernica*, Gerald de Barri mentioned Arthur as the overlord of Ireland, "famosus ille Britonum rex" [that celebrated king of the Britons], and in a context supportive of Henry II's claim to the island.[83] De Barri had entered royal service just a few years earlier, in 1184×1185, and the reference to King Arthur was not in the first (1187–88) edition of the *Topographia*. It looks as though it was only right at the end of Henry II's reign that the Welsh view of King Arthur began to be transmuted into something more acceptable to the English—and this by an author who was himself an Anglo-Welshman significantly younger than Walter Map. The earliest evidence for Arthur being turned into the model English king that he later became dates from the 1190s and from the reign of Richard I—in his military prowess a far more Arthurian king than his father had been, and a king who took Excalibur with him on crusade, i.e., a king who consciously associated himself with the legendary king. In his journal of the Third Crusade, Roger of Howden referred to the sword that Richard gave to Tancred of Sicily in March 1191 as "gladium optimum Arcturi, nobilis quondam regis Britonum, quem Britones vocaverunt Caliburnum" [The most splendid sword, which the Britons called Caliburn/Excalibur, and which belonged to Arthur, once the noble king of the Britons]. A few years later, when Roger rewrote this passage, he referred to Arthur as "rex Anglie."[84] It is also in the early 1190s that we must place the famous excavation at Glastonbury that uncovered the bodies of Arthur and Guinevere.[85] The abbot of Glastonbury responsible for this piece of theatre was Henry de Sully, formerly prior of Bermondsey, chosen abbot at an assembly at Pipewell in September 1189—an assembly dominated by the new king.[86] But if in the 1190s Arthur was being turned into an emphatically dead king of England, the loss of continental territories so soon afterwards, in 1202–04, had the effect of ensuring that the subsequent political resonance of an English King Arthur was restricted to that of a king intensifying his rule over the rest of Britain. In any case, as the romances of Chrétien of Troyes make plain, the literary magic of the court of King Arthur, of the Knights of the Round Table, of Lancelot, Gawain, Perceval, and the others, was so great that it had already overflowed the boundaries of the Angevin Empire and become part of the common currency of western-European literature.

Moreover, it does not seem likely that Henry II was interested in legitimizing his authority over Anjou and the Touraine at a lower level by claiming descent from Arthur's seneschal Kay, to whom, according to

Geoffrey of Monmouth, King Arthur had given Anjou.[87] The fact that the author of the mid-twelfth-century *Liber de compositione castri Ambazie* dwelt on this famous gift, and on Kay as the eponymous founder of Chinon, shows that the story was appreciated in the region, but this work was composed for the lords of Amboise in the Touraine, not for the comital court. Moreover, although the *Liber de compositione* appears as a kind of introduction to the "Breton d'Amboise" version of the *Gesta consulum*, when we get to the manuscripts of Jean de Marmoutier's version, the one version unquestionably intended for Henry II, we find that it has been omitted and replaced by a new introduction written specifically for the king himself.[88] The Trojan history was no doubt enjoyed, but there is no sign that at court it was taken seriously within the overlapping categories of history and legitimizing myth.[89] Neither Wace nor Benoît gave any more weight to the legendary Trojan origins of the Danes and hence of the Normans than Dudo or William of Jumièges had done. Their references are perfunctory at best; indeed Wace's few lines on the subject are in a fragment that the author himself may have discarded.[90]

It has been all too easy to overestimate the literary influence of the court of Henry and Eleanor, certainly so far as works in Latin are concerned. My sceptical approach to the role of this king and queen does not, of course, imply that in cultural terms the period was not a remarkable one. To quote Ian Short: "It would be only a slight exaggeration to conclude that for a short space of history, the courts of Henry I and Henry II and the Anglo-Norman baronage and Church had presided over a literary and intellectual efflorescence of remarkable brightness."[91] But as these words make plain, it is important to put the court of Henry II into the context of other twelfth-century courts. Between 1154 and 1189, with the exception of Walter Map's *De Nugis* and Gerald de Barri's two books on Ireland, the really impressive works of Latin literature were written by authors such as John of Salisbury, Joseph of Exeter, Walter of Châtillon, Nigel Whiteacre (Wireker), and Jean de Hauville who were attached to other courts. Although Jean de Hauville, for example, had a few nice things to say about a visibly aging Henry II, his *Architrenius* was dedicated, not to the king, but to Walter of Coutances as he moved from the see of Lincoln to the archiepiscopal see of Rouen.[92]

In a book about Henry II, however, it would no doubt be more courteous if I could conclude with a more positive view of Henry II's role in the history of literature. So I shall finish by linking him with an author virtually unknown when Haskins compiled his list of authors who dedicated their works to Henry, but one who has recently attracted quite a lot of attention.[93] This is Daniel of Beccles, author of the long Latin poem usually known as *Urbanus Magnus*—although *Liber Urbani*, "The Book of the

Civilized Man," is a more accurate title—and the most substantial courtesy poem in any language.[94] It ends "Explicit liber Urbani Danielis
Becclesiensis," after stating that it was "Old King Henry" who first gave
this teaching to the uncourtly [illepidis].[95] The Tudor bibliographer John
Bale called him Daniel Church (reading part of his name as "ecclesiensis"
instead of "Becclesiensis") and claimed to have found him mentioned in an
old chronicle as having been, for more than 30 years, at the court [curia] of
Henry II, a member of his "domus et familia" [house and household].[96]
Who was "Old King Henry"? Whether it was Henry I,[97] or Henry II, the
Old King as opposed to the Young King, his son, it is a plausible guess that
"the poem was produced at the Angevin court."[98]

With this in mind, it is worth looking closely at Walter Map's judgment
on Henry II. "He was acquainted with every polite accomplishment and
was learned as far as was fitting or useful" [nullius comitatis inscius, littera-
tus ad omnem decenciam et utilitatem].[99] In other words, he was even
more distinguished for his polished manners than for his learning. Indeed,
it was the king's courtliness, not his learning, that inspired anecdotes.
Consider one of Walter Map's anti-Cistercian stories:

> On a windy day recently a Cistercian monk was making his way on foot
> along the street when he looked round to see the lord king Henry II riding
> as usual at the head of his great train of knights and clerks. In his haste to get
> out of the way, the monk tripped over a stone and, unluckily for him—not
> just at that moment being borne up by angels—he fell over in front of the
> king's horse. The wind blew the poor man's habit right up over his neck
> exposing all his private parts. The king, that treasure-house of courtesy
> [omnis facetie thesaurus], pretended to see nothing and said nothing.[100]

Gerald de Barri also told admiring stories about Henry's courtliness,
even in later works written at a time when he generally took a hostile view
of the former king. In one such anecdote, some men were accused of
speaking ill [indecentia et inhonesta] of Henry; one of them admitted the
offence, saying "facete" it was nothing to what they would have said, had
the wine not run out. Everyone, Henry included, burst out laughing, and
the accused were let off.[101] There are obviously parallels here with the less-
amusing but better-known story of King Henry seeing the funny side
when Bishop Hugh of Lincoln's pointed remark about his "cousins of
Falaise" reminded him of the humble origins of William the Conqueror's
mother.[102] Academics have given too much attention to Henry's learning,
and not enough to his courtliness.[103] When he was a boy he may well have
been given the best tutors that money could buy, but there is no evidence

that he took so much trouble over the academic education of his own son and heir. Indeed, a letter written by Peter of Blois on behalf of the archbishop of Rouen strongly implies that he had not bothered.[104] We have been taught to think of Henry II as someone like us—a king whose "mind was of a decidedly intellectual bent," who preferred the arts of peaceful government to the arts of war, who liked to dress simply, and who "did not seek to buttress his regality with. . .the pretensions of *courtoisie* [courtesy]."[105] But his nickname, Courtmantle, should remind us of the fashionable and elegantly dressed young man, the king "whose power," in Walter Map's words, "almost the whole world fears and who is always robed in precious stuffs, as is right ('ut decet')."[106]

Notes

My thanks to Elisabeth van Houts and Jane Martindale for their kindness in reading and commenting upon a draft of this essay.

1. William Stubbs, *Seventeen Lectures on the Study of Mediaeval and Modern History* (Oxford: Clarendon Press, 1900), pp. 132–78.

2. In the second edition of his *Topographia Hibernica*, Gerald de Barri addressed Henry in the following words: "Quanto studio, quantaque et quam laudabili regio in sanguine diligentia, a primo aetate annisque pueritiae studia literarum amplexus fueris;. . .literatus princeps effectus, et in ethicis disciplinis decenter eruditus, inter universos mundi principes tanquam lucida gemma praefulseris," *Giraldi Cambrensis: Opera* vol. 5, ed. James F. Dimock, R[olls] S[eries] 21 (1867), 191–92. According to Peter of Blois, writing to a correspondent in Sicily: "Nam cum rex vester bene litteras noverit, rex noster longe litteratior est," *Petri Blesensis Bathoniensis in Anglia Archdiaconi opera omnia*, ed. J-P. Migne, PL 207 (Paris: J-P. Migne, 1855), 198.

3. See Emmanuèle Baumgartner, "Figures du destinateur: Salomon, Arthur, le roi Henri d'Angleterre," in *Anglo-Norman Anniversary Essays*, ed. Ian Short, Anglo-Norman Text Society Occasional Publications Series 2 (1993): 1–10, 7–10; and Siân Echard, *Arthurian Narrative in the Latin Tradition* (Cambridge: Cambridge University Press, 1998), pp. 1–2.

4. Charles H. Haskins, "Henry II as a Patron of Literature," in *Essays in Medieval History Presented to T. F. Tout*, ed. A. G. Little and F. M. Powicke (Manchester: Manchester University Press, 1925), pp. 71–77, at 76.

5. In conversation with Peggy Brown. See Elizabeth A. R. Brown, "Eleanor of Aquitaine Reconsidered: the Woman and her Seasons," in *Eleanor of Aquitaine: Lord and Lady*, ed. Bonnie Wheeler and John C. Parsons (New York: Palgrave Macmillan, 2002), pp. 1–54, at 54.

6. Reto R. Bezzola, *Les origines et la formation de la littérature courtoise en Occident (500–1200)*, 3 vols. (Paris: E. Champion 1944–1963), vol. 2, part 2: "La société féodale et la transformation de la littérature de cour" (1960). Rita Lejeune, "Rôle littéraire d'Aliénor d'Aquitaine et de sa famille,"

Cultura neo-latina 14 (1954): 5–57; eadem, "Rôle littéraire de la famille d'Aliénor d'Aquitaine," *Cahiers de civilisation mediévale* 1 (1958): 319–36.

7. The quotation is from Benoît de Sainte-Maure, *Roman de Troie*, ed. Leopold Constans, 6 vols. (Paris: Formin Didot, 1904–1912), p. 2: line 13,468. The passage in question can reasonably be taken to imply that Eleanor was likely to learn of Benoît's work, probably written between 1165 and 1170, but not that there was any closer connection between the queen and the poet. See Tamara F. O'Callaghan, "Tempering Scandal: Eleanor of Aquitaine and Benoît de Sainte-Maure's *Roman de Troie*," in Wheeler and Parsons, *Eleanor of Aquitaine,* pp. 301–17, at 303.

8. Peter Damian-Grint, *The New Historians of the Twelfth-Century Renaissance* (Woodbridge, Suffolk: Boydell and Brewer, 1999), p. 1.

9. V. H. Galbraith, "The literacy of the medieval English kings," *PBA* 21 (1935): 201–38, repr. in Galbraith, *Kings and Chroniclers* (London: Hambledon, 1982), 1:78–111, at 93; Walter F. Schirmer, "Die kulturelle Rolle des englischen Hofes im 12. Jahrhundert," in *Studien zum literarischen Patronat im England des 12.Jahrhunderts,* ed. Walter F. Schirmer and Ulrich Broich (Cologne: Westdeutscher Verlag, 1961), pp. 9, 18; Peter Dronke, "Peter of Blois and Poetry at the Court of Henry II," *Medieval Studies* 38 (1976): 185; Georges Duby, *Dames du XIIe siècle II. Le souvenir des aïeules* (Paris: Gallimard, 1995), p. 67; Echard, *Arthurian Narrative,* p. 2. For similar views see Egbert Türk, *Nugae curialium: le règne d'Henri II Plantagenêt (1154–1189) et l'éthique politique* (Geneva: Droz, 1977), xvii–xviiii and Elizabeth Salter, *English and International: Studies in the Literature, Art and Patronage of Medieval England* (Cambridge: Cambridge University Press, 1988), pp. 17–26.

10. But very likely there never was such an occasion. Quite apart from the fog of uncertainty surrounding Marie, Walter Map and Gerald de Barri proba-bly saw each other in the 1190s rather than at Henry II's court. On this, see A. K. Bate, "Walter Map and Giraldus Cambrensis," *Latomus* 31 (1972): 860–75.

11. Richard Mortimer, *Angevin England 1154–1258* (Oxford: Blackwell, 1994), p. 212.

12. In addition, it should be noted that in three songs, datable only to 1154–ca. 1180, the Limousin poet, Bernart de Ventadorn, implies that he sometimes attended Henry II's court, even when it took him across "the wild, deep sea" to England. See *Bernart von Ventadorn: seine Lieder,* ed. and trans. Carl Appel (Halle: M. Niemeyer, 1915), poems 21, 26, 33.

13. Giraldus Cambrensis, *Expugnatio Hibernica. The Conquest of Ireland,* ed. and trans. A. B. Scott and F. X. Martin, A New History of Ireland. Ancillary Publications 3 (Dublin: Royal Irish Academy, 1978), p. 132.

14. Broich, *Studien,* pp. 44–45.

15. Bernard Guenée, *Histoire et Culture historique dans l'Occident médiéval* (Paris: Aubier, 1980), p. 334. In Guenée's view they inherited this approach from both Norman dukes and Angevin counts. Cf. the description of the court of Henry and Eleanor "as a great melting pot in which elements of an

extremely wide range of traditions were analyzed, discussed and compared: the true melting-pot of the most significant developments of Old French literature" (Roberto Antonelli, "The Birth of Criseyde," in *The European Tragedy of Troilus*, ed. Piero Boitani [Oxford: Oxford University Press, 1989], pp. 21–48).

16. Peter Johanek, "König Arthur und die Plantagenets. Über den Zusammenhang von Historiographie und höfische Epik in mittelalterlicher Propaganda," *Frühmittelalterliche Studien* 21 (1987): 389.

17. Duby, *Dames du XIIe siècle II. Le souvenir des aïeules*, p. 68.

18. Amaury Chauou, *L'idéologie Plantagenêt. Royauté arthurienne et monarchie politique dans l'espace Plantagenêt (XIIe–XIIIe siècles)* (Rennes: Presses Universitaires de Rennes, 2001), pp. 45, 54–55; Amaury Chauou, "Arturus redivivus" in *Noblesses de l'espace Plantagenêt (1154–1224)*, ed. Martin Aurell (Poitiers: Université de Poitiers [Centre national de la recherche scientifique, Centre d'études supérieures de civilisation médiévale], 2001), pp. 67–78.

19. "This revival owed much to the influence of the royal court" (Antonia Gransden, *Historical Writing in England, c.550–c.1307* [London: Routledge & Kegan Paul, 1974], p. 219). Cf. "Henry II stood at the centre of a brief renaissance of vernacular and Latin historiography" (Andrew Galloway, "Writing history in England," chap. 10 in *The Cambridge History of Medieval English Literature*, ed. David Wallace [Cambridge: Cambridge University Press, 1999], 261), though a few lines later Galloway notes that "even Henry II's historiographical patronage was unpredictable."

20. Diana B. Tyson, "Patronage of French Vernacular History Writers in the Twelfth and Thirteenth Centuries," *Romania* 100 (1979): 180–222.

21. Karen Broadhurst, "Henry II of England and Eleanor of Aquitaine: Patrons of Literature in French?" *Viator* 27 (1996): 53–84, 69–70, 81–84. However if the author of the *Livre des manières*, Etienne de Fougères, was the royal chaplain appointed bishop of Rennes, then a case could be made for seeing it, too, as in some sense a product of the royal court, even though he dedicated it to the countess of Hereford; see *Etienne de Fougères. Le Livre des Manières*, ed. R. Anthony Lodge (Geneva: Droz, 1979), pp. 13–22.

22. Broich, *Studien*, pp. 92, 200. Wace's *Chronique ascendante* begins with nearly 100 lines devoted to an extremely flattering assessment of Henry II's rule. He says, moreover, that both Eleanor and Henry rewarded him with gifts and promises: Wace, *The Roman de Rou*, trans. Glyn S. Burgess with the text edited by Anthony J. Holden (St. Helier: Société Jersiaise, 2002), vol. 1: lines 17–107, esp. 19–21.

23. Wace, *The Roman de Rou*, vol. 3: lines 185–86, vol. 1: lines 1–4.

24. Benoît, *Chronique des ducs de Normandie*, ed. Carin Fahlin, 2 vols. (Uppsala: Bibliotheca Ekmaniana, 1951–54), vol. 2: lines 32,059–62. Cf. *The Chronicle of Robert of Torigni*, in *Chronicles of the Reigns of Stephen, Henry II and Richard I*, 4 vols., ed. Richard Howlett, RS 82 (1889): 4:212–13. Strikingly Wace tells us that he attended the ceremony, but does not mention the king's presence (*Roman de Rou*, vol. 3: lines 2241–46).

25. Frank Barlow, *Edward the Confessor* (New Haven and London: Yale University Press, 1997), appendices D and E.

26. Jean Blacker, *The Faces of Time* (Austin: University of Texas Press, 1994), pp. 102–17, 182–84. For further discussion of this matter see Jean-Guy Gouttebroze, "Pourquoi congédier un historiographe, Henri II Plantagenêt et Wace," *Romania* 112 (1991): 289–311; Matthew Bennett, "Poetry as History? The Roman de Rou of Wace as a source for the Norman Conquest," *Anglo-Norman Studies 5: Proceedings of the Battle Conference 1982*, ed. R. Allen Brown (Woodbridge, Suffolk: Boydell and Brewer, 1983), pp. 21–39; Elisabeth M. C. van Houts, "The adaptation of the *Gesta Normannorum ducum* by Wace and Benoît," chapter 11 in *History and Family Traditions in England and the Continent, 1000–1200*, Variorum Collected Studies Series (Aldershot: Ashgate, 1999), pp. 103–32.

27. Blacker, *Faces of Time*, pp. 190, 193.

28. Benoît, *Chronique*, lines 42,059–61.

29. Benoît, *Chronique*, lines 42,062–71. Discussed by Blacker, *Faces of Time*, pp. 49–50 and Damian-Grint, *New Historians*, pp. 104–5.

30. Matthew Strickland, "Arms and the Men: War, Loyalty and Lordship in Jordan Fantosme's Chronicle," in *Medieval Knighthood IV*, ed. Christopher Harper-Bill and Ruth Harvey (Woodbridge, Suffolk: Boydell and Brewer, 1992), pp. 187–220; Broadhurst, "Patronage," pp. 59–60. Broadhurst is even more dismissive of Eleanor's alleged role as patron of letters. Also skeptical of Eleanor's role is Ursula Vones-Leibenstein, *Eleonore von Aquitanien: Herrscherin zwischen zwei Reichen,* Persönlichkeit und Geschichte 160/161 (Göttingen: Muster-Schmidt, 2000), pp. 103–112. A searching investigation of Eleanor's links with Occitan poetry concludes: "The literary evidence suggests that the troubadours knew and frequented Eleanor's husband and sons, her daughters, her vassals and her enemies, but not her. In marked contrast to modern writers, the medieval Occitan poets—with the single exception of Bernart de Ventadorn—seem to have accorded her no importance at all" (Ruth Harvey, "Eleanor of Aquitaine and the Troubadours," in *The World of Eleanor of Aquitaine: Literature and Society in Southern France between the Eleventh and the Thirteenth Centuries*, ed. Catherine Léglu and Marcus Bull [Woodbridge, Suffolk: Boydell and Brewer, 2005]).

31. Osbert offered Duke Henry a ninety-seven-line poem shortly before he was anointed king. It is printed in E. W. Williamson, *The Letters of Osbert of Clare* (Oxford, 1929), pp. 130–32.

32. Robert of Cricklade, prior of St. Frideswide's, Oxford, from 1139×41 to 1174×80. The dedication of his *Defloratio* of Pliny's Natural History to Henry, whom he describes as "tot et tantarum regionum dominum et rectorem," might be thought to strike a sufficiently obsequious note: "Tibi illustrissime rex Anglorum Henrice ego tuus famulus Rodbertus hoc opus dedicavi. . .Siquidem notum est quia cum sis in bellicis negotiis invictissimus parto otio non minus es in litterali scientia studiosus," British Library MS Royal 16. C. XIV, fol. 1r. This approach may be connected with

the possibility that when he went to Scotland, it was on the king's business; see *Regesta regum Scottorum I: The Acts of Malcolm IV*, ed. Geoffrey W. S. Barrow (Edinburgh: Edinburgh University Press, 1960), nos. 223, 228. On Robert's works see Richard Sharpe, *A Handlist of the Latin Writers of Great Britain and Ireland before 1540*, revised ed. (Turnhout: Brepols, 2001), pp. 532–33. In an as yet unpublished study Elisabeth van Houts makes the very plausible suggestion that the *Defloratio* had been dedicated to Henry I first.

33. I do not include John of Salisbury, although Southern described his *Policraticus*, dedicated to Thomas Becket, as "evidence for the intellectual stimulus provided by the work of government in the time of Henry II"; see R. W. Southern, *Medieval Humanism* (Oxford: Blackwell, 1970), p. 176.

34. *Petri Blesensis Bathoniensis archdiaconi Opera omnia*, 4 vols., ed. J. A. Giles (Oxford: Parker, 1846–47), 3:19–20; R. W. Southern, "Peter of Blois: a twelfth-century humanist?," chap. 7 in *Medieval Humanism* (Oxford: Blackwell, 1970), pp. 105–132. There is no way of knowing whether or not Henry commissioned Peter's *Dialogus inter regem Henricum secundum et abbatem Bonevallis*, probably composed in 1188 or early 1189. On this see the edition by R. B. C. Huygens in *Revue Benedictine* 68 (1958), pp. 87–112; Martin Aurell, "Révolte nobiliaire et lutte dynastique dans l'empire Angevin, 1154–1224," *Anglo Norman Studies 24: Proceedings of the Battle Conference 2001*, ed. John Gillingham (Woodbridge, Suffolk: Boydell and Brewer, 2002): 31.

35. Walter Map, *De Nugis Curialium: Courtiers' Trifles*, ed. and trans. M. R. James, C. N. L. Brooke, and R. A. B. Mynors (Oxford: Clarendon Press, 1983), bk. 4, chap. 2: 282. If the following chapter, the *Dissuasio Valerii* (bk. 4, chap. 3), is the "libellus" referred to here, it might be construed as a wry comment on the rumors that Henry was hoping to re-marry; see Keith Bate, "La littérature latine d'imagination à la cour d'Henri II d'Angleterre," *Cahiers de civilisation médiévale* 34 (1991): 3–21, 15. The fact that an article, itself a fine study of three writers only one of whom, Walter Map, can be shown to have been attached to the court, should be given this title is testament to the magnetic pull of Henry II's court on the modern imagination.

36. "ad ipsius instanciam," Giraldus, *Expugnatio Hibernica*, 261. At the same time he asked that someone should translate his history, which in 1189 he dedicated to Richard I, into French [in Gallicum].

37. Haskins, "Henry II as a patron," pp. 77.

38. Giraldus Cambrensis, *Opera*, 6:7.

39. John Gillingham, "Henry II, Richard I and the Lord Rhys," *Peritia* 10 (1996): 225–36; repr. in *The English in the Twelfth Century* (Woodbridge, Suffolk: Boydell and Brewer, 2000), pp. 59–68, esp. 64–68.

40. In this Ailred addresses Henry as duke of the Normans and Aquitanians, count of the Angevins, and "hope of the English"; *Genealogia Regum Anglorum*, PL 195:711–13.

41. *Henry, Archdeacon of Huntingdon, Historia Anglorum*, ed. and trans. Diana E. Greenway (Oxford: Clarendon Press, 1996), 776. For discussion of the date of his death, which could have been as late as 1164, see p. lvii.

42. *Gesta Stephani*, ed. and trans. K. R. Potter and Ralph H. C. Davis (Oxford: Clarendon Press,1976), p. xii. If the author has been correctly identified as the bishop of Bath, it should be noted that he did not die until 1166.

43. Diana E. Greenway, *Fasti Ecclesie Anglicanae 1066–1300, VI York* (London: School of Advanced Study. Institute of Historical Research, 1999), p. 96, where she also shows that Prior Richard, John's predecessor at Hexham, and author of *De gestis regis Stephani*, was still alive in 1162.

44. For Howden in royal service see John Gillingham, "The Travels of Roger of Howden and his Views of the Irish, Scots and Welsh," *Anglo-Norman Studies 20: Proceedings of the Battle Conference 1997*, ed. Christopher Harper-Bill (Woodbridge, Suffolk: Boydell and Brewer, 1998): 151–69, repr. as chap. 5 in Gillingham, *The English in the Twelfth Century*, pp. 69–91, together with the references there to earlier work by Frank Barlow and David Corner; also John Gillingham, "Historians without Hindsight: Coggeshall, Diceto and Howden on the Early Years of John's Reign," in *King John: New Interpretations*, ed. S. D. Church (Woodbridge, Suffolk: Boydell and Brewer, 1999), pp. 1–26, at 9–23.

45. *Radulfi de Diceto Decani Lundoniensis Opera Historica*, ed. William Stubbs, 2 vols., RS 68 (1876), 2:viii–x.

46. Henry's confiscation, in 1157, of the estates of King Stephen's son, William, may also have had the unintended outcome of provoking the writing of the so-called "Hyde Chronicle"; see Elisabeth van Houts, "The Warenne View of the Past 1066–1203," *Anglo-Norman Studies 26. Proceedings of the Battle Conference 2002*, ed. John Gillingham (Woodbridge, Suffolk: Boydell and Brewer, 2003): 103–21.

47. Broich, *Studien*, pp. 89–92.

48. Leah Shopkow, *History and Community. Norman Historical Writing in the Eleventh and Twelfth Centuries* (Washington, D.C.: Catholic University of America Press, 1997), pp. 50–51, 113–115, 239–40.

49. PL 202:1307–09.

50. Howlett, *Robert of Torigni*, p. xx. This is based on the note in a partly autograph Mont St Michel manuscript of the chronicle: Bibliothèque municipale d'Avranches MS 159: "Ab eodem anno [1100] Robertus abbas fecit historiam continentem res gestas Romanorum, Francorum Anglorum usque ad presens tempus, continentem scilicet annos usque ad annum Dominicae incarnationis MCLXXXIIII, quem librum praesentavit karissimo domino suo Henrico regi Anglorum" (pp. lix–lx).

51. Howlett, *Robert of Torigni*, p. 211.

52. *Annales de l'Abbaye Royale de Saint-Pierre de Jumièges*, ed. Jean Laporte (Rouen: Lecerf, 1954).

53. "ad honorem dei vel patriae laudem," chap. 65 in Geoffrey of Vigeois, "Chronica," in *Novae Bibliothecae Manuscriptorum Librorum*, ed. Philip Labbe, 2 vols. (Paris: Cramoisy, 1657), 2:279–329. For a discussion of Geoffrey's outlook, see Michel Aubrun, "Le Prieur Geoffroy du Vigeois et sa chronique," *Revue Mabillon* 58 (1974): 313–26.

54. Edmond Martène, *Veterum Scriptorum et Monumentorum Historicum. Dogmaticorum, Moralium, Amplissima Collectio*, 9 vols. (Paris: Montalant, 1724–33), 5:1159–74, at 1173. The principal work on Richard the Poitevin remains Elie Berger, *Richard le Poitevin, moine de Cluny, historien et poète*, in his *Notice sur divers manuscrits de la bibliothèque Vaticane, Bibliothèque des écoles françaises d'Athènes et de Rome* 6 (Paris: E. Thorin, 1879), pp. 45–138.

55. This recension was printed in Lodovico Antonio Muratori, *Antiquitates Italicae Medii Ævi*, 6 vols. (Milan: Societatis Palatinae, 1741; repr. Bologna: A. Forni, 1965), 4:1077–1103, at pp. 1098, 1102.

56. Jean-Marie Martin, "Une 'Histoire' peu connue de Robert Guiscard," *Archivio storico pugliese* 31 (1978): 47–66, at 61–62. He suggests it might have been put together on the occasion of Joan's marriage to William II of Sicily in 1176.

57. For the text of the third recension, see Berger, *Richard le Poitevin*, pp. 123–26. This elaborates the praise for the verses of Peter of Saintes and quotes the opening, "Viribus arte nimis Danaum data Troia ruinis," closing, "Sic gens Romulea surgit ab Hectorea," lines from his poem on the fall of Troy. This is printed in PL 171:1451–53 as a supplement to the poems of Hildebert of Lavardin. On this see *Max Manitius: Geschichte der lateinischen Literatur des Mittelalters*, 3 vols. (Munich: Beck, 1931), 3:647. It has been suggested that "of Saintes" may be a copyist's mistake; see Barthélemy Hauréau, *Les mélanges poétiques d'Hildebert de Lavardin* (Paris: Pedone-Lauriel, 1882), pp. 164–65. But if early copies of Richard's chronicle were made in the Aunis region where it was composed, such a mistake is unlikely.

58. Martin Bouquet, et al, *Recueil des Historiens des Gaules et de la France*, 24 vols. (Paris: V. Palmé, 1869–1904), 12:418–21, at p. 419. See Berger, *Richard le Poitevin*, 75, and Eutropius: *Breviarium*, 7:23; see *Eutrope: Abrégé d'histoire romaine: texte établi et traduit par Joseph Hellegouarch, Collection des Universités de France* 356 (Paris: Les Belles Lettres, 1999).

59. *Chroniques des comtes d'Anjou*, ed. Louis Halphen and René Poupardin, *Collection de textes pour servir à l'étude et à l'enseignement de l'histoire* 48 (Paris: A. Picard, 1913), pp. xc–xciii, 37, 239–46.

60. In a document dated 1158 and witnessed by Hugues de Claye, Henry II announced that at Orleans "in communi audientia recognovit quod custodia abbatie sancti Juliani Turonensis ad me pertinet ex dignitate dapiferatus mei, unde servire debeo regi Francie sicut comes Andegavorum." *Recueil des Actes de Henri II, roi d'Angleterre et duc de Normandie, concernant les provinces françaises et les affaires de France*, ed. Léopold Delisle and Élie Berger, *Chartes et diplômes relatifs à l'histoire de France*, 3 vols. (Paris: Imprimerie nationale, 1909–1927), 1: no. 87. Twenty five other *acta* printed by Delisle and Berger show just how active Hugues de Claye was in the service of both Geoffrey Plantagenet and his son; see in particular, nos. 106, 129, 224, 226, 440.

61. Howlett, *Robert of Torigni*, pp. 240–41; *Gervase of Canterbury: Opera Historica*, ed. William Stubbs, RS 73, 2 vols. (1879–80): 1:166.

62. Jean's version seems to have been compiled between 1164 and 1173; Breton's earlier, but after 1155; see *Chroniques des comtes d'Anjou*, pp. xxxvi–xl, 140–41.

63. Halphen and Poupardin, *Chroniques des comtes d'Anjou*, pp. 162–65; Jean Dunbabin, *France in the Making 843–1180* (Oxford: Oxford University Press, 1985), p. 249.

64. Halphen and Poupardin, *Chroniques des comtes d'Anjou*, pp. 172, 231. I do not know on what evidence it has been said that Jean "fut sollicité par Henri II pour une biographie de son défunt père;" see Amaury Chauou, "La culture historique à la cour Plantagenêt," in *Culture politique des Plantagenêt 1154–1224, Civilisation Médiévale* 14, ed. Martin Aurell (Poitiers: Université de Poitiers, 2003), p. 278.

65. Halphen and Poupardin, *Chroniques des comtes d'Anjou*, p. 224.

66. A grant of 40 livres angevins annually for two priests "ut serviant cotidie ad altare illud quod est ante sepulchrum patris mei, pro anima patris mei." This grant was given at Winchester between 1155 and 1158. A later grant, for what was in effect the same amount, though expressed in livres mansois, made arrangements for payment of the revenues. *Recueil des Actes de Henri II*, 172–3, no. 70 and 494, no. 354.

67. *Recueil d'Annales angevines et vendômoises*, ed. Louis Halphen, *Collection de textes pour servir à l'étude et à l'enseignement de l'histoire* 37 (Paris: A. Picard, 1903), pp. 12–17. Apart from the slightly longer entry for 1158, most entries after 1154 consist of a just a few terse words.

68. PL 207, letters 4, 14, 19, 77.

69. *Richard FitzNigel: Dialogus de Scaccario*, ed. and trans. Charles Johnson; rev. ed. F. E. L. Carter and D. E. Greenway (Oxford: Clarendon Press, 1983), p. 27.

70. On this see John Gillingham, "Royal Newsletters, Forgeries and English Historians: Some Links between Court and History in the Reign of Richard I," in *La Cour Plantagenêt 1154–1204* ed. Martin Aurell, Civilisation médiévale 8 (Poitiers: Université de Poitiers, 2000), pp. 171–86.

71. Chauou, "La culture historique," p. 278.

72. *Itinerarium Peregrinorum et Gesta Regis Ricardi, Chronicles and Memorials of the Reign of Richard I*, vol. 1., ed. William Stubbs, RS 38 (1864); English translation by Helen Nicholson, *Chronicle of the Third Crusade* (Aldershot: Ashcroft, 1997), 1:29. This part of the text was written in the early 1190s.

73. Haskins, "Henry II as patron," p. 77. And this would fit with his decision (see Elizabeth van Houts' essay in this volume) to put the Constitutions of Clarendon into writing.

74. Virginie Greene, "Qui croit au retour d'Arthur?," *Cahiers de civilisation médiévale* 45 (2002): 321–40. Her answer to the question is: "Toujours les autres." On this see the observations of Martin Aurell, *L'Empire des Plantagenêt 1154–1224* (Paris: Perin, 2003), pp. 220–22.

75. Lesley Johnson and Alexander Bell, "The Anglo-Norman *Description of England*," in *Anglo-Norman Anniversary Essays*, ed. Ian Short, Anglo-Norman Text Society Occasional Publications Series 2 (London: Birkbeck College, 1993): 11–47, at 43. For a date in the 1140s, see John Gillingham,

"The Context and Purposes of Geoffrey of Monmouth's *History of the Kings of Britain*," *Anglo-Norman Studies 13: Proceedings of the Battle Conference 1990*, ed. Marjorie Chibnall (Woodbridge, Suffolk: Boydell and Brewer, 1992): 99–118, repr. in *The English in the Twelfth Century*, 19–39, at 33. If, as some have thought, the *Description* should be dated rather later, this would only strengthen the argument of this paper.

76. William of Newburgh: *Historia Rerum Anglicarum*, ed. Richard Howlett in *Chronicles of the Reigns of Stephen, Henry II and Richard I*, vols. 1 and 2, RS 82 (1884), bk. 3 chap.7. Both Howden and Diceto are oddly explicit that it was the Bretons who gave Arthur his name; see Roger of Howden, *Gesta regis Henrici II Benedicti abbatis: the chronicle of the reigns of Henry II. and Richard I. A.D. 1169–1192; known commonly under the name of Benedict of Peterborough*, ed. William Stubbs, 2 vols. RS 49 (1867), 1:361; *Diceto, Opera*, 2:48.

77. *Memoriale fratris Walteri de Coventria*, 2 vols., ed. William Stubbs, RS 58 (1873), 2:196. Cf. "The Arthurian legend had not been employed in any purposeful way to enhance the prestige of the Angevin dynasty in England. On the contrary, Breton resistance to Angevin hegemony was signaled when the heir to the duchy. . .was named Arthur" (Emma Mason, "The Hero's Invincible Sword," in *The Ideals and Practice of Medieval Knighthood, III*, ed. Christopher Harper-Bill and Ruth Harvey [Woodbridge, Suffolk: Boydell and Brewer, 1990], 131). Also skeptical, Stefano Maria Cingolani, "Filologia e miti storiografici: Enrico II, la corte plantageneta e la letteratura," *Studi medievali* 32 (1991): 815–32.

78. Lawman, *Brut*, lines 21–23; see *Layamon: Brut*, ed. G. L. Brook and R. F. Leslie, EETS OS 250 (Oxford: Oxford University Press, 1963).

79. Ian Short, "Patrons and Polyglots: French Literature in Twelfth-Century England," in *Anglo-Norman Studies 14: Proceedings of the Battle Conference 1991*, ed. Marjorie Chibnall (Woodbridge, Suffolk: Boydell and Brewer, 1992): 229–49, at 239.

80. Etienne de Roven, *Draco Normannicus*, in Howlett, *Chronicles*, 2: lines 946–1280, esp. 1218 [subridens sociis]; Johanek, "König Arthur," pp. 384–89. See Aurell, *L'Empire des plantagenêt*, pp. 170–172 for the "registre burlesque" in this scene, and Echard, *Arthurian Narrative*, pp. 85–93.

81. Dronke, "Peter of Blois and Poetry," p. 208, in Ian Short's translation, in *A Companion to the Anglo-Norman World*, ed. Christopher Harper-Bill and Elisabeth van Houts (Woodbridge, Suffolk: Boydell and Brewer, 2003), p. 202.

82. Map, *De Nugis*, xli, n. 1. As they observe, in Map's story of Offa and Gado, Offa seems to be given the role of an English hero to set against Arthur, though without mentioning Arthur. The story was probably written in the early 1180s.

83. Giraldus, *Topographia Hibernica*, p. 148.

84. Howden, *Gesta Regis*, 2:159; Howden, *Chronica*, 3:97. For this shift, see Gillingham, "Context and Purposes of Geoffrey of Monmouth's *History*,"

p. 23, n. 23. Moreover in October 1190 Richard had recognized his nephew Arthur as heir to the kingdom of England should he die without legitimate issue.

85. On this see Johanek, "König Arthur," pp. 379–84; Aurell, *L'Empire des Plantagenêt*, pp. 164–67. Charles T. Wood argues that finding King Arthur's body was Glastonbury's response to Richard's nomination of Arthur as heir presumptive; see Charles T. Wood, "Fraud and its Consequences: Savaric of Bath and the Reform of Glastonbury," in *The Archaeology and History of Glastonbury Abbey*, eds. Lesley Abrams and James P. Carley (Woodbridge, Suffolk: Boydell and Brewer, 1991), pp. 273–77. Cf. Catalina Girbea, "Limites du contrôle des Plantagenêt sur la légende arthurienne: le problème de la mort d'Arthur," in Aurell, *Culture politique*, pp. 287–301, esp. 292.

86. "Deinde dominus rex dedit. . .priori de Bermundeshaia abbatiam de Glastincbiria," Howden, *Gesta regis*, 2:85; Gervase, *Opera*, 1:458.

87. See above n. 18.

88. *Chroniques des comtes d'Anjou*, pp. vii–viii, lxxii–lxxv, 162 n. See also above p. 34.

89. How might Henry have responded to his teacher's poem (see above n. 57) on the fall of Troy? According to Raby, it is a dull poem without life or color, "which could serve no other use than the instruction of schoolboys" (F. J. E. Raby, *A History of Secular Latin Poetry in the Middle Ages*, 2 vols. [Oxford: Clarendon Press, 1934], 2:70–71).

90. Wace, *Roman de Rou*, Appendix, pp. 157–76; Benoît, *Chronique*, lines 645–60. For commentary see Emily Albu, *The Normans in their Histories* (Woodbridge, Suffolk: Boydell and Brewer, 2001), pp. 13–15, 62–63, 237–38 and Damian-Grint, *New Historians*, pp. 205–6.

91. Ian Short, "Language and Literature" in Harper-Bill and van Houts, *Companion to the Anglo-Norman World*, 212. Cf. the insertion of the words "and sons" in the following: "The courts of Henry II and his wife and sons sponsored and inspired an extraordinary volume and quality of writing" (Susan Crane, "Anglo-Norman cultures in England, 1066–1460," chap. 2 in Wallace, *Cambridge History of Medieval English Literature*, pp. 35–60, at 41).

92. On the questions of dedicatee and date of composition—1184–85, I follow Paul Gerhard Schmidt, *Johannes de Hautevilla: Architrenius* (Munich: W. Fink, 1974), pp. 14, 42. In 1:4–5 the dedicatee is explicitly likened to Phoebus and Maecenas, and then, in 5:17–18, a Phoebus of Trojan and Cornish descent is associated not with the king but with the church of Rouen.

93. Notably since Robert Bartlett gave half a dozen pages to him in his *England under the Norman and Angevin Kings 1075–1225* The New Oxford History of England (Oxford: Clarendon Press, 2000), pp. 579, 582–88. See also Frédérique Lachaud in "Littérature de civilité et 'processus de civilisation' à la fin du XIIe siècle: le cas anglais d'après l'*Urbanus magnus*," in *Les Échanges culturels au Moyen Âge: Actes du congrès des médiévistes français, Boulogne-sur-Mer 2001*, ed. D. Courtemanche et A-M. Helvétius (Paris: Publications

de la Sorbonne, 2002), eadem; "L'enseignement des bonnes manières en milieu de cour en Angleterre d'après l'*Urbanus magnus* attribué à Daniel de Beccles," in *Erziehung und Bildung am Hofe. 7. Symposium der Residenzen-Kommission in Celle*, ed. Holger Kruse and Werner Paravicini (Sigmaringen: Thorbecke, 2002); John Gillingham, "From *civilitas* to civility: codes of manners in medieval and early modern England," *Transactions of the Royal Historical Society*, 6th ser., 12 (2002): 267–89.

94. Jonathan Nicholls, *The Matter of Courtesy: Medieval Courtesy Books and the Gawain Poet* (Woodbridge, Suffolk: Boydell and Brewer, 1985), pp. 162–66, 185.

95. "Rex vetus Henricus primo dedit hec documenta/Illepidis, libro que subscribuntur in isto." *Urbanus magnus*, ed. J. G. Smyly, *Urbanus Magnus Danielis Becclesiensis,* Dublin University Press Series (Dublin: Hodges, Figgis, 1939, lines 2836–7.

96. Smyly, *Urbanus Magnus*, p. v.

97. Henry I's court was certainly seen as a school of good manners by those close to it. One of the nobles brought up there became King David I of Scotland and was congratulated by William of Malmesbury for his policy of offering tax rebates to any Scotsmen who would learn "to live in a more civilised style, dress with more elegance and eat with more refinement." David did this, in William's view, because "the rust of his native barbarism had been polished away by his upbringing among us"; see William of Malmesbury, *Gesta Regum Anglorum*, Volume 1, ed. and trans. R. A. B. Mynors, R. M. Thomson and M. Winterbottom (Oxford: Clarendon Press, 1998), p. 400.

98. Bartlett, *England under the Norman and Angevin Kings*, p. 583.

99. Map, *De Nugis*, p. 476.

100. Map, *De Nugis*, p. 102. For other anecdotes illustrating Henry's courtliness, see Map, *De Nugis*, pp. 486–94.

101. *Vita Remigii*, in *Girald: Opera*, vol. 7, ed. James F. Dimock, RS 21 (1877), p. 63. In another of Gerald's stories, also involving alcohol, Henry is said to have conducted himself "liberaliter et curialiter," *Speculum Ecclesie*, in *Giraldi: Opera*, vol. 4, ed. J. S. Brewer RS 21 (1873), p. 214.

102. Adam of Eynsham, *Magna Vita Sancti Hugonis* ed. Decima L. Douie and Dom Hugh Farmer, 2 vols. (London: Nelson, 1962), 1:115–18. According to Adam, Hugh spoke "comiter" and Henry enjoyed the "urbana invectio." It had, after all, been Hugh's combination of virtue with "morum elegantia" that made Henry choose him as bishop (1:94). As Karl Leyser pointed out, Henry may have enjoyed the joke partly because it "underpinned the rightfulness of the Angevin succession" (Karl J. Leyser, "The Angevin Kings and the Holy Man," in *Saint Hugh of Lincoln: Lectures delivered at Oxford and Lincoln to celebrate the eighth centenary of St. Hugh's consecration as Bishop of Lincoln*, ed. Henry Mayr-Harting (Oxford: Clarendon Press, 1987), p. 59).

103. Another side to Henry's courtliness was highlighted when Robert of Torigni said that he conducted himself "magnifice et dapsiliter" when he

visited Paris with a small following in 1158 (Howlett, *Robert of Torigni*, pp. 196–97).

104. The worries about the prince's education are said to reflect "religiosorum communis opinio," PL 207:210–13.

105. For emphasis on these traits in the "standard biography," see Wilfred Lewis Warren, *Henry II* (London: Eyre Methuen, 1973; repr. Yale University Press, New Haven and London), pp. 77–80, 207–10, 245, 629–30.

106. *De principis instructione*, bk. 3, chap. 28, in *Giraldi Opera*, vol. 8, ed. George F. Warner, RS 21 (1891), p. 304; Map, *De Nugis*, p. 116.

CHAPTER 2

LATIN AND FRENCH AS LANGUAGES OF THE PAST IN NORMANDY DURING THE REIGN OF HENRY II: ROBERT OF TORIGNI, STEPHEN OF ROUEN, AND WACE

Elisabeth van Houts

There was no shortage of interest in the past in Normandy during the reign of Henry II.[1] Although Latin was the conventional language employed by historians writing about the past, the vernacular became an important medium.[2] The juxtaposition of Latin and French raises various questions about patronage, authorship, audience, and gender. These can be explored through a study of the work of three contemporary Norman historians in particular: Robert of Torigni, monk of Bec (ca. 1128–54) and abbot of Mont Saint-Michel (1154–86), Stephen of Rouen, monk of Bec (d. after 1170), and Wace, born at Jersey, educated at Paris and Caen, and later canon of Bayeux (d. after 1174).[3] All three were clergymen: two monks and one secular clerk. All three were excellent Latinists, well versed in Latin historiography and court documentation, but only Abbot Robert and Stephen wrote, as far as we know, exclusively in Latin, while Wace used the vernacular. Yet, while Stephen and Wace preferred verse, Abbot Robert's work is in prose. The close connection between Henry II's mother, Empress Matilda (d. 1167), and the monastery of Bec no doubt explains the personal knowledge of her revealed by the monks Robert and Stephen.[4] Did they write as a result of her request or in expectation of patronage? Either way, a good knowledge of Latin on Matilda's part need not only be assumed but can be proven by other evidence. To what extent she may have been responsible for the choice of prose or verse and the selection of past events to be recorded are similarly intriguing questions. Wace, on the other hand, did endlessly appeal to King Henry II and Queen Eleanor (d. 1203) for gifts, money, and support.[5] These requests are woven into his vernacular verse-history of the dukes of Normandy. Are they simply to be explained by his position as a professional writer who lived off the proceeds of his literary skills? One theme that runs across all three works is that of filial war and fraternal strife. Abbot Robert and Wace are concerned with the wars between the sons of William the Conqueror (1035–87). Robert praises Henry I (1100–35) as a victimized brother who ultimately triumphed as king and duke, while Robert Curthose (1087–1106, d. 1134), the rebellious eldest son and negligent brother, is rehabilitated by Wace. Stephen attributes Henry II's survival (his brothers Geoffrey (d. 1158) and William (d. 1163/4) had predeceased him) as "unicus filius" [an only son], to the exceptional support of Empress Matilda. The theme of fraternal strife can be explained by reference to Henry II's troubles with his sons, Henry the Young King (d. 1183), Richard I (1189–99), and Geoffrey (d. 1186) during their rebellion in the early 1170s. The queen mothers, Empress Matilda and Queen Eleanor, provide a marked contrast in the Norman narratives. While praise is heaped on the former, the latter is virtually ignored. Hence only an evaluation of Empress Matilda's command of languages will be presented in this chapter.

Patronage

The three aforementioned Norman historians do provide information, at times tantalizingly ambiguous, about literary patronage as a contractual relationship between a patron who requests a work to be written, or translated, and an author who does this in return for remuneration.[6] The most explicit statement in this context concerns the potential rewards of writing history from the point of view of the author, and comes from Robert of Torigni in his letter to Gervase, prior of Saint-Cénery, asking him to write a history of Count Geoffrey of Anjou as duke of Normandy and count of Maine (ca. 1144–51).[7] In this letter, written not long after the count's death in September 1151, Robert sets out the advantages, as he sees them, for Gervase. He argues that not only would such a work bring Gervase fame, it would also bring him Robert's gratitude and indebtedness, and, most importantly, it might bring him the not-inconsiderable favor of the young duke Henry II.[8] At the time Robert was himself prior of Bec and the author of the updated *Gesta Normannorum Ducum* to which, as he explains in the letter, he added a book on Henry's grandfather, Henry I. Presumably, therefore, what Robert holds out as advantages for Gervase reflects in some measure his own experience as redactor of the *Gesta*

Normannorum Ducum.[9] Robert may also have picked up some knowledge of favors that Count Geoffrey of Anjou (d. 1151) and young Henry had recently bestowed on their favorite authors, who happened to be Henry's tutors. William of Conches (d. ca. 1154), a Norman philosopher from the neighborhood of Evreux, had dedicated his *Dragmaticon philosophiae*, a handbook on encyclopedic knowledge of human nature, to Geoffrey, who had asked for its composition probably in ca. 1147–49. Written as a dialogue between a duke and a philosopher, the book presents Geoffrey as the eager scholar asking questions while William is the philosopher providing the answers.[10] In the case of Adelard of Bath, who had dedicated to Henry his *Astrolabe* and also presented him with horoscopes, some dating around the time of his father Geoffrey's death, a reciprocal and contractual arrangement is more difficult to establish.[11] Robert of Torigni's own revision of the *Gesta Normannorum Ducum* had been completed in the first instance ca. 1139, more than a decade earlier, when Henry I's succession had not gone as planned. Stephen of Blois had succeeded to the throne in December 1135, but Empress Matilda did not cross to England until the time Robert picked up his pen. There is no doubt that Robert of Torigni worked as the Empress's partisan, praising her (as well as her mother, Edith/Matilda, and grandmother, St. Margaret of Scotland) in five long chapters, sketching her first marriage, the lofty origins of her second husband's family, her sons' position as the true heirs to Henry I's rule, and her benefactions to Bec.[12] He may have met her in 1134, when, as countess of Anjou, she spent some time in the late spring in Rouen, probably at Bec's priory, Notre Dame du Pré, recovering from the birth of her second son, Geoffrey.[13] His intention to secure the Empress' patronage for Bec, which was already impressive, is clear. Robert's estimation that historical writing would bring fame to the historian is borne out by his boasting about himself as "an avid reader and collector of religious and profane books."[14] Although the number of twelfth-century copies of his redaction of the *Gesta Normannorum Ducum* might have justified his pride—but not his arrogance—it does not quite explain how his audience (other than the monks of Bec, or Gervase of Saint-Cénery) would have known about him, since his revision of the *Gesta Normannorum Ducum* was done anonymously. Despite the later (anonymous) redactions, the *Gesta Normannorum Ducum* remained ostensibly the work of its original author, William of Jumièges.

When applied to Stephen of Rouen, Robert of Torigni's words to Gervase take on a further dimension of expectations of patronage. Writing just after the Empress's death in September 1167, an event mentioned on several occasions, Stephen acts very much as her and her son's champion and not entirely out of altruistic reasons.[15] His acquaintance with the Empress probably dated from the last stage of her life when she lived in retirement at Notre Dame du Pré. Perhaps, as seems likely, he was the monk of Bec who acted as messenger to announce her death to Henry II while the latter was on campaign in Brittany.[16] Stephen of Rouen's *Draco Normannicus* is often presented as not more than a verse abbreviation of the *Gesta Normannorum Ducum*, but, in fact, the dynastic-chronicle sections constitute less than a quarter of the *Draco Normannicus*.[17] The rest deals with the relations between Henry II and King Louis VII of France (1137–80), the papal schism of the 1160s, and, as we shall discuss below, the wars in Brittany in the late 1150s and 1160s. From other sources we know that the Empress had some involvement in all these affairs on behalf of her son Henry, so it seems not improbable that some of Stephen's information came through her. The topic closest to Stephen's heart, however, was the loss of Bec's priory at Poissy. Twice in his poem he discusses the priory's wealth—first, when he explores how, in 1077, King Philip I of France (1060–1108) had granted it to Bec; then, how twenty years later the same king gave it to the abbey of Molesmes—and, finally, at the end of his poem he points out that the peace treaty between Henry II and Louis VII in February 1167 (which Robert of Torigni and others place at Montmirail) was actually conceived of at Poissy.[18] This, surely, hints strongly at his expectations that a suitable reward for his work would be the restitution of Poissy to Bec. It is not unlikely that he had raised the matter with the Empress before her death. Neither Robert of Torigni nor Stephen explicitly mention in their own historical narratives the issues of commission, remuneration, or fame. As monks of Bec, however, they personally knew the Empress, and their attachment to her seems so strong that it is hardly believable that they wrote without her knowledge, without her blessing, or without her encouragement. What they wrote about her clearly indicates expectations of patronage by herself or her son for the abbey of Bec. As monks they were in no position to ask for anything much for themselves.[19]

The case of Wace, a secular clerk, is different for two reasons: first, because he explicitly sets out his expectations for remuneration; second, because he singles out Henry II as having rewarded him, presumably for his historical work. As is recognized by all, including Broadhurst, his is a clear case of literary patronage.[20] For Wace, the three pivotal figures whom he claims to have known were Henry I, Henry II, and Henry the Young King.[21] Whereas Robert of Torigni had told Gervase that he could expect fame and, perhaps, ducal favor, without specifying the form such favor might take, Wace was much bolder. He inserted a long passage spelling out how historians and chroniclers in the past used to be rewarded for their works, how they received more than words of praise alone.[22] He also spells out several times his expectations for his own labor.[23] He admits that King Henry II did give him a prebend at Bayeux and hints that it was in return for his services as a vernacular historian,[24] for he says that "in honour of Henry II he who was born of the lineage of Rou, I have spoken at length of Rou and his powerful family."[25] As a secular clerk Wace had to work to earn money, to buy parchment, and to hire, if necessary, scribes,[26] something that would not have been easy in the time before he received his prebend, unless he found patrons to provide him with the wherewithal to do so. Without institutional support of the kind that monks had, secular clerks were at the mercy of the bishops or the lay nobility to provide them with posts. Interestingly, Empress Matilda of all people recognized this occupational hazard of the clerks without livings or prebends, but without reference to Wace. In late 1164 she expressed her concern for wandering and penniless clergy in one of her discussions with Nicholas, prior of Mont-aux-Malades at Rouen, who paraphrased her words in a letter to Archbishop Thomas Becket.[27] It is therefore not surprising that of the three historians under discussion here, Wace was in the most vulnerable position, a circumstance that explains why he so frequently drew attention to his predicament.

Robert of Torigni's rewards, if they were for his ducal and royal service as dynastic chronicler, were his promotion in May 1154 to the abbacy of Mont Saint-Michel.[28] In his *Chronicle* he not only refers to his election but adds that it was ratified by Archbishop Hugh of Rouen and Empress Matilda. As abbot he remained a staunch supporter of Henry II and several years later, in 1161, stood godfather to Henry and Eleanor's daughter Eleanor.[29] Whether Stephen of Rouen ever found fame, or princely favor, is unknown. What we do know is that his campaign for the restitution of Poissy was unsuccessful. As for Wace, his prebend at Bayeux was given to him in the late 1160s, but his career as dynastic chronicler came to an end as he tells us himself when, probably in 1174, he was sacked by the king—an action that implies that he had been working in some official capacity—and replaced by Benôit de Sainte-Maure.

Brittany and King Arthur

The three Norman authors show a particular fascination with the southwestern borders of Normandy and Brittany. As abbot of Mont Saint-Michel since 1154, Robert of Torigni's interest in these borders was professional in that the abbey had many possessions on both sides of the frontiers.[30] Stephen of Rouen and Wace were experts on Arthurian knowledge and used their work as vehicles for its dissemination. The interest in King Arthur and stories centered on him began with Geoffrey of Monmouth's *Historia regum Britannie*, written between 1136 and 1138. The book was first publicly recorded by Henry, archdeacon of Huntingdon, during his visit to Robert of Torigni at Bec in 1139.[31] From Bec, Robert took the knowledge with him to Mont Saint-Michel, where in ca. 1155–60 under his guidance one of the monks, William of Saint-Pair, wrote a verse history of the abbey, the *Roman du Mont Saint-Michel*.[32] Divided into three books, of which book II is an abbreviated history of the Norman dukes based on the *Gesta Normannorum ducum*, it contains in book I a reference to King Arthur as uncle of the Helena buried at Mont Saint-Michel.[33] The fantastic story, molding Arthur into a national hero for the Britains, had a particular resonance from the mid-1150s, when, with moral backing from Abbot Robert of Mont Saint-Michel, Henry II began his campaign to acquire Brittany.[34] His initial, tentative moves date from 1155, followed by his acquisition of the county of Nantes in 1158. The final act was sealed when, in the summer of 1166, Henry II's son Geoffrey was promised in marriage to the Breton heiress Constance, an event that led to their wedding in 1181.[35] Therefore, it is perhaps worth noting that the marriage alliance was arranged while Empress Matilda was still alive, and that these events occurred a decade and a half or so before Stephen finished his *Draco Normannicus*. Firmly on the Plantagenet side, Stephen wrote the *Draco Normannicus* to legitimize Henry II's imperial policies: on the Continent by gradually enveloping Britanny into the Angevin realm and in the West by branching out into Ireland.[36] Stephen incorporated a series of fictitious letters, allegedly exchanged between Rolland of Dinant and King Arthur and between King Henry II and King Arthur himself.[37] King Arthur was resurrected for the occasion to speak on behalf of the Bretons, led by Rolland of Dinant, in an attempt to dissuade King Henry II from taking Brittany, without success. The alleged exchanges between Rolland and Arthur and between Arthur and Henry are lengthy texts. As a very interesting testimony to Stephen of Rouen's clever use of the past, they provide the three protagonists with historical precedents justifying their claims.[38] Stephen himself was by no means the first to have King Arthur resurrected for propaganda reasons, for at least one other letter allegedly written by King Arthur was already in circulation.[39] The letter, dated to July 1157, was addressed to Hugh, chaplain of Braine, the Avre castle of Agnes de Baudemont and her second husband (since 1152), Robert of Dreux, brother of King Louis VII.[40] Its contents are not time-specific, but they interestingly refer to Arthur as the king of the two Britains, one of the "seven of God's servants who have revealed to us seven times the dark wishes of the heart on the seventh night of the seventh month (July)."[41] Arthur ends his letter by expressing his hope that the two parts ("climates") of the world will be strengthened by his rule and by his wish that "the land from Jupiter to Isis may be freely subject to you on account of the dignity of your promotion."[42] As Julia Crick has suggested, it is tempting to place the letter in the context of the Plantagenet campaign for rule over Brittany,[43] which by 1157 was in full swing, followed in the summer by Henry's successful campaign in Wales. Nevertheless, at present the precise significance of the events of July 7, 1157 in relation to Hugh of Braine escapes us.[44] The symbolism of the number seven was well known in Normandy. Following the author of the *Brevis Relatio*, written in ca. 1114–20, Robert of Torigni changed the numbering of the books of the *Gesta Normannorum Ducum* from I–VIII into I–VII, thereby turning book VIII into book VII in order to underline the fact that Henry I represented the seventh generation of dukes.[45]

To return to Stephen of Rouen's *Draco Normannicus*, there is no doubt that Stephen was well informed about the most-recent Latin Arthurian tradition. More or less in a dialogue with Wace, and probably with Robert of Torigni as well, Stephen cross-referenced between events in the Norman past, contemporary events, and parallels in Arthurian history. He explained how Merlin's prophecies had been fulfilled on several occasions, such as the marriage of Empress Matilda and Henry V, the divorce of Queen Eleanor and Louis VII, and the deaths of the two Williams, the eldest sons of Henry I (in 1120) and of Henry II (1156).[46] He also bolstered the imperial theme by including parallels with Alexander the Great. His sources were the Arthurian texts of the so-called Nennius and Geoffrey of Monmouth's *Historia regum Brittanie*, as well as the Alexander canon. Significantly, all narratives existed bound-up with Robert of Torigni's own copy of the *Gesta Normannorum Ducum* as one volume in the library of Bec.[47] The physical link between Robert's authoritative history of the Norman dukes and the Latin narratives of Arthur and Alexander the Great is proof, so Stephen seems to imply, that, for the Bec community, Arthur and Alexander were inextricably bound up with Henry II's ancestors. Stephen, however, went one step further than Robert of Torigni by composing a Latin narrative weaving together the Norman dukes, King Arthur, and Alexander the Great into one seamless imperialistic fabric. At the same time, the *Draco Normannicus* is a Latin challenge to Wace's earlier work *Roman de Brut*, a verse adaptation of Geoffrey of Monmouth's Arthurian tale, which crucially left out the link with Alexander the Great. By employing Latin, the language of authority, and by binding Henry II to Arthur and Alexander the Great, Stephen went further than both his contemporaries Robert of Torigni and Wace, who much more closely stuck to their sources. In the eyes of Stephen, the Empress's *unicus filius*, Henry II, was the equal of Arthur and Alexander on a scale that was truly imperial.

Filial Rebellion, Fraternal Strife, and
Maternal Concern

The third theme that binds the three Norman authors is that of filial rebellion, fraternal strife, and maternal concern.[48] All three writers lived through a period in Anglo-Norman and Angevin history in which kings faced rebellion from sons, brothers fought brothers, and mothers chose sides; the most fiercely fought battle was that between the cousins Stephen and Matilda. William the Conqueror's succession in 1087 was characterized by rivalry between his three sons; Henry I's succession in 1135 was marred by the contest between Stephen and Matilda; while Henry II experienced trouble with his brothers in the 1150s, and with his sons in the early 1170s. Robert of Torigni began his biography of King Henry I in the *Gesta Normannorum Ducum* with an account of Henry's struggle for survival against his two older brothers, Robert Curthose, duke of Normandy (1087–1106), and William Rufus, king of England (1087–1100).[49] Robert of Torigni does not disguise his delight in the fact that ultimately Henry succeeded where both brothers failed and were condemned to their just ends: death for William and captivity for Robert. Henry's porphyrogenity and legitimacy as king (from 1100) and as duke (from 1106) is the main theme of the eighth book of the *Gesta Normannorum Ducum*.[50] According to Robert of Torigni, Henry combined Robert Curthose's skill in warfare with William Rufus's secular expertise, but he also possessed qualities that both brothers had lacked, namely love for the church and, most crucially, wisdom. If we are right in attributing some role to Empress Matilda in the genesis of Robert of Torigni's account of her father's reign, we may come close to a family sentiment (shared by father and daughter) that, as a result of Henry I's emergence as king and duke, justice had been done.[51] In such a context (datable to ca. 1139 when King Stephen had succeeded Henry I), it is then no surprise to find Robert of Torigni expressing his (and the Empress's?) belief that her three sons, Henry (II), Geoffrey, and William, were their grandfather's true heirs.[52] Thirty years later, in ca. 1169, this view was outdated, as it had been overtaken by events. By the time Stephen of Rouen picked up his pen, two of Henry II's brothers, Geoffrey and William, had died, the former at Nantes in 1158 and the latter of illness in 1163/4.[53] Their deaths left, as in the case of Henry I, one brother as the legitimate heir, in this case Henry II. Several times in the *Draco Normannicus*, Stephen of Rouen praises Henry II and Empress Matilda, always pointing out that the *unicus filius*, the only son, survived because of the unique support of his mother, the anchor to his ship.[54] The bond between mother and son came to an abrupt end with Matilda's death in September 1167. Thus the two Bec historians, Robert of Torigni and

Stephen of Rouen, construct the same pattern of divine justice, a sentiment, I argue, that was shared by Empress Matilda, respectively daughter and mother of the two kings Henry. The fact that both Henrys had survived was truly a sign of God that they were both divinely chosen kings. Wace does not follow the Bec interpretation of the two Henrys emerging rightfully from fraternal strife. Instead, he highlights the triumvirate of three Henrys by including Henry the Young King, even though his (alleged) support of the Young King may have contributed to his fall from royal favor after the siege of Rouen in 1174.[55] But what is striking about Wace's judgement is that for him the right of the eldest son stands out. For Wace, the young Henry, even though his father was still alive, was wronged by his father in the same way that Robert Curthose had been wronged by William the Conqueror. Neither had received any income or power in Normandy during their fathers' lifetime, despite promises to the contrary.[56] Wace used the *Roman de Rou* to highlight the tragedy of Robert Curthose, older brother of Henry I, who had lost out on the English throne twice (in 1087 and 1100) and who then lost the duchy so dramatically at Tinchebrai (in 1106).[57] If anything, the *Roman de Rou*'s emphatic rehabilitation of Curthose's cause, at the same time as Wace's potential defense of the Young King, may well have precipitated Wace's demise as court historiographer. Significantly, Wace's work on the *Rou* was contemporary to Robert of Torigni's ongoing work on his *Chronicle* and to Stephen's *Draco Normannicus*. It followed the *Gesta Normannorum Ducum*, though not, as might have been expected, Robert of Torigni's recent version written in ca. 1139. Instead, ca. 1160 Wace, provocatively, used Orderic Vitalis's E redaction.[58] This allowed him the leeway to write his own continuation of the *Gesta Normannorum Ducum*, which he did by supplying the missing section on Robert Curthose as duke of Normandy up to the Battle of Tinchebrai in 1106, a section which William of Jumièges had originally intended to write himself but was prevented from doing.[59] Consequently, Robert of Torigni's Latin justification of the rule of Henry I was publicly snubbed by Wace, who deliberately put forward a vernacular case for Curthose. In turn, within a decade, Stephen reacted to Wace and, again, put forward the case for the two Henrys, in Latin. The switches in language and genre are intriguing and are probably linked to the various audiences. Wace's choice of the vernacular for his subversive, relatively unpopular (see below) continuation of the *Gesta Normannorum Ducum*, left unfinished by the lack of an account of Henry I, remains a baffling act on the part of an intelligent and ambitious clerk in search of royal patrons.

Of the three authors it is, interestingly, neither Robert of Torigni nor Wace, but only Stephen of Rouen who makes space in his narrative for the concerned mother. Even where Wace was given the chance by his source to elaborate on a mother's concerns, for example in the long section preceding the Battle of Hastings where Vitalis had introduced Gyrth, who was supported by Gytha, Wace left out Harold's mother.[60] Similarly, he did not elaborate on Matilda of Flanders as Robert Curthose's mother. Instead, Wace attributes a semi-maternal role to Henry I's wife, Queen Edith-Matilda, who, he suggests, had a soft spot for her brother-in-law. He reports how the birth of her child deflected Robert Curthose from attacking Winchester and how the queen in turn intervened in the issue on behalf of Robert. The inversion is the more interesting considering that Robert had in fact stood godfather to her.[61] In contrast, there is little mention of Empress Matilda and nothing about her role in supporting her son.[62] According to Wace, the Empress was so harassed by Stephen that "she recognized his right and gave him the kingdom as an inheritance."[63] It is intriguing that Wace did not follow his sources' guidance in this respect. Perhaps he felt he was justified by the fact that in his own time he did not know Empress Matilda. It is equally noteworthy that he did not have much to say about Queen Eleanor.[64]

Languages of the Past

All three authors were excellent Latinists, although of varying degrees of competence. Robert of Torigni's Latin was dull and administrative or utilitarian, while that of Stephen was highly sophisticated and literary. Wace's knowledge of Latin can only be assessed indirectly because all his surviving work is in Old French. Yet, we know that as translator his Latin was excellent, but whether it was as basic as Robert's or as highly developed as Stephen's is unknown. What can we learn from their use of languages for the past by considering them as contemporaries living and working in the same sociocultural and intellectual climate of the second half of the twelfth century in Normandy?

Robert of Torigni, the only Latin-prose author of the three, rigorously sticks to the chronological order of events, both in his revision of the *Gesta Normannorum Ducum* and in the *Chronicle*. The blueprint for his ideas about the writing of history and chronology can be found in his letter to Gervase of Saint-Cénery:

> If you are going to write this work, I wish that you do it in this order. First you sum up, briefly as if you are recapitulating, the names, genealogy and succession of the counts of Anjou from Ingelgerius to Geoffrey, how many years each of them has reigned as count and what famous deeds they have performed either in secular or in religious affairs which are worthy to commemorate; and under which king of the Franks the Angevins had Count

Ingelgerius. And when you have reached Count Fulco, Geoffrey's father, on account of the fact that his wife was the daughter of Count Helias of Maine, just as you drew up an epilogue of the counts of Anjou, I want you to do the same for the counts of Maine plus all that you have observed about them [i.e., the Angevins] as I above suggested that you do.[65]

Thus the names, origin, and succession of the counts of Anjou as well as their most important actions and the number of years for which they reigned had to be recorded. Secular and religious deeds would be considered worthy of noting down. Owing to the marriage of Geoffrey's parents (Count Fulk V, 1106–31, d. 1142 and Eremburga of Maine), an excursus on his maternal ancestors, the counts of Maine, had to be compiled as well. Clearly, what mattered was the claim that Geoffrey, and through him his three sons, could exercise on Anjou and Maine. The plan for the historical narrative was simple and straightforward, however dull any reading of it would be.

And dull it might have been in medieval eyes as well. Compare for example Gaimar's critique of the now-lost verse history of Henry I, commissioned by his widow, Adeliza of Louvain, from one David.[66] Gaimar complains that it lacked any detail on "festivities, drinking and boasting bouts, courting and love affairs" as well as on "hunting, pomp and ceremony, the acts of generosity and display of wealth," in fact, just the sort of information Gaimar himself would have liked to add to the book on Henry. None of Gaimar's desiderata can be found in Robert of Torigni's Latin prose histories, yet some can be identified in Stephen's *Draco Normannicus*, while many indeed are present in Wace's *Roman de Rou*. In fact, Wace's adaptation of the *Gesta Normannorum Ducum* reads like a faithful translation of the Latin with Gaimarian touches added. The same can be said of William of Saint-Pair's adaptation of the Latin charters and miracles of Mont Saint-Michel, carefully collected in Latin under the guidance of Abbot Robert in the abbey's cartulary but expanded according to Gaimar's "blueprint."

In contrast to Robert of Torigni, and perhaps David's lost verses on Henry I, the poets Stephen of Rouen and Wace are much more flexible in their use of chronology and time. Stephen certainly jumps forward and backward between the past and the present in a clear attempt to catch the attention of the audience. On the whole, Wace sticks to the chronological order of his sources, of which, as we have seen, the *Gesta Normannorum Ducum* was the most important. Nevertheless, he frequently interrupts his narrative with excurses, occasionally bursts into commentary on contemporary events or praise of members of the ducal family, or, as discussed earlier, complains about the lack of remuneration. Commenting on contemporary times by using historical precedents, or alternatively by explaining the past in terms of contemporary examples, is an age-old rhetorical device employed not only to catch the attention of the audience, but to keep it. Thus genre, that is, prose narrative determined by chronological order as opposed to verse narrative with a more flexible approach to the timing of events described, is an important dividing line between the three authors. What did this mean to their audience?

First of all, if we stick with Gaimar, it ought to be noted that though he might have been scathing about David's shortcomings, his criticism did not prevent either Queen Adeliza or Gaimar's patron, Constance, or any of the other owners of copies of the work—which Gaimar reported as circulating—from reading about King Henry I's achievements. There clearly was then, as is now, an audience for obituaries, but whether it included Robert of Torigni we do not know for sure. If he did know David's work, he considered its existence no obstacle for his own expansion of the *Gesta Normannorum Ducum* with a biography of Henry I, and Empress Matilda probably concurred. We have already noted that all three Norman authors had contacts with the royal-ducal family, especially with Empress Matilda (Robert of Torigni and Stephen) and with Henry II (Wace, Robert of Torigni, and Stephen), and that although active patronage bestowed on them by the royals cannot be proven, except in the case of Wace, there is certainly evidence of considerable interplay between authors and royal family to the effect that all three had some expectation of rewards in one form or another. They must therefore have been part of the intended audience. But what about others?

Manuscript evidence suggests that the prose narrative in Latin, that is, Robert of Torigni's work, was by far the most popular. Both his *Gesta Normannorum Ducum* and *Chronicle* have survived in more than twenty manuscripts.[67] In contrast, Wace's *Roman de Rou* and Stephen of Rouen's *Draco Normannicus* have survived in only a handful.[68] The *Draco Normannicus* had an exclusively local audience restricted to Bec, and the only proven provenance for a *Rou* manuscript is the early-thirteenth-century manuscript from Battle Abbey, the memorial foundation to the Norman Conquest. But before we jump to the conclusion that the contemporary audience was uninterested in Latin and vernacular historical verse, we would do well to remind ourselves of the success of Wace's earlier work the *Roman de Brut*, the popularity of which was on the scale of the *Gesta Normannorum Ducum* and the *Chronicle*.[69] The evidence also underlines that whenever we can establish provenance, it is invariably monastic or ecclesiastical, mostly confined to Normandy, England, or the neighboring French areas. There is virtually no trace of any active ownership by or audience of the laity.

The internal evidence for audience suggests an aristocratic public that would be listening to rcitations of the text. One such occasion for the reading of *Roman de Rou* might have been the splendid gathering on the occasion of the translation of the bodies of dukes Richard I and Richard II at Fécamp ca. March 11, 1162, an occasion attended by King Henry II and his entourage, amongst which we may guess were his mother, Empress Matilda, as well as Wace himself. However, the charter issued at this time does only mention the king and his advisors.[70] Whether this was the occasion Wace had in mind when he explicitly referred to his audience at the abbey in connection with certain jongleurs' tales he had heard there is unknown.[71] There is no difficulty in imagining a vernacular verse being performed on such or similar occasions. Everyone knowing French, whether of the continental or the English variety, would have been able to understand the contents.[72] After all, the stories are easy to follow, there are many repetitions, and the frequent passages that adapt the text to a contemporary audience by elaborating in descriptive passages on hunts, festivals, warfare, or interior-decorating would have appealed to many people. However, to assume that the vernacular implies an unlearned or unsophisticated lay audience is wrong. Monks too would have enjoyed literature that was slightly less demanding than Latin prose or poetry. Yet, William of Saint-Pair in his verse history of Mont Saint-Michel specifically states that he wrote the text for the instruction of the pilgrims visiting the abbey and unable to read Latin.[73] At the same time it was a text aimed also at a domestic audience of monks and their *familia* [wider circle] of lay benefactors and friends. One of its themes was the monks' right to free abbatial-elections, a hotly debated point because most abbots, since the abbey's reestablishment, had been appointed by the dukes of Normandy. Robert of Torigni himself had been elected even though his election had been approved, as we have seen, by the Empress and her son. His accession, however, had ended a troubled period (post tribulationem) as he himself reported in his *Chronicle*.[74] Perhaps, he had approved of William of Saint-Pair's vernacular defence of this right in the hope that it would reach a wider audience than a Latin text might have done. Alternatively, as in the case of Wace's *Roman de Rou*, with its provocative section on Robert Curthose, the vernacular allowed more leeway in political terms to express views that might clash with those of opponents. Since William of Saint-Pair wrote at the same time in which Robert ordered the composition of the abbey's Latin cartulary, opening with the very documentation translated into the vernacular by William, the *Roman du Mont Saint-Michel* may be seen as a commentary and contemporary exegesis of what the Latin documentation meant in practice. Any such commentary in Latin was deemed to be an authoritative legal interpretation, which could have been thought to be inflammatory and thus unwise.

The Latin of Robert of Torigni's historical work is, as we have seen, relatively uncomplicated. The annalistic form of the *Chronicle* is accessible and relatively simple though also fairly boring to listen to or even to read. The *Gesta Normannorum Ducum* has more literary pretensions. The language is certainly more variable and sophisticated than that of the *Chronicle* with longer sentences, more subclauses and a greater variety of vocabulary. Nevertheless, a Romance-speaking aristocratic audience, many of the members of which were probably also bilingual in that they possessed the skills of oral Latin, should not have had too much difficulty with understanding the contents of Robert of Torigni's work.[75] For precisely such an audience Stephen of Rouen added the *argumenta*, the Latin prose summaries at the head of each verse chapter. Those knowing oral Latin could easily have coped with the prose, although they might have been defeated by the complex hexameters that followed. Where amongst these various categories of audience do we fit the members of the royal family, whom we have seen in contact with the three authors?

Henry II had received an excellent education.[76] Walter Map tells us that he was skilled in many languages, but that normally he spoke in either Latin or French.[77] I presume, but cannot find any confirmation of this hunch, that he also had a rudimentary knowledge of English.[78] His father, Geoffrey of Anjou, was literate, well educated, and often praised for his literary taste. This at least was the praise heaped upon him by Geoffrey's only known-biographer, John of Marmoutiers, who dedicated the work to the bishop of Le Mans.[79] Geoffrey appointed several well-known scholars as Henry's teachers, foremost amongst whom were, as we have seen, Adelard of Bath, William of Conches, and Master Matthew.[80] Henry's mother, Matilda, was literate too, and we have some very good evidence for the extent of her literacy. But whether we should interpret this as basic and adequate skills that most queens would have possessed, or, as Miriam Büttner-Shergold recently has suggested, as sophisticated and learned skills, depending on individual ability and intelligence, remains a matter of interpretation.[81] Empress Matilda fits the category of well-trained, highly skilled, and literary sophisticated aristocratic women. According to Robert of Torigni, Matilda was a young girl when she was sent to Germany to be educated in the language and customs of that country.[82] This means that she must have added to French, her native tongue, others such as German, Latin, and perhaps Italian.[83] The evidence for the latter depends on the interpretation of her role as judge in two north-Italian court cases in 1117 and 1118, when, uniquely for a German queen-consort, she was in charge of the juridical proceedings, something that is difficult to believe if she had not been able to speak Latin or Italian. One could interpret the source material conservatively by arguing that the proceedings themselves would have been conducted by the bishops present, while Matilda's presence guaranteed the legality of the sessions.[84] In contrast, Amalie Fössel, in her study of the medieval queens of Germany, emphasizes the uniqueness of Empress Matilda's role on both occasions and warns her readers not to trivialize Matilda's expertise, actions, or the authority with which she acted.[85] Her education in Trier under the supervision of Archbishop Bruno and her administrative experience in Germany and Italy had made her familiar with legal texts, the bulk of which consisted of charters that she witnessed as queen consort, countess of Anjou, as lady of the English, and as caretaker for her son in Normandy. So, what do we know about her Latin expertise?

Empress Matilda and Languages

There is evidence strongly suggesting that in 1126 Matilda brought back with her from Germany some Latin chronicles. First is the famously unique autograph of the anonymous imperial chronicle with an illustration of her wedding breakfast that is now preserved in the Parker Library of Corpus Christi College, Cambridge.[86] Next, there is the tantalizing evidence of two English copies (one mid-twelfth century and one late-twelfth century) of the so-called *Annals of Ottobeuren*, a historical narrative ending in 1113.[87] Whereas the latter is a historical narrative of the sort of chronicle one might expect a newly arrived queen to have to read in order to familiarize herself with her new country's past, the imperial chronicle provided an account of her early time in Germany and was dedicated to her first husband, Henry V. Both chronicles also fit the mold sketched by Robert of Torigni to Gervase as being of the type that would acquire the favor of a new ruler. Their Latin is comparable to that of Robert of Torigni's work. We are on safer ground with the two (now lost) gospel manuscripts, no doubt in Latin, amongst the treasure which the Empress bequeathed to Bec in 1167.[88] Otherwise, there are the Latin chronicles dedicated to her, such as Hugh of Fleury's *Liber qui modernorum regum Francorum continet actus*, written while she was a young queen to Henry V. Interestingly, in the prologue, Rollo's dynasty is given in order to enable her to graft her native family onto that of the kings of France, a tactic similar to that employed by Robert of Torigni when he fitted the history of the counts of Anjou into his version of the *Gesta Normannorum Ducum*.[89] William of Malmesbury's *Gesta Regum Anglorum* was originally commissioned by Queen Edith/ Matilda, who asked for it to be written, and which was then dedicated to her daughter in the late 1120s.[90] Otherwise, the mother–daughter link is made explicit by Robert of Torigni in the *Gesta Normannorum Ducum*, where he extends it backward in time by linking both to St. Margaret of Scotland, the Empress's maternal grandmother. Robert reports, in what seems to be an address to

Empress Matilda, how the *Life* of Margaret had been dedicated to her daughter. He continues by saying that he intends to add it to the *Gesta Normannorum Ducum*; sadly there is no manuscript evidence that he ever did so.[91] Neither do we know if the Empress herself possessed a copy of her grandmother's *Life*, although it is fairly safe to assume, from the way Robert of Torigni refers to it, that she knew of it.

The most important evidence for Empress Matilda's knowledge of Latin prose comes from a letter written in the Christmas period of 1164 by Nicholas of Mont aux-Malades at Rouen to Thomas Becket, then in exile.[92] In it he tells how Matilda, after an initial refusal, was finally persuaded to acquaint herself with the *Constitutions of Clarendon*, the very document at the heart of the conflict between her son Henry II and the then Archbishop of Canterbury. She ordered Nicholas to read the document in Latin aloud to her ("precepit nobis eas latine legere"), a gesture that suggests that she could perfectly understand the Latin language. We do not know why she did not read it for herself, but failing eyesight (she was well into her sixties) or the nature of the script would have been obvious reasons. On the other hand, it was common for the aristocracy—kings, queens, abbots, bishops—to have their letters read out to them by secretaries, not because they could not read them themselves but because it was thought to be a task proper for servants to perform.[93] After Nicholas had finished the reading, the Empress then asked him to explain the contents in French ("et exponere gallice"). This suggests that although she could understand the Latin she desired to have an exposition of the contents in French.[94] The Latin of *Constitutions of Clarendon* is not unduly complicated.[95] However, it was a controversial legal text drafted in a concise form. Hence any understanding of the text necessitated not only a bare translation, but comprehension as to its meaning and implications. In terms of Latin complexity, I would rate the *Constitutions* as very similar to Robert of Torigni's prose, and vastly simpler than Stephen's hexameters. Nicholas's letter is incontrovertible evidence that the Empress was able to cope with Latin prose narrative.

We cannot be so unequivocal as to her understanding of Latin hexameters. It is therefore difficult to assess whether she would have been able to cope with Stephen of Rouen's verses had she had knowledge of them. Several poems have been addressed to her: one to her and her first husband to celebrate their entry in Canossa, one relatively easy Latin poem on Rouen as the second Rome at the time of Count Geoffrey that celebrates her imperial title, and a short one by Hildebert of Le Mans addressed to her alone.[96] Tantalizing evidence suggests that we may be able to link another Latin poem to her. Bishop Guy of Amiens's *Carmen de Hastingae Proelio*, the song on the Battle of Hastings, an epic poem written in Latin hexameters in ca. 1067, exists in two manuscripts of the monastery of St. Eucharius-Matthias at Trier.[97] Since the older of the two, which is also the most complete, dates from the second or, less likely, third decade of the twelfth century, it is tempting to argue that its presence can be linked in one way or another with Empress Matilda, who, as we have seen, was educated at Trier. If it was not meant for her, it is puzzling to see who else in Trier at that time would have been interested in a poem celebrating William the Conqueror's victory over King Harold in 1066. If the young Matilda was taught Latin partly on the basis of her grandfather's deeds in verse, and if we assume that she kept up her Latin all through her life, there is no reason to doubt her ability to read Stephen of Rouen's work, even though in its present form the *Draco Normannicus* dates from after her death.

As to Empress Matilda's native knowledge of French, the only Anglo-Norman text addressed to her was the *Livre de Sibile*, attributed to Philippe de Thaon.[98] Its dedication was fueled by the author's hope that his maternal inheritance would be restored to him through the intercession of the Empress.[99] What is interesting about the *Livre de Sibile* is that the text, though predominantly Anglo-Norman, contains a fair smattering of (easy) Latin. Again on these grounds it would be easy to picture the Empress able to digest the text. As for its prophetic contents, apart from the fact that there may be a link between the *Livre* and the griffin eggs that formed part of her legacy to the abbey of Bec,[100] they remind us that interest in the Sibyls coincides with the royal demand for horoscopes, as we have noted, in the 1150s. Interest in the past went hand in hand with fascination about the future. Latin and French were languages employed to understand and interpret both. The evidence presented in this chapter underlines that various degrees of authority were attached to the two tongues, depending on the topic, the political circumstances, and the patronage involved. Latin prose remained the standard language of authority for narratives of the past, but the result was often a fairly dull affair. Latin verse allowed more scope for chronological inversion and inclusion of literary detail. French, which inherently meant verse, became very popular, not least because it allowed its authors to embark on greater detail, enlivening the historical narrative with contemporary imagery, which permitted the audience to picture the past before their very eyes. Normandy, like England, provided fertile soil for dynastically inspired historiography in Latin, and more imaginatively, in French. All signs are that its authors hoped that it would be enjoyed by men as well as by women.

Notes

1. For useful introductions, see Leah Shopkow, *History and Community: Norman Historical Writing in the Eleventh and Twelfth Centuries* (Washington, Catholic

University of America Press, 1997), Emily Albu, *The Normans in their Histories* (Woodbridge, Suffolk: Boydell and Brewer, 2001), and Elisabeth van Houts, "Historical Writing," *A Companion to the Anglo-Norman World*, ed. Christopher Harper-Bill and Elisabeth van Houts (Woodbridge, Suffolk: Boydell and Brewer, 2003), pp. 103–22.

2. Peter Damian-Grint, *The New Historians of the Twelfth-Century Renaissance: Inventing Vernacular Authority* (Woodbridge, Suffolk: Boydell and Brewer, 1999); a comparative study of Latin and French is presented by Jean Blacker, *The Faces of Time: Portrayal of the Past in Old French and Latin Historical Narratives of the Anglo-Norman Regnum* (Austin: University of Texas Press, 1994). For the intellectual climate, see Ian Short, "Language and Literature," *A Companion to the Anglo-Norman World*, ed. Christopher Harper-Bill and Elisabeth van Houts (Woodbridge, Suffolk: Boydell and Brewer, 2003), pp. 191–214.

3. For Robert of Torigni, see *The Gesta Normannorum Ducum of William of Jumièges, Orderic Vitali and Robert of Torigni*, ed. Elisabeth M. C. van Houts, 2 vols. (Oxford: Oxford University Press, 1992–95), 1: lxxvii–xci, et al., and *The Chronicle of Robert of Torigni*, ed. Richard Howlett, *Chronicles of the Reigns of Stephen, Henry II and Richard I*, 4 vols. RS 82 (1884–89), p. 4; for Stephen of Rouen, see *Le dragon normand et d'autres poèmes d'Etienne de Rouen*, ed. Henri Omont, *Société de l'histoire de Normandie* (Rouen: Charles Métérie, 1884) and *The Draco Normannicus of Etienne de Rouen*, ed. Howlett, *Chronicles*, 2:589–762 (all references here are to Howlett's edition); for Wace, see *The History of the Norman People: Wace's Roman de Rou*, trans. Glynn S. Burgess, ed. Anthony Holden, annot. Glynn S. Burgess and Elisabeth van Houts (St. Helier: Société Jersiaise, 2002).

4. Marjorie Chibnall, "The Empress Matilda and Bec-Hellouin," *Anglo-Norman Studies* 10 (1987): 35–48, repr. as chap. 11 in Marjorie Chibnall, *Piety, Power and History in Medieval England and Normandy*, Variorum Collected Studies Series, 11 (Aldershot: Ashgate, 2000), pp. 35–48.

5. See p. 57.

6. The definition is from Karen M. Broadhurst, "Henry II of England and Eleanor of Aquitaine: patrons of literature in French," *Viator* 27 (1996): 53–84, at 54. See also the classic work, Walter F. Schirmer and Ulrich Broich, *Studien zum literarischen Patronat im England des 12. Jahrhunderts*, Arbeitsgemeinschaft Für Forschung des Landes Nordrhein-Westfalen. Wissenschaftliche Abhandlungen, 23 (Cologne: Westdeutscher Verlag, 1962); for a recent critique on Broadhurst's definition as too narrow, see Amaury Chauou, *L'Idéologie Plantagenêt: Royauté arthurienne et monarchie politique dans l'espace Plantagenêt (XIIe–XIIIe siècles)* (Rennes: Presses universitaires de Rennes, 2001), pp. 79–88.

7. The full text can be found in *Venerabilis Guiberti abbatis b. Mariae de Novigento Opera Omnia*, ed. Dom Luc D'Achéry (Paris: Jean Billaine, 1651), pp. 715–16 and Elisabeth M. C. van Houts, *Gesta Normannorum Ducum: een studie over de handschriften, de tekst, het geschiedwerk en het genre* (Meppel: Krips Repro, 1982), p. 172, n. 116.

8. *Venerabilis Guiberti*, ed. D'Achéry, pp. 715–16: "Hoc enim ad augmentum famae tuae proficiet, et gratiosum me tibi, et remunerationis debitorem efficiet; et quod his omnibus majus est, novi ducis favorem non modicum forsitam adquiret."

9. *Gesta Normannorum Ducum*, 2:196–289.

10. *Guillelmi de Conchis. Dragmaticon philosophiae*, ed. Italo Ronca, Corpus Christianorum Continuatio Mediaevalis, 152 (Turnhout: Brepols, 1997), pp. xvii–xxii.

11. Adelard's address to Henry was printed by C. H. Haskins, "Adelard of Bath and Henry Plantagenet," *English Historical Review* 28 (1913): 516–17. Emmanuel Poulle, "Le traité de l'astrolabe d'Adélard de Bath," *Adelard of Bath. An English Scientist and Arabist of the Early Twelfth Century*, ed. Charles Burnett, Warburg Institute Surveys and Texts, 14 (London: Warburg Institute, 1987), pp. 119–32; J. D. North, "Some Norman Horoscopes," *Adelard of Bath*, ed. Burnett, 147–61, at 159–61 and Louise Cochrane, *Adelard of Bath the First Scientist* (London: British Museum Press, 1994), 97–98, 105. Recently, it has been suggested that the horoscopes may be by Robert of Chester, see *Adelard of Bath, Conversations with his Nephew: On the Same and the Different, Questions on Natural Science and On Birds*, ed. and trans. Charles Burnett, et al., Cambridge Medieval Classics 9 (Cambridge: Cambridge University Press, 1998), p. xvi, n. 26.

12. *Gesta Normannorum Ducum*, book 8, chap. 11, pp. 25–28, ed. van Houts, 2:216–19, pp. 240–47.

13. *Robert of Torigni*, pp. 123–24; Marjorie Chibnall, *The Empress Matilda. Queen consort, Queen Mother and Lady of the English* (Oxford: Blackwell, 1991), p. 61 and "Matilda and Bec-Hellouin": 46.

14. *Gesta Normannorum Ducum*, 1:lxxviii, n. 223.

15. Matilda's death is mentioned at the start of *Draco Normannicus* books 1: chaps 2 and 3: 1 and at the end of book 2: chap. 23 (ed. Howlett, pp. 597, 713 and 708). For the Empress as his patron, see Chibnall, "Matilda and Bec-Hellouin," p. 47.

16. *Draco Normannicus*, book 2: chap. 23 (ed. Howlett, p. 708): "Interea Mathildis obit regique repente/Beccense monachus mittitur, exit, abit."

17. *Draco Normannicus*, book 1: chaps 14–30 (ed. Howlett, pp. 610–48) on Rollo to the Norman conquest of England.

18. *Draco Normannicus*, book 2: chap. 2 (ed. Howlett, 661–63), book 3: chap. 16 (ed. Howlett, pp. 753–57); see also Adolphe André Porée, *Histoire de l'abbaye du Bec*, 2 vols. (Evreux: Hérissey, 1901), 1:240.

19. But see p. 65 for a discussion of Robert's election as abbot of Mont Saint-Michel, reported by himself with close reference to the Empress's agreement.

20. Broadhurst, "Henry II of England," pp. 56–58.

21. *Wace*, book 3, lines 177–79, 11431–32 (trans. Burgess, pp. 112–13, 338–39).

22. *Wace*, book 3, lines 143–66 (trans. Burgess, pp. 110–11).

23. *Wace*, book 2, lines 1359, 4423 (trans. Burgess, pp. 40–41, 106–7).

24. *Wace*, book 3, lines 172–75 (trans. Burgess, p. 111).

25. *Wace*, book 3, lines 185–88 (trans. Burgess, p. 112).

26. *Wace*, book 3, lines 155–56 (trans. Burgess, p. 110). Gaimar records that the copy of the now lost verse history of Henry I by David had cost his patron Constance one mark of silver; see *L'Estoire des Engleis by Geffrei Gaimar*, ed. Alexander Bell, Anglo-Norman Texts, 14–16 (Oxford: Blackwell, 1960), line 6492, at p. 205.

27. *The Correspondence of Thomas Becket Archbishop of Canterbury 1162–70*, ed. and trans. Anne J. Duggan, 2 vols. (Oxford: Clarendon Press, 2000), 1: no. 41, pp. 158–69, at 166–67.

28. *Robert of Torigni*, p. 179.

29. *Robert of Torigni*, p. 211.

30. Elisabeth van Houts, "Le roi et son historien: Henri II et Robert de Torigni," *Cahiers de Civilisation médiévale* 37 (1994): 115–18; for the frontier position of Mont Saint-Michel, see Cassandra Potts, "Normandy or Brittany? A Conflict of Interests at Mont Saint-Michel (966–1035)," *Anglo-Norman Studies* 12 (1989): 135–56.

31. *Henry, Archdeacon of Huntingdon, Historia Anglorum. The History of the English People*, ed. and trans. Diana E. Greenway (Oxford: Clarendon Press, 1996), liv–v, clxviii and 558 n. g.

32. *Der Roman du Mont Saint-Michel von Guillaume de S. Paier. Wiederausgabe der beiden Handschriften des Brittischen Museums*, ed. Paul Redlich, Ausgaben und Abhandlungen aus dem Gebiete der romanische Philologie, xcii (Marburg: Elwert, 1894). I am most grateful to Ian Short for discussing this text with me.

33. *Roman Mont Saint-Michel*, line 64 (ed. Redlich, p. 11).

34. J. A. Everard, *Brittany and the Angevins. Province and Empire 1158–1203*, Cambridge Studies in Medieval Life and Thought, 4th ser., 48 (Cambridge: Cambridge University Press, 2000), pp. 34–75, at 34–45 for a political guide to the chronology.

35. Everard, *Brittany and the Angevins*, p. 99.

36. Judith Everard, "The 'Justiciarship' in Brittany and Ireland under Henry II," *Anglo-Norman Studies* 20 (1997): 87–106.

37. *Draco Normannicus*, book 2, chap. 18 (ed. Howlett, p. 696): Rolland to Arthur; book 2, chap. 19 (ed. Howlett, p. 696): Arthur to Rolland; book 2, chap. 20 (ed. Howlett, pp. 697–705): Arthur to Henry; book 2, chap. 21 (ed. Howlett, pp. 705–7): interval on how Henry had Arthur's letter read aloud to his followers; book 2, chap. 22 (ed. Howlett, p. 707): Henry's reply to Arthur. For the identification of Rolland, see Everard, *Brittany and the Angevins*, pp. 44, 56–57 where it is noted that in 1169 Rolland and Henry II established peace, which is just about the time that Stephen of Rouen was writing the *Draco Normannicus*.

38. Peter Johanek, "König Arthur und die Plantagenets," *Frühmittelalterliche Studien* 21 (1987): 346–89, at 384–86, where it is suggested that Stephen may have used an existing fictional correspondence in prose which he put

into verse; Julia Crick, *The Historia Regum Brittanie of Geoffrey of Monmouth. IV Dissemination and Reception in the later Middle Ages* (Cambridge: D. S. Brewer, 1991), pp. 92–93; Chauou, *L'idéologie plantagenêt*, pp. 71–72.

39. Crick, *Historia Regum Brittanie*, pp. 92–93 where the full text is printed. The identification of "Hugoni cappellano de Branno" with Hugh of Braine is mine.

40. For Agnes de Baudemont, see Theodore Evergates, "Aristocratic women in the county of Champagne," in *Aristocratic women in Medieval France*, ed. Theodore Evergates (Philadelphia: University of Pennsylvania Press, 1999), pp. 74–100, at 101.

41. Crick, *Historia Regum Brittanie*, p. 93: "Occulta cordis desideria .uii. nocte mensis septimi septem Dei famuli nobis sepcies reuelauerunt."

42. Crick, *Historia Regum Brittanie*, p. 93: "Terraque a Ioue [sic] ad Isium [sic] libere tibi pro dignitate tue promocionis famulabitur."

43. Crick, *Historia Regum Brittanie*, p. 92.

44. The Braine connection with the court of Henry II in the context of Arthurian interest would benefit from further investigation. In the early 1160s Walter of Châtillon was engaged in discussion with Baldwin of Valenciennes, a canon at Saint-Yves de Braine, on the Jews, comparing the Jewish wait for the Messiah with the Breton wait for Arthur (*Tractatus sive dialogus magistri Gualteri Tornacensis et Balduini Valentianensis Contra Judaeos*, PL 202:423–53, at 424: "ut Britones Arturum primum ipsius praestolatur aduentum;" I owe this reference to Anna Abulafia). A few years later, in January 1165, John of Salisbury gossips to Thomas Becket about Agnes and her husband giving 300 ells of linen to Henry II for the making of shirts in the hope of establishing marriages for their children with Anglo-Norman/Angevin nobles; see Duggan, *Correspondence*, 1, no. 42, at pp. 170–73. Around 1200 a copy of the *Gesta Normannorum Ducum* was available in the library of Saint-Yves at Braine (*Gesta Normannorum Ducum*, 1:cvii–cviii).

45. *Gesta Normannorum Ducum*, 1:lxxxiv–v; 2:196–97 n. a.

46. *Draco Normannicus*, book 1, chap. 4, line 172 (ed. Howlett, p. 597); book 2, chap. 2, lines 115–16 (ed. Howlett, p. 663); book 1 chap. 36, lines 165–67 (ed. Howlett, pp. 654–5), and book 1 chap. 11, line 421 (ed. Howlett, p. 607).

47. Now preserved as Leiden Universiteitsbibliotheek MS BPL 20. *Gesta Normannorum Ducum*, 1: cix–cx, and Crick, *Historia Regum Brittanie*, pp. 23 and 45, both note the links with the Alexander material.

48. For a differently focussed discussion of the theme of filial strife, see also Blacker, *Faces of Time*, pp. 184–85.

49. *Gesta Normannorum Ducum*, 2:200–203.

50. Note that Robert of Torigni changed the original numbering of the books; cf. n. 45.

51. The sentiment can be detected already in Hugh of Fleury's prologue to his *Liber qui modernorum regum Francorum continet* (ed. Georg Waitz, *Monumenta Germaniae Historica: Scriptores* 9 (1851): 376–95, at 376), addressed to Empress Matilda as a young queen to Henry V. In it Hugh skips from

William the Conqueror to Henry I without mentioning either of Henry's older brothers.

52. *Gesta Normannorum Ducum*, 2: 240–41: "heredes legitimos Anglici principatus."

53. *Robert of Torigni*, pp. 196 and 318 (Geoffrey's death) and *Robert of Torigni*, p. 221; *Draco Normannicus* book 2: chap. 8 (ed. Howlett, p. 676).

54. *Draco Normannicus* book 1: chap. 10, book 2: chaps 22 and 23 (ed. Howlett, pp. 605–607, 707, 708).

55. *Wace* (trans Burgess, pp. xiv–v). The suggestion is based on the work by Matthew Bennett who argued that the list of the conqueror's companions might have reflected names representing enemies of Henry II in 1173/4; see Matthew Bennett, "Poetry as History? The Roman de Rou of Wace as a source for the Norman Conquest," *Anglo-Norman Studies* 5 (1982): 21–39; see also Blacker, *Faces of Time*, p. 185.

56. For Henry the Young King, see Warren, *Henry II*, pp. 117–36; for Robert Curthose, see Judith Green, "Robert Curthose Reassessed," *Anglo-Norman Studies* 22 (1999): 95–116.

57. Elisabeth van Houts, "Wace as Historian," *Family Trees and the Roots of Politics. The Prosopography of Britain and France from the Tenth to the Twelfth Century*, ed. K. S. B. Keats-Rohan (Woodbridge, Suffolk: Boydell and Brewer, 1997), pp. 103–32 and Green, "Robert Curthose Reassessed," pp. 95–96.

58. Elisabeth van Houts, "The adaptation of the *Gesta Normannorum Ducum* by Wace and Benoit," *Non Nova sed Nove: Mélanges de civilisation médiévale dédiés à Willem Noomen*, ed. Martin Gosman and Jaap van Os, Mediaevalia Groningana 5 (Groningen: Bouma's Boekhuis, 1984), 115–25; *Wace* (trans. Burgess, p. xxxi).

59. *Gesta Normannorum Ducum*, 2: 184–5.

60. *Wace*, book 3: lines 6905–6948, 6985–7050 (trans. Burgess, pp. 247–9, 249–51).

61. For Edith-Matilda, see *Wace*, book 3: lines 11137–39, 10338–40, 10645–10704 (trans. Burgess, pp. 312–13, 316–17, 322–25); for the godparents, see Lois L. Huneycutt, *Matilda of Scotland. A Study in Medieval Queenship* (Woodbridge, Suffolk: Boydell and Brewer, 2003), p. 10.

62. Chibnall, *Empress Matilda*, passim; see *Wace*, book 3: lines 11437, book 1: lines 110–36, book 3: lines 10143–8, 11437 (trans. Burgess, pp. 4–5, 312–13, 338).

63. *Wace*, book 1: lines 132–33 (trans. Burgess, pp. 4–5): "tant le destrainst li roiz que son droit recongut, / du regne l'erita, qui a cues moult crut. . . ."

64. *Wace*, book 1: lines18, 24–34 (trans. Burgess, pp. 2–3).

65. See n. 7 above.

66. *L'Estoire*, lines 6495–97, 6505–6511 (ed. Bell, pp. 205–6). I am most grateful to Ian Short for allowing me to use his unpublished translation.

67. *Gesta Normannorum Ducum*, 1:cix–cxix and *Robert of Torigni*, xxxvii–lxv; see also Damian-Grint, *New Historians*, pp. 194–99.

68. *Wace* (trans. Burgess, pp. xxv–vi); *Draco Normannicus* (ed. Howlett, pp. xci–xcix).

69. *Wace's Roman de Brut: A History of the British. Text and Translation*, trans. Judith Weiss (Exeter: University of Exeter Press, 1999), pp. xxvii–xxix.

70. *Wace*, book 3, line 2242 (trans. Burgess, pp. 52–3); *Recueil des actes de Henri II, roi d'Angleterre et duc de Normandie, concernant les provinces françaises et les affaires de France*, ed. Leopold. Delisle and Élie Berger, 4 vols. (Paris: Imprimerie nationale, 1909–27) no. 223, at pp. 1, 2, 3, 4:360–61. I am most grateful to Judith Everard for providing me with a copy of the new edition of this charter (no. 598H).

71. *Wace*, book 2: line1356 (trans. Burgess, pp. 40–41).

72. Short, "Language and Literature," p. 204.

73. *Roman Mont Saint-Michel*, lines 1–27 (ed. Redlich, 1); K. S. B. Keats-Rohan, "Bibliothèque municipale d'Avranches, 210: Cartulary of Mont Saint-Michel," *Anglo-Norman Studies* 21 (1998): 95–112, at 107–108; Damian-Grint, *New Historians*, pp. 66–67, 119–20 and 131.

74. *Robert of Torigni*, p. 179.

75. Short, "Language and Literature," pp. 198–99 on spoken Latin.

76. V. H. Galbraith, "The literacy of the medieval English kings," *Proceedings of the British Academy* 21 (1935): 1–40, at 15–16; Warren, *Henry II*, pp. 38–39, 207–208.

77. *Walter Map, De nugis Curialium. Courtiers' Trifles*, ed. and trans. M. R. James, C. N. L. Brooke and R. A. B. Mynors (Oxford: Clarendon Press, 1983), pp. 476–77.

78. The periods in his youth spent at Bristol suggests this to me.

79. *Chroniques des comtes de'Anjou et des seigneurs d'Amboise*, ed. Louis Halphen and René Poupardin, Collection de textes pour servir à l'étude et à l'enseignement de l'histoire 48 (Paris: A. Picard, 1913), p. 162; for the dedication of John of Marmoutiers' text to Henry II, see pp. vii–viii.

80. *Dragmaticon philosophiae*, ed. Ronca, pp. xvii–xxii; Cochrane, *Adelard of Bath*, pp. 97–8, 105; *Gervase of Canterbury: Opera Historica*, ed. William Stubbs, RS 73, 2 vols. (1879–80): 1: 125; Warren, *Henry II*, pp. 38–39. See also Peter of Blois' interesting letter, on behalf of Archbishop Rotrou of Rouen, on the education of Henry II's son Young Henry (PL 209:210–13).

81. Chibnall, *Empress Matilda*, pp. 33–34, 46, 47–48 argues against overestimating the empress's skills. Miriam Büttner-Shergold is inclined to give more credence to learning and literary skills in Latin and the vernacular of high aristocratic women and queens ("The Education of Queens in the Eleventh and Twelfth Centuries," PhD. diss., University of Cambridge, 2003, pp. 168–203).

82. *Gesta Normannorum Ducum*, 2:216–17; Chibnall, *Empress Matilda*, pp. 25, 47–48.

83. The Empress's knowledge of English is not recorded. However, I would suggest that with an English born mother, Edith/Matilda, and having lived in England until the age of eight, it is highly likely that she knew some English. Anyone with a knowledge of spoken Latin, which as we will see

Matilda possessed, Italian would not have been too difficult to pick up. Alternatively, spoken Latin would have helped the empress in court.

84. Chibnall, *Empress Matilda*, pp. 33–34, 48.

85. Amalie Fössel, *Die Königin im mittelalterlichen Reich* (Stuttgart: Thorbecke, 2000), pp. 106–107 and 159–61, at 161: ". . . übernahm Königin Mathilde nicht nur den Vorsitz, sondern auch die Rolle der Richterin, ausgestattet mit den entsprechenden Befugnissen: Sie leitete die Verhandlung, beriet mit den Beisitzern, verkündete den Urteilsspruch, investierte in Besitzungen, verhängte den Bann, verfügte die Ausstellung der Urkunde."

86. Corpus Christi College, MS 373. *Anonymi Chronica Imperatorum Heinrico V dedicata*, ed. Franz-Joseph Schmale and Irene Schmale-Ott, Ausgewählte Quellen zur Deutschen Geschichte des Mittelalters, 15 (Darmstadt: Wissenschafliche Buchgesellschaft, 1972), 211–65 for the section from 1095 to the end in 1114. For the authorship and date of composition ca. 1112–14, see pp. 39–42; see also Chibnall, *Empress Matilda*, p. 26.

87. Martina Giese, "Die sogenanten Annales Ottenburani," *Deutsches Archiv* 58 (2002): 69–121. Two of the four manuscripts of the "Annals of Ottenbeurani" contain the *Gesta Normannorum Ducum*, books 1 and 3 (*Gesta Normannorum Ducum* 1:xcvii–viii), and 01 and 02 in Giese's work. I am grateful to Dr Martina Giese for discussing the potential link with Empress Matilda with me; we agree that it is likely that the work came to England with Matilda, but at the same time we realize that conclusive proof is missing.

88. Porée, *Histoire de l'abbaye du Bec*, pp. i, 293–95, 650–51, 653; Chibnall, *Empress Matilda*, pp. 189–90.

89. Waitz, *Liber regum Francorum*: 376–95, with prologue at 376–77; Chibnall, *Empress Matilda*, p. 46. For Hugh of Fleury's text, see Alexandre Vidier, *L'Historiographie à Saint-Benoit-sur-Loire et les Miracles de Saint Benoit* (Paris: A. Picard, 1965), pp. 79–80.

90. *William of Malmesbury, Gesta Regum Anglorum*, ed. and trans. R. A. B. Mynors, completed R. M. Thomson and M. Winterbottom, 2 vols. (Oxford: Clarendon Press, 1998–99), 1:6–9 and Chibnall, *Empress Matilda*, pp. 46–47.

91. *Gesta Normannorum Ducum*, 2:242–43. For the *Life of St. Margaret*, see now Huneycutt, *Matilda of Scotland*, pp. 161–78.

92. Duggan, *Correspondence*, no. 41, at pp. 158–69 and Chibnall, *Empress Matilda*, pp. 170–71. Jacques was prior of Mont aux-Malades from ca. 1164 to 1173/80.

93. C. Bougy, "Comment lisait-on une lettre au Moyen Age? Le témoignage du *Roman du Mont Saint-Michel*," *Tabularia. Documents* 3 (2003): 1–12.

94. I do not think that Nicholas meant simply that he was only translating the text for her, as Anne Duggan (*Correspondence*, 1: 166–67) suggests by translating "exponere" as "translating"; Chibnall, *Empress Matilda*, p. 170 is no doubt right in her preference for "explaining."

95. *Councils and Synods with Other Documents Relating to the English Church. Vol. I AD 871–1204, Part II 1066–1204*, ed. Dorothy Whitelock, M. Brett,

Christopher N. L. Brooke, 2 vols. (Oxford: Clarendon Press, 1981), 2:877–83.

96. For the Canossa lines, see Chibnall, *Empress Matilda*, pp. 30–1 and quoted by Fössel, *Die Königin*, p. 106; the Rouen poem is printed in Charles Homer Haskins, *Norman Institutions* (New York: Ungar, 1918), p. 144, n. 72; *Hildeberti Cenomannensis episcopi Carmina Minora*, ed. A. Brian Scott (Leipzig: Teubner, 1969), no. 35, at pp. 21–22 and Chibnall, *Empress Matilda*, p. 47.

97. *The Carmen de Hastingae Proelio of Guy, Bishop of Amiens*, ed. and trans. Frank Barlow (Oxford: Clarendon Press, 1999), pp. xix–xx.

98. *Livre de Sibile by Philippe de Thaon*, ed. Hugh Shields, Anglo-Norman Text Society 37 (London: Westfield College, 1979), pp. 89–90 (lines 1207–18).

99. Shields (*Livre de Sibile*, p. 24) suggests a date while the empress was active in England, i.e., between 1139 and 1147/8—a date upon her return in Normandy, where she was often acting on behalf of her son, is as realistic.

100. Chibnall, *Empress Matilda*, p. 190. Elisabeth van Houts, "Gender, Memories and Prophecies: Adeliza of Louvain," in *Medieval Narrative Sources: A Gateway into the Medieval Mind*, ed. Werner Verbeke, Ludo Melis and Jan Goossens, Mediaevalia Lovaniensia, Series 1: Studia 34 (Louvain: Louvain University Press, 2005), pp. 21–36, at 35–36.

CHAPTER 3

AN INTRUDER AT THE FEAST? ANXIETY AND DEBATE IN THE LETTERS OF PETER OF BLOIS

Neil Cartlidge

Of all the writers associated with Henry II's court, Peter of Blois could perhaps be seen as the most representative, the one who defines with the greatest clarity the intellectual coordinates of the Angevin world.[1] His letters repeatedly suggest a particular willingness to occupy the common ground of literary discourse in this period[2]—to make use of apparently conventional themes, images, citations, and arguments, in a way that, on the face of it, clearly provides a basis for Sir Richard Southern's allegation that the "attractive exterior of his work" covers nothing more than "a deep emptiness, a lack of thought, of originality, of anything but conventional feelings."[3] Yet Peter is rarely as simple, as unintelligent or as predictable as such an assessment might imply. Indeed, his dedication to convention is in many ways the most perplexing aspect of his literary persona, for the certainty and self-complacency that usually accompany most kinds of conventionality are, in his work, conspicuously lacking. As I hope to be able to show in this essay, it is precisely by recognizing and reworking conventions, adapting and juxtaposing particular routines of argument and association—sometimes in ways that are surprising and/or self-contradictory—that Peter makes his letters a vehicle both for a provocative description of the cultural landscape in which he lived and for a teasingly evasive display of his own personality.

It is still worth respecting Southern's terms, since Peter's apparent facility and his accommodation of conventional modes of thinking are indeed the most-immediately striking qualities of his work—even if they mask more complexity and more unease than Southern ultimately allows. At least some of the letters can certainly be seen as thin pretexts for the rehearsal of rhetorical set-pieces on familiar and broadly applicable themes.[4] Letter VII, for example, is addressed to a man who, Peter says, entertains his friends with irresponsibly generous amounts of alcohol; it begins with a vividly realized anecdote about the drunken behavior of one of these friends, which, as it turns out, provides the occasion for a summary of the biblical pronouncements on the evils of intoxicating drink.[5] Letter LVI proposes to rebuke an elderly bishop for his addiction to hunting, but quickly develops into a rather abstract disquisition on the immorality of the sport—much of it adapted from John of Salisbury.[6] Neither of these letters is at all original in substance, nor are they energetic or individual enough to suggest any deep feeling, for all the apparent care with which their author describes the occasions on which they were sent. They are marked much more by their density of quotation and allusion than by any pronounced assertion of personality. In this respect, it could be argued, Peter's letters only conform to the expectations of the genre in which he was working, since medieval letter-collections usually aspire to just the kind of mannered urbanity he displays, and in most of them biographical actuality is implicitly subordinated to the conscious demands of an often rather impersonal form of art.[7] Yet Peter conforms to the expectations even of this most conservative of genres almost too amply, modeling and polishing sometimes already well-worn opinions and quotations so intensively, and with such evident satisfaction, as to suggest an unusually profound satisfaction with intellectual artifice.

In Letter LV, to take another example, Peter congratulates the young woman Adelitia on her decision to become a nun, with a masterfully lapidary summary of the conventional arguments in favor of virginity. This is completely beside the point, since she has already made her decision to enter a religious life and needs no more persuasion. At the same time it is precisely the fluency with which Peter slips into the stream of the argument that makes this letter such an elegant congratulation to her. There is something of the well-oiled machine here, the soft click of the gears as the writer accelerates into an exhilarating display of rhetorical power: "You have wisely resolved to relinquish the world before it relinquishes you. Blessed are you who have rejected the sons of men," and so on.[8] Such fluidly mechanical control is the effect of a cultivated refinement of discourse and learning; and in the context of this celebration of piety any conspicuous display of originality could only have seemed—to its author at least— merely churlishly obtrusive.[9] Peter himself praised John of Salisbury's *Policraticus*, not for any innovations of style or matter, but for its well-honed erudition and pleasingly artful variety of opinions [artificiosum sententiarum varietatem]. This perhaps explains both his readiness to quarry John's work for its erudition, and the criteria on which he would have own liked his own work to be assessed.[10] Yet there are differences between the two writers—differences that sometimes amount to a significant tension. Most obviously, Peter's language and imagination remain predominantly biblical, despite his apparently bare-faced raids on John of Salisbury's more distinctly classical learning.[11]

It may in fact have been precisely this ability to distil so many of the characteristic preoccupations of his age, and often with such precise and accessible grace, that enabled Peter to find such an extensive and appreciative reception for as long as he did; and it is roughly on these grounds that Southern ultimately chooses to justify his own long-standing engagement with Peter's work. "However coolly we may assess his absolute importance as a man of thought and feeling," he says, "the wide and long-lasting distribution of his letters throughout Europe illustrates his continued utility."[12] As he points out, there are over 250 medieval manuscripts of Peter's letters still extant, most of them dating from the fourteenth or fifteenth centuries, and to this long history of scribal copying can be added three printed editions before the end of the sixteenth century.[13] Given the sheer size of the collection, this is a publication history that amounts to a canonicity bordering on the monumental.[14] Yet to define the literary significance of these texts only in terms of this combination of volume, popularity, and influence risks presenting Peter as a mere cipher—a writer so absolutely representative as to have absolutely no profile of his own. From this perspective Peter starts to look like a kind of twelfth-century John Lydgate—or at least the particular Lydgate so persuasively invoked by Derek Pearsall, who sees the fifteenth-century monk's work as profoundly, essentially typical, and thus in itself a kind of "introduction to medieval literature, presenting its themes and methods in their basic form, without the complications of experiment, ambiguity, or even, sometimes, of individual thought."[15] Certainly, the work of both writers could be seen as almost encyclopedic in its range and patience, and to that extent, both offer the literary historian a fairly comprehensive record of the general temper and interests of their respective ages. Even if the differences between the two writers eventually turn out to be more important than the similarities (which I think is the case) the specific similarities do still exist—the conspicuous display of copiousness in eloquence and opinion, for example, and the accretive, deeply syncretic sensibility. It is perhaps these similarities that explain why it is that both Peter of Blois and John Lydgate have tended to be received by modern critics in such similar terms—at its worst, a mix of back-handed respect for their industry with condescending scorn for their supposedly uncritical allegiance to the literary norms of their day.[16] If Peter is to be critically rehabilitated, it may well be that the best route to doing so will be through the recognition in his work of some of the same kinds of "energy" or "ambivalence" that some recent critics have tried to demonstrate in the work of Lydgate.[17]

Whether or not this analogy holds, there are certainly problems with reading Peter's literary personality as an essentially flat or "empty" one—despite his seemingly impersonal style. If he has any claim at all to be the most representative writer of Henry II's reign, indeed, then that claim rests not in those qualities that have made him for so long seem like a reassuringly transparent figure, but in those that allow him to disclose an uncomfortable strain of crisis or conflict throughout his creative work. If Peter of Blois is indeed more "representative" than any other writer of Henry II's reign, it is not in the sense that he is so at home in his environment as to be culturally invisible, but in the sense that he registers more clearly than anyone else the cultural and social tensions implicit in the sprawling and precarious new Plantagenet polity—"in tam spatiosis et diffusis regionibus" [in regions so scattered and widespread] as he himself put it.[18] On the one hand, it was Henry's inheritance of (or claims to) this complex set of dominions—the kingdoms of England, Scotland, Ireland, and Wales, the duchies of Normandy, Aquitaine, and Brittany, and the counties of Anjou and Maine[19]—that broadened the field of administrative[20] and literary[21] opportunities on which ambitious Latin-speaking courtier-clerks like Peter of Blois depended. On the other hand, such "clerici aulici"[22] paid the price for their social and cultural mobility in the literal mobility of Henry's court—an entity so fundamentally elusive as to belong, in Peter's rhetoric, only to a kind of virtual reality.[23] The cosmopolitanism that was both the product and the condition of belonging to the Angevin affinity precluded its members in the end from the comfortable stability of any identity predicated on language, local origin, or class. As a result, there is a pervasive ambivalence in the literature of Henry II's reign, particularly when it pretends to take a moral or satirical perspective on the court itself. What purports to be a detached commentary on the values of the king's political community generally reveals itself to be an essentially reflexive exercise—a more or less rueful or self-mocking acknowledgment of the values that the courtier-clerk brings to it.[24] The restless ambition apparently embodied in the Angevin court turns out to be a figure of the writer-critic's own uneasy subjectivity, the supposedly mad career of the king's household throughout his lands a reflection on the careerism of its individual members.

In Peter's case, the general uncertainties of the age are specifically realized as an insistence on his sense of his own rootlessness or lack of identity. This is expressed in his work in several different ways. For example, he frequently alludes to his own literal "foreignness"—his awareness of not being English, and of not speaking English, even when neither Englishness nor the use of English in any way defined the cultural horizons of the Angevin court: "Wandering in England for twenty-six years I have listened to a language that I do not understand. . .Am I always to be 'a wanderer and a fugitive' on the earth? Will no one put an end to my wandering, so that I might breathe the air of my native land one last time before my spirit breathes its last?"[25] This is not just the expatriate's inevitable unease, but something much deeper—the sense of exile as an essential state of being, rather than just an accident of circumstance.[26] In effect, there is an attempt here to interpret the centrifugal, inchoately "national" tensions in Henry's dominions into symbolic terms, as a figure for a kind of moral condition. Yet Peter's apparent identification with the exiled Cain is so extreme, even in the context of a consciously rhetorical contrast, that it begs questions about the very categories that Peter employs—living abroad is one thing, but bearing the mark of Cain is quite another. Does Peter really mean to imply that his life in England is a punishment ordained by God—and, if so, for what crime? Or, if Cain's exile is used here simply as a symbol for the common condition of fallen humanity, banished to a "regio dissimilitudinis" [a land of unlikeness], how is Peter's condition actually any different, or worse, than any other human being's?[27] In any case, there are occasions when he is prepared to argue, pointedly, in England's favor, such as when he urges Richard, bishop of Syracuse, to come home from Sicily: "England fosters me now in my old age, just as it fostered you as a child. I wish you would leave behind you that monstrous, mountainous country and return to the sweetness of your native air."[28]

Another apparent aspect of this rhetoric of disorientatedness is a lack of confidence in the hierarchies of social class. So, for example, he writes to a nobleman who had expressed scorn for the low birth of his chaplain: "Vague and uncertain is the heredity of men; for even a prince's son might turn out to be the bastard of some gigolo from the kitchens. As the poet [Juvenal] testifies: 'No matter how many candles adorn your altars, nobility depends solely and exclusively on virtue.' "[29] This could be taken as a characteristically clerical emphasis on meritocratic (as opposed to aristocratic) values, but then Peter also defines virtue as the ability to transcend any desire for worldly honor in a way that suggests some doubt about social advantage itself, not just the means by which it is achieved. As he says, "to triumph over the pomp of the world and, as you crush the riches of the world under your heel, to think yourself rich only in being poor—this is what constitutes a preeminent claim to virtue. The Lord of Worlds has taught us to flee the privileges of this world."[30] He defends the nun Anselma from the suggestion that her religious vow could be seen in any

way as a disparagement of her rank;[31] and, even though his own family
origins were apparently noble,[32] he proudly asserts that his father was a
self-made man: "my father had no patrimony in the territory of Blois, but
through his own industry he acquired enough to be able to marry all of his
daughters honorably."[33] Peter's indifference to rank is clearly not as great
as these instances might suggest, for in practice he is fiercely defensive of his
own "estate" and its prerogatives. Here again, it looks as if he is challenging a category of identity largely in order to assert his own sense of standing imaginatively outside such categories. It is as if he needs to express
skepticism about the status quo, not so much because he really was—or
thought he was—a social outsider, but because it is another means of
expressing an underlying sense of moral alienation.

This posture of estrangement from the environment in which he found
himself is expressed, most famously, in his satire on the "miseries" of life at
Henry's court, Letter XIV. This is now perhaps the best-known of all
Peter's letters, and deservedly so, for it combines an amusingly trenchant
complaint about the discomforts and dangers of the courtier's life—the
hazards of travel, horrible food, and the malevolence of the court's
marshals—with a rueful, even ironically self-mocking awareness of his own
folly in pursuing ambition so far. Peter's rhetoric is so deliberately inflated
that it again suggests a moral as much as a personal condition: courtiers are
"martyrs to the world, professors of worldliness, disciples of the court,
soldiers of Herlekin [the king of the wild hunt]."[34] As he admits, he was
driven there only by his own worldly ambition: "Urged on, indeed, by a
certain spirit of ambition I immersed myself wholly in the waves of civil
business; leaving behind me God, the church and my own [clerical] status,
I anxiously concerned myself not with how much God could do for me,
but with how much wealth I could accumulate for myself."[35] Ambition, in
fact, is one of the key terms in Peter's work. "O inanis gloria! O ambitio
caeca!" [O empty glory! O blind ambition!], he declares in Letter XXIII,
with an emphasis that suggests his own perception of its centrality as an
idea, and as a problem, in the world around him.[36] Admittedly, he was not
alone among his contemporaries in thinking in these terms, since anxiety
about ambition could be defined as one of the characteristic preoccupations
of twelfth-century social commentary;[37] but there are still ways in which he
seems to develop such ideas further—or, rather, to integrate them more
consistently into his own subjectivity—than anyone else. The alienating
itinerancy of the court can in fact be seen as an image of his own sense of
inner conflictedness—an instrument of self-criticism, rather than a political
critique intended to have any real effect. Certainly, criticism of the
courtier-clerk's role is a theme to which Peter returns with something like
obsessiveness, though also with varying emphases—on the court itself, on

ambition, or on worldliness in general.[38] At times his sense of the sinfulness of a clerk's immersion in secular matters seems absolute—"It is not fitting for an educated man and a man of the church to involve himself in worldly affairs," he declares emphatically.[39] Yet at other times he argues the opposite view, taking pride in the importance of the role taken by clerks in the business of government—"all the difficult, knotty problems of the kingdom were referred to us"[40]—and even arguing that it is a holy duty for a clerk to counsel his king—"I say indeed, that it is a holy thing to assist the lord of a kingdom, since 'he is holy and anointed by the Lord.' "[41] This vacillation might be read in biographical terms, as a change of opinion produced by some kind of moral crisis, or by a series of them,[42] but they are almost too pervasive in his work to be explained so categorically. It seems much more likely that these contradictions are deliberately cultivated—that this obsessive problematization of the clerk's role in society is Peter's means of denying or destabilizing the particular forms of social situatedness that determine identity. The "rootlessness" expressed so frequently in his work, and echoed so often in Angevin writing generally, could perhaps be seen as the condition and effect of a dialectic of personality that is, in his case, peculiarly acute.

The general picture of Peter's literary persona that I have tried to draw is by no means a new critical departure. Indeed there seems to be a developing critical consensus that his creative mind is, as I have suggested, distinctively shaped by conflict—not just in the sense that he conveys his anxieties and self-doubts in ways that are strikingly persuasive, but also in the sense that he deliberately and characteristically seeks out and stylizes oppositions and contrasts, both formally and thematically. So, for example, even Southern acknowledges that Peter was a more complicated figure than his own uneasy allegation of superficiality might indicate. As he puts it, using terms that are suggestively binary: "Peter of Blois was a man of many hesitations and uncertainties; hesitating between old and new, between the religious life and the world, between solitude and business, between faith and unbelief."[43] E. C. Higonnet amplifies this suggestion of a much more complex, divided mentality concealed behind the confident polish of his letters, arguing that the collection's "appeal, not only to the men of the late Middle Ages, but also to readers today, results from these essentially human qualities it displays: Peter's inner conflict, indecision, hesitation, the tension running through his view of man's place in the universe, and especially the preoccupation with himself and his own condition implied by these uncertainties."[44] Yet the most thoroughgoing attempt so far to present Peter both as an index of the sensibility of the age and as an artist characterized fundamentally by the play of contradiction has been made by Peter Dronke, who argues that his namesake "exemplifies the quality of *sic et non* [yes and no] perhaps more remarkably than any of his contemporaries"—"that *sic et non* which characterizes not only Abelard's contradictions and inner tensions but also the outlook of many of his most sensitive successors in the twelfth-century clerical world."[45] He goes on to point out that debate is central to Peter's work, not just as an organizing principle, but as a characteristic means of mediating between mind and literary matter. Several of Peter's letters can be seen as contrasting diptychs, for example, while several of his poems show affinities with the genre of medieval debate-poetry.[46] As Dronke points out, one of the most remarkable of these poems, the sophisticatedly confessional "Olim militaveram / pompis huius seculi" [Once I used to march in the pomps of this world], has long passed under the title, "Cantilena de luctu carnis et spiritus" [the song of the conflict between body and spirit].[47] This is a formulation that clearly suggests an awareness of the medieval "Body and Soul" tradition, as exemplified most influentially by the Latin poem known generally as the "Visio Philiberti" and its many translations into the vernacular.[48] Similarly, the poem on the prodigal son that Dronke ascribes to Peter begins "Non carnis est sed spiritus / hoc meum natalicium" [My birthright is not the body's, but the soul's] in such a way as to connect the body/soul opposition with another characteristic theme—that of exile.[49] Meanwhile, "Quod amicus suggerit," a debate on the advantages and disadvantages of the courtier's life (and a poem certainly written by Peter), could reasonably be seen as a direct contribution to the tradition of medieval *Streitgedichte*.[50] This is also true of a text for which the evidence of Peter's authorship is again more tenuous, "Quam velim virginum" [a contrast between the erotic attractions of maidens and of wives].[51] Finally, in another poem possibly by Peter, "Vacillantis trutine / libramine" [In the balance of the quivering scales][52] we find not so much a debate-poem in itself, as an extraordinarily sensitive use of the poised oppositions of formal debate in order to depict the precarious subjectivity of the mind at work.[53] It is in these debates or debate-like poems particularly, Dronke argues, that "we can come closest to perceiving the essential in [Peter's] mind and artistry, and through this, gain a sharper sense of the imagination of the age."[54]

Whether or not the canon of Peter's poetry can be extended as far as Dronke extends it,[55] all of these suggestions about the nature of Peter's creative mind can be developed further by looking at his letters; and, far from contradicting the image of the "impersonal" Peter with which I began this essay, these perceptions of his work actually help to explain how it is that his individuality can at times seem so stubbornly evasive, and so much like a function of his own eloquence. The letter to Adelitia quoted above, for example, immediately succeeds one in which he argues vigorously for her right not to be placed in a nunnery against her will and to marry if she chooses. The almost jaunty fluency of his subsequent letter celebrating her vow of celibacy seems to reflect both his relief in discovering that she had no need of his defense of her right to marry and his satisfaction with the opportunity to balance it, artistically, with an exhortation to virginity. These two letters, like many of the others, bear out Giles Constable's observation that "Peter was particularly interested in practical moral dilemmas";[56] and this interest is clearly expressed in his willingness to define and analyze problems explicitly phrased as scholastic "quaestiones."[57] That Peter saw the discussion of questions of this kind as an intrinsic part of literary practice is shown by the terms in which he praises Henry II's learning: "But yet at the court of the King of England, there is a daily academy of the most learned men, the continual discussion and analysis of problems [quaestiones]."[58] Southern argues that his interest in debating such "quaestiones" intensified towards the end of his life as a result of finding himself in less-elevated, but more sociable, circumstances—and this might be true, though it poses no contradiction to Constable's general perception of Peter's quality of mind.[59] Peter's playful use of wine as a figure of identity (as explored in this chapter) and his apparently nonjudgmental acknowledgment of Henry II's love of hunting (Letter LXVI) already suggest that he is not quite the austerely rigid moralist that his diatribes against alcohol (Letter VII) and hunting (Letter LVI) might imply. Indeed it seems to me that the appeal of such pieces lies in their deliberate one-sidedness, the provocativeness with which they seem to invite the balance of an opposing or moderating argument.[60] Moreover, Peter's peculiar sensitivity to forms of literary debate, and the particular influence of debate-poetry, is perhaps indicated by his willingness to employ a terminology drawn from the more distinctively oppositional topoi of twelfth-century poetry in general, such as his use of the satirical tag "per fas et nefas" [through right and wrong].[61] and his tendency to think in terms of a contrast between body and soul [cor et anima]—even when this apparently contributes nothing more to what he is saying than a rhetorical periphrasis.[62] Finally, Dronke's suggestion that his method might be characterized in terms of the Abelardian "sic et non" is challenged—but also perhaps ultimately supported—by the occasional appearance in Peter's own vocabulary of a near-parallel expression, the "Est et non" of St. Paul's Second Letter to the Corinthians (2 Cor 1:17).[63] The Apostle uses the phrase only to deny its applicability to himself, reading the very opposition between "it is and it is not" as a figure of moral indecision and uncertainty that borders on a loss of faith; nor does Peter use it to describe his own vacillations, only that of others. Yet by using the idea at all both Paul and Peter express a sense that the even the most elemental structures of thought and speech can have moral significance—to the extent that, in Peter's work, the shapes of intellectual method define his poetic sensibility. From this perspective it is perhaps Paul, rather than Abelard, who demonstrated for Peter the metaphorical force of opposition itself, and thus Paul who justifies Peter's insistent cultivation of forms of irresolution as a means of describing his own characteristically divided, dividing, mind.

What emerges from this is that the "impersonal Peter" is more of a "multiple Peter," an author who generates an uncomfortable tension in his work and in his implied subjectivity by refracting it into a range of different opinions and perspectives.[64] It is a technique peculiarly well adapted to addressing what seems to me the predominant concern in his work—his anxiety about defining his own place in an environment constantly demanding a new "self-fashioning"—the court of Henry II and the circles of clerkly careerists associated with it.[65] In other words, the poise and balance that make Peter in many ways such a fascinatingly evasive figure are part and parcel of the sense of alienation that he expresses so strongly. The "emptiness" in his work identified by Southern is a sounding-board for his uncertainties—a function of the gap between the confident eloquence of his artistic persona and the uneasy flexibility with which he contemplates his own identity. In what remains of this essay, I try to develop further one particular perception that is a central element in the case for the essential and self-conscious conflictedness of Peter of Blois as a writer; and this is Dronke's observation that Peter's artistic methodology connects rather strikingly with the distinctive poetics of medieval debate-poetry. My point is that the letters reflect this connection not just in style, structure, and theme, but also, on occasion, in their direct engagement with ideas and issues that are so intrinsically bound up with the literary appropriation of formal contention as to be almost incomprehensible except as part of an ongoing, conscious attempt to define and extend the poetics of contention. The mentality that they express is so peculiar—both to the genre of medieval debate-poetry and to Peter of Blois—that the one serves almost necessarily as a commentary on the other. This is a point I hope to be able to make by reference to one of Peter's so-called later letters—Letter 31 in Elizabeth Revell's recent edition.[66] This is not a text to be found in the "standard" collection of the letters and indeed, like most of the letters printed by Revell, it is very rare in manuscript. It is extant only in two copies, one of which is derived from the other—the older one in Erfurt, commissioned at the beginning of the fifteenth century by the humanist Amplonius Ratinck; the younger in Bamberg, written by the Carmelite Matthias Farinator in the winter of 1472–73. Despite the scarcity of the witnesses, there seems to exist no reason to doubt that Peter wrote the letters unique to Ratinck's collection. Revell thinks the internal evidence for

their authenticity "overwhelming,"[67] and she points out that there are
several explanations available for why they failed to be included in the standard collection—perhaps most simply that their author never got round to
making sure that they were.[68] More difficult to explain is Letter 31's curious combination of themes and its peculiar line of thought, but these features do make sense if the letter is read as an expression of its author's
distinctive—and perhaps, as Southern suggests, growing—interest in the
dynamics of formalized debate.

   Letter 31 opens with the writer's assertion that his correspondent had
accused every nation in the world of avarice, with the exception of his
own—apparently England—which he had lauded for its generosity.[69]
National difference here serves as a grid for moral difference, in a way that
is typical of Peter's thinking. At the same time, the contrast between
avarice and generosity immediately suggests one of his other major preoccupations, the dynamics of the courtier-clerk's relationship with his patron.
Yet what Peter goes on to do is to accuse his correspondent of confusing
generosity with prodigality and avarice with frugality, elaborately defining
the contrasts between the four qualities according to a symmetrical pattern
of oppositions.[70] This could be described, in rhetorical terms, as a strikingly
extended instance of the figure of "paradiastole"[71]—the rhetorical distinction between two apparently similar things, here used in such a way as to
create two pairs of converses, "prodigus/largus" [generosity/avarice] and
"parcus/avarus" [prodigality/frugality].[72] Alternatively, in dialectical terms,
Peter could be seen as using these ethical contrasts in order to establish a
scheme that looks rather like the so-called square of opposition, a diagram
that explains the way in which logical contradiction is modified by the
terms "and" and "or" in a way that could be seen as typical, or even defi-
nitional, of medieval dialectic.[73] The two converse pairs of ethical contraries in this scheme—like the types of logical propositions for which the
diagram was designed—are most conveniently expressed as four points,
arranged as a square, and connected by eight lines expressing their possible
relationships.[74] What the analogy suggests is that Peter's tendency to think
in terms of oppositions and contrasts is driven by the same impulses that
drive dialectical thinking in general. Not only is contradiction made an elemental principle in a system that generates complexity only from geomet-
rical progression, but also this mode of thinking itself becomes a means of
analyzing thought. This model also applies well to the way in which most
medieval debate-poetry actually works: for it is generally not simply binary
in its effects, as modern literary critics tend to assume, but tetradic—that is,
governed by an essentially four-fold pattern, in which each of the two
speakers both defends his or her own position and attacks his or her opponent's, very often in such a way as to create a square of ethical contrasts just

like the one that Peter defines so elaborately here. It also tends to have a self-reflexive quality, generating complexities from the binary positions it characteristically begins with—and just in such a way as to make the reader or audience sharply aware of the workings of the reasoning mind.[75]

This particular set of moral qualities—generosity, avarice, prodigality, and frugality—is, of course, a distinctively Aristotelian one. Aristotle considers the relationships between them in book 2 of the *Nichomachean Ethics* (to which Peter would certainly have had access as part of the "older" Latin Aristotle) and also, at more length, in book 4 (which was one of the "newer" parts of the Aristotelian corpus, but still possibly would have been available to Peter in some form, as Revell suggests).[76] Even so, Peter's departures from Aristotle's handling of the theme are perhaps more important than his inheritances from it: for, while Aristotle's analysis of this set of concepts is wholly in the service of his argument for the inevitable superiority of the middle term—of moderation as a self-sufficient principle—Peter never gets as far as offering such a resolution. Indeed, he seems to be much more interested in the moral oppositions that Aristotle sets up for the sake of argument, than he is in the philosopher's method of negotiating between them.[77] Instead of any calm confidence in his ability to identify the golden mean, Peter's analysis is much more anxious, but also more realistic, in that his emphasis on the multiplication of the complexities implicit in moral opposition draws attention to the fact that they are functions of the perceiving, moving mind—and not so obviously or stably calibrated as to make it easy for anyone to identify the golden mean, or at least certainly not so easy as Aristotle's calmly reasonable assurance suggests. In any case, the set of contrasts at issue here were probably already a commonplace by the time that Peter was writing, for Peter quotes the saying "Prodigus a largo dissentit, parcus avaro" [the prodigal is opposed to the generous, as the frugal to the miserly] as if it should have been instantly recognizable to his readers. It perhaps ultimately derives from one of Horace's Letters,[78] but it may already have been a proverbial tag even in Peter's day—as it certainly later became.[79]

At this point, we seem to have been taken a long way from the nationalist identity-politics that supposedly provoked this letter; and this raises the question of quite why its author chose this particular square of moral oppositions as a means of challenging a moment of jingoistic banter. The answer, it seems to me, lies not so much in the nature of medieval thinking on nationalism, as in the way it serves to express Peter's recognition of the nature of the literary game that his opponent, was playing—the game of literary debate. Indeed his analysis of the "prodigus/largus, parcus/avarus" problem [prodigal/generous, frugal/miserly] could be read as an attempt to demonstrate mastery of the rules of that particular game—elaborately claiming a sophisticated understanding of the rules of opposition and contradiction only in order to deny, more or less playfully, that his antagonist is capable of making those same discriminations. In effect, what Peter offers us—using this issue as a representative example— is a guide to the construction of formal literary debates; and in this sense, his disquisition on moral economics could be seen, to a large extent, as an exercise in literary criticism. Only in the wake of all this does he at last explain that his opponent's attempt to fight for his country [pro pugnare pro patria] in fact amounted to nothing more elevated than a rhetorical defense of the characteristically English liking for beer—an argument that Peter goes on to declare impudent, imprudent, and superlatively obtuse [imprudenter et impudenter omnium hominum cervicosissimus pro cervisia pugnat].[80] In other words, for all the extravagance of his language, all he is doing is responding to an argument in favor of drinking beer with one in favor of drinking wine—a topic for debate perhaps ultimately related to the extensive medieval tradition of poetic debates between wine and water.[81] In this context his analysis of the "prodigus/largus, parcus/avarus" square serves not just as a means of declaring his correspon- dent's critical incompetence, but also as a means of expressing an interest in the intellectual patterns implied by such oppositions.

Yet there is a particular relevance to his analysis of "prodigus/largus" and "parcus/avarus" in that so many of the genres of medieval literary debates typically convert the issues that they address into terms that closely resemble the ethics of economics analyzed so elaborately here. So, for example, poetic debates between Winter and Spring or Summer frequently devolve on what might be described as the seasons' sumptuary personae— their supposed participation in an economics of consumption implied by climate. In the Carolingian debate between Winter and Spring sometimes attributed to Alcuin, Winter admits to being a kind of miser, counting over his beloved treasures in their chests [optatas gazas numerare per arcas], but is eventually condemned by the shepherds who judge the debate, as a dreadful prodigal [rerum tu prodigus atrox].[82] In Nicolas Bozon's four- teenth-century French debate between Winter and Summer, "De l'Yver et de l'Ésté," Winter claims overlordship on the basis of his great generosity [pur ma très grant largesse] (line 65), while Summer retaliates by accusing him of waste [vus le avez gasté] (line 115).[83] In this instance, Summer goes on to evoke both Aristotle's ethics and precisely the same imagined antag- onism—between wine and beer—that supposedly provoked the writing of Peter's Letter 31: "Quar en vus n'est point de mesure / Tant come vyn ou cervoise dure" [as long as there's any wine or beer left, you're incapable of moderation] (lines 119–20). The most explicit realization of the "prodigus/ largus, parcus/avarus" opposition as a debate-poem can be found in the fourteenth-century English debate *Winner and Waster*,[84] but it had an even-wider currency in the slightly more disguised form of the conflict between Carnival and Lent, which was fought all over western Europe throughout the later Middle Ages—and in such a way as to provide what has come to be seen to be one of the leitmotifs of the age.[85]

As it turns out, Peter is so sensitive to the dynamics of debate here, not simply because he has been invited to take part in a formal literary debate, but because his letter, in effect, constitutes his acceptance of that invitation. For all his long preamble—his pedantic analysis of the logical dimensions of opposition—he turns out to be perfectly happy to argue one side of an argument; and he goes about his task with all his characteristic fluency and panache. Beer does *not* smell like nectar, no matter what his opponent Thomas might think. No indeed—beer is a horror from the swamp of hell [Stygie paludis horrorem], beer is made from that suspicious substance, yeast, otherwise only good for making bread, beer is beneath the contempt even of barnyard animals, beer makes people stutter and spit and vomit, and so on. He even deploys with apparent relish the venerable pun on "populorum"/ "poculorum" that so often provides matter for amusement in medieval parody: "He thinks beer is the sovereign-queen not just of all the cups [poculorum] but also of all the nations [populorum]."[86] Yet the bland vigor with which he presses home his attack on beer only makes his disquisition on the dialectics of generosity and avarice look rather ironic— and, I think, deliberately so. The discrepancy between his claims to a superior understanding of dialectical opposition, on the one hand, and his amusingly crude and exaggerated abuse of beer, on the other, is very much the same as the one on which much of the humor is founded in *The Owl and the Nightingale*—one of the most brilliant of all medieval debate-poems. Here the birds of the title are imagined ruminating on their forensic technique with all the self-regard of a pair of legal advocates or university professors, and yet much of what they actually say to each other is pettily, wittily spiteful, and more at the level of playground-abuse than of learned disputation.[87] From this point of view, Peter's Letter 31 might be seen most simply as an epistolary version of his two poetic contributions to the tradition of debates between wine and beer—his two pro-wine poems in an exchange with Robert of Beaufeu.[88] Much the same arguments recur in these: beer is manufactured from strange and poisonous ingredients [infumata seges], beer makes people so drunk they can't walk straight, it confuses their minds and incites them to sin, to drink beer is to drink from the swamps of the river Lethe, and so on. In effect, Letter 31 is one side of a debate-poem, or a letter intended to be read very much like a speech in a debate-poem. Yet it is also an analysis of opposition that works in such a way as to play Peter's intellectual interest in theoretical patterns of conflict and debate against an illustration of the apparently sincere enjoyment he found in practicing such patterns. From this point of view, it simultaneously offers us both a particular insight into Peter's own literary motivations and his testimony to the general validity of the notion of debate as a distinct literary genre in this period.

There is another respect in which Letter 31 seems to participate in the evolving poetics of medieval debate: and this is its use of inserted narrative—or, more accurately, of allusion to narrative—as a means of providing raw argument with "anecdotal" evidence to work on. So, for example, Peter tells us:

> We read that a certain fellow who'd been brought up on swamp-water, coming to Ravenna and taking a sip of wine, was suddenly taken with vomiting and retching; nor could he obtain any hope of recovery until, returning to the swamp that had nourished him, to muddy and dirty drinking-water, he was immediately revived. We have heard from many people and in some cases seen that those accustomed to public filth cannot smell aromatic spices without a disturbance or defect of the heart, which is popularly called a fit. They can easily be revived from their fit, however, if some truly disgusting manure or horse-dung is placed under their nose. It is thus fitting that "those who are [wallowing] in the filth should become filthy."[89]

The story of the man in Ravenna is clearly a calque of the Old French fabliau known as "Du Vilain Asnier" in which a dung-carter turns into the spicers' street in Montpellier, passes out, and is only revived when a forkful of dung is waved under his nose.[90] Indeed, it makes little sense unless the allusion to the fabliau-version of the table is recognized. Paradoxically, Peter presents his story of the man in Ravenna as one he has read, though in fact it seems much more likely that it is a nonce-version created in order to adapt the tale to the occasion. Meanwhile, the story with which he compares it— the story recorded in the fabliau—is presented as a matter of both hearsay and personal experience. Indeed, there are several details here that suggest Peter's direct familiarity with a version of the story very like that of "Du Vilain Asnier" itself—even though his letter clearly predates any extant texts of the vernacular tale. Peter's reference to the "publicis fetoribus assueti" [those accustomed to public filth] is almost incomprehensibly elliptical except as a euphemistic reference to the dung-carter of the fabliau. The unfortunates he refers to are overcome by "species aromaticas," just like the peasant in Montpellier; and he elaborates the medical effects of this— "syncopi seu defectu cordis, qui vulgariter dicitur *spasmatio*" [a syncope or defect of the heart, which is commonly known as a spasm]—in a way that recalls the wording of the fabliau—"chiet *pasmez* isnelepas / autresi con së il fust morz [he falls straightaway into a spasm, just as if were dead]." The cure for this condition is the same in both cases: like the fabliau–poet, Peter testifies to the efficacy of an inhalation of dung as a means of reviving peasants knocked unconscious by pleasant smells.

This technique of appropriating apparently well-known tales to the cause of argument was to become a distinctive feature of medieval debate-poems, if it was not so already. For example, in *The Owl and the Nightingale*, the story of the owlet in the hawk's nest is also presented in the debate as a reported event—not as a separate fiction, but as a reality in the shared world of fiction—in much the same way that Peter testifies to the actual misfortunes of "publicis fetoribus assueti." In both cases it is suggested that indifference to ordure should be interpreted as a sign of an opponent's moral and critical incapacity.[91] It is as likely that *The Owl and the Nightingale* belongs to the late thirteenth century as to the late twelfth, as I have argued elsewhere, but even in twelfth-century Latin debates there are references to stories drawn from apparently traditional narrative.[92] In the "Visio Philiberti," for example, the devils use the fable of the toad and the harrow as a means of taunting the soul as they haul it off to hell.[93] In this respect, Peter's use of the tale of the dung-carter is another instance of the openness of clerical culture to material generally thought of as typically "popular," vernacular, or bourgeois—and of the perennial dangers of thinking of medieval writing in terms of categories drawn too rigidly along linguistic boundaries. It also suggests a deliberate attempt to stretch the possibilities of the debate-form. Peter's employment of this story in the debate between wine and beer is audaciously ingenious, precisely in the sense that it is relevant here only with a certain amount of strain. For Peter to caricature his beer-drinking opponent as a version of the "vilain asnier" is amusingly hyperbolic, but it also assumes an audience with a sophisticated interest in the game of debate, since Peter's line of thought is by no means easy to follow.

Indeed one way of explaining Letter 31, and particularly its variety of implicitly debate-like or "debatable" motifs, is as an experiment with—or illustration of—the essentially metonymic nature of debate. This in turn reflects Peter's characteristic tendency to see identity in metonymic terms. So, for example, it is apparently because Wine and Beer could serve as figures of national identity—as his opponent Thomas seems to have so loudly insisted—that Peter felt moved to read his praise of beer as a kind of literary challenge to himself personally. His argument that Thomas has in fact failed to recognize the principles on which such a metonymy could be constructed—confusing the "generosity" of his beer-drinking compatriots with prodigality, and the avarice of other nations with prudence—in no way prevents him from accepting the figural significance of wine for his own "French" identity. This could be seen as a recognition and acceptance of another of the conventions of literary debate—the twelfth-century debate between wine and beer in the Herdringen miscellany draws attention to its own nationalistic connotations,[94] while the debate between the Englishman and Frenchman found in British Library MS Cotton Titus A.xx refers their differences, conversely, to the realm of Wine and Beer—and does so, moreover, in terms of avarice and prodigality.[95] By accepting Thomas's identification of Englishness with beer and then choosing to identify beer-drinking with drunkenness, Peter makes it possible for himself to create an argument against English national self-esteem out of the list of biblical pronouncements against drinking that he had already rehearsed elsewhere—for exactly the same series of authorities appears in Letter 31 as in Letter VII, Peter's critique of Master A. for too generously supplying his guests with alcohol.[96] The effect of all this is to draw attention to the constructedness of all such figures of identity—national and moral identities as much as identities based on preferences for particular beverages—and to that extent it demonstrates that the construction of any given identity depends on the manipulation of cultural signifiers that are essentially arbitrary. At the same time, it could be argued that to make such self-conscious game out of categories of identity is a means of breaking down the barriers thrown up by linguistic and political differences. The absurdity of interpreting the contrast between Wine and Beer, for example, as a critical index of national difference, perhaps implicitly dissolves any real sense of cultural antagonism. From that point of view, the game of debate effectively socializes those who play it, creating a community defined by an understanding of its rules.

Yet the insistent, almost obsessive, concern with figures of opposition, and the extension of those figures, metonymically, into complex, shifting systems of identification and antagonism, still suggests a doubt about community—since all there is, in such a view of the world, is difference. From this perspective, the dynamics of debate—as Peter explores them here—might be seen as an aspect of his rhetoric of disorientation, another means of asserting the irreconcilability of the various cultural and moral forces at work on writers in the Angevin world. Perhaps the conclusion that Peter invites us to draw is that if there is no metaphorical truce between wine and beer, then there can be none in reality between being English and being French. Furthermore, if national difference is expressed not just by the opposition between "largitas" and "parcitas," "avaritia" and "prodigalitas," but also by the fact of being able to negotiate between them—as the "French" Peter supposedly can and the "English" Thomas cannot—then even the capacity to make moral discriminations, to find the golden mean if any is to be found, itself becomes a proof of the finality of national difference.

At a much simpler level, it is striking that Peter unquestioningly accepts Thomas's assumption that both the moral question about the nature of "largitas" and the competition between national identities must inevitably be discussed with reference to the idea of hospitality. He concludes his account of Thomas's limitations (both moral and national) in Letter 31 by imagining him simultaneously as a bad host and a bad guest, taxing him with being "forever forgetful of liberality in your own guest-rooms, but at the feasts of the great a foolish, impudent and even violent intruder."[97] Perhaps only someone very aware of being a foreigner would have quite so automatically located a discussion of "largitas"/"parcitas" versus "avaritia"/ "prodigalitas," or of national identity, in an evocation of unsatisfactory lodgings and antisocial behavior at banquets. Admittedly, Peter was continuing a line of thought already established by his opponent, who had provoked him to begin with by linking Englishness, beer, hospitality, and liberality so aggressively together. Yet in responding at all to Thomas's claims about the preeminence of English hospitality, Peter implicitly states his dissatisfaction with being himself a guest of the English. From this perspective, it is clearly not Thomas, but Peter, who is most obviously described as the intruder—not, of course, the riotous and foolish intruder that he accuses Thomas of being, but an intruder in what is probably a much more fundamental sense—someone who is deeply conscious of not belonging at the feast in the first place. It is thus impudently ironic that he should choose to contradict Thomas's cultural confidence by accusing him, not just of misunderstanding the nature of hospitality, but of being *himself* an intruder at the feast.

Much more remains to be said about the various kinds of cultural discomfort expressed in the letters of Peter of Blois, and about their engagement with the poetics of debate more generally in this period; but I hope at least to have shown that Peter's literary persona might be described as essentially refractive—individual, that is, only in so far as it embodies a self-conscious cultivation of difference (both a sense of difference and ideas about difference) under the mask of a polished urbanity of style. From this perspective, there emerges a striking contrast between, on the one hand, Peter's superficial ease of expression and his apparent derivativeness and, on the other, his deep-seated poetic and ideological unease. Indeed, the certainty and clarity of Peter's rhetoric could perhaps be seen as the necessary still point in a world of images and ideas that is otherwise constantly turning. The reassurances provided by the apparently conventional aspects of Peter's letters, in other words, perhaps create the necessary counterpoint to a literary disposition that is anything but safely or simply uncritical. The intensive analysis of opposition found in Letter 31, for example, and the drive towards continual metonymy so self-consciously disclosed there, might be seen as a specific instance of Peter's rhetoric of disorientedness—and as such, a continuation both of the self-collapsing postures of his anticurial satire and of the complex, mobile subjectivity glimpsed in his poetry.

Notes

1. As Rolf Köhn observes, Peter has often been cited "als typisches Beispiel für die bildungsgeschichtlichen Kennzeichen der Renaissance des 12. Jahrhunderts und die literarischen Zentren der höfischen Gesellschaft" [as a typical illustration of the features of the twelfth-century Renaissance in cultural history and of the literary centers of courtly society], in *Magister Peter von Blois (c. 1130 bis 1211/12): Eine Studie zur Bildungsgeschichte der Geistlichkeit in der höfischen Gesellschaft* (Ph.D. diss. University of Konstanz, 1973), p. 23.

2. I have cited the letters from *Petri Blesensis Bathoniensis in Anglia Archdiaconi opera omnia*, ed. J-P. Migne, PL 207 (Paris: J-P. Migne, 1855), despite its many misprints, since this is still the most recent edition, and more widely accessible than either of the two earlier editions on which it is based, those of Pierre de Goussainville (Paris: Piget, 1667) and J. A. Giles in his *Patres ecclesiae anglicanae*, 4 vols. (Oxford: Oxford University Press, 1846–47). A thorough critical edition of Peter's letters remains a *desideratum*, but the difficulties of such an undertaking are immense. Southern even described it as a "jungle" ("there is none more impenetrable than the tangle of a widely disseminated collection of letters": R. W. Southern, in "Peter of Blois: A Twelfth-Century Humanist?," chap. 7 in *Medieval Humanism and Other Studies* (Oxford: Blackwell, 1970), pp. 105–32, at 129). Efforts to provide the necessary groundwork for a critical edition can be found in E. S. Cohn, "The manuscript evidence for the letters of Peter of Blois," *English Historical Review* 41 (1926): 43–60; Southern, in *Medieval Humanism*, pp. 129–32; and, most recently, in Lena Wahlgren, *The Letter Collections of Peter of Blois: Studies in the Manuscript Tradition*, Studia Graeca et Latina Gothoburgensia 58 (Göteborg: Acta Universitatis Gothoburgensis, 1993). Some of the hazards still lurking in the jungle are suggested by the way in which Wahlgren has been accused of concerning herself both too much and too little with hypotheses about the development of the collection as a whole: see the reviews by Monika Asztalos, *Speculum* 69 (1994): 1291–95 and Southern, *English Historical Review* 110 (1995): 925–37. The so-called later letters are cited from the edition by Elizabeth Revell in *The Later Letters of Peter of Blois*, Auctores Britannici Medii Aevi 13 (Oxford: Oxford University Press, 1993); and I have cited these by arabic numeral, as she does, in order to distinguish them from the main body of letters in PL, which are listed in Roman numerals.

3. Southern, *Medieval Humanism*, p. 107.

4. The letters may have been intended to serve as dictaminal models, even if they nevertheless "reflect a genuine correspondence," as A. G. Rigg suggests in *A History of Anglo-Latin Literature 1066–1422* (Cambridge: Cambridge

University Press, 1992), p. 85. This interpretation of Peter's purposes is reinforced by the possibility that he wrote the *Libellus de arte dictandi rhetorice* now extant only in a single Cambridge manuscript (Cambridge University Library MS Dd. 9. 38). Martin Camargo has cast serious doubt on this ascription: see "The *Libellus de arte dictandi rhetorice* Attributed to Peter of Blois," *Speculum* 59 (1984): 16–41, esp. 39. Southern, however, rejects these doubts out of hand: see his review of Wahlgren, pp. 929–30, n1.

5. Ep. VII, PL 207:19–21.

6. Ep. LVI, PL 207:169–171. Cf. John of Salisbury, *Policraticus*, ed. C. C. I. Webb, *Ioannis Saresberiensis Episcopi Carnotensis Policratici sive De Nugis Curialium et Vestigiis Philosophorum*, 2 vols. (Oxford: Clarendon Press, 1909; repr. Frankfurt a. M., 1965), Book 1, chap. 4, vol. 1, 21–35, esp. 21–22. This is an example of the tendency towards derivativeness that Southern also finds deeply troubling—"that terrible plagiarism," as he calls it (*Medieval Humanism*, p. 107). This is a charge leveled most vigorously by Philippe Delhaye in "Un témoignage frauduleux de Pierre de Blois sur la pédagogie du XIIe siècle," in *Recherches de Théologie Ancienne et Médiévale* 14 (1947): 329–31.

7. See Giles Constable, *Letters and Letter-Collections*, Typologie des Sources du Moyen Age Occidental (Turnhout: Brepols, 1976), esp. 11–12. This does not mean that any of the circumstances described in his letters can be shown to have been fictional, only that the particular reality Peter chooses to describe seems to have been selected, in many cases, for its convenience to his theme. Southern still insists that "even with all the additional rhetoric and changes of emphasis in later recensions, the reality of the events described in the letters remains unimproved. There is no sign anywhere, so far as I have been able to discover, of any invention of persons or events" (R. W. Southern, "The Necessity for Two Peters of Blois," in *Intellectual Life in the Middle Ages: Essays presented to Margaret Gibson*, ed. Lesley Smith and Benedicta Ward (London and Rio Grande: Hambledon, 1992), pp. 103–118, at 105). Nevertheless it does seem that Peter was capable of "adapting" his experiences—as, for example, when he made changes in order to accommodate altered loyalties; for a complex case in point, see Lena Wahlgren, "Peter of Blois and the Later Career of Reginald fitzJocelin," *English Historical Review* 111 (1996): 1202–15.

8. Ep. LV, PL 207:167: "mundumque relinquere decrevisti prudenter, antequam relinquaris ab eo. Beata es, quae spretis filiis hominum."

9. This is implicit in Peter's defense of his "compilative" practices in Ep. XCII, PL 207:289–91.

10. Ep. XXII, PL 207:82: "ibi optima forma est, et propter artificiosum sententiarum varietatem inaestimabilis materia voluptatis."

11. For an illustration of Peter's ambivalence about the use of classical literature, see, e.g., Ep. LVI, PL 207:170: "Quae tamen comparatio est gentilium ad sacerdotem Christi, qui mortis cruciatus praeeligere debuisset, antequam ad talia posset cogi?" [What comparison is there among the pagans for the

priest of Christ who would have chosen the suffering of death before he could be driven to such things?]. This comes after a "comparatio gentilium" entirely lifted from John's *Policraticus*.

12. R. W. Southern, *Scholastic Humanism and the Unification of Europe*, vol. 2, *The Heroic Age* (Oxford: Blackwell, 2001), p. 218. This is also the position from which Ethel Cardwell Higonnet begins her assessment of Peter's work, in "Spiritual Ideas in the Letters of Peter of Blois," *Speculum* 59 (1975): 218–44, at 218.

13. Southern, *Scholastic Humanism*, 2: 217. There were three editions before de Goussainville's in 1667: the Brethren of the Common Life (Brussels, ca. 1480); Jacobus Merlinus (Paris, 1519); and Johannes Busaeus (Mainz, 1600).

14. Peter's reputation seems to have remained high even among "Renaissance" writers like Coluccio Salutati: see Richard B. Donovan, "Salutati's Opinion of Non-Italian Latin Writers of the Middle Ages," *Studies in the Renaissance* 14 (1967): 185–201, at 194, 197.

15. Derek Pearsall, *John Lydgate* (London: Routledge & Kegan Paul, 1970), pp. 298–99.

16. See, for example, *The Catholic Encyclopedia*, s.v. "Peter de Blois": URL: <http://www.newadvent.org/cathen/11765a.htm> [accessed 17/8/04]. Here we are told that Peter "wrote numerous letters, models of his epoch, but full of the bad taste of the twelfth century."

17. See, for example, James Simpson, "The Energies of John Lydgate," in his *The Oxford English Literary History*, vol. 2, *1350–1547: Reform and Cultural Revolution* (Oxford: Oxford University Press, 2002), pp. 34–67; and Lee Patterson, "Making Identities in Fifteenth-Century England: Henry V and John Lydgate," in *New Literary Historical Study*, ed. Jeffrey N. Cox and L. J. Reynolds (Princeton, N.J.: University of Princeton Press, 1993), pp. 69–107.

18. Ep. XCV, PL 207:298.

19. Peter enumerates these dominions in Ep. LXVI, PL 207: 200–201.

20. For some illustrations of the ways in which clerks were redefined as a class by the emergence of such opportunities, see R. W. Southern, *Scholastic Humanism and the Unification of Europe*, vol. 1, *Foundations* (Oxford: Blackwell, 1995), pp. 141–45; Ralph V. Turner, "Changing Perceptions of the New Administrative Class in Anglo-Norman and Angevin England: the *Curiales* and Their Conservative Critics," *Journal of British Studies* 29 (1990): 93–117; M. T. Clanchy, "*Moderni* in Education and Government in England," *Speculum* 50 (1975): 671–88; and C. Stephen Jaeger, "The Courtier Bishop in *Vitae* from the Tenth to the Twelfth Century," *Speculum* 58 (1983): 291–325.

21. On Henry II's court as a literary center, see C. H. Haskins, "Henry II as a patron of literature," in *Essays in Medieval History presented to T. F. Tout* (Manchester: Manchester University Press, 1925), pp. 71–77; W. Stubbs, *Seventeen Lectures on the study of Mediaeval and Modern History* (Oxford: Clarendon Press, 1900), chaps. 6–7; Reto R. Bezzola, *Les origines et la*

formation de la littérature courtoise en Occident (500–1200), 3 vols. (Paris: Champion 1944–1963), vol. 2, part 2: "La société féodale et la transformation de la littérature de cour" (1960), pp. 3–311; Rita Lejeune, "Rôle littéraire d'Aliénor d'Aquitaine et de sa famille," *Cultura neo-latina* 14 (1954): 5–57; Walter F. Schirmer and Ulrich Broich, *Studien zum literarischen Patronat im England des 12. Jahrhunderts* (Cologne and Opladen: Westdeutscher Verlag, 1962).

22. For this term, and the criticism attached to it, see, for example, Peter Damian's *Contra clericos, aulicos, ut ad dignitates provehantur*, PL 145:464–72.

23. See, for example, Ep. XLI, PL 207:121–122, in which Peter wearily but whimsically adds the royal court to the four "investigibilia"—things that leave no trace—of Prov. 30:18–19. This kind of imagery is not unique to him in this period: see, for example, Walter Map, *De Nugis Curialium (Courtiers' Trifles)*, ed. and trans. M. R. James, revised by C. N. L. Brooke and R. A. B. Mynors (Oxford: Clarendon Press, 1983), Book I, chaps 1–12, 2–37; and also the discussion by Andreas Bihrer, "Selbstvergewisserung am Hof: Eine Interpretation von Walter Maps *De nugis curialium* I, 1–12," *Jahrbuch für internationale Germanistik* 34 (2002): 227–258, esp. 236–42.

24. On twelfth-century curial satire in general, see Claus Uhlig, *Hofkritik im England des Mittelalters und der Renaissance: Studien zu einem Gemeinplatz der europäischen Moralistik*, Quellen und Forschungen zur Sprach- und Kulturgeschichte der germanischen Völker, n.s. 56 (Berlin and New York: Walter de Gruyter, 1973); Joachim Bumke, *Höfische Kultur: Literatur und Gesellschaft im hohen Mittelalter* 10th ed. (Munich: Deutscher Taschenbuch Verlag, 2002, first pub. 1986), pp. 583–94.

25. Ep. CLX, PL 207:455: "Viginti sex annis in Anglia peregrinans, linguam, quam non noveram audivi. . .Numquid semper ero *vagus et profugus* [Gen. 4:14] super terram? Nemo finem imponet peregrinationi meae, ut saltem semel ante supreme spiritus exhalationem in aere nativo mihi liceat respirare?" On the relationship between language and national identity in Anglo-Norman England, there is now an extensive bibliography: see, for example, Ian Short, " 'Tam Angli quam Franci': self-definition in Anglo-Norman England," *Anglo-Norman Studies* 18 (1996): 153–75.

26. In this respect, Peter might be said to be participating in an extensive literary tradition: see Ernst Doblhofer, *Exil und Emigration: Zum Erlebnis der Heimatferne in der römischen Literatur* (Darmstadt: Wissenschaftliche Buchgesellschaft, 1987); and *Exil, Fremdheit und Ausgrenzung im Mittelalter und früher Neuzeit*, ed. Andreas Bihrer, Sven Limbeck and Paul Gerhard Schmidt (Würzburg: Ergon, 2000).

27. For the history of this idea, see Charles Dahlberg, *The Literature of Unlikeness* (Hanover and London: University Press of New England, 1988).

28. Ep. XLIV, PL 207:137: "Fovet Anglia me jam senem, quae vos fovit infantem. Utinam relinqueretis terram illam, Pater, montuosam et monstruosam, et ad nativi aeris dulcedinem redireris." Elsewhere, Peter contrasts the vices of Sicily with the virtues, not of England, but of "sweet France": see Ep. XCIII, PL 207:293.

29. Ep. III, PL 207:8: "Vaga et incerta est hominum generatio, et quandoque putatur filius principis, qui filius est culinarii histrionis, testimonio poetae: 'Cum tua multiplices exornent undique cerae, / Atria, nobilitas sola est atque unica virtus.' " The reference is to Juvenal's *Satires*, ed. E. G. Hardy (London: Macmillan and co., 1895), 8:19–20, at p. 44.

30. Ep. XCIII, PL 207:291: "insignis autem virtutum titulus est, triumphare de saeculi pompa, mundique divitiis conculcatis se in paupertate sola divitem reputare. Dominus saeculorum fugere nos docuit saeculi dignitates."

31. Ep. XXXV, PL 207:113.

32. See, for example, Ep. XLIV, PL 207:147: "Sicut publice notum est, pater meus et mater mea de optimatibus minoris Britanniae traxerunt originem" [as is public knowledge, my mother and father traced their descent from the noblest in Brittany].

33. Ep. 6, ed. Revell, p. 38: "pater meus in territorio Blesensi nichil patrimoniale habuit, sed acquisivit industria sua unde omnes filias suas honorifice maritavit."

34. Ep. XIV (B), ed. Wahlgren, p. 155: "martyres saeculi, mundi professores, discipuli curiae, milites Herlekini."

35. Ep. XIV (B), ed. Wahlgren, p. 152: "Ductus equidem quodam spiritu ambitionis me totum civilibus undis immerseram; Deumque et ecclesiam eius atque ordinem meum post terga reiciens, non quantas mihi fecisset Dominus, sed quantas mihi possem aggregare divitias, anxius attendebam."

36. Ep. XXIII, PL 207:82.

37. See for example, John of Salisbury, *Policraticus*, Book 7, chaps. 17–19, pp. 160–181, and Alexander Murray, *Reason and Society in the Middle Ages* (Oxford: Clarendon Press, 1978), chap. 4, "Ambition," pp. 81–109.

38. See Rolf Köhn, " 'Militia curialis': Die Kritik am geistlichen Hofdienst bei Peter von Blois," in *Soziale Ordnungen im Selbstverständnis des Mittelalters*, Miscellanea Mediaevalia 12, ed. Albert Zimmerman (Berlin and New York: De Gruyter, 1979), pp. 227–57.

39. Ep. XXV, PL 207:89–90: "Virum litteratum et ecclesiasticum non sic decebat saecularibus negotiis implicari."

40. Ep. VI, PL 207:17: "omnes quaestiones regni difficiles et nodosae referentur ad nos."

41. Ep. CL, PL 207:440: "Fateor quidem, quod sanctum est domino regi assistere; sanctus enim et *christus Domini est* [1 Sam. 24:7, 24:11]."

42. This is the approach taken by Higonnet, "Spiritual Ideas," p. 229, for example, and by Southern, *Scholastic Humanism*, 2:204–5.

43. Higonnet, "Spiritual Ideas," p. 129.

44. Higonnet, "Spiritual Ideas," p. 244.

45. Peter Dronke, "Peter of Blois and Poetry at the Court of Henry II," *Mediaeval Studies* 28 (1976): 185–235; repr. in *The Medieval Poet and his World* (Rome: Edizioni di storia e letteratura, 1984), pp. 281–339, at 287, 285.

46. The best survey of this genre is still the one by Hans Walther, *Das Streitgedicht in der lateinischen Literatur des Mittelalters* (Munich: C. H. Becksche Verlag,

1920); repr. with supplementary material by P. G. Schmidt (Hildesheim: Olms, 1984); but see also Peter Binkley, "Dialogues and Debates," in *Medieval Latin: An Introduction and Bibliography*, ed. F. A. C. Mantello and A. G. Rigg (Washington, D.C.: Catholic University of America Press, 1996), pp. 677–81. For anthologies of debates in the vernacular languages, see Michel-André Bossy, ed. & trans., *Medieval Debate-Poetry: Vernacular Works*, Garland Library of Medieval Literature, Series A, vol. 52 (New York and London, 1987); and John W. Conlee, ed., *Middle English Debate Poetry: A Critical Anthology* (East Lansing, Mi.:, Colleagues Press, 1991).

47. Ed. Dronke, "Peter of Blois and Poetry," pp. 337–38; also, with commentary, by C. Wollin, *Petrus Blesensis Carmina*, Corpus Christianorum Continuatio Medievalis 128 (Turnhout: Brepols, 1998), pp. 229–38.

48. The most accessible edition is by Thomas Wright, in *The Latin Poems commonly attributed to Walter Mapes* (London: Camden Society, 1841; reprinted Hildesheim: Olms, 1968), pp. 95–106. See further Neil Cartlidge, "In the Silence of a Midwinter Night: A Re-evaluation of the *Visio Philiberti*," *Medium Aevum*, forthcoming. Peter explicitly acknowledged the influence of Hildebert of Le Mans (Ep. CI, PL 207:314), so he was probably also familiar with Hildebert's *Liber de Querimonia et Conflictu Carnis et Spiritus seu Animae*, PL 171:989–1004.

49. Ed. Dronke, "Peter of Blois and Poetry," pp. 338–39; Wollin, *Petrus Blesensis*, pp. 525–32, who classes it as a poem of doubtful authenticity: "doch ist aufgrund der Überlieferungslage eine sichere Zuschreibung an Peter von Blois weder möglich noch besonders wahrscheinlich," at p. 525.

50. Ed. Dronke, "Peter of Blois and Poetry," pp. 304–308; Wollin, *Petrus Blesensis*, pp. 263–74.

51. Ed. Wollin, *Petrus Blesensis*, pp. 617–19.

52. Ed. Dronke, "Peter of Blois and Poetry," pp. 298–300; Wollin, *Petrus Blesensis*, pp. 474–81.

53. Ed. Dronke, "Peter of Blois and Poetry," pp. 300–301. Wollin shows that this depiction of the "vacillating" mind is indeed characteristic of Peter's idiom: see the parallels he provides for the str. 1a, at p. 476. Even so "Vacillantis trutine . . ." also recalls the striking emphasis on interiority found in parts of the work of Chrétien de Troyes: see, for example, *Cligés*, ed. Charles Méla and Olivier Collet (Paris: Gallimard, 1994), lines 472–527.

54. Ed. Dronke, "Peter of Blois and Poetry," p. 290. On the particular influence of debate and/or dialectic on "the imagination of the age," there are now several studies available: see, for example, Thomas L. Reed, Jr., *Middle English Debate Poetry and the Aesthetics of Irresolution* (New York: Columbia University Press, 1990); Helen Solterer, *The Master and Minerva: Disputing Women in French Medieval Culture* (Berkeley, Los Angeles and London: University of California Press, 1995); Catherine Brown, *Contrary Things: Exegesis, Dialectic, and the Poetics of Didacticism* (Stanford, Calif.: Stanford University Press, 1998).

55. Southern defines the canon of Peter's work very much more narrowly than Dronke: see his summary in "The Necessity for Two Peters of Blois,"

p. 117. Wollin is also much more cautious: indeed, he describes his own discussion of the "Zuschreibungsfrage" only "als vorbereitende Darstellung der Schwierigkeiten und der jeweiligen Argumente, die den Leser in die Unsicherheiten der Problematik einführen soll, ohne ihm ein vermeintlich sicheres Urteil aufzuzwängen" [as a preliminary description of the difficulties and current arguments, designed to introduce the reader to the uncertainties of the controversy without pressing him towards any supposedly certain conclusion] (*Petrus Blesensis*, p. 9).

56. Giles Constable, review of Revell, *The Later Letters*, in *Journal of Medieval Latin*, 5 (1995): 246–53, at 249.

57. An interesting example is Letter 39, ed. Revell, pp. 186–87, which offers a discussion of some "questiones de resurrectione Lazari." These correspond in spirit at least, as well as in some details, to the curious debate-poem entitled "Discussio litis super hereditate Lazari et Marie Magdalene, sororis eius, videlicet quis eorum debeat habere eorum hereditatem" [The debate about the dispute over the inheritance of Lazarus and his sister Mary Magdalene—that is, about which of them should get their inheritance], which is edited by Walter, *Das Streitgedicht*, pp. 234–48. The creative possibilities perceived by twelfth-century writers in the form and practice of the "quaestio" are only just beginning to be realized: see, for example, A. G. Rigg, "Walter Map, the Shaggy Dog Story, and the *Quaestio Disputata*," in *Roma, magistra mundi. Mélanges offerts au Père L. E. Boyle à l'occasion de son 75e anniversaire*, ed. Jacqueline Hamesse, vol 2 (Louvain-la-Neuve: Université Catholique de Louvain, 1998), pp. 723–735.

58. Ep. LXVI: PL 207, p. 198: "Verumtamen apud dominum regem Anglorum quotidiana ejus schola est litteratissimorum conversatio jugis et discussio questionum."

59. Southern, *Scholastic Humanism*, 2:209–12.

60. Such arguments existed. In favor of hunting, for example, is the *Dialogus de Scaccario* (*The Course of the Exchequer by Richard, Son of Nigel*), ed. and trans. Charles Johnson (London: Nelson, 1950), p. 60; in favor of wine-drinking is Alexander Neckam's *De Commendatione Vini*, ed. M. Esposito, "On some unpublished poems attributed to Alexander Neckam," *English Historical Review* 30 (1915): 450–71 (Book I) and H. Walther, "Zu den kleineren Gedichten des Alexander Neckam," *Mittellateinisches Jahrbuch* 2 (1965): 111–29 (Books II and III). Defenses of alcohol, moreover, are implicit in the tradition of poetic debates between Wine and Water: see, for example, "Cum tenerent omnia medium tumultum," ed. Wright, *Latin Poems*, pp. 87–92—a contest in which Wine emerges with the upper hand. Johannes de Hauvilla rehearses the arguments both for and against "Bacchus" in *Architrenius*, ed. Paul Gerhard Schmidt (Munich: W. Fink, 1974); reprinted with trans. by Winthrop Wetherbee (Cambridge: Cambridge University Press, 1994), Book 2, caps 9–10 (Wetherbee, 46–51).

61. Ep. XVIII, PL 207. 66; Ep. XXII, PL 207. 83; Ep. XXVI, PL 207. 92; Ep. CXX, PL 207. 353. For the use of this tag as a satirical leitmotif, see Walter

of Châtillon, "Fas et nefas ambulant/ pene passu pari. . ." *Carmina Burana*, no. 19, ed. A. Hilka, O. Schumann and B. Bischoff, in *Carmina Burana: Die Lieder der Benediktbeurer Handschrift: Zweisprachige Ausgabe* (Munich: Deutscher Taschenbuch Verlag, 1979), pp. 46–49.

62. Peter gives serious consideration to the relationship between body and soul in Letter 50, ed. Revell, pp. 226–29.

63. Ep. XX, PL 207:72; Ep. LI, PL 207:155.

64. This tendency has rendered the debate about the identity of the "Peter of Blois" addressed in Letters LXXVI and LXXVII—historical individual or artistic alter-ego—rather more complicated than it might have been: see Bezzola, "La société féodale," 41; Dronke, "Peter of Blois and Poetry," pp. 293–95; Southern, "The Necessity for Two Peters of Blois" and *Scholastic Humanism*, 2: 178–81.

65. I borrow the term from Stephen Greenblatt's *Renaissance Self-Fashioning: From More to Shakespeare* (Chicago: University of Chicago Press, 1980; reprinted 1984); and I do so pointedly—there seems to me much to be gained from comparing the ways in which twelfth-century writers expressed "increased self-consciousness about the fashioning of human identity as a manipulable, artful process" (Greenblatt) with the way in which sixteenth-century writers did so.

66. The existence of the "later letters" was first signaled by Southern, in "Some new letters of Peter of Blois," *English Historical Review* 53 (1938): 412–24.

67. Revell, *Later Letters*, p. xxiv.

68. Revell, *Later Letters*, pp. xxx–xxxi.

69. On English national consciousness in the Middle Ages, see Thorlac Turville-Petre, *England the Nation: Language, Literature and National Identity 1290–1340* (Oxford: Clarendon Press, 1996)—though this study, unfortunately, only addresses a rather narrow time-frame. For a broader view, see also Paul Meyvaert, " 'Rainaldus est malus scriptor Francigenus'—Voicing National Antipathy in the Middle Ages," in *Speculum* 66 (1991): 743–63, and the useful bibliographical survey he provides on page 743. Meyvaert also notes as a problem the use of the expression "largitas incomparabilis Anglicorum" [incomparable generosity of the English] in the context of verses otherwise only hostile to the English. Peter's Letter 31 may provide the necessary explanatory context—"largitas" may have been claimed often enough by pro-English partisans like Peter's antagonist, Thomas, for the anti-English to use it with implicit and unqualified irony. The verses in question are edited by Hans Walther, "Scherz und Ernst in der Völker- und Stämme-Charakteristik mittellateinischer Verse," *Archiv für Kulturgeschichte* 41 (1959): 263–301, at 284.

70. Peter's questioning of the idea of "largitas" at the beginning of Letter 31 broadly resembles Horace's questioning of the same idea at the beginning of one of his *Satires*, I, 2, p. 24, ed. H. Rushton Fairclough, *Satires, Epistles and Ars Poetica* (Cambridge, Mass.: Harvard University Press, 1926), p. 20.

71. See *M. Fabi Quintiliani Institutionis Oratoriae Libri XII*, ed. Ludwig Radermacher, 2 vols. (Leipzig: B. G. Teubner, 1965), Book IX, 3, p. 65,

vol. 2, p. 187: "huic diversam volunt esse distinctionem, cui dant nomen παραδιαστολην, que similia discernuntur: 'cum te pro astuto sapientem appelles, pro confidente fortem, pro inliberali diligentem' " ["They choose to oppose this with [the device called] 'distinctio,' which they call paradiastole, according to which we distinguish between similar things: 'When you call yourself wise instead of astute, brave instead of confident, careful instead of mean' "].

72. Contrasts and conflicts between pairs of these four qualities are commonplace in twelfth-century literature. For avarice against prodigality, see, for example, Walter of Châtillon, "Fas et nefas ambulant/ pene passu pari. . .," which continues "prodigus non redimit / vitium avari"; and also Map, *De Nugis*, p. 438. For avarice against generosity, see John of Salisbury, *Policraticus*, Book VIII, chap. 4, II:241–43; and Alan of Lille, *Anticlaudianus*, 9:8, PL 210:573–74. Vernacular texts, by contrast, are much more likely to advocate unqualified *largesse*: for example, the emperor's advice to his son at the beginning of Chrétien de Troyes's *Cligés* (lines 192–217) is to be liberal, without any counterbalancing warning against prodigality. This might be seen as a deliberately one-sided appropriation of the moral scheme employed by Peter.

73. See Terence Parsons, "The Traditional Square of Opposition," in *The Stanford Encyclopedia of Philosophy*, ed. Edward N. Zatta (Summer 2004): URL = http://plato.stanford.edu/archives/sum2004/entries/square.

74. Peter's apparent use of the square of opposition in a broadly "literary" context is not unparalleled among twelfth-century writers: Alan of Lille seems to refer to it in his description of Nature's zodiacal crown in *De Planctu Naturae*, II, pr. 1, trans. James J. Sheridan, *Alan of Lille: The Plaint of Nature* (Toronto: University of Toronto Press, 1980), pp. 77–81—though not directly in connection with the ethical contrasts at issue here. Even so, elsewhere in his poem, there can be found contrasts between avarice and generosity (Prose 8, ed. Sheridan, p. 203) and between generosity and prodigality (Prose 9, ed. Sheridan, p. 214). Sheridan prints the square on p. 77, n. 14.

75. See, for example, *The Owl and the Nightingale*, ed. Neil Cartlidge (Exeter: University of Exeter Press, 2001), lines 933–54. For a recent discussion of the way in which this poem might be said to constitute a criticism of criticism itself, see Christopher Cannon, "*The Owl and the Nightingale* and the Meaning of Life," *Journal of Medieval and Early Modern Studies* 34 (2004): 251–78.

76. Revell, *Later Letters*, p. 161, n8—though as Revell herself remarks: "In general, Peter's handling of scholastic questions reflects the intellectual traditions in which he had been brought up, not the new dialectical education in Paris (see especially Letter 28)" (Revell, *Later Letters*, p. xxvi).

77. In the sense that the Aristotelian affirmation of the mean amounts to a claim to the wisdom of moderation, or that, as Horace puts it, "dum vitant stulti vitia, in contraria currunt" (*Satires*, I, 2, p. 24, ed. Fairclough, p. 20), Peter's apparently deliberate failure to make the same affirmation could be read as a means of identifying himself—ruefully—with the "stulti" of Horace's dictum.

As Horace's association of fools with contraries suggests, the golden mean could be (and was) used as a satirical argument against ambition: see, for example, "Missus sum in vineam circa horam nonam," ed. Wright, *Latin Poems*, pp. 152–59, lines 205–8: "Audi, qui de Socrate disputas et scribes,/ miser, vaca potius potibus et cibis; / quod si dives fieri non vis aut nequibis,/ inter utrumque tene, medio tutissimus ibis" [Listen now, you who dispute and write about Socrates, you wretch, you'd better devote yourself to food and drink; because if you don't want to or can't get rich, stick between the two [extremes], you'll go most safely down the middle].

78. Horace, *Epistulae*, II. 2, pp. 192–94, ed. Fairclough, 438–41: ". . . et tamen idem/ scire volam, quantum simplex hilarisque nepoti / discrepet et quantum discordet parcus avaro" [and yet I shall want to know how much the man who is artlessly good-natured differs from the prodigal, how much the frugal contrasts with the avaricious].

79. Hans Walther, *Initia Carminum ac Versuum Medii Aevi Posterioris Latinorum* (Göttingen: Vandenhoeck & Ruprecht, 1959), no. 14787; *Proverbia Sententiaeque Latinitatis Medii Aevi* (Göttingen: Vandenhoeck & Ruprecht, 1965), no. 22570.

80. There is an untranslatable pun here on "cervisia," "beer," and "cervicosus," "obstinate."

81. See J. H. Hanford, "The Mediaeval Debate between Wine and Water," *PMLA* 28 (1913): 315–67; Walther, *Das Streitgedicht in der lateinischen Literatur*, 46–53; Rigg, *History of Anglo-Latin Literature*, 143–44. For the vernacular "bataille des vins," see *Les "Dits" d'Henri d'Andeli*, ed. Alain Corbellari (Paris: Champion, 2003), pp. 51–57. It is interesting to compare these medieval debates between beverages with the encounter between Coffee and Tea described in an Arabic debate poem first published in 1955: see C. D. Holes, "The Dispute of Coffee and Tea: A Debate-Poem from the Gulf," in *Tradition and Modernity in Arabic Language and Literature*, ed. J. R. Smart (Richmond, Surrey: Curzon Press, 1996), pp. 302–15.

82. Alcuin (?), "Conflictus Veris et Hiemis," ed. & trans. Peter Godman, *Poetry of the Carolingian Renaissance* (London: Duckworth, 1985), pp. 144–49, lines 32, 45. In a Latin debate-poem now extant in a fourteenth-century manuscript in Göttingen ("Phebus libram perlustrabat. . .," ed. Walther, pp. 191–203), Summer even accuses Winter of being an Epicurean (str. 52, 197).

83. Nicole Bozon, "De l'Yver et de l'Esté," ed. Bossy, 2–15; also A. Jubinal, *Nouveau Recueil de contes, dits et autre pieces inédites des XIIIe, XIVe et XVe siècles*, 2 vols. (Paris: Pannier, 1839–42), 2:40–49.

84. *Wynnere and Wastoure*, ed. Stephanie Trigg, EETS os 297 (Oxford: Oxford University Press, 1990); also ed. Thorlac Turville-Petre, in his *Alliterative Poetry of the Later Middle Ages: An Anthology* (London: Routledge, 1989), pp. 38–66, and in *The New Pelican Guide to English Literature: 1. Medieval Literature: Part One: Chaucer and the Alliterative Tradition* (Harmondsworth: Penguin, 1982; revised 1994), pp. 398–415. The "Aristotelian" background to the poem is drawn by Thomas H. Bestul in *Satire and Allegory in "Wynnere and Wastoure"* (Lincoln, Nebr.: University of Nebraska Press, 1974), esp. pp. 5–17.

85. See Neil Cartlidge, "The Battle of Shrovetide: Carnival against Lent as a Leitmotif in Late Medieval Culture," *Viator* 35 (2004): 517–41.

86. Ed. Revell, 163: "Vult quod cervisia regina et domina sit, non solum omnium poculorum sed etiam omnium populorum."

87. See Cartlidge, *The Owl and the Nightingale*, p. xxiv.

88. See E. Braunholtz, "Die Streitgedichte Peters von Blois und Roberts von Beaufeu über den Wert des Weines und Bieres," *Zeitschrift für Romanische Philologie* 47 (1927): 30–38; André Wilmart, "Une suite au poème de Robert de Beaufeu pour l'éloge de la cervoise," *Revue bénédictine* 50 (1938): 136–40.

89. Ed. Revell, p. 163: "Legimus quod quidam nutritus ex aquis palustribus, Ravennam veniens, vino modico sumpto incurrit vomitum et singultum, nec spem sanitatis optinere potuit donec ad nutriciam paludem rediens ad lutosum et fetidum potum continuo respiravit. De multis audivimus et de quibusdam vidimus quod publicis fetoribus assueti non sine syncopi seu defectu cordis, qui vulgariter dicitur spasmatio, species aromaticas poterant odorare; pasmati autem leviter sanabantur si ad nasum eorum fimum fetidissimum vel equorum stercora ponerentur. Decet igitur ut *qui in sordibus est sordescat adhuc* [Apoc. 22:11] [. . .]."

90. "Du Vilain Asnier," ed. B. J. Levy and C. E. Pickford, in *Selected Fabliaux: Edited from B.N. Fonds Français 837, Fonds Français 19152 and Berlin Hamilton 257* (Hull: University of Hull Department of French, 1978), pp. 1–2.

91. *The Owl and the Nightingale*, lines 101–26.

92. Neil Cartlidge, "The Date of *The Owl and the Nightingale*," *Medium Ævum* 65 (1996): 230–47. Dronke suggests that both Peter's poetry and *The Owl and the Nightingale* can be seen as instances of a significant upsurge of literary achievement in the debate-form in the two decades or so after 1200 ("Peter of Blois and Poetry," pp. 312–13). Even if it is no longer clear that the Middle English poem can be placed so early, I still share with Dronke the sense that medieval writers' engagement with the debate-form is a significant and revealing intellectual development, even if over a longer period than Dronke suggests.

93. "Visio Philiberti," ed. Wright, *Latin Poems*, lines 289–90. Cf. Odo of Cheriton, no. 53, ed. Léopold Hervieux, in *Les fabulistes latins depuis le siècle d'Auguste jusqu'à la fin du moyen âge*, 5 vols (Paris: Firmin-Didot, 1884; 2d ed., 1893–98), 4:224: "Traha semel transiuit super Bufonem, et unus dens percussit eam in capite, alius in corde, alius in renibus. Et ait Bufo: 'Deus confundat tot dominos!'." Cf. also Hans Walther, *Proverbia Sententiaeque Latinitatis Medii Aevi*, 6 vols (Göttingen: Vandenhoeck & Ruprecht. 1963–69), nos 2180, 2184, 2185, 2186, 6160, 29463.

94. "Altercatio vini et cervisie," ("Ludens ludis miscebo seria. . ."), ed. Aloys Bömer, "Eine Vagantenliedersammlung des 14. Jahrhunderts in der Schlossbibliothek zu Herdringen (Kr. Arnsberg)," *Zeitschrift für deutsches Altertum* 49 (1908), pp. 161–238, at 200–202, str. 5: "Eius [Beer's] regnum est alemannia, / hannonia, brabantis, flandria, / frederici regnum, saxonia, . . ." [His [Beer's] kingdom is Alemannia, Hainaut, Brabant, Flanders, Frederick's realm, Saxony. . .].

95. "The Dispute between an Englishman and a Frenchman," ed. Thomas Wright, *Political Poems and Songs relating to English History composed during the period from the accession of Edward III to that of Richard III*, 2 vols., RS 14 (1859, 1861), 2:91–93, lines 25–40.

96. Ed. Revell, p. 164, §11; PL 207:20. Peter's readiness to "plagiarize" his own work in this way needs to be taken into account when addressing the problem of his "plagiarism" from other people.

97. Ed. Revell, p. 164: "semper in hospitio tuo largitatis immemor, sed ad magnatum dapes infrunitus et impudens atque violentus intrusor."

CHAPTER 4

"I WILL NOT STAY SILENT": SOVEREIGNTY AND TEXTUAL IDENTITY IN WALTER OF CHÂTILLON'S "PROPTER SION NON TACEBO"

Simon Meecham-Jones

The recognition by twelfth-century rulers of the seminal role of literature in the consolidation and self-mythologizing of royal authority—understood at the court of Henry II as it was in the circles around Frederick Barbarossa—was to find curious echoes in the parallel processes of textual colonization and the exercise of self-construction and projection that characterize the work of the most original and accomplished poet of the age, Walter of Châtillon. Indeed, the two strands of Walter's literary career—as the creator of an epic detailing the career of a warrior whose appetite for new conquest is insatiable, and as the author of febrile and phantasmagoric satires on human corruption—could both be read, in part, as critical commentaries on the exercise of "imperial" notions of power.[1] Walter's writing can be read as formulating an act of textual resistance to the apparently relentless exercise of worldly and ecclesiastical prerogative authority.

The extent of Walter's personal involvement with the court of Henry II remains contentious. Tradition has identified the poet with the "Walter de Insula" mentioned in the letters of John of Salisbury as a leading functionary (and man of conscience) in the service of King Henry. This Walter is described in the letters of John of Salisbury, and in letters to Thomas Becket, as having held the senior post of deputy keeper of the king's seal—a position from which he was to be removed.[2] Critics such as

Hauréau and Colker have cast doubt on the identification of this Walter
with the poet,[3] Colker's skepticism deriving from the fact that none of the
biographical *Vitae* inscribed on manuscripts of the *Alexandreis* describe
Walter as having held office in England. The *Vitae* were, though, written
after Walter's death and in a different political climate—perhaps at a time
when it was no longer politic to draw attention to Walter's services to the
English crown. Certainly the Walter described by John of Salisbury found
that the demands of royal service placed him in situations in which his conscience was compromised and his position as a cleric within the church was
undermined:

> Accitis ergo nuper ad colloquium Chinon(ense) magnatibus suis cum
> familiaribus, qui rerum malarum industriam habere dinoscuntur et usum, et
> sapientes sunt ut dicent et faciant mala, studiosius inquisiuit cum promissis,
> minis et obstestatione quam-plurima, quonam consilio sibi utendum esset
> aduersus ecclesiam,. . .et rex (quod ad uestram notitiam uenisse non ambigo)
> uirum bonum magistrum Galterum de Insula misit in Angliam cum litteris a
> colloquio Chinon(ensi), ut insulanos super facta appellatione praemuniret et
> portus et transitus faceret diligentius obseruari et clerum ab obediendo sus-
> penderet, cum tamen nondum facta sit appellatio et archiepiscopus possit
> facile inueniri. Nec dubito quin praedicto Galtero machinatio ista displiceat
> cum omnibus quae presumuntur aduersus ecclesiam Dei, quoniam Deum
> timet.

> [Lately he gathered to the conference at Chinon his nobles and his
> household, who are known to be assiduous in pursuit of evil works, and are
> experts in recommending and doing evil. . .the king meanwhile (as I do not
> doubt has come to your notice) sent that good man master Walter de Insula
> to England with a letter from the Chinon conference, to warn the islanders
> of the appeal that had been made, to see that harbours and cross-Channel
> routes are more closely watched, and to keep the clergy from obedience to
> their superior—although in fact the appeal is not yet made and it is easy to
> get in touch with the archbishop. I have no doubt that this scheme is
> distasteful to Walter along with all other attempts against God's Church,
> since he is a God-fearing man.][4]

Duggan further complicates an identification with the poet Walter by
proposing that the deputy keeper of the king's seal, whom she describes as
Master Walter de Insula, be distinguished from a second Walter de Insula,
mentioned in the records of the royal household for 1167–68, who appears
to have been a trusted counselor of the king in the months that preceded
the murder of Becket.[5] The involvement of this Walter as a trusted advisor
to Henry during the conflicts that preceded the murder of Becket would
seem to make him a more plausible candidate for identification with the

poet than the "Master Walter" who fell from grace in 1166, but there is no
surviving evidence to justify such an identification. The evidence from
Walter's poetry, though suggestive, is no less inconclusive. Through the
Alexandreis, Walter is at some pains to set his poem in a relationship to the
English crown, opening the work with a reminder of his patron's mem-
bership in the Norman royal house: "At tu, cui maior genuisse Britannia
reges / Gaudet auos" [But you, among whose ancestors Great Britain
proudly numbers its kings][6]

Later in the poem, he turned his eyes from the antique past, adding a
brief (yet damning) reference to the death of Becket, which some early
scribes felt obliged to make more explicit:

> Non caderent hodie nulo discrimine sacri
> pontifices, quales nuper cecidisse queruntur
> viciniae modico distantes equore terrae.

> [Holy archbishops would not fall today indiscriminately, such as those whose
> recent fall is the subject of complaint by neighboring countries, separated by
> but a narrow sea.][7]

Even if Walter had refrained from incorporating into the text a
reference to the murder of Becket, the potential applicability of the story of
the *Alexandreis*, with its warning of the limits of earthly power, to the
career of England's conquering hero must have been apparent to Henry's
contemporaries.[8] The inclusion of glancing references to events of his own
time added a taste of satirical grit to the texture of Walter's epic, though
these hints at contemporary reference prove merely that Walter observed
the English royal house, not that he served it.

Nonetheless, throughout the satirical poems there are interesting verbal
echoes that reveal Walter's closeness to the intellectual elite that had gathered around Becket's predecessor, Archbishop Theobald. In the satirical
poem "Propter Sion non Tacebo" [I will not keep silent about Sion], for
example, Walter uses, or (less probably) coins, the term "sterlingorum,"
[English currency] a word the first appearance of which is not recorded
before the late 1150s.[9] It is certainly a word used by John of Salisbury, in a
letter addressed to Pope Adrian IV:

> Petit hoc ipsum dominus Cant(uariensis), apud quem centum marcas
> sterlingorum deposui, quas ad mandatum uestrum inplendum a praefato
> episcopo acceperam.[10]

> [I am joined in this petition by the lord archbishop of Canterbury, with
> whom I have deposited a hundred marks sterling, which the bishop had
> transferred to me for the execution of your mandate.]

The appearance in a poem that berates the sins of the Universal Church of a word associated only with English (or Scottish) currency demands explanation, raising puzzling questions as to the relationship of the poem, and poet, to English ecclesiastical authority.[11] It may be that the Goddess referred to as being not (and presumably far less than) the legendary Thetis was meant to satirize the church in England,[12] or, less probably, some notable English woman (Eleanor of Aquitaine? Or the Empress Matilda, in which case the nonidentification of Henry's mother with the mother of Achilles carries perhaps a hint of rebuke). It is as likely, though, that Walter's echoing of a word used by John of Salisbury was designed as a discreet textual in-joke, through which Walter saluted an esteemed colleague. Such allusion is scarcely without precedent in the text: later in the poem Walter makes a reference to the prophet Elisha in the clause "nisi latus Helisei / Giezi corrumperet," [had Giesi not counterfeited the person of Elisha] which either copies or inspires a similar idea, similarly phrased, in the poem "De Avaritia et Luxuria Mundi," attributed to Walter Map: "At si fortis videris velut Helisaeum. . .habebit Gyezim leprae Syri reum."[13] Whether this echoing shows contact between the poets, or imitation by Map, is unclear. Map's poem is found in British Library MS Harley 978, at folio 108, while the verso of folio 109 contains another poem by Map, "De Mundi Cupidate" which, in its use of imagery of Rome and of the monstrous dog Cerberus to denounce avarice and corruption, reworks (or predicts) the concerns of "Propter Sion non Tacebo." Though the poems are unlike in meter and poetic structure, the continuity of their ideological concerns is clearly more than accidental, even if it is impossible to determine beyond question the direction of influence.

The overlapping of themes and lexical items between Walter of Châtillon's texts and those of other writers of his own time should be understood not as reflecting a serendipitous congruence of styles but as a conscious gesture of affiliation, through which each poet draws other writers within his texts in a gesture of mutual support.

The extensive imitation by many later poets of Walter's poetic forms and diction provided an appropriate homage to Walter's own creative practices, in which the texts of classical antiquity were alluded to and borrowed from with a remarkable confidence and thoroughness. Processes of verbal allusion and appropriation from anterior texts are central to the structuring of Walter's lyrical texts and contribute to the aggression with which his satirical muse is expressed. Walter composes his lyrics not by the faithful imitation of classical models but, in part, by the seizure of materials from prior texts.[14] Rather like the plundered sculpture of the Tetrarchs set into the corner of St. Mark's Cathedral in Venice, the shards of classical poetry set within Walter's lyrics function as a statement of cultural rivalry, their disturbing incongruity guaranteeing Walter's triumph as heir to, reader of, and emulator of the classical poetic tradition.

The satirical lyric "Propter Sion non Tacebo" is typical in its demonstration of the ambition of Walter's subversive aesthetic.[15] At first it seems as if the classical poetic tradition will not be his major source in framing a satire on ecclesiastical corruption. There is something fitting, or almost inevitable, in this most outspoken of satirists beginning the poem by declaring that he will not be silent:

> Propter Sion non tacebo
> set ruinas Rome flebo,
> quousque iustitia
> rursus nobis oriatur
> et ut lampas accendatur
> iustus in ecclesia.
>   (1.1–6)

> [I will not keep silent about Sion, but I will weep for the ruins of Rome, until justice arises again for us, and so that the lamp of justice might be kindled again in our church.]

But the words with which he does so have a familiar ring, having been borrowed from the prophetic verses of Isaiah:

> Propter Sion non tacebo et propter Hierusalem nonquiescam
> donec egrediatur ut splendor iustus
> eius et salvator eius ut lampas accendatur

> [For Sion's sake will I not hold my peace, and for Jerusalem's sake I will not rest, until the righteous thereof go forth as a lamp that burneth.]

As Walter shifts the focus of his poem from Jerusalem to Rome, Isaiah's thought is broken to fit the meter, and the words that constitute his utterance ("iustus" [justice], "lampas" [lamps]) are reordered. Walter creates a stanza that asserts its independence of its revered source even while the understanding of Walter's lyric is perhaps dependent on, and certainly enhanced by, the recognition of the debt it owes to the Hebrew prophet. But it is not the Old Testament alone that Walter adapts to his own purpose. In the fifth stanza, his borrowing of the word "bitalassum" [touched by two seas] from the Acts of the Apostles allows Walter to infuse his imagery with a recollection of the stormy and dangerous journey of St. Paul to Rome, adding another level of ironic humor to the poet's account of his imagined experience of the Holy City: "Et cum incidissemus in locum bithalassum impegerunt navem" [And falling into a place where two seas met, they ran the ship aground.][16]

There is a deftly mimetic edge to Walter's adaptation of this unfamiliar word—"touched by two seas." The word is a post-classical coining, code-mixing into Latin a term that had been expressible in Greek but not Latin. The word is itself manifoldly "touched by two seas"—the Greek and Latin languages, which thereby represent the classical (and pagan) tradition and the post-classical (and Christian) tradition. The word is used as an early pointer of Walter's awareness of the multiple and overlapping figuration of ideas of identity within his verse.

At a time when detailed familiarity with the scriptural texts was regulated by the hierarchy of the church, Walter's technique of unattributed extraction allowed him a striking freedom in adapting and altering words from the scriptures, which suggests a remarkable self-confidence in dealing with the always delicate topic of a holy text guarded (and obscured) by the priesthood's control of access. Sometimes Walter's changes to his sources are merely playful, perhaps a textual curtsy to his clerical audience, as when, for example, in stanza 25, a tag from Psalm 34: "egenum et pauperem a diripientibus eum" [the poor and the needy from him that spoileth him?] is reversed, presumably for metrical reasons: "pauper autem et egenus" (25.5). But Walter concludes the poem with words taken from another psalm, Psalm 38:

> Dixi custodiam vias meas
> ut non delinquam in lingua mea
> posui ori meo custodiam
> cum consisteret peccator adversum me
>
> [I said, I will take heed to my ways, that I sin not with my tongue: I will keep my mouth with a bridle while the wicked is before me.]

From this, Walter extracts a single phrase:

> . . .ori meo
> posui custodiam. . .
>   (30. 5–6)

isolating the words from their Psalmic context in a way that requires the reader to supply the missing words and to speculate why Walter has chosen to suppress them.

Walter's use of scriptural material raises many questions—about the creative freedom claimed by clerical authors, and about the nature of the audience for such works—but its originality should not be overstated. Medieval learned-lyric perpetually faced the challenge of justifying its existence, of proving itself a worthwhile medium for learned men (and thereby justifying the implicit claim that the experience of a particular individual was worthy of textual preservation). Such an assertion implicitly cut across Christian notions of humility and, perhaps, denied the value placed on spiritual discretion, rather than spiritual or emotional "show." These potential inhibitions on the development of a genre of learned lyric were perhaps magnified by the profusion of "worthless" popular lyric, with its scant claim to scholastic respect. There was, though, biblical precedent for the expression of the lyric mode in a few key scriptural texts: the Book of Job, the Song of Songs, and most significantly, the Psalms (as well as, more problematically, the Revelation of St. John). The protracted medieval reinvention of the lyric voice as an instrument of "High Art" drew much of its justification from these biblical precedents, and the lyric poems of writers such as Abelard show an overwhelming debt to scriptural texts. The survival of Abelard's learned and biblically inspired lyrics, and the loss of the lyrics he claimed to have written during his involvement with Heloise, seems to demonstrate the relative value accorded to lyrics valorized by biblical precedents and those which did not display this "guarantee" of value:

> Quem etiam ita negligentem et tepidum lectio tunc habebat, ut iam nichil ex ingenio sed ex usu cuncta proferrem, nec iam nisi recitator pristinorum essem inventorum, et si qua invenire liceret, carmina essent amatoria, non philosophie secreta; quorum etiam carminum pleraque adhuc in multis, sicut et ipse nosti, frequentantur et decantantur regionibus, ab his maxime quos vita, similis oblectat. Quantam autem mestitiam, quos gemitus, que lamenta nostri super hoc scolares assumerent, ubi videlicet hanc animi mei occupationem immo perturbationem presenserunt, non est facile vel cogitare.

> [What is more, my reading then found me so careless and apathetic that I produced nothing new from inspiration—but everything from previous experience. And no longer was I anything more than a mere reciter of what I had discovered previously, and if I could produce creative writing, they were love songs not the secrets of philosophy. Also, most of these songs are still popular and are still sung in many places by those who enjoy a similar life style. What sadness, what groans, what lamentations our scholars would take up considering my life style (when, of course, they became aware of this preoccupation, or rather, this disturbance to my mind) is beyond contemplation.][17]

In the lyrics of Walter of Châtillon, the debt to biblical models is no less present, but the poet's response to the scriptural texts is muddied by an alternative and prominent sequence of allusions to, and extractions from, secular classical texts. In "Propter Sion non Tacebo" these allusions take a variety of forms. Some of the figurative machinery is borrowed, as when Walter adapts Ovid's account of Scilla and Charybdis (*Metamorphoses*

7:62–68; *Amores* 2:11, 18–20). Even this proves more complex than it ini-
tially appears: Walter had (presumably) previously adapted this figure in the
Alexandreis, so the allusion to Ovid also provides an opportunity for Walter
to remind us of the existence of his own *magnum opus*:

> Hic syrtes habuere suas. Hic altera sicco Scilla mari latrat, hic puluerulenta
> Cribdis.[18]

> [Here the syrtes have their well-known storms, here a second Scylla barks on
> a dry sea, here one finds a dust-covered Charybdis.][19]

Another reason for Walter's employment of a recurring pattern of allusion
to precedent texts derives from the opportunities this afforded for punning,
misquotation, and ironically inappropriate citation. Sustained wordplay has
long been recognized as central to the "Goliardic" aesthetic, and Jill Mann
has drawn attention to the ways by which in Walter's work "moral
perversion goes along with—and is revealed by—linguistic perversion."[20]

Mann draws on Jolivet's account of "Grammatical Platonism" to
illuminate the ethical seriousness achievable and embodied in the humor of
verbal quipping,[21] but it is important also not to deny the ways in which
the playfulness of Walter's punning introduce an exhilarating and potentially transgressive energy into the text. Often Walter exploits the expressive possibilities inherent in the ways in which, through the long
development of Latin, words had developed alternative, sometimes unrelated, meanings. In a line like "id est [there is] cardinalium" (4.6), Walter
can frame a statement with assertive confidence, knowing that the meaning
of the line has been rendered inevitably ambiguous by the diverse meanings
of the key term. For the adjective "cardinalis" Lewis and Short note as
meanings both "of or pertaining to a door hinge" and "that on which
something depends i.e. principal, chief."[22] Walter allows both these possibilities to color his line, while at the same time inferring the implied contrast with the cardinals of the church who should be "principal, chief,"
and to be relied on like a hinge, but who are failing in the duties spelled out in
their name.

In describing the sea as "duplex," Walter forces the reader to decide
whether he is describing the sea as "twofold/double/bipartite" or if the
word carries some of its metaphorical meaning ("[of words] ambiguous, [of
character] false, deceitful"). In his list of Medieval lexical items, Niermeyer
notes a further meaning, "a gold coin," adding an addition level of nuance
(and untranslatability) to Walter's use of the term.[23] Sometimes Walter's
wordplay can be translinguistic, as when he declares: "ibi panni submerguntur" (7.2). "Pannus" may refer to cloth (the brown of the poor, and the
purple vestments of the Curia) but also carries a hint of the Greek word

pan—everything. As a cleric trained within a tradition that had proclaimed that "In the beginning was the Word, and the Word was with God, and the Word was God,"[24] Walter seems to display a glee, tinged with dizziness, at the ability of words to signify in unexpected ways. Occasionally, this delight in his own facility is crystallized in an allusion of potent accusatory force. It is appropriate that a satirical poem should show a familiarity with the works of Juvenal, the classical master of the form, but it is a familiarity Walter demonstrates through discreet verbal echo. The monstrous figure of clerical vice is described in stanza 20 in terms that borrow an apparently incidental detail from Juvenal's *Satires*. Walter's sneering words "ventre grosso, lota cute" (21.4) [huge belly, washed skin] are stiffened by the incorporated recollection of Juvenal's observations: "ad moechum lota veniunt cute.[25] [Her lover she will meet with a clean-washed skin.]

The identification of the corrupt churchman with Juvenal's vain and preposterous woman preparing to cheat on her husband is the more damning because, in its (for Walter) apparently uncharacteristic understatement, it demands a knowledge of the original context to appreciate the force of the insult concealed in the two not-obviously pejorative words "lota cute." It is only when we recall that the cleric bears the name of Pilate that we realize the true meaning of the reference to washed skin.

Elsewhere in the poem, Walter's sense of an almost occult pleasure in verbal manipulation perhaps explains the presence of a wealth of adapted classical material, which seems almost to be concealed. Often Walter alludes to phrases from texts that were not generally familiar. In 13.6 the unfamiliar word "supinant" seems designed to make a veiled reference to a phrase from Virgil's *Georgics*: "ante supinatas Aquiloni ostendere glaebas" [to expose the upturned clods to the North-wind].[26]

The praise of the larger harbor as "fetus ager" similarly imbeds in the text a reference to a comment by the Muse as recounted in Ovid's *Fasti*: "seminibus iactis est ubi fetus ager" (It is when the seed has been sown and the field fertilized).[27]

The connotations of the imagery of the fertilized field threaten to problematize the apparently sincere praise of the pope, Alexander III, but in Ovid's text the Muse uses "fetus ager" as a symbol of constancy—"sic tempora certa" (the season is fixed)—which might be interpreted as an obscure but welcome tribute to Alexander's authority. Nonetheless the overall effect is to add difficulty to an understanding of the text, a difficulty which is increased rather than diminished if the allusion is noticed.

The quotation from the *Fasti* is typical of Walter's technique in using the adaptation of apparently unproblematic words from inappropriate or unexpected contexts to create a sense of ambiguity within the text.

This ambiguity exists at both a verbal and a structural level. Through the conflation of material extracted from the classical lyric tradition and from the scriptures, Walter achieved a disturbing stylistic instability, characterized by giddying shifts of key signature. In the past this perpetual instability of tone was read as evidence of a lack of technical command, but such readings underestimated the sophistication of Walter's texts, and of its presumed audience. All of Walter's career must be understood as a response to the oppressive and potentially inhibiting burden of the perceived achievement of classical literature. Walter's response can be seen to have evolved into two contrary aesthetics—the respectful and reasonably faithful imitation of classical forms attempted in the *Alexandreis* and the disordering of classical structures achieved in the lyrics. Both forms amply demonstrate the depth and critical engagement of Walter's involvement with classical poetry but, whereas in his exercise in the mode of post-Christian epic (or failed epic) in the *Alexandreis*, Walter was able to demonstrate the skill of his craftsmanship, it was in the lyrics that he was able to demonstrate the cutting edge of his originality as a poetic voice. Compared to the more stately music of the *Alexandreis*, Walter's satirical poems must have seemed to his contemporaries exercises in a mongrel form—but he had fashioned a mongrel that had sharp satirical teeth:

> Canes Scille possunt dici
> veritatis inimici,
> advocati curie,
> qui latrando falsa fingunt,
> mergunt simul et confringunt
> carinam pecunie.
> (9.1–6)

[The dogs of Scilla can be called the enemies of truth, the supporters of the senate who, by their barking make false statements; at the same time they submerge and smash open the ship of money.]

Strangely, the originality and vehemence of Walter's satires have caused critics to set limits on their applicability to contemporary ecclesiastical practice. In particular, scholars have found difficulty imagining a context and an audience for which these poems might have been written. Schmidt has argued that the particular form of the "quotation poem" can be linked to the *Festum Stultorum* (the Feast of Fools)—that one day a year when traditional structures of authority were parodically overturned.[28] He notes that two of Walter's poems in this form mention the *Festum Stultorum* and, following Spanke,[29] proposes that another five, including "Propter Sion non Tacebo," were written as entertainment for this singular festival. There is, though, something unduly restricting in Schmidt's interpretation. Though

Walter's excoriation of ecclesiastical corruption is forthright, it is also general in its scope—that is, it attacks the idea of corruption rather than its practice by named individuals. As such, however uncomfortable reading they might have seemed, Walter's criticisms cannot be considered to be contrary to the dictates of the church which also castigated unworthy conduct in its midst—at least in theory. It is surely as plausible that Walter used the *Festum Stultorum* merely as an image within his verse—a version of the "world turned upside down" topos noted by Curtius[30]—as that it provided the occasion for the writing of the poems (and their preservation in a variety of manuscript sources).

Schmidt's reading threatens to obscure both the intellectual ambition of a poem like "Propter Sion non Tacebo," and the creative anxiety crystallized within the text. Walter's citation of unfamiliar words from lesser-known corners of the classical repertoire uncovers, in its very thoroughness, the extent to which he was involuntarily measuring his work against the achievements of the past. If the idea of Alexander the Great or King Arthur functioned as both an inspiration and an implicit rebuke to the imperial aspirations of Henry II, so Virgil, Ovid, and Juvenal are an ever-present threat in Walter's creative universe, an unimpeachable reminder to Walter of the probable inadequacy of his work by comparison. This must have been a grievous concern for a writer who boasted to his patron of the immortality of his talent:

> Nam licet indignum tanto sit presule carmen,
> cum tamen exuerit mortales spiritus artus,
> viuemus pariter. Uiuet cum uate superstes
> gloria Guillermi nullum moritura per euum.[31]
>
> [For, though my poem is unworthy of so great a prelate, we shall, nevertheless, live on together after the soul has cast aside these mortal limbs. Along with the poet, William's glory will survive and live on, destined never to die.][32]

This anxiety, which scarcely ruffles the serenity of the *Alexandreis*, is revealed in a more aggressive light in Walter's lyrics, as bleeding chunks of classical texts are torn from their context and reused to Walter's purposes—in the process often becoming ironized by their proximity to scriptural material. There is a violence in Walter's appropriation of textual extracts that is marked also in his less-than-respectful handling of biblical material, and which is quite different from the more genial, jostling "mis-quotation" poetry of the Arch Poet.[33] In his constant allusion to prior texts, Walter seeks to set himself in a relationship of inheritance of past forms, but in a lyric like "Propter Sion non Tacebo," that relationship is reconfigured as one of conquest. Perhaps we can see a transference of this creative anxiety into the prose work *Tractatus sive dialogus contra Iudaeos*,[34] a polemic that attempts to "rescue" the ethical values derived from Judaism from their association with the Jews. In that work, Walter's resentment of the prior claims of an earlier culture encourages him to attempt to depose that culture's right to intellectual and ethical respect by "carrying off" the culture's (intellectual) goods. Something of that same resentment can be seen in his free handling of psalmic material, canonical expressions of that culture he had elsewhere berated. In this creation within his work of a dialectic between the expressions of two past literary cultures—the classical and the biblical—Walter fashions a discourse of exile and divided loyalties, which both satirizes and mimetically recreates his experience as a man living, not merely imagining, repeated experiences of exile within his own time. Walter was to experience exile in many forms. As a priest in a church that had only recently enforced clerical celibacy, he was exiled from the experiences of love and parenthood most of his contemporaries, and at least some of the poets he drew on as sources, could have expected—and Walter attempts to understand the experience he has been denied by (presumably) imagining fatherhood in the lyric "Verna redit tempories."[35]

Then there is the linguistic exile, enacted in the poems. As a student of the classics, he experienced the potent regret of one born too late—an awareness of an intellectual exile that was to be expressed more openly in the writings of Boccaccio, Chaucer and, pre-eminently, Petrarch, but which is the more poignant in Walter's work for being denied. Like Alan of Lille or Bernard Silvestris, Walter had trained himself as a Latin poet, but as a Latin poet condemned to write more than a thousand years after the zenith of the traditions he sought to emulate, and in a form of Latin that morphologically and lexically proclaimed its immense distance from the Augustan Golden Age. The use of Latin rather than the vernacular was an inevitable gesture in the framing of the epic *Alexandreis*, less so in the creation of a lyric voice, for which contemporary vernacular analogues (albeit for the most part of less involved complexity and ambition) survive. It was a decision that, though in part designed to project Walter's creative ambition, simultaneously reaffirmed his self-diagnosed perception of his status as an intellectual exile, set apart through the awareness of virtue and the recognition of vice literature has taught him. This "exile" can be seen as expressing both a literary pose and a dilemma; in their different traditions, Juvenal and Isaiah had proclaimed the status of the honest man as set apart from his less-aware contemporaries, a "voice crying in the wilderness," but the unabashed display of corruption in Walter's (or any satirist's) time must cause any poet with the faculty of self-awareness to ask why what seems so obvious to him seems invisible to others. If the "message" has not been heard by others, the honest poet must question the efficacy, or adequacy, of the voice through which he seeks to make himself heard. This "questioning of the voice" is at the core of Walter's method and preoccupations, and must be considered the primary theme of "Propter Sion non Tacebo," rather than a secondary theme in a poem primarily concerned with the denunciation of ecclesiastical corruption.

Though Eldredge several times describes elements of Walter's satirical expression in "Propter Sion non Tacebo" as "commonplace,"[36] he misreads Walter's citation of textual sources as a decorative literary technique rather than as a primary satirical subject of the poem. For Walter to write a poem so clearly concerned with its relationship to past literature must be considered a striking gesture, a gesture in which Walter seeks to weigh the value of "lived" experience against that of textual experience. The extracts from past literature function in the figurative role of body armor as Walter asserts his sense of exile, in a combative gesture of dissociation from the fallen concerns of the temporal sphere. The citation of the past provides witnesses that such corruption has previously been noted, even if it rather weakens Walter's satirical point by suggesting the universal and insoluble recurrence of such behavior. But the calling up of the venerable literary ancestors also changes the nature of Walter's poem, in lending it an abstract quality, framed to express a general truth rather than to comment on a specific set of circumstances. Rather than addressing the inevitable misery of everyday experience—poverty, disease, and conflict—and set in contrast to the corruption he so grotesquely figures, the very-present machinery of the textual tradition transforms the poem into a structure that acknowledges its own artifice and that, thus reserved from the courtesies and obligations of the merely physical life, provides a place of fictive *asylum* within which the poet can find sanctuary.

The lyric "Propter Sion non Tacebo" is unusual, though, among Walter's work in its engagement with another aspect of the representation of identity—the assertion of a sense of "national" identity. Whereas lyrics such as "Tanto viro locuturi" or "Missum sum in Vineam" are set entirely within the imaginative confines of their biblical and classical sources and could be said to exist in a plane of geographical abstraction, the material of "Propter Sion non Tacebo" is set in a complex relationship between locations which speak of the literary source (as, for example, St Paul's "in locum bithalassum") and those that place the poem in a recognizable contemporary setting. The most important of these occurs when the poetic persona is identified by the Sirens (whose voice is later revealed to be that of the cardinals) as being "de Francia"—from France:

Dulci cantu blandiuntur
ut Sirenes et loquuntur

primo quedem dulcia:
"Frare, ben je te cognosco,
certe nichil a te posco,
nam tu es de Francia.

Terra vestra bene cepit
et benigne nos recepit
in portu concilii.
Nostri estis, nostri—cuius?
sacrosancte sedis huius
speciales filii.

Nos peccata relaxamus
et laxatos collocamus
sedibus ethereis.
nos habemus Petri leges
ad ligandos omnes reges
in manicis ferreis."
                    (14.1–6, 15.1–6,
                         16.1–6)

[They are flattered with sweet singing like the sirens and at first they are told some sweet words: "brother, I know you well, I am certainly demanding nothing from you for you are from France. Your land has done well to capture us and has received us kindly in the harbor of the council. You are ours, and ours will be whose? You are the special sons of this Holy seat. We absolve our sins and we place those who are released in their Heavenly seats. We have Peter's laws to bind all the kings in iron fetters."]

This gesture of recognition forms the center-point of a sequence of references to France that show that the focus of the poem is not, as Eldredge asserted, "Rome. . .the center of two worlds,"[37] but rather the relationship of France, and those born in France, to the two worlds of the classical inheritance and church hierarchy isthat are represented in the imagery of Rome. In dramatizing this relationship, Walter introduces into his text an ambiguity which editors and critics have chosen to ignore. The repeated iteration of *ibi* ("there") succeeds in conflating Rome not merely with the straits of Messina, and Crassus, as Eldredge notes, but also with the demon hidden in men's hearts, which is then followed by a return to Walter's preoccupation with the corruption of the French:

Vidi, vidi caput mundi,
instar maris et profundi
vorax guttur Siculi;
ibi mundi bitalassus,
ibi sorbet aurum Crassus
et argentum seculi.

Ibi latrat Scilla rapax
et Caribdis auri capax
potius quam navium;
fit concursus galearum
et conflictus piraturum
id est cardinalium.

Sirtes insunt huic profundo
et Sirenes toti mundo
minantes naufragium;
os humanum foris patet
in occulto cordis latet
informe demonium.

Habes iuxta rationem
bitalassum per Franconem
quod ne credas frivolum:
ibi duplex mare fervet,
a quo non est qui reservet
sibi valens obulum.

Ibi venti colliduntur,
ibi panni submerguntur,
bissus, ostrum, purpure;
ibi mundus sepelitur,
immo totus deglutitur
in Franconis gutture.

Franco nulli miseretur,
nullum sexum reveretur,
nulli parcit sanguini;
omnes illi dona ferunt,
illuc enim ascenderunt
tribus, tribus domini.
                    (stanza 3–8)

[I have seen, I have seen the capital of the world, like the greedy throat of the deep Sicilian sea; there, at the crossing-place of the world, there Crassus swallows up the gold and silver of the age. There rapacious Scilla roars, as does Charybdis, greedy for gold even more than for the ships [which carry it]. There the galleys meet and there, there, the clashing of the pirates—there is the hinge of fate (the cardinal point). There are shallows in this sea and sirens threatening shipwreck for all mankind. The words of clear for all to see whereas in the hidden depths of his heart there lies an ugly demon. You have reason to believe that this is the passage for France, which you ought not to take lightly. There a two-fold sea rages, from which there is no one can res-cue for himself a coin of value. There the winds clash, there everything is swallowed up, there the world is buried, or rather the whole of it is swallowed down the throat of France. France pities no one, has regard for no gender, spares no blood. All bring gifts to her, the tribes, the tribes of the leader made their way there (to pay homage).]

The sequence of *ibi* clauses begins in the Straits of Messina but ends in the throat of France, and it must be for the reader to determine where it is that "the galleys meet" and "the clashing of the pirates" occur—but the presence there of the Sirens who, a few stanzas later, hail the *persona* for being "de Francia," [of France] would suggest that this "crossing place of the world" can be found in France, and that the "Canes Scille" [the dogs of Scylla] whose vices are described might also be "de Francia"—whether their corruption is executed in their homeland, or in the Curial circles of the Vatican.

The sustained critical failure to notice this poem's engagement with issues of national identity is, in itself, very revealing. Strecker read the references to "Franco" as referring to a fictional character, identified with the perils of Scylla and Charybdis and satirized within the text. In his summary of the poem he merely notes "Der Doppelstrudel ist Franco" [the double whirlpool is Franco],[38] and seems oblivious to the fact that the only characteristic of this fictional character that Walter chooses to share with his readers is his place of origin. We might note that "Franco's" identity is constituted merely from his being French. Eldredge follows Strecker and seems notably uncurious as to the reasons why Walter has introduced "an unidentified Franco" into the text.[39] Though Eldredge sees this introduction as "an abrupt change of imagery," he makes no effort to explain what constitutes this change and does not allow this supposed "change" any value in determining the meaning of the text.

In both cases it seems reasonable to assume that neither critic would have expected to find any questioning of the nature of "national" identity of the sort that Walter attempts in this lyric. It is a critical commonplace that the ideology of the nation-state, with fixed and determinable boundaries, is a concept developed in and after the Renaissance, and that medieval writers would have had no discourse of nationalism from which to draw. But the ideology of the nation-state developed, in response to deep-rooted assumptions of difference—difference of language, difference of culture, perceived "difference" of race—and it is absurd to imagine that medieval writers were less aware of difference, or less concerned by it, than their Renaissance successors. Rather, it is the absence of a clear and easily recognizable ideology of national identity which makes the subject such a deep source of questioning and anxiety for a writer like Walter. Though the Sirens declare Walter "de Francia" it is clear that that statement requires careful clarification—for what does it mean to be "de Francia" in the 1170s? Faced with the paucity of medieval dispositions on nationality, much recent research has sought to investigate medieval concepts of territorial boundaries and frontiers as a means of approaching the complex balancing of boundary and nationality implicitly synthesized in medieval understandings of what it meant to be the subject of a particular monarch. Ellenblum quotes from Isaac's work on Roman imperial concepts of frontiers to interpret medieval ideas of the frontier:

> "The limits of the empire," he wrote, if at all defined, were expressed in terms of power and military action. . .According to him, the fact that a certain Roman province was defended during a certain period of time by a wall is not proof of the existence of a borderline.[40]

From this, Ellenblum hypothesizes a model of "nationhood" in which:

> Medieval political communities, on the other hand, are more easily characterized by their centers or by their common association with a ruler than by their physical space.[41]

In a world in which territories had moved between the royal houses of England and France for reasons of inheritance, rather than conquest and re-conquest, it becomes clear that to be defined "de Francia" was not something which could easily be defined territorially, or relied on to remain constant over time. Abulafia has drawn attention to the differing and complex conceptions of kingship associated with monarchies like that of Henry II, which drew together distinct titles from diverse geographical and genealogical sources under the physical control of a single ruler:

> Though rulers in the years around 1200, like the governments of modern states, might see an advantage in controlling contiguous territories rather than a multitude of scattered slices of land, they also saw advantages in holding those lands in different ways to suit local exigencies: here as a king, there as another king's vassal, here creating an extensive royal demesne, there granting palatine rights to responsible feudatories. This was as true of the highly centralized Sicilian state as it was of Capetian France, in which royal power was much more obviously circumscribed.[42]

The exercise of bonds of "common association with a ruler," forging working relationships developed and judged in personal rather than national terms, made the exercise of loyalty a more personal, more contingent (and less predictable) act than it might have been in territorially defined monarchies—a situation implicitly proved by the presence at the

English court, in the service of the English royal household, of Peter of Blois and, perhaps, of Walter himself.

Finally, Walter was debarred from declaring a national identity on linguistic grounds at a time when the ruling class of England spoke Anglo-Norman, and their command of English was almost certainly sporadic and limited. In the development of the Francophone Angevin court, Walter witnessed the development of a phenomenon that must have seemed set fair to become a France beyond France, French in language and general culture, but finally English in its economic and territorial preoccupations. It was a rivalry embodied in the "transfer" of Eleanor of Aquitaine from the bedchamber of one French king to that of another. Perhaps it was this sense of being caught between two incomplete insufficient models of "Francia" that Walter sought to capture in the strange image of:

Habes iuxta rationem
bitalassum per Franconem
quod ne credas frivolum:
ibi duplex mare fervet,
a quo non est qui reservet
sibi valens obulum.
                    (6.1–6)

[You have reason to believe that this is the passage for France, which you ought not to take lightly. There a two-fold sea rages, from which there is no one can rescue for himself a coin of value.]

The competing claims of Angevin England and Capetian France together form one interpretation of the image of the "duplex mare," even as the competing claims of the classical past and corrupt present offer another.

But in a poem that constantly asserts that nothing is what it seems—from the "dulci cantu" [sweet singing] of the Sirens' song to the cardinal virtues of the higher clergy—Walter raises the issue of his national identity not as a matter of pride, or of regret. Rather it is a move in his strategy to escape the implied burdens of loyalty dependent on that conception of identity. In his evocation, through adaptation and allusion, of the writers of the past he suggests the possibility of constructing an alternative discourse of identity, an identity that is not "given" but worked for and deserved, as the inheritor of the skills (and words) of the great writers of the past. But his freedom to declare a "nationality of the learned" is limited by the inescapable fact of the unchosen nationality of his physical body: "de Francia." Walter uses the learned language in the composition of his lyrics to mark out his independence from the loyalties of kingdom and race, but in this poem he reminds us also of his recognition of the impossibility of any such attempt to deny the quality of "Frenchness" he had not chosen but which he cannot disavow. National identity figures in this lyric as an image of those physical realities which the intellect cannot change or deny, though it may seek to conceal them, and once again it is the device of verbal play that allows Walter do this. Niermeyer notes the two distinct meanings of "Francus"/"francus" in medieval texts—as representing a Frenchman and also a freeman "enfranchised, [a] dependent who is exempted from certain manorial obligations."[43] In Walter's figuration of identity, in so far as he is French—"Francus"—he is not a freeman— "francus"—that is, he is not free to invent or interpret himself within any tradition except that within which he was born.

In this way, Walter embodies in the text a discourse between those elements of human conduct that are chosen, and those that are "given" by accidents of birth. In "Propter Sion non Tacebo," Walter introduces a subtle but unsettling new term into the vehemence of his satire. As a self-declared scholar of Juvenal, Walter uses the discreet allusion to the discourse of nationality as a means of reorienting the ethics of his source, inflecting his imitation of a classical model with a distinctively Christian questioning of the nature of sin. Setting the "given" qualities of the poetic *persona* against those qualities he has pursued, or chosen, he invites the reader to utilize the same distinction in understanding the sins of the church hierarchy. Have these great men of the church chosen the path of sin, when their position of power has laid the chance open to them, or is corruption a "given" quality of fallen humanity, magnified in its operation by the wealth of opportunity their eminence has thrown open? To berate the sins of the corrupt is the vocation of the satirist, but even to begin the process of accounting for their corruption demands the skills of a more perceptive and original moralist.

But in giving this satirical lyric a historical and geographical particularity, Walter achieves an additional purpose, of the most unexpected kind. Walter's lyric unerringly, if (probably) unconsciously represents and gives a recognizable form to the uneasy cultural identity of the court of Henry II's court, synthesizing a poetic voice that, in claiming a rebellious kinship with the authority of classical texts, refuses to be identified solely with his native France, but which reveals an underlying anxiety about the meaning of, and the burden of, ideas of national identity. In its use of the language of doubleness and division—"duplex, bitalassum," Walter's lyric both captures and casts judgment on the cultural neuroses of his own time. With brutal prescience, "Propter Sion non Tacebo" uses the power of the text to construct a concrete physical expression of the psychical dilemma ever-present in Henrician court culture—not anchored in the dry land of a valorized national tradition but adrift on uncertain transnational waters, where the possibility remains that "surgunt venti, mare crescit," not comfortably

English, or British, but not French either, multilingual by choice and by perceived necessity, and driven to perpetuate (and distort) projections of the culture of the past as a means of justifying an otherwise-baffling present.

Notes

1. Walter of Châtillon, *The Alexandreis*, trans. R. Telfryn Pritchard, Mediaeval Sources in Translation 29 (Toronto: Pontifical Institute of Mediaeval Studies, 1986).

2. *The Letters of John of Salisbury, in Two Volumes, Vol. 2: The Later Letters*, ed. W. J. Millor and C. N. L. Brooke (Oxford: Clarendon Press 1979), pp. 76–79, 114–115, 192–7, 254–57; *The Correspondence of Thomas Becket*, ed. Anne J. Duggan, 2 vols. (Oxford: Clarendon Press, 2000). The reasons for Walter's dismissal are described in letters to Becket by Brother Nicholas of Mont-Rouen and an anonymous friend (letters 112 and 113, ed. Duggan, *Correspondence*, at 1:540–553). Duggan also suggests Master Walter de Insula as a possible author for letter 227 to Becket, a letter which she characterizes as "an extremely valuable eye-witness account, totally devoid of the rhetorical tricks which obscure unwelcome truths." Duggan, *Correspondence*, 1:lvi, 2:978–987.

3. Barthelemy Hauréau, "Notice sur un manuscript de la reine Christine a la Bibliotheue du Vatican," *Notices et extraits des manuscripts de la Bibliotheque Nationale et autres bibliotheques*, 29.2 (1858): 295–98; Marvin L. Colker, *Galteri De Castellione Alexandreis* (Padua: Antenore, 1978), xvii. The likelihood of Walter's having served Henry is also considered by Pritchard, *Alexandreis*, 2–3 and in J. R. Williams, "William of the White Hands and Men of Letters," in *Anniversary Essays in Medieval History by Students of Charles Homer Haskins*, ed. Charles Taylor (Boston: Houghton Mifflin, 1929), pp. 365–87.

4. *John of Salisbury, Later Letters*, Letter 168 (ed. Millor and Brooke, at pp. 108–9, 114–15). The letter is dated 1166. In letter 180 from later that same year, John comforts Walter for the loss (or resignation) of his post as keeper of the King's Seal, an estrangement from Henry which long pre-dates the murder of Becket (ed. Millor and Brooke, at pp. 192–97).

5. Perlectis vero litteris, nobis amotis, consilium inde rex se captutrum respondit. Tunc, uocato Walterio de Insula, et cum eodem habito consilio, reuocati sumus. . .[After the letters [from Becket] were read, with us removed from the room, the king declared that he would take counsel on the matter. Then, having summoned Walter de Insula and taken counsel with him, we were recalled. . .] (Duggan, *Correspondence*, 2:1302–09).

6. *Alexandreis*, 1:12–13 (ed. Colker, 7, trans. Pritchard, p. 36).

7. *Alexandreis*, 7:328–30 (ed. Colker, p. 187, trans Pritchard, p. 171). Both Colker and Pritchard reject the additional line (in two variants) in some manuscripts as being an early scribal addition: Flandria robertum thomam dolet anglia cesum / Flandria Robertum, caesum dolet Anglia thomam

imprimunt (ed. Colker, at p. 187). [Flanders grieves for Robert, and England for the murdered Thomas] (trans. Pritchard, at p. 178).

8. Scathing criticism of Henry's behavior is found in another satirical poem attributed to Walter; see Karl Strecker, *Die Lieder Walters von Châtillon in der handschrift 351 von St. Omer* (Berlin: Wiedmannsche Buchhandlung 1925), p. 27.

9. Latham proposes "approximately 1160" as the date of first usage; his source, though not cited, must therefore be presumed to be the letters by John of Salisbury; see R. E. Latham, *Revised Medieval Latin Word-list from British and Irish Sources* (London: Oxford University Press for the British Academy, 1965). The dating of Walter's lyrics has generally been assumed to be the 1160s or 1170s.

10. John of Salisbury, Epistola XXX, *Opera Omnia*, PL 199:20. This letter, together with a related letter (Epistola XXXI) are also reproduced and translated in Millor and Brooke, *Later Letters*, pp. 76–77. PL places both letters in the period 1156–58, while Millor and Brooke specify Mid-December 1157 as the probable date of composition.

11. Gillingham makes much of the political consequences of the fact that Henry's dominions in England and France made use of separate currencies; John Gillingham, *The Angevin Empire* (London: Arnold, 2001), pp. 116–117.

12. Eldredge believes that she "clearly represents avaritia" but he offers no explanation for the use of the figure of Thetis; see Laurence Eldredge, "Walter of Châtillon and the *Decretum* of Gratian: an Analysis of 'Propter Zion Non Tacebo'," *Studies in Medieval Culture* 3 (1970): 59–69, at 66.

13. *The Latin Poems commonly attributed to Walter Mapes*, collected and edited by Thomas Wright (London: Camden Society, 1846), p. 166.

14. Walter's texts, in their turn, were to act as models for imitation and borrowing by later writers. Walter's influence was geographically and stylistically wide-ranging—Schmidt details the imitation of Walter's lyric forms while Ashurst describes the adaptation of a scene from the *Alexandreis* (itself adapted from a scene in the *Aeneid*) in Icelandic Saga; see Paul Gerhard Schmidt, "The Quotation in Goliardic Poetry: the Feast of Fools and the Goliardic Strophe *cum auctoritate*," in Peter Godman and Oswyn Murray, *Latin Poetry and the Classical Tradition: Essays in Medieval and Renaissance Culture* (Oxford: Clarendon Press, 1990), pp. 39–55; David Ashurst, "The Transformation of Liebestod in Sagas Translated from Latin," *Saga-Book* 26 (2002): 67–96.

15. Walter's satirical poems were edited by Strecker; see Karl Strecker, *Moralisch-Satirische Gedichte Walters von Châtillon* (Heidelberg: Carl Winter 1929). Strecker's edition of "Propter Sion non Tacebo" (used throughout the present essay) makes use of eleven manuscript sources, including one from the *Carmina Burana* collection. The numbering of stanzas follows Strecker; the translation into English is my own.

16. Acts 27:41.

17. Peter Abelard, *Historia Calamitatum*, ed. Jacques Monfrin (Paris: Vrin, 1962).

18. *Alexandreis*, 3:379–80 (ed. Colker, p. 82).

19. *Alexandreis*, 375–78 (trans. Pritchard, p. 90).

20. Jill Mann, "Satiric Subject and Satiric Object in Goliardic Literature," *Mittellateinisches Jahrbuch* 15 (1980): 63–86, at 69.

21. Jean Jolivet, "Quelques cas de 'platonisme grammatical,' " in *Melanges offerts a Rene Crozet à l'occasion de son soixante-dixième anniversaire*, 2 vols., ed. Pierre Gallais and Yves-Jean Riou (Poitiers: Société d'Etudes Médiévales, 1966), 2:93–99.

22. Charlton T. Lewis and Charles Short, *A Latin Dictionary* (Oxford: Clarendon Press, 1958).

23. Jan Frederic Niermeyer, *Mediae latinitatis lexicon minis*: A Medieval Latin/French/English Dictionary (Leiden: Brill, 1976), p. 451.

24. John 1:1.

25. Juvenal, Satire 6: 464 (*Juvenal* and *Persius*, ed. and trans. G. G. Ramsay, Loeb Classical Library (Cambridge, Mass.: Harvard University Press, 1940 (repr. 1990), pp. 120–21).

26. Virgil, *Georgics* 2:261 (*Virgil, Eclogues, Georgics, Aeneid I–VI*, trans. H. Rushton Fairclough, rev. G. P. Goold, Loeb Classical Library (Cambridge, Mass.: Harvard University Press, 1999), pp. 134–35).

27. Ovid, *Fasti*, 1:662 (ed. and trans. Sir James George Frazer, revised G. P. Goold, Loeb Classical Library (Cambridge, Mass.: Harvard University Press, 1989), pp. 50–51).

28. Paul Gerhard Schmidt, "The Quotation in Goliardic Poetry," pp. 43–45.

29. Hans Spanke, "Zu den Gedichten Walters von Châtillon," *Volkstum und Kultur der Romanen: Sprache, Dichtung, Sitte* 4 (1931): 197–220, at 204.

30. E. R. Curtius, *European Literature and the Latin Middle Ages*, trans. Willard R. Trask (London: Routledge & Kegan Paul, 1979), pp. 94–980.

31. *Alexandreis*, 10:466–69 (ed. Colker, p. 231).

32. *Alexandreis*, 466–69 (trans. Pritchard, p. 231).

33. *Archipoeta, Die Gedichte des Archipoeta*, ed. Heinrich Watenpuhl (Heidelberg: Winter, 1958).

34. *Tractatus sive dialogus contra Iudaeos*, PL 209:421–58. The role of Walter's text as part of a wider twelfth-century intellectual engagement with the disputation of Judaism—a debate which absorbed, also, Peter Abelard, Peter the Venerable and Peter of Blois—is considered (briefly) by Berger; see David Berger, "Mission to the Jews and Jewish-Christian Contacts in the Polemical Literature of the High Middle Ages," *American Historical Review* 91:3 (1986): 576–91.

35. *The Oxford Book of Medieval Latin Verse*, ed. F. Raby (Oxford: Clarendon Press, 1959), pp. 176–7.

36. Eldredge, "Walter of Châtillon and the *Decretum*," in p. 60, 68, 69.

37. Eldredge, "Walter of Châtillon and the *Decretum*," in p. 60.

38. Strecker, *Moralisch-Satirische*, p. 17.

39. Eldredge, "Walter of Châtillon and the *Decretum*," p. 62.

40. Benjamin H. Isaac, *The Limits of Empire: The Roman Army in the East* (Oxford: Clarendon Press, 1990) quoted in Ronnie Ellenblum, "Were

there Borders and Borderlines in the Middle Ages? The Example of the Latin Kingdom Of Jerusalem," in *Medieval Frontiers: Concepts and Practices*, ed. David Abulafia and Nora Berend (Aldershot: Ashgate, 2002), pp. 105–119, at 106.

41. Ellenblum, "Borders and Borderlines," p. 108.
42. David Abulafia, Introduction: "Seven Types of Ambiguity, c. 1100-c. 1500," in Abulafia and Berend, *Medieval Frontiers*, pp. 1–34, at 1–2.
43. Niermeyer, *Mediae latinitatis lexicon*, p. 451.

CHAPTER 5

SEX, GHOSTS, AND DREAMS: WALTER MAP
(1135?–1210?) AND GERALD OF WALES
(1146–1223)

Tony Davenport

Christopher Brooke called Walter Map "a kind of thermometer of the
temperature of [his] age,"[1] and Gerald de Barri, too, has been seen as
one of the "pioneers of medieval historical writing,"[2] and as some kind of
mirror of his time:

> The entire corpus of his writings is perhaps the best literary measure we have
> of the scope of the century's learning and interests.[3]

It is understandable that these two highly educated men with parallel
careers in church and court, both of whom provide vivid physical descriptions of Henry II, should be looked to for a picture of court and society and
a sense of what the period stood for. They were both educated at the
University of Paris and may, before that, have attended the same school
(St. Peter's Abbey, Gloucester), and were thus trained in rhetoric, theology, and the liberal and scientific arts of the time; both became professional
churchmen, and, though neither rose higher than archdeacon, both were,
at various times, in the running for promotion to bishop—both were plu-
ralists and had secure, well-to-do lives at least until their later years; both
were court servants for part of their lives, closely, if intermittently, involved
with the affairs of Henry II's court in the last twenty years of his reign;
both were writers, with a strong critical streak, of the failings and follies of
the great, of women, of religious orders—the Cistercians in particular.

They are often referred to as friends, but they need not have been so: they were far enough apart in age to have missed each other until perhaps the mid-1180s, when Walter would have been about fifty and Gerald in his late-thirties. Keith Bate in a closely argued essay pointed out that Walter never mentions Gerald and that, although Gerald refers to Walter a dozen times, some of these allusions are essentially quotations where Gerald is plagiarizing Walter for jibes against the Cistercians, while others are quoted compliments (sometimes a little ambiguous) on Gerald's writings; even Gerald's naming of Walter as a possible candidate for the see of St. David's after he himself had been denied the office for the second time in 1203 is debatable as evidence of close personal friendship. The only direct expressions of acquaintance between the two are the texts referring to the gift of a staff or walking stick, the head a natural piece of wood but with a carved foot, sent as a gift to Walter by Gerald accompanied by complimentary verses; Gerald records both his own series of twelve Latin elegiac couplets, from which Walter was to choose the one he admired the most, and Walter's reply, supposedly a compliment to Gerald, but arguably, as Bate suggests, such a fulsome expression of friendship, laying on praise, esteem, and *amicitia* with a trowel, that it could be read as a parody of friendship poetry. Map was no lover of pretentiousness and this praise of Gerald, which Gerald quotes, in his "incomparable vanity," as Bate puts it, can be read as undermining while apparently praising.[4] Certainly the contrast between Gerald's endless facility for rhetorical amplification and Walter's barbed wit is one that strikes the reader elsewhere, and is recognizable as the base of Gerald's own report of Map's comparison of the two as writers:

> Multa, magister Giralde, scripsistis, et multum adhuc scribitis; et nos multa diximus. vos scripta dedistis, et nos verba.

> [You have written many things, master Gerald, and still do; I have spoken much. You produced writings, I produced words.][5]

And though Walter is (as one can tell from what follows) speaking of his own ephemeral efforts in conversation, and in English, as opposed to Gerald's composed written Latin, there is a wider appropriateness in the comment. In their different ways they both claim to be recording contemporary events: Walter says of *De Nugis Curialium* that he has "jotted [it] down by snatches at the court of King Henry," and Gerald, in the second and third books of *De Principis Instructione*, gives an account of the main events of Henry's reign. Yet one does not have to read far into the writings of Walter Map and Gerald de Barri before questions arise, not only as to how far they are reliable as historians, but as to whether they should be considered as historians at all. Antonia Gransden treats them as satirists and journalists who were historians only incidentally,[6] while Map's modern editors offer a less-solemn version of the idea of his representativeness:

> The *De Nugis* is not only very entertaining; it is a rough inventory of the mental furniture of a learned and witty 12th-century clerk, a marvellous guide to a fascinating lumber-room.[7]

My title is obviously designed to draw attention to the extraordinary content of the work of these supposed reflectors of their time. Here are two twelfth-century ecclesiastics, writing in Latin for an educated church and court audience, recording all sorts of the stuff of dream-books, hearsay, and old wives' tales, erotic, violent, supernatural, and fantastic. Gerald's writings on Ireland and Wales and Walter's first, second, and fourth sections are full of the material of folklore, tales of magic, apparitions, and marvels. Gerald tells of poltergeists in Wales, throwing refuse, ripping up people's clothes, arguing with the house-dwellers; he tells curious tales such as that of Simon, the helpful red-haired devil, an always punctual servant who encourages everyone to enjoy themselves, who loses his job merely because someone sees him at night conversing with a few fellow-demons, and another story of the discreet, hard-working archbishop's assistant who absentmindedly reveals that he once escaped from Jesus' presence (this was during Christ's life on earth, you understand, when devils' working conditions were more than usually hazardous) by jumping down a well—realizing what he has said, he blushes for shame and disappears. Among his many scrappy and indiscriminate tales of miracles and divine punishments, Gerald inserts some longer folk tales, such as the story of Elidyr's visits, when he was a twelve-year-old boy, to the under-ground realm of the "little people" at whose court he was taught to love truth and to live on milk until he tried to bring back to the upper world a golden ball as a present to his mother, after which he could never find the way back to the lost world. Gerald's stories of demon lovers and tormen-tors even include joking on the subject as when he tells us that the Welsh soothsayer Meilyr, when unduly bothered by devils, placed St. John's Gospel on his lap, and then they all flew away like birds, but when Geoffrey of Monmouth's *History of the Kings of Britain* is put in his lap instead, "The demons would alight all over his body, and on the book too, staying there longer than usual and being even more demanding."[8]

Walter's tales tend to be more sinister ones of phantom knights, night-time companies of dancing ladies, a respectable-looking female ghost who is a child-murderer. He tells the story of the ancient British king Herla to illustrate the restlessness of Henry II's court, which he compares to Hell: Herla's pact with the pygmy king traps him in the wild hunt which will go on for eternity; the hunters are later referred to again as the Herlethinga, night-wanderers, the troop of the dead (an image taken up by both David Jones and Tolkien in modern times).[9] Walter tells several fairy-mistress stories, some Welsh legends, the myth of Nicholas Pipe, the Man of the Sea, several tales associated with the Crusades, and a wonderfully Gothic version of the story of the Gorgon's head which Edgar Allan Poe would have been proud of: this is the story of the haunted shoemaker of Constantinople that Walter tells in Distinction 4, chapter 12. A young man whose brilliant craftsmanship attracts a beautiful maiden to order a pair of his shoes becomes obsessed with the girl, sells his trade to become a soldier of fortune, becomes powerful and piratical, still determined to possess the maiden to the extent that, when he hears that she has died, he breaks into her tomb and has intercourse with her; from this act of evil horrors grow— after due time the corpse gives birth to the Gorgon head, which becomes the agent of violence, death, and pestilence, until eventually cast into the sea to become the whirlpool of Satalia. The story is an ancient one and appears in various forms in medieval writing—in Mandeville's *Travels*, for instance—but Walter's version is the darkest and he tells it with a particularly chilling verve.[10]

How then does one account for the sensational quality of these supposed measuring-rods for the culture of their time? One possibility is to explain their cast of mind as the product of their shared education at the University of Paris, which one must suppose to have inculcated the habit of reading classical and other texts as the providers of illustrative instances and striking figurations. Robert Levine suggests that we should read *De Nugis* as a rhetorical textbook, with the "grotesque fantasies of impotence, castration, necrophilia and decapitation" deliberately fabricated to hold the attention of adolescent students.[11] It may certainly be read as an exemplum-book, or, in Geoffrey Shepherd's phrase, "a book about stories and their status."[12] Literary sources are augmented from oral narratives— and in Gerald too one is always meeting examples quoted, attributed to people (usually important ones) that he had met; the writing of both is full of names, of authorities, sources, contemporary figures in power, examples from the ancients, and so on. In Walter's case the miscellaneous and unedited nature of the text contributes to its picturesqueness: it is a mixture of satire and commonplace book, where lengthy literary narratives sit cheek-by-jowl with gossip. Perhaps only the antifeminist tract, the *Dissuasio Valerii* (now part of the fourth section of *De Nugis*), which was evidently written before the rest, was circulated in Map's lifetime; the work was begun in the early 1180s but its arrangement in the only manuscript is some sort of shuffling of separate passages written at various times (some as late as two years after Henry II's death). Walter insists in his several *Tristram*

Shandy-ish prologues that his writing is not to be taken seriously:

> I do not touch upon suits of the lawcourts or upon grave pleas: it is the
> theatre and the arena that I haunt. . .You bid me record examples for
> posterity, such as may serve either to excite merriment or edify morals.
> Though it is beyond my powers to obey. . .it is not hard to gather or write
> something which may turn to profit.[13]

It is in the epilogue he wrote in 1191 (which confusingly appears at the
beginning of Distinction 4) that he says:

> This little book I have jotted down by snatches at the court of King
> Henry. . .now after hearing of the death of the king. . .[and] after two years
> of memorial services [I] realise for the first time the inestimable gain of being
> freed from the court. . .Therefore I can approach the task I used to fear in
> confidence and unarmed.[14]

From these passages we may conclude that such direct recordings of
experience as occur in *De Nugis* are, as it were, accidental.

The range of Gerald's writings gives a more sequential picture of
interests developing and changing with his career and the shifting areas of
his social experience. His first works, written in his early forties, relate to
his family background, his travels, and the apparently marginal situation in
which he found himself.[15] Although he was born in Wales and had a Welsh
grandmother, it is debatable whether it is appropriate to think of him as
Welsh. He did not speak, read, or understand Welsh when he accompanied
Archbishop Baldwin on his tour of Wales (recruiting for the Third
Crusade) in 1188—they preached in Latin and French—but Gerald claims
that the common people wept in untold numbers nevertheless.[16] The most
Gerald does is to explain the meaning of a few Welsh words and
place-names. His father, William de Barri, was a Norman knight; his mother
was the daughter of another Norman, Gerald of Windsor, Constable of
Pembroke. Gerald's Welshness depends on his grandmother, Nest, daughter of Rhys ap Tewdwr, mistress of Henry I and married twice: hence the
mother of a Fitzhenry, as well as at least four Fitzgeralds, and a Fitzstephen
from her later marriage to Stephen, Constable of Cardigan. Gerald took on
Welshness as part of the patriotic rhetoric of his case to succeed his uncle,
David Fitzgerald, Bishop of St. David's 1148–76; in this he failed twice,
first in 1176 when his uncle died, and more lengthily in 1199–1203,
when his election was vetoed, after a long campaign by Gerald, by Pope
Innocent III and King John. He became identified with the ambition not
only to become bishop but to do so without acknowledging the supremacy

of Canterbury and with the hope that he might become Archbishop of Wales; this was a major reason for his failing to achieve the appointment, and in 1199–1203 he was accused of fomenting Welsh rebellion and declared an enemy of the realm. In his autobiography he represents his nomination to the see in 1199 as the apex of his career, but it is arguable that, as Bartlett says, "his patriotism was a rhetorical and polemical stance."[17] Gerald's identification with the Welsh more or less petered out after 1203 and in his later writings he speaks of them with disillusion, just as he had in the *Description of Wales* in the early 1190s. Even in the *Invectiones* (a polemical work of self-justification which he began to write about 1200) a dream of his rise to episcopacy is tempered by contempt: he sees himself in the dream being led past twenty bishops' thrones (all occupied) representing the sees of England, "wherein at this time he placed all his hope" and also those of Wales "which, at that time, he completely rejected from consideration because of the poverty of the land and the wickedness of the people."[18] In the vision, however, only St. David's is offered to him, and this appears as a disappointment rather than a triumph. When in 1215 he was again offered the see of St. David, he rejected it.

Gerald identified himself more often with the culture of France and of his Norman father and grandfather and his Norman uncle who had settled in Ireland. This explains the curious stance of his writings on Ireland in which his sympathies are neither with the Irish nor with Angevin ambitions to rule Ireland but with the Anglo-Norman conquerors and settlers. Reading the *Topographia Hibernica* reminds one of the experience of being guided round the historical monuments of Sicily by a tour-leader from Milan, whose interest in the Roman and Norman past goes along with scorn, despite his sharing a nationality, religion, and language, for the present-day people of Sicily, whose idleness, criminality, and filth seems to him signs of virtual barbarity. And so with Gerald whose description of Ireland is often classed as his best work, because of its recording of natural history, geography, and local traditions, and yet whose view of the feckless people indulging in incest or having sex with goats and other livestock is understandably deeply offensive to the Irish.

Gerald himself was very pleased with his *History and Topography of Ireland*[19] and describes, in *De Rebus a se Gestis*,[20] the "magnificent and costly achievement" of his presentation of the work "before a great audience at Oxford," in which he read the three parts on three consecutive days: first day, on the geography and natural history, to the poor of the town; second day, on the marvels and miracles of Ireland, to the doctors of diverse faculties; third day, on the inhabitants of the country, to more scholars and to knights and citizens. Archbishop Baldwin read it too and, so Gerald tells us, liked it so much that he never tired of reading it—to

Baldwin's praise of the elegance of Gerald's style (Gerald had not only learned the arts of rhetoric in Paris but taught the subject too) we may owe the several revisions, whereby Gerald kept on expanding the text with more and more passages of moralization, allegorical interpretation, quotation, wordplay, and legend, so that the final version is more than twice as long as the first.

The success of the *Topography* was obviously its novelty: an interest in the natural history and in the myths of a little-known country. If Gerald had a model it was presumably Tacitus's *Germania*, but to modern eyes it falls between stools: it is, in a sense, the beginning of ethnography (and interestingly the current standard students' introduction to ethnography features a paragraph from Gerald, thus identifying him in some sense as a founding father of the subject); the problem is not just the bestiary lore and the acceptance of fantastic folklore, however unlikely, but the treatment of the inhabitants. A modern assessment of the work sees it as of little value, because it presents

a written landscape that is inhabited by a bizarre menagerie of outlandish monstrosities and vitiated by inflections of scorn, disdain and slander.[21]

The claims that such creatures as a prophetic werewolf and fish with golden dentures exist alongside kingfishers and badgers and that the Irish were lustful and perverted barbarians do tend to undermine the degree of credence that one gives to the whole. Rollo argues that the work reflects Gerald's years of education at the University of Paris, in the decade in which Alain de Lille composed *De Planctu Naturae*, and his absorption of contemporary neo-Platonist teaching: Alain's work is a satire on vices of language and depravities of sex and Gerald can be thought to have appropriated Alain's patterns of thought as part of a prejudicial account of a colonized territory. The characterization of the people as sexually immoral, immoderate, and perverted is part of a familiar rhetoric of classifying peoples as barbarian in order to justify conquest and occupation. The fact that Gerald himself had an ambiguous attitude towards Angevin expansionism produces some contradictions and cross-currents, but his intentions in writing the work were clearly a good deal less simple than to provide a twelfth-century travel-book or journal of natural history.

Similarly with the *Journey through Wales* and *The Description of Wales*: the first is controlled by the recording of the stages of the actual journey, but there is more room in the second work for comments on the Welsh, and if they are credited with looking after their teeth, with musical skill in part-singing and a witty way with words, they are also the target of some less-than-patriotic comments such as:

The fact that the Welsh have now given up homosexuality, which they were unable to resist in their more prosperous days, must be attributed not to any

improvement in their morals, but to their indigence now that they are exiled
and expelled from the kingdom of Britain. How can they say that they have
done penance and more than paid the penalty, when we see them still sunk
in sin and in a deep abyss of every vice—perjury, theft, robbery, rapine,
murder, fratricide, adultery, incest, and obstinately ensnared and entangled
in wrongdoing, which grows worse as day follows day?[22]

His sequel to the *Topography*, which Gerald claims was written at the
behest of Henry II but which was dedicated to his son, Richard, the
Expugnatio Hibernica (or *Conquest of Ireland*), is a combination of family saga,
as Gerald recounts the exploits of his kinsfolk in the Norman occupation of
Ireland, and contemporary history. It is here that his most-often-quoted
passages of dream occur and that his vivid description of Henry II is found.
Gerald begins his portrait with physical description (Henry's reddish, freck-
led complexion, powerful torso, restless energy, and so on, his pliant wit in
conversation and his other likeable ways), but he gradually becomes more
critical, exposing Henry's adulteries and his neglect of religion. In Gerald's
writings about Henry we are faced with a flat contradiction between the
tone of adulation towards the king that Gerald adopted when dedicating
the *Topography* to him as "our western Alexander":

Truly you are king and conqueror, ruling your courage by your virtue, and
conquering your anger with your temperance.

and his readiness, at the end of his reign, to express a hostile view. In his
account of events leading to the king's death, Gerald embellishes the
circumstances with the heavy trappings of references to the death of Becket,
foreboding, and prophecy. He tells us that he was at the Castle of Chinon
during the period of strife between Henry and his sons and how on the
10th of May he had a dream of a great crowd of men staring heavenward,
as a bright light parts the clouds to reveal the court of heaven: the court is
being attacked from all sides with hideous violence—heads and arms being
lopped off by swords, men pierced by arrows, and the bloodstained
murderers eventually attacking Christ himself, "seated in majesty among
his people, just as he is shown in paintings"; they drag him from the throne
and pierce his side with a spear; a terrifying voice cries, "Woch, Woch,
Pater et Filius, Woch, Woch, *Spiritus Sanctus!*," and in terror he awakes.[23]
Gerald interprets the dream at some length, concluding that the mournful
complaint, beginning in German and ending in Latin, can be understood as
meaning that the nations which speak in the Germanic and Latin tongues
are the ones troubled by wrongs done to their savior.

This oblique reference to the Third Crusade has become explicit
criticism of Henry's failure to support it when Gerald reuses the material

(as he was always doing—transferring whole chapters of works from one place to another) in *De Principis Instructione*.[24] He began to write this as a conventional (and completely derivative) "Mirror of Princes," with one or two comments on contemporary affairs, at the same time as he was writing the *Journey through Wales* (1191), but the second and third books (written in John's reign) are an account of the reign of Henry (book 2 up to 1185, book 3 the last few years) composed as a pattern of pride and fall and dominated by the image of fortune's wheel. Here the references to Becket are more judgmental and the dream is interpreted as prophesying the failure of the Crusade. Other dreams are added: he sees the body of the king carried into a church where a flock of crows and jackdaws extinguish all the lights; he reports a vision of Baldwin in which the corpse of the king, lying on a bier in a church, suddenly raises itself and says "a church is no place for me—carry me out," and when the Archbishop approaches the altar to celebrate mass he finds it desecrated with human excrement.

And so the classical language of visionary omens and portents and the implication of divine judgement become part of the rhetoric of Gerald's revised treatment of Angevin power. Elsewhere in the work Gerald presents the view of Henry's stock as tainted. He is one of the contemporary authors who give us the ideas of the descent of the Angevins from a "demon countess"—that myth of the "Devil's brood:" according to this model of twelfth-century history, Henry's father and mother were guilty of sexual crimes and the blood had been further tainted by Eleanor of Aquitaine, herself descended from an immoral union and having had sexual relations with Henry's father while still married to Louis, and then having left him for Henry:

> Since the root was completely corrupt, how can fruitful or virtuous offspring come from it?[25]

Gerald uses similar language of family stock, blood, and descent in his account of his quarrel with his own nephew, which is the subject-matter of *Speculum Duorum (A Mirror of Two Men)*,[26] when he explains his nephew's perverse behavior—as he saw it—in terms of his mother's family, the Baskervilles [*Bascrevillana natura perversa*].

In contrast to the Angevin inheritance Gerald sees the "natural princes" of France, portrayed as sexually virtuous, avoiding blasphemy, ruling in mild simplicity with little unnecessary court ceremony, dealing out justice promptly and impartially:

> They always acquire the royal patrimony through hereditary succession and natural right. They zealously preserve moderation, modesty, and mercy

towards their subjects and avoid any atrocity or cruelty in the rule. As a
result, their reigns are long, prosperous, and tranquil, by command of
God. . .they die a blessed death and receive eternal reward in heaven for
such just and pious rule, leaving their realm happily to their sons and heirs.[27]

Here again modern understanding of the period is unlikely to see Gerald's
version of things as a mirror of history, but Gerald's exaggerated images
leave their mark: here, as elsewhere, he is more interesting as a creator of
pictures than as a recorder of fact.

As remarked earlier in this chapter, it is not easy to see the historical
current of Walter Map's writing in the same way, though one can identify
a similar mixture of autobiography, contemporary history, anecdote, and
literary example in *De Nugis*. Walter also describes Henry, in some of the
last-written pages of the book, and it has been suggested that he imitates
Gerald in *De principis* in doing so. There are some significant differences
though, particularly in references to Henry's illegitimate son, Geoffrey,
who became Archbishop of York: Gerald wrote a fairly sympathetic (not
to say in places sycophantic) life of this man in 1194,[28] but he is the butt of
Walter's wit;[29] Walter clearly thought him a pretentious fool and he not
only names his mother ("a common whore named Hikenai") but even
questions whether Henry was actually the father. The anecdotal, malicious
quality of Walter's writing has a good deal more individuality than Gerald's
well-polished smoothness of expression, and Walter's portrait of Henry is
better balanced. Often inaccurate about facts, Walter is more interested in
intellectual play. Even the collection of exempla strung together in the
antifeminist *Dissuasio Valerii* are treated with some wit, sometimes erudite
and pedantic, as with this grammatical quibble:

> Metellus made answer to Marius (whose well-dowered, beautiful daughter . . .
> he refused to marry): "I would rather be mine than hers." Quoth Marius:
> "Nay, but she will be yours." "Nay," said he, "the husband is bound to be the
> wife's; it is a maxim of logic—'Predicates will be what their subjects allow.' "[30]

Map was interested in sex but Gerald was troubled by it. He shares with
Walter his antifeminist outlook, but Gerald's expression of it might seem
obsessive. In his saints' lives, for instance, comparison with his sources shows
that Gerald significantly expanded antifeminist material, as Robert Bartlett
has pointed out.[31] So, for example, in the *Life of St. Ethelbert* (1195), based
on a mid-twelfth-century Latin *Life* by Osbert of Clare, the description of
Ethelbert's reaction to pressure to marry goes as follows in the source:

> although virgin innocence pleased him more than married chastity or the
> union of wedlock, he nevertheless bent a favorable ear to his magnates' wish.[32]

In Gerald's version this becomes:

> he had read of the absurdities of foolish women, the loathing of the ugly, the haughtiness and pride of beautiful and well-born women, adultery, uncertainty about offspring. . .anger, quarrels, deep jealousies and suspicions . . . As their pressure upon him grew and grew and they gave him no respite. . .he eventually decided to yield to their wishes.[33]

This sounds rather as if personal preoccupation is taking the writer into over-insistence, and it is no surprise that when Gerald deals with examples of sexual misconduct in *Gemma Ecclesiastica* his choice of stories can be unsettling.

Gerald defines the purpose of *Gemma Ecclesiastica* as that of compiling "from the disparate ideas of others something like a compendium";[34] there are over five hundred Biblical allusions and examples, many verbatim passages from a variety of sources, including Gratian's *Decretals* and the writings of Peter Lombard and Peter the Cantor, as well as references to Ambrose, Augustine, Bede, Isidore, Bernard, Gregory, and Jerome on the one hand, Virgil, Ovid, Horace, Lucan, Cicero, Seneca, and Terence on the other, which may be signs of Gerald's scholarship, but equally could be from a florilegium, the kind of source that Gerald can be shown to have made use of in some of his works.[35] The whole thing is a fine example of Gerald's skilful writing by mosaic. Intended for the clergy, it is a work in two parts. Distinction 1 deals with canon law (mainly the sacraments including such fascinating details as what the priest should do if consecrated wine gets spilt and what penance he must observe if he is neglectful enough to let the communion wafers be eaten by a mouse); chapters 18–27 are made up of stories concerned with diabolical possession, magic, and exorcism among which one of the most interesting is the story of the father Poterius, whose hope of dedicating his virgin daughter to the service of God is frustrated by his servant whose desire for the girl leads him to sign a pact with the devil; the result is that "the tortuous serpent, the corrupter of souls" inflames the girl with love for the young man. Though the young pair have to suffer later before the Faustian compact can be undone, the father is defeated, the "iniquitous marriage" is made, and the "diabolical villainy completed" (which is as much as to say the girl is no longer a virgin and in a different kind of work might be said to have achieved the beginning of a happy ending, since the marriage survives and the young couple find a way for the husband to return to the Christian fold).

Distinction 2 consists of exhortations to holy living and illustration of offences against moral law; there are many exempla, often with an antifeminist streak and many on the themes of continence and sexual temptation.

Gerald's selection of stories here seems to me revealing. So, in chapter 14
we are told of "a strange apparition and an unheard-of defilement": the
story is of a young monk who, as he lies prostrate in prayer, is approached
by an evil spirit, which

> places its hand on his genital organs, and does not stop rubbing his body with
> its own until he is so agitated that he is polluted by an emission of semen.

The story is quoted from Hildebert, later Archbishop of Tours, who
disputes whether the monk can accurately be described as a virgin, since
emission of semen has occurred, and considers the case dubious, concluding "I do not know how the temptation can go this far unless he wants it
to": Gerald hedges his bets in commenting on the tale. In chapter 11
Gerald tells a story (the source of which is not known) of a nun burning
with lascivious thoughts for a handsome cleric: he appears to her in a dream
desiring intercourse; she manages to resist and, applying her reason to the
scene perceives the young man not as desirable but as unnaturally huge and
threatening; terrified she leaps from bed, seizes a scythe and chops him
in half; all her lustful thoughts are cured by the stench that rises from
the body.

More developed narratives are found that afford some interesting
comparisons with contemporary romance and with Map's tales. In chapter
13 is a story (credited to Archbishop Baldwin and not told elsewhere) of a
cleric amorously approached by a beautiful woman at noon in an orchard;
she apparently "proves" that she is not a demon by receiving communion,
but the young priest is still hesitant when, again in the orchard, her sexual
desire for him is being given its head. He calls to his dog, called Galiena,
and to avoid lovemaking plays with the dog. The woman is furious and,
swearing that Galiena will avenge her, disappears. Later the clerk falls for a
girl whom he sees with her mother at the ferry near his father's house; he
sickens with love for her, but is rejected; he becomes a monk but is still
tormented and even prayers said throughout the order (Cistercian, of course)
are without effect and he dies. The hard-hearted girl is, as you would have
guessed, called Galiena. Though Gerald tries to wrest a moral from the tale
to make it appear a divine test, he does not really succeed in taking it
beyond the idea that "there are many things in this tale to be wondered at,"
though we may find in the intriguing echoes of Marie de France's "Lanval"
more to ponder.

Most interesting of these tales, not least because we recognize a variation
on the plot that became Chaucer's Franklin's Tale, is the story (told in
chapter 12) of a distinguished soldier, Reginald de Giens, who loves the
wife of a fellow-soldier but is rebuffed; after a tournament the husband and

his friends all agree that Reginald is a champion unequalled in performance. "Is this soldier.. so very good?" asks the wife and when her husband
praises Reginald she is "conquered by evil desire" and sends a message to
which Reginald responds immediately; as they go to bed and "are enjoying each other's desired embraces before intercourse" he asks her why she
has changed her mind about him and when she tells him that it is because
of her husband's praise, Reginald replies:

> Then I too will change my mind. . .I will never illicitly love my beloved to
> the extent of injuring her husband who spoke those praises, and for his sake
> I will abstain forever from these embraces I have so greatly desired.

And Gerald concludes by calling it "a laudable example of continence."

In this case we can make a direct comparison with Walter Map's
storytelling because he includes the same story in Distinction 3 of *De Nugis*
(and, though the names are different, Map is presumably a possible source
for Gerald). In Map's version the would-be lover is Resus, a handsome,
noble youth, who when repulsed by the wife of the chivalrous hero, Rollo,
determines to make himself more worthy of love by seeking deeds of arms
and adventure. He is so successful that Rollo knights him and he becomes
so filled with the spirit of chivalry that his continuing love appears as
weakness, and Map describes him as:

> effeminated, nay, rather infeminated by himself, since it passed into the
> weakness of a woman: womanlike pursuing its wishes without thought, a
> lamb within and a lion without; and the overthrower of castles abroad,
> unmanned by his inward cares, grew soft, wept, prayed and mourned.[36]

However, Rollo thinks well of the young man and, meeting him when
with his wife, praises him as "the noble wonder of our time." As in
Gerald's version the wife is so impressed by this that she changes her mind
about Resus and makes a secret assignation, where he too is able to restrain
himself when he learns of Rollo's praise, though the terms of his self-denial
are rather different:

> Never shall Rollo be requited by Resus with wrong for his goodness: it
> would be discourteous [*inurbanum*] to stain that couch.[37]

So, says Walter, "contrary to what Ovid would have us believe," the lady
was returned to her husband unsullied by a young and ardent man: "he
who controls his flesh escapes wrath." The tale is thus as much an
exemplum for Walter as for Gerald, but the more courtly emphasis and the

greater degree of intellectual analysis of the feelings mark Map's far greater literary subtlety. Even from this story, with its reference to Ovid and its obvious awareness of contemporary interest in debating degrees of honor and love, we might challenge the statement (made by the editors of *De Nugis*) that "The ideals of courtly love were foreign to him."[38] Even more is this the case in the story of Sadius and Galo, Map's longest and most complex narrative.

The central thread of this story is the theme of friendship between men versus a woman's lust and vengeful frustration. Sadius, nephew of the king of Asia, has a friend and companion at court, Galo, who is the object of the queen of Asia's passionate, frenzied, and prolonged love: he resists her pursuit of him with steadfast modesty and chastity— "against the beauty and delights of the queen and the warfare of his own flesh"; Sadius diverts the queen's attention by pretending that Galo is impotent. The second phase of the story is initiated by the queen's sending one of her attendant women, Ero, to test this. Walter's treatment of this episode is remarkable: we remain with the queen as her jealousy and lustful imagination grow, rather than experience directly the scene between Galo and Ero. It is developed as a scene in three parts: (1) the queen's soliloquy, as she releases a stream of frustration at Galo's refusal of her, and then allows her mind to dwell on a prurient, vicarious imagining of what will happen between Galo and Ero, as her doubts about his impotence fester into frenzy; (2) then she questions another of her women, Lais, about Ero's departure, what time she left, how she was dressed, etc.; (3) with the return of Ero, her jealousy boils over and she attacks the girl. All this turns the story into a compelling drama, much of it in direct speech, implying an audience interested in the moment-by-moment shifts of feeling and the acting out of quixotic love-madness; it is a powerful portrait of "cruel anger, the pitiless revenge of women. . .the violence of love," as the queen is driven into hatred and the desire to humiliate Galo.

The banquet scene which follows develops a tale within the tale, as Galo is forced to tell of his encounter, when weak after illness, with a silent maiden, whom he attempts to rape until prevented by a giant who easily overcomes him. He is saved from death by the intervention of a second maiden and by the giant's own chivalry; the day of their postponed combat has now arrived. The vengeful queen never ceases to press until Galo's full shame is exposed: he is forced to confess his fear of the giant and his determination to avoid the fight—he rushes from the table leaving the queen to proclaim his cowardice. Again the dramatic structure is striking.

The climax is the duel, in which Galo fights disguised as Sadius; the scene is full of descriptive detail in the blow-by-blow account of the phases of the fight, the reactions of the onlookers, and the queen's spiteful comments, supposedly made to Galo but in reality to the disguised Sadius. In the fighting Galo repeatedly behaves with the utmost chivalry, refusing to take advantage when the giant's sword snaps and again when the giant stumbles: "Honor must be gained by valor not by luck"; the giant's second sword is invincible but Galo, covered in blood, fights with the utmost concentration, biding his time until the giant has a moment of carelessness and Galo chops off his hand. When, after the fight, the young men resume their own identities, the queen is stupefied, "as if she beheld a Gorgon" and "like a snake at evening [she is]. . .left only with the will to hurt."[39]

The story is full of fascination and of suggestive echoes of other narratives: of Ovid, for a start, in the queen's erotic imaginings which resemble those of Tarquin in the *Fasti* as he recalls the exact details of the appearance of Lucretia. There are reminders too of Latin drama: a specific allusion to Terence's *Adelphi*, and his *Eunuch* uses the pretended impotence idea; less specifically there are similarities to contemporary Latin *comedia*[40] which shares some of the themes (impotence, humiliation, disguise, frustration of malice), as well as an element of slapstick (as when Galo falls flat on his face through weakness and is thrown into a tree by the giant, and when the second maiden is kicked in the teeth by the first). In another direction there are resemblances to the treatment of love in the lays of Marie de France and in the Arthurian romances of Chrétien, with more specific similarity to Chrétien's *Yvain* in the banquet scene and to *Perceval* in the double plot. The interest in the subtleties of inner debate and the scenes of emotional see-sawing have qualities in common with the contemporary tellings of the story of Tristan and Yseult by Thomas, Béroul, and Gottfried. Whether or not this tale should be read as a comment on Henry's court, with the figure of the queen as a caricature of Queen Eleanor, or as a parody of romance situations and expressions of feeling,[41] Map is surely in some way reflecting French courtly taste and sophistication through Latin rhetoric. Apart from Walter's Parisian education and cultural contacts, it is known that he had personal acquaintance with court circles in France: when in 1178, Walter set off for the Third Lateran Council to be held in the following year he went via the court of Champagne, and on his return visited the court of King Louis in Paris. Direct knowledge of Chrétien's poetry is an obvious possibility.

This story confirms the sense, which I hope I have communicated already, that, if Walter and Gerald are the mirrors or the thermometers of their age, then the reflections and the temperature are not steady ones. The elements of the grotesque, sensational, and fantastic in their writings can be related to the cross-currents in their nationality and education, to twelfth-century taste for legends and marvels, to their combining in their writing as well as in their lives the, at times contradictory, roles of civil

148 TONY DAVENPORT

servant and churchman, and their consequently mixed literary purposes. What they really record about the culture of their age are some of the ways in which fiction interrelated with the personal lives of two educated and, in their different ways, detached courtier-writers. The result is an intriguing combination of sophistication and uncertainty: both capable of assertive expression of their own wit and self-confidence, they nevertheless betray their various instabilities of personality and position. It is as well to be reminded—particularly for those of us who look at the period mainly through writings in English—that between the last entries in the Peterborough Chronicle and Laȝamon's *Brut* lie the products of a rhetorical book-culture that draws on classical Latin authors to provide the language in which educated court-men can treat contemporary history, society, and morality, and the themes of fashionable French court literature. But, like old mirrors, that language has become blurred and pockmarked, leaving it by no means easy to read.

Notes

1. Christopher Brooke, *The Twelfth-Century Renaissance* (London: Thames & Hudson, 1969), p. 172.
2. H. E. Butler, Introduction to *The Autobiography of Giraldus Cambrensis* (London: Cape, 1937), p. 10; this is a translation mainly of passages from *De Rebus a se Gestis* (written post 1208) and *De Iure et Statu Menevensis Ecclesie* (written ca. 1218) with interpolated extracts from other works.
3. *The Jewel of the Church: Gerald of Wales; a translation of* Gemma Ecclesiastica *by Giraldus Cambrensis*, trans. John J. Hagen, Davis Medieval Texts and Studies 2 (Leiden: Brill, 1979), xxxii.
4. A. K. Bate, "Walter Map and Giraldus Cambrensis," *Latomus* 31 (1972): 860–75.
5. *Expugnatio Hibernica: The Conquest of Ireland, by Giraldus Cambrensis*, ed. and trans. by A. B. Scott and F. X. Martin (Dublin: Royal Irish Academy, 1978), pp. 264–65.
6. Antonia Gransden, *Historical Writing in England c.550 to c.1307* (London: Routledge & Kegan Paul, 1974), pp. 242–46.
7. Walter Map, *De Nugis Curialium (Courtiers' Trifles)*, ed. and trans. by M. R. James, rev. C. N. L. Brooke, and R. A. B. Mynors (Oxford: Clarendon Press, 1983), p. xix. Though *Courtiers' Trifles* continues to be used as the English title, one can think of better translations—*Of the Follies of the Court*, for instance.
8. Gerald of Wales, *The Journey Through Wales and The Description of Wales*, trans. Lewis Thorpe (Harmondsworth: Penguin, 1978), *Journey Through Wales* 1, chap. 5, pp. 117–18.
9. See Helene Newstead, "Some Observations on King Herla and the Herlething," in *Medieval Literature and Folklore Studies: Essays in Honor of Francis Lee Utley*, ed. Jerome Mandel and Bruce A. Rosenberg (New Brunswick, N. J., Rutgers University Press, 1970), pp. 105–10.

10. See L. Harff and Marie-Noëlle Polino, "Le gouffre de Satalie: survivances médiévales du mythe de Méduse," *Moyen Age* 94 (1988): 73–101.

11. Robert Levine, "How to read Walter Map," *Mittellateinisches Jahrbuch* 23 (1991): 91–105.

12. G. T. Shepherd, "The Emancipation of Story in the Twelfth Century," first published in *Medieval Narrative: A Symposium*, ed. by Hans Bekker-Nielsen et al. (Odense: Odense University Press, 1979), 44–57, at 53; repr. in Geoffrey Shepherd, *Poets and Prophets: Essays on Medieval Studies*, ed. T. A. Shippey and John Pickles (Cambridge: D. S. Brewer, 1990), pp. 84–97.

13. Map, *De Nugis*, Distinction 3, Prologue, ed. James, p. 211.

14. Map, *De Nugis*, Distinction 4, chap. 2, ed. James, pp. 283–87.

15. *Topographia Hibernica* (written in 1188 but subsequently revised three or four times); *Expugnatio Hibernica* (first version written 1189, but the text "evolved" over the years until the version dedicated to Prince John in 1209); *Itinerarium Kambriae* (written 1191 but revised at least twice); *Descriptio Kambriae* (written in 1194 and revised at least once). The Latin texts of Gerald's works were edited as *Giraldi Cambrensis: Opera* by J. S. Brewer, James F. Dimock, and G. F. Warner, 8 vols., RS 21 (1861–91); see 5: 191–92. The textual information is conveniently summarized by Robert Bartlett in his biography *Gerald of Wales, 1146–1223*, Oxford Historical Monographs (Oxford: Clarendon Press, 1982), Appendix 1, "The Chronology and Manuscripts of Gerald's Works," pp. 213–21.

16. Gerald of Wales, *Journey Through Wales*, 1:11.

17. Bartlett, *Gerald of Wales*, p. 56.

18. Bartlett, *Gerald of Wales*, p. 48.

19. *The History and Topography of Ireland*, translated into English by John J. O'Meara, (Dundalk: Dundalgan Press: 1951; repr. Harmondsworth: Penguin, 1982).

20. *De Rebus*, chap. 16, in *Opera*, I:72–3; trans. in Butler, *Autobiography*, p. 97.

21. David Rollo, *Historical Fabrication, Ethnic Fable and French Romance in Twelfth-Century England*, Edward C. Armstrong Monographs on Medieval Literature 9 (Lexington, Ky.: French Forum, 1998), p. 251.

22. Gerald of Wales, *Description of Wales*, 2:7.

23. *Expugnatio Hibernica*, p. 213.

24. *De Principis Instructione* was begun in the early 1190s, as Gerald mentions in the preface to the *Journey Through Wales*, but was not completed until about 1218. A translation of books 2 and 3 by Joseph Stevenson, entitled *Concerning the Instruction of Princes*, was published by Seeleys of London in 1858; there is a repaginated facsimile reprint of this called *On the Instruction of Princes* (Felinfach, Dyfed: J. M. F. Books, 1991).

25. *De Principis Instructione*, pp. 301–302.

26. Giraldus Cambrensis, *Speculum Duorum, or A Mirror of Two Men*, edited by Yves Lefèvre and R. B. C. Huygens, with an English translation by Brian Dawson, Board of Celtic Studies, University of Wales. History and Law Series 27 (Cardiff: University of Wales Press, 1974).

27. *De Principis Instructione*, p. 320.

28. *De Vita Galfridi Archiepiscopi Eboracensis*; RS 21: 4; see above, n15.

29. Map, *De Nugis*, ed. James, pp. 496–97.

30. Map, *De Nugis*, 4:3, p. 303.

31. Robert Bartlett, "Rewriting Saints' Lives: The Case of Gerald of Wales," *Speculum* 58 (1983): 598–613.

32. Bartlett, "Rewriting Saints' Lives," 602.

33. Bartlett, "Rewriting Saints' Lives," 603.

34. Gerald of Wales, *The Jewel of the Church*; see n 3 above.

35. See A. A. Goddu and R. H. Rouse, "Gerald of Wales and the *Florilegium Angelicum*," *Speculum* 52 (1977): 488–521.

36. Map, *De Nugis*, ed. James, p. 273.

37. Map, *De Nugis*, ed. James, p. 275.

38. Map, *De Nugis*, ed. James, p. xxi.

39. Map, *De Nugis*, ed. James, p. 245.

40. See *Three Latin Comedies*, ed. A. K. Bate (Toronto: Center for Medieval Studies by the Pontifical Institute of Medieval Studies. 1976); A. G. Rigg, *A History of Anglo-Latin Literature, 1066–1422* (Cambridge: University of Cambridge Press, 1992).

41. As is argued by Siân Echard, "Map's Metafiction: Author, Narrator and Reader in *De nugis curialium*," *Exemplaria* 8 (1996): 287–314.

CHAPTER 6

OLD ENGLISH TEXTUAL ACTIVITY
IN THE REIGN OF HENRY II

Mary Swan

Introduction

The focus of this chapter and the one by Elaine Treharne which follows it is on the body of texts written in Old English during Henry's reign. This Old English textual production could be seen as a kind of subculture, marginal to, and arguably competing with, the dominant literatures in Anglo-Norman and Middle English that form the focus of other chapters in the volume. It has often been obscured and overlooked by scholarly surveys of the literature of the period, and its very existence raises some important questions about the linguistic and literary map of twelfth-century England. In particular, this material highlights the importance of always envisaging textual production and use in the period in a plurilinguistic context, in which language choices are made by writers and readers for different reasons at different moments, in which those choices always carry implications for cultural identity, and in which the carrying forward of pre-Conquest English linguistic and literary traditions must bear very particular meaning.

This chapter sets out the extent and nature of Old English textual activity in the latter half of the twelfth century and gives an assessment of scholarly engagement with it to date, and an indication of work to be done, in the form of crucial current research-questions. The ways in which some of these questions can be addressed are explored with reference to one particular manuscript. One key issue addressed in this chapter is that of the problems generated by modern categories and the labels which accompany them. The category label "post-Conquest Old English textual activity" is itself not free of difficulties. It is used here as a title of convenience to refer to the production of texts after 1066 the language of which shows many of the features of standard late West-Saxon-written Old English, even if lexical and grammatical updating are also evident. It is not, however, intended as a purely linguistic categorization, but rather as a way of identifying texts composed in Old English in pre-Conquest England that were recopied and adapted after 1066, and also—in a few cases—texts newly composed in English after 1066 of which literary style and sensibilities, as well as the language, fit much more closely with Old English traditions than with Middle English ones.[1] Finding accurate terminology with which to identify this material without reinforcing the notions that Old and Middle English are distinct entities and that anything which appears to have features of both is somehow by definition more transitional, and therefore less fixed and less significant than either, is fraught with complications. For the purposes of the current survey, "post-Conquest Old English" as a label is not meant to imply an acceptance of a need to categorize the textual evidence in question as belonging on one side of a dramatic divide, but rather is intended to highlight an interwoven continuity and transformation of English linguistic and cultural identity.

This blend of continuity and transformation is shown by both of the major categories of surviving post-Conquest Old English texts. Those that are copies of pre-Conquest Old English works bring their pre-Conquest sources forward into the twelfth century by updating them stylistically and linguistically so that, whilst they must have been identifiable to twelfth-century audiences as having the basic characteristics of pre-Conquest Old English language and literature, they are also subtly transformed into something current. The second of the categories is made up of surviving post-Conquest Old English texts that have been shown to be newly composed after the Conquest. These include the *Lives* of Saints Giles and Nicholas,[2] and perhaps also the *Life* of St. Margaret,[3] which were probably written in England after 1066,[4] and—as argued later in this chapter—some of the Old English items in Lambeth Palace manuscript 487, which may also have been newly composed in the later twelfth century. These post-Conquest Old English texts demonstrate in a different way the vitality of the tradition and its meaningfulness in the twelfth century, by carrying forward and updating the traits of pre-Conquest vernacular language and style as a medium for new work.

The Evidence for Old English Textual Production

Of the eighty or so surviving post-Conquest Old English manuscripts, fourteen substantial ones were written between ca. 1150 and 1200. As can be seen from the list below, these contain a variety of texts, the majority of which are of popular and key religious genres, including preaching texts and saints' lives, but there also survive laws, one version of the Anglo-Saxon Chronicle, copies of Classical texts, and some interesting miscellaneous items, including prognostications and medical recipes.

Principal Manuscripts Containing Old English Texts Produced between ca. 1150 And 1200

Homilies and hagiography

1. Cambridge, Corpus Christi College MS 303: s.xii[med]; probably Rochester.[5]
2. Cambridge, Corpus Christi College MS 367: s.xii[2]; southern; Rochester or Christ Church, Canterbury.
3. London, British Library MS Cotton Vespasian D. xiv: s.xii[med]; Christ Church, Canterbury or Rochester.
4. London, British Library MS Cotton Vespasian A. xxii: s.xii[ex]; probably Rochester.
5. Oxford, Bodleian Library MS Bodley 343: s.xii[2]; West Midlands (Worcester or Hereford).
6. Cambridge, University Library MS Ii. 1. 33: s.xii[2]; southern; Rochester or Christ Church, Canterbury.
7. London, Lambeth Palace Library MS 487: s.xii/xiii[in]; West Midlands; possibly Worcester area.
8. Cambridge, Trinity College MS, B. 14. 52: s.xii[ex]; provenance unknown.

Gospels

9. London, British Library MS Royal I. A. xiv: s.xii[2]; probably Christ Church, Canterbury.
10. Oxford, Bodleian Library MS Hatton 38: s.xii/xiii; Christ Church, Canterbury.

Glossed Psalter

11. Cambridge, Trinity College MS R. 17. 1: s.xii[med]; Christ Church, Canterbury.

Benedictine Rule adapted for women

12. London, British Library MS Cotton Claudius D. iii: s.xii/xiii; provenance unknown.

Ælfric's version of Bede, "De Temporibus Anni"

13. Cambridge, Corpus Christi College MS 367: s.xii^2; southern; Rochester or Christ Church, Canterbury.

Laws

14. London, British Library MS Harley 55: s.xii^{med}; provenance unknown.

"Anglo-Saxon Chronicle"

15. Oxford, Bodleian Library MS Laud Misc. 636: s.xii^{med}; Peterborough.

Apothegms and dialogue literature

16. London, British Library MS Cotton Vespasian D. xiv: s.xii^{med}; Christ Church, Canterbury or Rochester.

Augustine's "Soliloquies", Gospel of Nicodemus, debate of Solomon and Saturn, homily on St. Quentin

17. London, British Library MS Cotton Vitellius A. xv: s.xii^{med}; provenance unknown.

Metrical prayer, dialogue between Adrian and Ritheus, miscellaneous notes and Distichs of Cato

18. London, British Library MS Cotton Julius A. ii: s.xii^{med}; provenance unknown.

Prognostications

19. Oxford, Bodleian Library MS Hatton 115: s.xi^2 and s.xii^{med}; provenance unknown.

Medicinal texts

20. London, British Library MS Harley 6258 B: s.xii^2; provenance unknown.

Scholarship to date

Post-Conquest Old English has never been studied holistically. The tendency has been not to consider the whole range of surviving manuscripts but rather to treat individual ones as isolated, marginal productions, and not indicators of wider Old English textual activity. The material has thus been studied piecemeal, as a postscript to Old English or as a precursor to Middle English textual and linguistic culture, or as dialectically idiosyncratic. Furthermore, almost no scholarship has taken a comparative cultural or interlinguistic approach by working across material in English, Anglo-Norman, and Latin.

In disciplinary terms, work on this period has also been uneven: there is relatively abundant work on social history, but little work on cultural, linguistic, or literary history, and work on ecclesiastical history has focused on Anglo-Norman and Latin materials. Moreover, since—as the list above shows—most surviving Old English texts from the second half of the twelfth century are practical in character, they have almost always been omitted from literary surveys of the period, since they do not fit the narrower definitions of what constitutes a "literary" text. Neither do these texts, with the exception of the *Peterborough Chronicle*, usually qualify as "historical" in the traditional disciplinary sense.

The traditional boundaries of periodization and disciplinarity, therefore, have limited work to date in this field. One increasingly powerful trend in medieval textual research, however, has the potential to counter these limitations and oversights. Materialist philology—the holistic study of manuscripts—has made considerable inroads into medieval literary and historical scholarship in the last decade and has resulted in a shift of focus away from the single text, interpreted in isolation from the context of its production and the context of its preservation in a manuscript, and toward an understanding that these contexts are vital evidence for the meaning of any text and the cultural work it was intended to perform.

Post-Conquest Old English manuscripts reveal a great deal about the viability of the literary output of Anglo-Saxon England after the Conquest, and the ways in which the political and literary identity of such material is reshaped and reinvigorated for new reasons and a new context: to perform new cultural work. However little we might know about the precise motives for the production of Old English texts in the Henrician period, it is increasingly clear that this is never an unconscious, unreflective, automatic sort of activity. In the complex political and linguistic climate of the second half of the twelfth century, writers in England were always in the position of making linguistic choices, and the majority of them chose Anglo-Norman or Latin. Those who elected to write in Old English, therefore, must have done so in response to an imagined audience or patron, and with some idea of their own cultural identity or agenda and that of their audience. In the context of widespread Latin and Anglo-Norman textual activity, and the dominant status of these two languages,

Old English texts that were composed before 1066 might, on the face of it, seem to be of little relevance after the Conquest. In fact their very difference—their lack of conformity to the dominant linguistic options— means that those Old English texts that were recopied or glossed or annotated between ca. 1150 and 1200 are deemed, or made, to be valid and meaningful for their copyists and users.

Detailed research on post-Conquest Old English texts has begun to take shape in the last few years.[6] The consensus to date is that, in the overwhelming majority of cases, Old English texts were not copied after 1066 for purely antiquarian reasons. Almost all of the examples that have been studied can be argued to have been chosen for copying because they were considered to be relevant to post-Conquest concerns and audiences. This is clear in several respects: from the predominance of performance texts— mostly homilies—that were copied and that serve a practical function in the ongoing cycle of religious devotion; from the ways in which items are carefully gathered together into manuscripts that do not always reproduce the contents and ordering of their exemplars; and from the ways in which some manuscript collections have edited earlier Old English pieces to produce either collections of abbreviated texts,[7] or new, composite preaching texts from earlier materials, some of which join together their Old English source excerpts with compiler-written link passages.[8] These newly ordered manuscripts and newly adapted texts show evidence of having been put together freshly, to a predetermined plan, and for new use. Above all, the adaptations made to earlier Old English texts to update them linguistically and thematically for twelfth-century use mark this textual production as useful and indicate that it is being undertaken in response to a perceived need for utilitarian texts, not for facsimile reconstructions of a dead tradition. Furthermore, the preponderance of homiletic texts amongst the Old English materials adapted in the Henrician period is a key to a potential ideological motivation for this recopying: preaching texts are, of course, representations of preaching events, and therefore of performances; they are also performative in the sense of having the function of producing, defining, and upholding identities and ideologies. As such, they are crucial evidence for the vitality of Old English in the period and of its central importance in delineating identity for its producers and users. Fundamental to a rounded picture of textual production in the Henrician period and its relationship with national identity are the questions of exactly what sort of identity is being delineated by the production and use of Old English texts in the period, and in particular of whether this identity is marked as specifically English in a way intended to contrast with and resist Anglo-Norman textual production and cultural markers,[9] or instead to coexist with them.

Research Questions for Future Work on Post-Conquest Old English

To determine exactly what post-Conquest Old English textual activity means in a Henrician context, many basic questions need asking of the material and many basic scholarly assumptions should be reexamined. The following set of research questions approaches the issue holistically by plotting the most important coordinates of the field and identifying key issues and key gaps in current understanding.

1. What was copied and produced in English from 1050 to 1250?
2. Where and when was this material produced?
3. Is there an identifiable program of copying in English or is it a marginal activity?
4. How were manuscripts written in English disseminated?
5. Who had access to post-Conquest Old English manuscripts?
6. Whom are post-Conquest Old English religious texts aimed at?
7. What languages did monks, nuns, and priests use for speaking, preaching, and teaching?

The full answer to the question of what was copied in English should provide the data for all future research on the topic, and the list of manuscripts above gives an indication of what has been identified to date for the time period from 1150 to 1200. To produce a full and accurate list for the whole of the relevant period will require some manuscripts—especially those which are now dated to a band that spans the decades on either side of 1050 and 1250—to be dated more precisely, on grounds of script, codicology, and/or contents. It also necessitates the creation of a unified list of all textual material produced in English in the period: texts of all generic types, including charters and other documents, as well as narrative and exhortatory texts, and of all shapes, including annotations, marginalia, and corrections, as well as whole texts. Such a unified list will make it possible to gauge the scale of writing activity in English and will provide a full set of data for analyzing dates and places of production. A related question is that of how what was copied in English relates to texts copied in Anglo-Norman and Latin. Collaboration between Old English, Anglo-Norman, and twelfth-century Anglo-Latin specialists will be of central importance in understanding this topic. A full and informed comparative survey of materials copied in all three languages will generate a much clearer picture of how their producer and user communities differ, the points at which they overlap, and of the functions textual production in each language might have been intended to serve.

In order to explore when and where the English material was produced, it is first necessary to identify all known scriptoria; to identify specifically all scriptoria known to have produced texts in English; to assess how accurately the relevant manuscripts can be dated within the time frame; to pinpoint what sort of occupation or rank their scribes held, and in particular which scribes are likely to have been professional, which amateur, which monks, which nuns, and which secular clergy; to determine whether scribes working in English were likely to be of different profession or rank from scribes working in Anglo-Norman or Latin; and to analyze the extent to which scribes of Old English texts and the manuscripts that they wrote traveled, where to and from, and for how long. The results of this analysis should allow a detailed mapping of the place of Old English textual production in terms of geography, networks, institutions, and social rank.

When more substantial work has been done on scriptoria and manuscript production and movement, it will be possible to estimate whether or not the majority of surviving post-Conquest manuscripts containing Old English are just one-off productions, undertaken as individual pieces of work separate from the other activities of their compilers, scribes, and places of production, or whether they represent structured programs of copying Old English in particular scriptoria. Once again, comparison with Anglo-Norman and Latin manuscript-production will be crucial for the accurate assessment of this possibility. Mary Richards's work has already shown that Rochester Cathedral appears to have followed a program of assembling manuscripts and of copying Old English homiletic texts on basic Christian instruction after its refoundation as Benedictine in 1075.[10] Richards speculates that, since Rochester Cathedral would have served also as a parish church, its canons might have needed such materials to train others for parochial duties. An important future research-topic is the investigation of whether or not this continued into the twelfth century.

It is also clear that Worcester and other centers in its locality went through a relatively concerted period of copying Old English texts on into the late twelfth or early thirteenth century.[11] At Worcester itself, the impetus for this is thought to have been generated during the time when Wulfstan was bishop, from 1062 to 1095. Research on Worcester in this period has identified what appears to amount to a sort of cultural self-fashioning as English on the part of the cathedral community.[12] Links with Saint Wulfstan are emphasized, Old English texts are recopied and are also reworked into new, composite pieces. Recent work on women readers of post-Conquest Old English texts has, as noted below, highlighted the West Midlands in general, and Worcester in particular, as a possible focus for the production of particular sorts of Old English texts for both lay and female readers. The question of the impetus for the production of English texts, in terms of patronage and commissioning, and its implications for the cultural identity expressed by their producers and users, is key to the understanding of the consumption milieu of the texts and to how this relates to their contexts of production.

In terms of the dissemination of manuscripts written in Old English, the availability of some now-lost pre-Conquest Old English texts and manuscripts can be ascertained by extrapolating from surviving post-Conquest copies of them. Here again, regionally concentrated data is informative: thus, for example, scribes working in the Worcester area must have had access to a range of homilies by Ælfric, since they make use of some of his work in the production of new, composite or adapted homilies.[13] It can also be shown that several surviving pre-Conquest Old English manuscripts must have been in Worcester, since they were annotated there in the late twelfth and early thirteenth century by the scribe known as the "Tremulous Hand."[14] What is not clear is how these manuscripts, not all of which are thought to have been produced at Worcester, got there. Were they bought in as part of a post-Conquest Old English library restocking campaign, or did the Tremulous Hand scribe assemble them in order to read and work on them? Or, as an alternative hypothesis, were these manuscripts never at Worcester, but rather at one or more other religious houses in the Worcester neighborhood to which the Tremulous Hand had access? Careful scrutiny of a wider range of manuscripts will determine whether there is evidence of similar post-Conquest annotating of pre-Conquest Old English manuscripts in other regions, and thereby provide some comparative examples.

It is important, moreover, to remember that there is not always evidence that post-Conquest copies of earlier Old English texts were produced by scribes working from an earlier manuscript, and that the possibility that any copies of Old English texts were made by scribes working from memory, not from manuscripts, is one which should always be considered. The nature of some of the pre- and post-Conquest copies of material from Ælfric's *Catholic Homilies* makes it much more likely that they were produced by memorial copying than from manuscript exemplars.[15] This possibility, of course, raises the very interesting question of the circumstances under which a scribe might read or hear, and memorize, Old English texts after the Conquest and on into the Henrician period.

In the case of the Tremulous Hand scribe, it can be seen that at least one individual, probably a monk, had access to Old English manuscripts in the twelfth century. Until more is known about the intended function of post-Conquest Old English manuscripts, it will not be possible to ascertain whether in general they were only available to their scribes, and never read subsequently by anyone else; or whether they were also available to occasional individual readers or users, perhaps including preachers, who sought out Old English material; or whether they had wider circulation than this scenario would imply. The question of regionality is also very important in addressing this question, since—even allowing for the many factors that, from the later Middle Ages to the nineteenth century, led to the wholesale exporting or destruction of Old English manuscripts from particular areas, and to their concentration in others—the evidence of surviving Old English manuscripts indicates that it is likely that, in the twelfth century, access to them was much more easily had in some areas of the country than in others.

The distinction between regional and national identity, and the relative importance of each, is crucial to a full appreciation of the nuances and ideology of language use in the period and is touched on in the discussion of Lambeth Palace manuscript 487 that follows. The relationship between regional and national identities has too often been overlooked in research on the period, and in addressing it fully, comparison with Anglo-Norman and Latin textual culture will be vital, and the evidence for intraregional and interregional networks of textual transmission must also be considered.[16]

The question of for whom post-Conquest copies of Old English texts were made is often asked of pre-Conquest Old English religious texts too, and of course of Anglo-Norman and Anglo-Latin ones as well. Even in the case of surviving pre-Conquest collections of Old English homilies and saints' lives, the precise intended audience is rarely known. For the Henrician period, it is not simply a question of whether Old English religious texts were intended to be read privately or to be read aloud to a monastic, or a secular audience: the question of language use is also central. If post-Conquest Old English religious texts were designed for private reading, who might have commissioned them? If they were designed for public preaching, what sort of community, in what part of the country, might have found them suitable? Further close study of individual manuscripts is one way to frame the range of possible answers to this question, as is demonstrated by the discussion below of Lambeth Palace manuscript 487.

On the question of what languages monks, nuns, and priests used for which aspects of their activities, there survive a few references to preaching in Old English after the Conquest, and these identify a number of prominent male ecclesiastics as at least capable of speaking in public in English: Godfrey de Jumièges, abbot of Malmesbury in 1081; Samson, abbot of Bury St. Edmunds; Odo of Battle; Hugh de Eversden, abbot of St. Albans; and Robert Grosseteste, Bishop of Lincoln.[17] As regards the language of everyday speaking, first-language-English speakers would have been amongst the population of some monasteries and nunneries for decades after the Conquest, even if the Anglo-Saxon holders of more senior

monastic offices before the Conquest were replaced with Norman candi-
dates after 1066. Presumably those monks and nuns who were accustomed
to reading English before 1066 and who remained after this date would not
have switched their linguistic codes immediately so that they only read
Anglo-Norman, and in some cases may never have done so.

Some significant recent work by Sarah Foot has drawn attention to
previously ignored or underestimated "paramonastic" activity by women
in late Anglo-Saxon England who are identified in the historical record as
"nunnan"—secular vowesses, not professed nuns.[18] As I argue elsewhere,
this raises the possibility that groups of Anglophone secular vowesses
survived the Conquest and formed an audience for Old English texts in the
late eleventh and twelfth centuries. It is also tantalizingly possible—if not
yet provable—that, in the West Midlands, these groups of women form
the bridge between eleventh- and early-twelfth-century readers of Old
English and the readers of thirteenth-century "Katherine Group"-type
English prose.[19]

In considering any of the above points, it is important also to reassess
how valid for the Henrician period modern definitions of linguistic,
cultural, and professional categories and distinctions are. These have been
crucial factors in framing and articulating research to date, but they have
often been unscrutinised, and their applicability to the period in question is
underexplored. In order to assess their validity, the following definitions
must be reassessed: Latin versus the vernacular(s), in terms of their use by
individuals and in different situations; the identity categories of Saxon and
Norman, how long they persisted after 1066, and how they fed into a definition or definitions of Anglo-Norman; the relevant institutional ranks
and the relationships between them, such as monk, nun, secular vowess,
canon, priest, abbot, and bishop; relationships between and the hierachies
that qualified those who copied manuscripts and their superiors, monks and
nuns and secular clergy, and secular clergy and parishioners.

The status of all of these categories has implications for textual production and consumption and the identities these activities create, and so too
does the complicating but often-forgotten factor that any one reader or listener might well consume texts in more than one language, depending on
the situation and the genre.

Lambeth Palace Manuscript 487: A Case Study

Lambeth Palace manuscript 487 was written in the late twelfth or early
thirteenth century, probably in the West Midlands.[20] The contents of the
manuscript are listed below. Where the title of an item is not given in the
manuscript, but is supplied by Richard Morris, the manuscript's first and to

date only editor,[21] it is given in square brackets. Where an item has an explicitly homiletic beginning ("dearly beloved" or some equivalent phrase) and/or end (most commonly a prayer followed by "Amen"), it is labeled "homily"; where neither the beginning nor the end is explicitly homiletic, but the main body of the text contains such markers as addresses to an audience, use of the homiletic "we," and exhortation, it is labeled "homiletic in content."

Item 1. [In Dominica Palmarum] Homily. Echoes of Old English homilies.
Item 2. Hic Dicendum est de Quadragesima. Homily. Reuses Wulfstan.
Item 3. [Dominica Prima in Quadragesima] Homily. Echoes of Old English homilies.
Item 4. In Diebus Dominicis. Homily.
Item 5. Hic Dicendum est de Propheta. Homily.
Item 6. Pater Noster. Poem.
Item 7. [Credo] Exposition.
Item 8. [De Natale Domini] Homily.
Item 9. [In Die Pentecosten] Homiletic in content. Reuses Ælfric.
Item 10. De Octo Uiciis & De Duodecim Abusiuis Huius Seculi. Homily. Re-uses Ælfric.
Item 11. [Dominica V. Quadragesimæ] Homiletic in content. Reuses Ælfric.
Item 12. [Dominica Secunda Post Pascha] Homily.
Item 13. [Sermo in Epist. 2 ad Corinth. ix. 6] Homiletic in content.
Item 14. In Die Dominica. Homily.
Item 15. [Sermo in Marcum viii. 34] Homily.
Item 16. [Estote Fortes in Bello] Homily.
Item 17. [Sermo in Ps. Cxxvi. 6] Homily.
Item 18. Poema Morale. First-person address.
Item 19. [On Ureisun of oure Louerde] Prayer (by hand of s.xiii med).

The first eighteen items in the manuscript were all written by a single scribe around the year 1200,[22] possibly in the West Midlands. These items are therefore, on the chronological face of it, Early Middle English, not Old English. The first seventeen items are commonly known as the "Lambeth Homilies"; they cover a range of church festivals, including Palm Sunday, three Sundays in Lent, and the Nativity, and in three cases provide commentaries on specific gospel readings. All of the "Lambeth Homilies" are written in prose except for item 6, "Pater Noster," a rhyming running commentary on the Lord's Prayer which does not have a homiletic opening, but is full of direct addresses and expressions of encouragement from the speaker to the audience of a sort common in the exhortations to confession often copied into earlier homiletic manuscripts.

Four of the items in Lambeth 487 (items 2, 9, 10, and 11) are altered copies of pre-Conquest Old English religious texts,[23] an Old English homiletic source has recently been identified for the conclusion of item 3,[24] and item 1 reads as if it may well be using a so-far unidentified Old English source or as if it is a newly composed post-Conquest writing which is consciously drawing on pre-Conquest Old English style. These six or so items, then, are more strongly marked as late Old English than early Middle English. The remaining items are all much more like Middle English in a range of ways.

Five of the items in the manuscript which have no apparent connections to Old English texts (items 7, 13, 15, 16, and 17) also survive in the slightly earlier manuscript Cambridge Trinity College B. 14. 52, which appears to have no links with Old English traditions. The nineteenth and final item in the manuscript, "On Ureisun of Oure Louerde," is in a mid-thirteenth-century hand. Some of these items in Lambeth 487 with no apparent connections to Old English texts show an interest in themes and a spiritual sensibility much closer to post-Conquest than to Anglo-Saxon England. They include an exposition of the Creed (item 7), one piece on the necessity of praising and loving God which focuses on Christ's blood (item 12), and another which meditates on the theme of tears (item 17). In tone and subject-matter, these pieces foreshadow the thematics of Christocentric devotion, which becomes so popular in Anglo-Norman, Anglo-Latin, and Middle English literature from the twelfth century onward. Some of these trends are present, if in less-prominent positions, in later pre-Conquest English writings,[25] but they certainly gather momentum in the Henrician period in England, and as such are more a feature of post-Conquest Old and Middle English, rather than pre-Conquest Old English literary traditions.

In terms of how—and for what purpose—some of the Old English–affiliated items in the manuscript have been remade, comparison of the Ælfric rewrites in Lambeth 487 with earlier versions of the source texts shows that they have been adapted for an audience less interested in the details of monastic life than Ælfric, and, since they include a reference to tithing, presumably for a secular one.[26] There is a fleeting indication that one of the reused Ælfric pieces, item 9, might have been grammatically adapted for a female audience,[27] and I have argued elsewhere that the Ælfric material in this item is rewritten for an audience with less formal education in exegesis and with a preference for a more conversational sermon style.[28] Item 10 implies a similar sort of shift of audience.

Beyond the examples noted above, clues as to the intended audience of Lambeth 487 are scarce. The range of texts in the manuscript provides for reading, or for reading and preaching, on central Christian topics from a

didactic and exhortatory and also an individualized perspective. The manuscript is thus usable in a variety of potential contexts. It contains no signs
of use, such as marginal additions and alterations,[29] and is all (items 1–18)
the work of a single, and not terribly neat, scribe, who must have had training
in the art of copying, but whose work in this manuscript is not of the
quality normally evidenced in large and prestigious scriptoria. It may be the
case that the scribe had assembled the manuscript for personal use, and if
this is so, then the following hypotheses present themselves: perhaps the
scribe of Lambeth 487 was a parish priest who had access to a monastic
library that contained a range of English preaching and general devotional
materials, both brand new and pre-Conquest, and who drew on that library
to assemble material that he intended to use in another context or
contexts—for his private devotional reading, or for recycling in preaching
or writing in English in another context; or alternatively for reading aloud
to an Anglophone acquaintance, perhaps a secular vowess, so that the
acquaintance has access to it as devotional material. Or perhaps, as I have
argued elsewhere,[30] the putative Anglophone secular vowess, desirous of a
varied collection of reading materials on old and new themes, was herself
the collector of the material and the scribe of the manuscript. In any of
these cases, the user or users of the manuscript are marked by it as English
in a Henrician context and in a very particular sense, which assimilates pre-
and post-Conquest texts, traditions and styles, and which thus deploys both
change and continuity to make a particular point, and a particular identity.

Conclusion

The aim of this overview of Old English textual activity in the latter half of
the twelfth century has been to show that, if textual culture in England in
this period is to be mapped accurately, a significant body of material is in
urgent need of scholarly attention alongside Anglo-Norman and Latin productions. The range of types of Old English texts copied in the period—
including preaching texts, saints' lives, Gospels, the Psalter, monastic rules,
patristic texts, prognostications, and medicinal texts—and the evidence
offered by detailed studies of individual examples, such as the adaptations to
and recontextualization of pre-Conquest English texts in Lambeth 487,
show that Old English textual production in these decades is varied and
purposeful. This highlights the central questions of who produced and used
Old English texts in the Henrician period, and of the place of those texts
relative to those in Latin and Anglo-Norman that were produced and used
alongside them. A fully rounded picture of literature of the plurilinguistic
reign of Henry II will be alert to the nuances of language as a signifier of
affiliation and identity, and to the place of the continuing production of

Old English texts in the carrying over of old traditions and identities and their transformation into new ones.

Notes

1. See Susan Irvine, "The compilation and use of manuscripts containing Old English in the twelfth century," in *Rewriting Old English in the Twelfth Century*, ed. Mary Swan and Elaine M. Treharne, Cambridge Studies in Anglo-Saxon England 30 (Cambridge: Cambridge University Press, 2000), pp. 41–61 (at 47).
2. *The Old English Life of St Nicholas with the Old English Life of St Giles*, ed. Elaine Treharne, Leeds Texts and Monographs, n.s. 15 (School of English, University of Leeds: Leeds, 1997).
3. In Cambridge, Corpus Christi College MS 303. Discussed and edited by Mary Clayton and Hugh Magennis, *The Old English Lives of St Margaret*, Cambridge Studies in Anglo-Saxon England 9 (Cambridge: Cambridge University Press, 1994). See also Hugh Magennis, "Listen Now All and Understand: Adaptation of Hagiographical Material for Vernacular Audiences in the Old English Lives of Margaret," *Speculum* 71 (1996): 27–42. On CCCC 303, see further Elaine M. Treharne, "The production and script of manuscripts containing English religious texts in the first half of the twelfth century," in Swan and Treharne, *Rewriting Old English*, pp. 11–40.
4. In the following chapter, Elaine Treharne discusses in detail another Old English text which can be shown to have been composed after 1066.
5. Details of manuscript dates and provenance are taken from N. R. Ker, *A Catalogue of Manuscripts Containing Old English* (Oxford: Oxford University Press, 1957; reprinted 1990) and Swan and Treharne, *Rewriting Old English*.
6. From 2005 to 2010, a new research project, "The Production and Use of English Manuscripts, 1060 to 1220," funded by the UK Arts and Humanities Research Council and directed by Elaine Treharne of the University of Leicester and Mary Swan of the University of Leeds, will identify, analyze and evaluate all manuscripts containing English produced between these dates, and will study them against the backdrop of the production of texts in Latin and Anglo-Norman, in order to advance our understanding of textual and linguistic culture. The project will produce a new analytical corpus to enable innovative scholarship on fundamental questions about this field. Some of its major research questions and directions will be discussed below.
7. An example of such a manuscript is British Library, Vespasian D. xiv, discussed in Elaine Treharne's chapter, which contains a large number of devotional and homiletic texts, almost all of which have been substantially edited and reworked.
8. Examples include some of the preaching texts in Cambridge, Corpus Christi College MS 303, Oxford, Bodleian Library MS Bodley 343, and Lambeth Palace MS 487, discussed below.

9. For a detailed treatment of the possibility of resistance, see Treharne, *Living Through Conquest: The Politics of Early English*, forthcoming (Oxford: Oxford University Press, 2006).

10. Mary P. Richards, *Texts and Their Traditions in the Medieval Library of Rochester Cathedral Priory*, Transactions of the American Philosophical Society 78.3 (Philadelphia, Pa.: American Philosophical Society, 1998), and "Innovations in Ælfrician Homiletic Manuscripts at Rochester," *Annuale Medievale* 19 (1970): 13–26.

11. See Mary Swan, "Mobile Libraries: Old English Manuscript Production in Worcester and the West Midlands, 1090–1215," in *Manuscripts of the West Midlands*, ed. Wendy Scase, forthcoming from Brepols.

12. The most important study to date on this topic is Emma Mason, *St Wulfstan of Worcester c.1008–1095* (Oxford: Blackwell, 1990).

13. Some of the adaptations of Ælfrician homilies in Lambeth Palace MS 487, discussed below, exemplify this.

14. See Wendy Collier, "The Tremulous Worcester Hand and Gregory's *Pastoral Care*," in Swan and Treharne, *Rewriting Old English*, pp. 195–208.

15. See Mary Swan, "Memorialised Readings: Manuscript Evidence for Old English Homily Composition," in *Anglo-Saxon Manuscripts and their Heritage*, ed. Phillip Pulsiano and Elaine M. Treharne (Aldershot: Ashgate, 1998), pp. 205–17.

16. For some of the evidence for the existence of post-Conquest Old English textual networks, see Swan, "Mobile Libraries."

17. See William of Malmesbury, *De Gestis Ponificum. Anglorum*, ed. A. Hamilton, (London, 1870), RS 52: 431–32: William's monks "vulgares tantum litteras balbutievant." According to Rokewoode, Samson sometimes preached in the dialect of Norfolk; see *Chronica Joscelini de Brakelond*, ed. J. G. Rokewood, RS 96 (London, 1879–80), I:245. Odo preached in French and Latin, and "ad edificationem rudis vulgi lingua materna publice pronunciabat." See *Chronicon Monasterii de Bello*, ed. J. S. Brewer, Anglia Christiani 1 (London: Anglia Christiani, 1846), p. 163. Hugh was fluent in English. See Thomas Walsingham, *Gesta Abbatum Monasterii Sancti Albani*, ed. T. Riley, RS 28 (London, 1867), III:113. Grosseteste preached in English and exhorted priests in his diocese to do so too. See J. Stevenson, ed., *Chronicon de Lanercost*, Publications of the Bannantine Club 65 (Edinburgh: Bannantine Club, 1839), p. 43 and Robert Grosseteste, *Epistolae*, RS 25:155.

18. Sarah Foot, *Veiled Women: The Disappearance of Nuns from Anglo-Saxon England*, 2 vols. (Aldershot: Ashgate, 2000).

19. See Mary Swan, "Constructing Readerships for Post-Conquest Old English Manuscripts," in *Imagining the Book*, ed. John Thompson and Stephen Kelly (Turnhout: Brepols, 2006).

20. The description and list of the contents of Lambeth Palace MS 487 which follow necessarily repeat some details from the article referenced in n 19 above.

21. Richard Morris, ed., *Old English Homilies and Homiletic Treatises of the Twelfth and Thirteenth Centuries*, EETS os 29 and 34 (London: Trübner, 1868). In the Notes and Emendations to his edition of the manuscript, *Old English Homilies*, Morris comments on some of the comparisons between items in Lambeth 487 and earlier Old English texts, but he does not provide thorough collations. Some of the manuscript's contents are edited by Sarah M. O'Brien, "An Edition of Seven Homilies from Lambeth Palace Library MS 487," Ph.D. diss., University of Oxford, 1985. The prose items in the manuscript are described by Veronica O'Mara in O. S. Pickering and V. M. O'Mara, *The Index of Middle English Prose. Handlist XIII: Manuscripts in Lambeth Palace Library* (Cambridge: D.S. Brewer, 1999), pp. 40–43, and the manuscript has been published in the Early English Manuscripts in Microfiche Facsimile series, with an introduction by Jonathan Wilcox: *Wulfstan Texts and Other Homiletic Materials*, EEMF 8 (Tempe, Ariz.: Arizona Center for Medieval and Renaissance Studies, 2000). Dr O'Mara and Dr Wilcox both generously made their descriptions of the manuscript available to me before publication. I am currently re-editing the manuscript for publication in the Arizona Medieval and Renaissance Texts Series.

22. N. R. Ker does not include Lambeth 487 in his *Catalogue of Manuscripts Containing Anglo-Saxon* (Oxford: Clarendon Press, 1957; repr. with supplement 1990), on the grounds of what he describes as its "tenuous" connection with Old English manuscripts (at p. xix). He also notes that the manuscript "may have been written before 1200" (at p. xix).

23. For a fuller analysis of item 9, see Mary Swan, "*Ælfric's Catholic Homilies* in the Twelfth Century," in Swan and Treharne, *Rewriting Old English*, pp. 62–82 (at 74–75). For a study of item 11, see Mary Swan, "Old English Made New: One *Catholic Homily* and its Reuses," *Leeds Studies in English*, n.s. 28 (1997), pp. 1–18.

24. In a recent conference paper by Elaine Treharne, "Unoriginal Sin: Textually Transmitted Deviancy in Old English Prose." The detailed findings will be published in *Living Through Conquest* (see n9).

25. For a discussion of how one element of the Cult of the Passion might have been developed in later Anglo-Saxon England, see Swan, "Remembering Veronica in Anglo-Saxon England," in *Writing Gender and Genre in Medieval Literature*, ed. Elaine Treharne (Cambridge: D. S. Brewer, 2003), pp. 19–39.

26. For a fuller analysis of Item 9, see Mary Swan, "*Ælfric's Catholic Homilies* in the Twelfth Century," in Swan and Treharne, *Rewriting Old English*, pp. 62–82 (at 74–75). For a study of item 11, see Mary Swan, "Old English Made New: One *Catholic Homily* and its Reuses," *Leeds Studies in English*, n.s. 28 (1997): 1–18.

27. See Peter Clemoes, ed., *Ælfric's Catholic Homilies. The First Series. Text*, EETS ss 17 (Oxford: Oxford University Press, 1997), pp. 50 and 153. Peter Clemoes suggests that one alteration in item 9 implies that its intended audience may be nuns.

28. Swan, "*Ælfric's Catholic Homilies* in the Twelfth Century," pp. 74–75.

29. The preachability of some of its rewritten Old English homilies as they stand might be deemed to be questionable, since in places they seem to have garbled the sense of their sources, but, as suggested in Swan, "Constructing Readerships," this might not present a real barrier to their delivery by an experienced preacher.
30. See n 19.

CHAPTER 7

THE LIFE OF ENGLISH IN THE MID-TWELFTH CENTURY: RALPH D'ESCURES'S HOMILY ON THE VIRGIN MARY

Elaine Treharne

Throughout the post-Conquest period, manuscripts written in English continued to be produced,[1] usually at monastic centers, in much the same way as they had been during the Anglo-Saxon period. The preponderance of surviving material based on Old English exemplars that was copied and adapted from ca. 1100–1200 is homiletic and hagiographic in nature. Its recontextualization in the twelfth century provides opportunities for investigating textual transmission and dissemination, for codicological and paleographical analyses, for assessing the uses of English texts, and for determining the characteristics and aims of the native literate elite.

A particular manuscript of note that is representative of the trends in English textual production in this period is London, British Library MS Cotton Vespasian D. xiv. Compiled in the mid-twelfth century, probably at Christ Church, Canterbury, this extensive codex contains fifty-two English texts, including homilies written by the Old English author Ælfric, a unique *Life* of St. Neot, a version of the *Dicts of Cato*, and two twelfth-century translations—excerpts from Honorius Augustodunensis's *Elucidarium* and a homily on the Virgin Mary by Ralph D'Escures.[2]

These two post-Conquest translations are especially interesting for being witnesses to the latest compositions in Old English, or, as some scholars would have it, the earliest in Middle English.[3] Thomas Hahn, for example, has stated of the *Elucidarium* and the Marian homily that:

> These renderings of near-contemporary Latin texts stand among the first specimens of eME, and, like the heterogeneous character of the *Anthology*

> [Vespasian D. xiv] as a whole, document how the native tongue had begun
> to negotiate various domains of cultural production.[4]

The linguistic demarcation of texts in this transitional period into "Old" or
"Middle" English has, of course, no basis outside our present-day insistence
on labeling and categorizing. For the compiler(s) of Cotton Vespasian D.
xiv there seems to have been no recoverable distinction between the way
in which the language of the texts was regarded: some of the texts are relatively closely copied from pre-Conquest exemplars, and some use later
forms of language. The compiler(s) did not distinguish between these; Old
and early Middle English, then, coexist harmoniously, indicating that the
rigid chronology we assign nowadays to language evolution simply has no
relevance within the context of the twelfth century.

To these manuscript compilers, and the scribes with whom they
worked, it seems there was no incongruity in placing texts that appeared
phonologically or morphologically very different next to each other; to a
greater or lesser extent, these were simply the compilers' required vernacular materials, which, we must accept, were considered as equally intelligi-
ble to the intended audience. There appears, prima facie, then, to have
been a tolerance of linguistic variability within written texts in the
post-Conquest period, very much foreshadowing the emergence of
remarkably divergent dialectally marked texts in the later twelfth century
and thereafter. Variability seems not to have prompted too great an anxiety
for contemporary manuscript writers or, indeed, for users. English materials copied in the post-Conquest period, particularly those based on Old
English exemplars, should therefore not be written off simply as archaic or
as a corrupt form of some linguistic koiné previously more perfect, as
indeed they often are.[5]

The precise environment in which these early-English texts were read
and used in the twelfth and thirteenth centuries is difficult to determine.[6] It
is generally thought that religious manuscripts such as Cotton Vespasian D.
xiv were compiled because homiletic and hagiographic texts were "needed
for religious instruction in the vernacular, to lay people as well as to nuns
and monks."[7] In the case of Oxford, Bodleian Library MS Bodley 343, a
West Midlands' manuscript containing English and Latin homilies and
hagiographies dating from ca. 1170, it may have been intended to act as
"devotional reading for English speaking monks and nuns" and as "a
reading book for secular clergy which could be assimilated and adapted for
use in preaching."[8] These conclusions assume that preaching was, on
occasion, performed in English, and that secular clergies were able to read
and assimilate, or copy for themselves, the materials included in these
manuscripts.

These theories could indeed account for the post-Conquest compilation of manuscripts containing English texts. But, often, such conjecture cannot be entirely substantiated by the meager evidence that the manuscripts themselves provide.[9] In addition, although the surviving homiletic and hagiographic manuscripts can be treated as a group, particularly because of the shared codicological aspects of the volumes, their intended uses may have been varied depending on where and when they were produced.[10] In practical terms, the production of manuscripts must have depended on available personnel and materials: the institution had to have at least one compiler or supervisor who recognized the need for English texts; one or more scribes capable of writing English; at least one Old English exemplar from which texts could be copied; and facilities to enable the copying to proceed. Contemporary evidence suggests that such a combination of conditions was rare and only a limited number of religious institutions appear to have engaged in the copying of English. Moreover, only four of these—Rochester, Christ Church, Canterbury, and Worcester—have more than one significant or extensive vernacular manuscript attributed to them.[11]

In theory, Cotton Vespasian D. xiv could have been written for preachers as a form of homiliary or general religious miscellany; as a collection of texts for monastic students; or, as a compilation of works suitable for female readers; or a volume always generally intended for private, devotional reading. It seems most likely, though, that this is a monastic production originally intended for an exclusively monastic audience. Of particular note for assessing the importance of English in the period is the fact that Cotton Vespasian D. xiv was very probably compiled in the scriptorium of the primate, where one might presuppose the greatest compliance with the Norman overlordship, and a lack of regard for the subordinate native vernacular. *The Eadwine Psalter*, however, produced at Christ Church in the mid-twelfth century, demonstrates beyond doubt the relative value attached to the three languages current in England during the reign of Henry II.[12]

That the potential contemporary audience for a codex such as Vespasian D. xiv is monastic in the first instance can be substantiated by evidence that is extratextual—in that monastic institutions alone seem to have produced vernacular manuscripts in the twelfth century, as far as our current knowledge of certain localization permits.[13] Intratextual evidence also clearly points to this immediate audience: texts have been adapted and manipulated throughout the codex, in such a way as to eliminate references to material that is not relevant for strictly monastic recipients. It is crucial to note that within the term "monastic recipients" is to be understood a variety of audience members—not simply a uniform group of Latinate and educated men in the coenobitic order. The monastic community would be home to many differing individuals (from *conversi*, to lay brothers, to members of the confraternity), whose language, intellectual talents, commitment to the order, and roles within their particular institution would merit a diversity of textual materials for a variety of purposes.

Vespasian D. xiv, then, is a well-produced, thoughtful, and extensive compilation that confirms the literary relevance and cultural usefulness of English in this post-Conquest period. Reinforcing the contemporary relevance of English (as opposed to its "antiquarian" function[14]) is the inclusion of the translation of Ralph D'Escures's homily on the Festival of the Virgin Mary. Ralph D'Escures, at one time abbot of Séez, and then the Benedictine bishop of Rochester (to 1114), and archbishop of Canterbury until his death in 1122, wrote his Latin homily for the Assumption of St. Mary in ca. 1100. Until the work of Wilmart, the homily was thought to be by Anselm.[15]

The homily concerning Mary, with its pericope of Luke 10:38–42, was intended by its author to be used at the Assumption of the Virgin, celebrated on August 15. D'Escures's homily is one of five English pieces in Vespasian D. xiv that center on Marian feast-days, and indicates that the place of origin of this codex was very much participant in the emerging Marian cultus in the twelfth century[16] and paid especial attention to the Feast of the Assumption. Included in Vespasian D. xiv are D'Escures's piece (rubricated here as *Sermo in festis Sancte Marie virginis*), three texts, or parts of texts, for the Assumption of the Virgin,[17] and an extract from Ælfric's Homily on the Annunciation from his *Catholic Homilies I*. The occurrence of these homilies in two parts of the codex, correctly sequenced—three in one cluster, the D'Escures piece some one hundred folios later, and the Annunciation of Mary appearing as the penultimate text—indicates an organizational scheme very loosely approximating to two separate, thin sequences of *temporale* and *sanctorale* pieces, interspersed with other, less easily definable texts.

The English version of D'Escures's text was, it seems, part of the original design of the manuscript, copied by the main scribe, and occurring at folios 151v–57v, following the unique *Life* of St. Neot (feast-day July 31)[18] and preceding a brief, integral extract in English from the *Trinubium Annae*. The latter text, the earliest vernacular rendition of its source, is intimately linked with the Festival of Mary by its provision of the lineage of the Virgin, and an explanation of the various Marys of the New Testament attempting to clarify the protagonists of Luke 10:38–42 who form the main homily's focus.

Interestingly, in terms of the homily's mode of composition, Ralph D'Escures writes that he delivered it first in French to his chapter before transcribing it into Latin.[19] In itself, this nugget of information is of immense importance in overturning scholarly perceptions that preaching to a monastic audience would have been in Latin.[20] That preaching in chapter could be in a vernacular becomes particularly useful for the inter- pretative and performative reversal indicated by the translation into English, possibly, then, for delivery to an audience of monoglot monks, novices, or, perhaps most likely, lay brothers and *conversi*.

This early English adaptation stays fairly close to its source, which will have been a Latin text of the homily similar to that edited by Kienzle in 1997 from the early twelfth-century manuscript, Worcester Cathedral Library MS F. 94.[21] Retaining the pericope, but in English, the vernacular version then omits D'Escures's preface outlining his dedication and exposition of how the homily came about, as well as his more general series of statements about exegesis and a particular allegorization of *castellum* [castle] with its obvious resonances for interpreting the Virgin from scriptural reference.

The structure of the main body of the Old English homily follows precisely that of the Latin source. The exposition of the symbolism of Mary as the "castle" into which Christ entered, signified by Martha's house, becomes the impetus for the detailed allegorization of Mary's walls of virginity and tower of humility. This leads into a narration of the Annunciation, which is employed to exemplify the Virgin's unique quality of both mother and virgin, her words "Ic eam Drihtenes þenen" [I am the handmaid of the Lord], being used to support her humility. From this, the homily proceeds to expand the discussion: the gate of faith through which Christ entered the Virgin was not despoiled, since he is, as his name signifies, the savior.

The second half of the homily concerns the elucidation of Mary and Martha as symbols of the contemplative and active lives, respectively: two facets of life that are unified within the Virgin Mary herself. Neither Mary nor Martha could achieve the accomplishments of Christ's mother, but each in their own chosen tasks is following Christ's commands. The active life of Martha is demonstrated in the Virgin's merciful acts, an aspect of the symbolism that allows the homilist to allude to the care of the baby Jesus, the Flight to Egypt, the Massacre of the Holy Innocents, and the Crucifixion and Resurrection. In all these things was the Virgin troubled. The contemplative aspect of Mary's life in Luke 10:38–42 is enacted through the care with which the Virgin listened to Gabriel, and literally interiorized the wisdom and virtue of God. Since the Virgin, in being "lifted up over the angels" and reunited with Christ, was no longer trou- bled, this contemplative aspect represents the best part, that which shall never be taken away.

The symbolism of the roles of Martha and Mary as active and contem- plative was widely commented on throughout the medieval period, by

Gregory, Jerome, Bede, Augustine, Hrabanus Maurus, Ælfric,[22] Honorius Augustodunensis, and many other commentators. While the unification of the aspects of both of Lazarus's sisters within the singular figure of the Virgin emerged from at least the ninth century,[23] it does not appear to be until the later eleventh and twelfth centuries that the interpretation of Mary as unifying the active and contemplative, and choosing the latter as the best part, becomes fully advanced. Thus, not only was Ralph D'Escures's homily reflecting very contemporary theological developments, but also the English translation in Cotton Vespasian D. xiv was a deliberate effort to ensure that innovative and current exegesis was made available in the native vernacular. It is, in sum, the earliest allegorization of Mary as "cæstel" [castle] in English.

The Old English translation begins with the Gospel story itself in a relatively full discussion of chapters 38–42. This section closes with the point that:

> Sume ungelærede mænn wundrigeð hwæt þiss godspell belimpe to þære eadigen Marien Cristes moder, and hwi man æt hire þenunge geræde þiss godspell; ac us þincð þæt hit rihtlice to hire gebyreð beo þan þe ure larðeawes us doð to understandene.

> [Some unlearned people wonder in what way this gospel relates to the blessed Mary, Christ's mother, and why this gospel is read at her service; but it seems to us properly to pertain to her as our teachers help us to understand.]

Within this short passage, which comes before the translation proper from D'Escures's Latin source, and which is thus unique to the English text, the adapator is clearly addressing not the "ungelærede mænn" [unlearned people] themselves, but others—the "us"—who set themselves apart from this group: a theologically aware audience for whom clarity is equally necessary, but who would not doubt the appropriateness of the Lucan passages to an exegetical interpretation of the Virgin.

After the introductory statements, the English follows the Latin homily by relating the relatively complex exegesis that links the distinctive qualities of Mary and Martha—as contemplative and active—as united characteristics centered in the Virgin's single person. The Latin source is closely followed throughout the English homily: the same structure is adhered to; and the same tropes for explaining the interpretation are present. For example, the following quotation figuratively elucidates the image of the *castellum* of Mary and Martha into which Christ entered as guest as the Virgin Mary herself:

> Tamen hic castellum, in quod intravit Iesus, singularem et intemeratam Virginem eiusdem Iesu genitricem, salva Scriptuarum regula, per similitudinem

accipimus. Castellum enim dicitur quaelibet turris, et murus in circuitu eius. Quae duo sese invicem defendunt, ita ut hostes per murum ab arce et a muro per arcem arceantur.

Huiusmodi castello non incongrue Virgo Maria assimilatur, quam virginitas mentis et corporis, quasi murus, ita undique vallavit ut nullus unquam libidini ad eam esset accessurus nec sensus eius aliqua corrumperentur illecebra. Et quia virginitatem, cum libido non possit, solet impugnare superbia, est in eadem virgine turris humilitatis, qua a muro virginitatis omnem repellit superbiam. Et quia humilitatem, cum superbia non possit, solet impugnare libido, murus virginitatis a turre humilitatis omnem repellit libidinem. Itaque hae duo, murus videlicet virginitatis et turris humilitatis ab alterutro muniuntur; ut nunquam in humili Virgine fuerit nec superba virginitas, nec inquina humilitas, sed semper in eadem permanserit et humilis virginitas et virgo humilitas.[24]

Ðes cæstel þære ure Drihten in com betacneð rihtlice þæt synderlice unwæmme mæden Maria Cristes moder. For cæstel is geclypod sum heh stepel, þe byð mid wealle betrymed, swa þæt æigðer oðre bewereð wið unwinen gewinne.

Ðyssen cæstele is rihtlice wiðmeten þæt synderlice mæden Marie Cristes moder, for heo wæs fæstlice betrymed mid mæigne unwæmmes mægeðhades on lichame and on geðanca swa swa mid strangen cæstelwealle swa þæt hire næfre ne mihte genelæcen nan lichamlic galnysse ne forðen to hire geðanca nan ungelefed hæmeðe; and for þan þe mægðhad stranglice mæig wiðstanden þære galnysse þæt hit ne byð þurh þæt oferswiðen modignysse gelomen gewinð þa infare, for þan wæs eadmodnysse stepel on hire, and wal þe aferseð ealle modignysse fram þan mægðhade.

[This castle into which our lord came signifies properly that singularly undefiled maiden Mary, Christ's mother. For a castle is protected by a high tower which is enclosed by walls so that each protects the other against enemies in conflict. This castle is rightly compared to that unique maiden Mary, Christ's mother. For she was securely enclosed with the might of pure virginity in body and in mind as if with strong castle walls, so that no bodily lust might ever come near her, nor penetrate her mind; not one illicit act of fornication. And therefore virginity strongly might withstand that lust so that it cannot be overcome by it. Pride might frequently attack the entrance yet humility was the tower in her and the walls which resisted all pride because of that virginity. (Lust might frequently attack the entrance but for the wall of virginity in her which resolutely resisted all lust from the tower of humility. And thus is the wall of virginity and the tower of humility and both are strengthened by the other. That in her virginity might never be overcome by pride, but humility and virginity and pure piety was always in her.)]

As the figurative *cæstel*, Mary is protected by the tower of humility and the walls of virginity in body and mind such that no pride or lust can enter.[25] The translator stays close to the source phrase by phrase, sense by sense, abbreviating some clauses slightly, and expanding with minor details for clarity (by, for instance, adding "Cristes moder" [Christ's Mother] in the third sentence). Interestingly, the English version is linguistically traditional in terms of the very high proportion of Old English lexis employed.[26] The phonology and inflectional morphology, though, are recognizably transitional Old English—such as the consistent leveling of the dative and the preterite plural, in particular, to the unstressed *en*—and as such this piece is very much a product of the post-Conquest period.

Apart from the language used in this text,[27] other aspects of the translator's techniques demonstrate a concern to achieve the greatest possible clarity in the English version. This adherence to clarity does not imply simplification, such as is often associated with the composition of texts in the vernacular from identifiable Latin sources. A small amount of extraneous matter, not pertinent to the specific emphasis of this text's main interpretation is excised; for example, the name of Elizabeth, mother of John the Baptist, is excised in the English. Her Annunciation is employed as a comparison to the Virgin's in the Latin source,[28] whereas in the English "Hit wearð fullfremod on hire [Mary] þæt þæt se ængel hire sæde" [It was fulfilled in her just as the angel told her]. The vernacular version effectively emphasizes its focus on the Virgin, therefore, but may also here be foreshadowing the genealogical clarification that comes in the *Trinubium Annae* appended to the homily, and which thus renders unnecessary the comparison with Elizabeth at this point.

Other excisions from the Latin include the attempt to explain Mary's humility and virginity. D'Escures reminds his audience that any virgin, like Mary, who was about to get married would ponder the significance of Gabriel's statement of the immaculate conception:

> Si cuilibet virgini desponsatae in animo suo disponenti nubere diceretur, filium habetis, non miraretur neque interrogaret quomodo istud fieret utpote quae se desponsatam et in proximo nupturam sciret et a viro gravidari usu naturae speraret. Haec autem non immerito mirata est, et quomodo quod promittebatur fieret, sciscitata quoniam quamvis desponsatam, tamen se nunquam nupturam, neque virum cognituram certissime sciebat.[29]

The English abbreviates this to:

> Gyf ænige mædene þe hæfde gemynt were to underfone and wære gesæd þæt heo scolde sune geberen, ne þuhte hit hire sellic, ne heo axigen nolde: "Hwu sceal hit gewurðen þæt ic sune gebide?" Ac eaðe þeos mihte axigen: "Hwu sceall þiss gewurdeðen þæt ic sune habbe?" For þeh heo Josepe gehandfæst wære, þehhweðere he hæfde anrædlice on hire gemynte þæt heo næfre weres gemænnysse nolde cunnen.

[If any virgin who had a mind to be married to a man were told that she would bear a son, might it not seem strange to her? Might she not ask: "How can it be that I should expect a son?" But easily might this woman [Mary] ask: "How shall it come about that I shall have a son?" For though she was engaged to Joseph, nevertheless she had resolutely resolved that she would never participate in intercourse with a man.]

In this excerpt, then, the "natural order" of marriage and pregnancy seen in the Latin is omitted in the English, retaining the focus on the miraculousness of the Virgin's conception, and yet highlighting the normal human reaction she showed to Gabriel's extraordinary news. Mary's statement of intent to remain a virgin permanently is emphasized in the English through the addition of Joseph's name, amplifying the audience's understanding of the direct speech, and demonstrating, through the impact of the double negative ("nunquam. . .neque" "næfre. . .nolde"); Mary's life-long commitment to her purity.[30]

The minor addition of Joseph's name in the English version is typical of the translator's method of enhancing the clarity of the Latin by adding small details such as "Cristes moder" [Christ's mother] to the Latin "Maria" in order, presumably, to ensure that the audience understands to which Mary the text refers. Similarly, in maintaining its focus, the English adaptation insists at all points on the superlative nature of Mary's endeavors. The Latin, discussing the manner in which Martha and Mary's attributes are brought together uniquely in the Virgin, states:

> Nunquam in aliqua persona, immo in omnibus, Martha sic operata est; nunquam in sic alias, Maria contemplationi vacavit. Nunquam sic alias haec vel illa quod suum est exhibuit.[31]

The English adds to this description of the uniqueness of the Virgin:

> On nanre oðre næs Marthe studdinge on nanen time swa fullice geforðed toweard Gode and toweard his leomen swa on ures Drihtenes moder. Ne Marien besceawunge ne hire hlystinge to Godes worden næs næfre on nanre oðre swa fullice geforðed swa on ure Drihtenes moder.

> [In no other was Martha's labor at any time as fully accomplished toward God and toward his body as in our Lord's mother. Nor was Mary's contemplation nor her listening to God's word ever in any way as fully accomplished as it is in our Lord's mother.]

The English version thereby augments the focus of the Latin, and seeks to intensify the superlative nature of the Virgin, both in her role as the perfect embodiment of the active and contemplative, and in her role as the mother of God. This movement towards the specific identification of the Virgin as glorious perfection is very much in keeping with theological developments in the twelfth century, which strove to stress the importance of Mary as mediatrix and Virgin Mother.[32] The English version of the D'Escures homily, to a greater extent than the original, is testimony to this Mariological process.

Inextricably linked with the glorification of Mary in this period is the reminder of the humanity of the Mother of God. Again, the English adaptation of D'Escures's homily gives more weight to this element of the Marian presentation than does its source. This emphasis comes more from the incremental buildup of related expansions in the English, some of which are discussed above, rather than from any explicit statement. In the enumeration of the six corporal mercies, Mary is shown in the role of young mother to the baby Christ. The Latin explains that Mary clothed Jesus, fed him, quenched his thirst, looked after him during sickness, bathed him, comforted him, helped him; in the English version, she "wrapped and clothed him with her body; when he was hungry and thirsty, she graciously filled him with her milk. In his childhood sickness, she bathed him, and warmed him, and anointed him, and carried him, and comforted him, and rocked him." This enhanced description of the mother's concern for her child encourages the personal engagement of the audience in the relationship between Mary and her baby, before the sudden transition to Mary's grief at Christ's Crucifixion, where Christ's death "þurheode hire sawle" [pierced her soul]. In the Latin, "a sword passed through her soul." Albeit written in a third-person narrative, this demand for empathy on the audience's part is broadly reminiscent of the affective piety of Anselm's prayers; this moment in the homily preempting the much more introspective devotion to the Virgin evinced in later texts, such as *On God Ureisun of Ure Lefdi*, which is similarly inspired by the office for the Feast of the Assumption.[33]

A more significant expansion of the original Latin text, which again demonstrates the contemporary validity of the English version, concerns the definition of what constitutes the active and contemplative lives as represented by Martha and Mary. Both lives, and their meaning, had been the cause of considerable, prolonged debate for centuries, some authors, such as Gregory and Bede, distinguishing between the two in a temporal sense, and others, such as Abbo of Fleury, distinguishing between them in a practical sense.[34] This debate was to take on added force for some writers inasmuch as the contemplative life signified by Mary became associated with the monastic life as the *optima pars* [best part]. By the twelfth century, although the lives were distinguished, it was their compatibility and unification either in Mary or in Christ that appears to dominate both artistic and textual discourse.[35]

In the Latin text of D'Escures's homily, he comments of Mary and Martha that:

> Duae istae sorores, sicut sancti patres plenissime nobis exposuerunt, duas in sancta ecclesia vitas designant: Martha scilicet, activam; Maria, contemplativam. Ista laborat ad exhibenda indigenti omnia humanitatis officia; illa vacat et videt quoniam Deus est. Ista circa exteriora occupatur; illa interiora contemplatur.[36]

This interpretation of Martha and Mary—with the former working by showing all the occupations of humanity for the needy, and the latter devoting herself to search for God—has been altered in the English in an interesting way:

> Ðas twa gesustre, beo þan þe ure larðeawas us cyðeð, betacnigeð þa twa lif þe man lætt on rihtwisnysse: Martha þæt geswyncfulle lif þe we one drohtnigeð; Maria þæt ece lif þe we to willnig[eð]. Martha swanc and becarcade to geforðigene þan Hælende and his þeowen þa lichamlice behefðen; Maria fæstlice wunede abuten þan Hælende and hlyste his worden. Seo studdede emb þa uterlice þing; þeos oðer þa inweardlice þing gemyndelice besceawode.

> [These two sisters, about whom our teachers reveal to us, signify the two lives that are permitted to a person in righteousness: Martha is that active life, which we lead;[37] Mary that eternal life, which we desire. Martha labored and was anxious to take care of the Savior and serve his physical needs; Mary resolutely stayed around the Savior and listened to his words. The one troubled about the outer things; the other woman contemplated spiritual things in her heart.]

The ostensibly insignificant alteration in the English has consequences for interpreting the way in which the translator understood or wished to convey the meaning of the active and contemplative lives. There is no doubt that while the two figures of Mary and Martha were uniquely united in the Virgin Mary, the distinction between the two lives was very real for this writer. For Ralph D'Escures, the distinction appears to be one of pastoral and charitable activity versus a metaphorical and spiritual *peregrinatio pro amore Dei* [pilgrimage for the love of God]. Rather like the structure of the *Ancrene Wisse* and the stipulations of the author, the outer concerns, although necessary, are secondary to the inner: the physical and temporal in opposition to the spiritual and eternal.

For the English translator, D'Escures's practical distinction is adapted explicitly into one that signifies the time lived in this present life from the time to come. The variance between the Latin and the English is subtle, but it is notable. The English writer seems deliberately to have altered the emphasis away from the need of the *vita activa* [active life] to undertake specifically pastoral or charitable work, to a life on earth in and of itself. The hope for the *vita contemplativa* [contemplative life] is necessarily the hope expressed through Mary's "best part" of being reunited with Christ in heaven: a part, which, as the translator says, "us geunne God þurh hire þingunge" [God might grant us through her ministry]. This interpretation belongs specifically to the Augustinian conception of the two lives: "What Martha did is what we are; what Mary did is what we hope for."[38] Moreover, the translator's alteration of his source to encapsulate Augustine's interpretation can be directly linked to Ælfric, in his homily on the Assumption of the Virgin from his *Catholic Homilies II*, which takes Augustine's *Sermons* 103 and 104 as a major source.[39] It is likely that the English writer borrowed from Ælfric at this point in the text, since Ælfric's own Assumption homily appears earlier in Cotton Vespasian D. xiv,[40] in which the text reads (at fol. 55v): "On þyssen twam gesustren wæron getacnode twa lif, þiss geswyncfulle þe we onwuniged, and þæt ece þe gewillniged" [The two lives were symbolised in these two sisters: this laborious life in which we dwell, and that eternal life which we desire].[41] In this way, as well as in terms of the lexis of the English text, the translator marries earlier vernacular traditions with innovations in homiletic and theological writings. This praxis of tradition and innovation entirely typifies the corpus of English religious writings in this period.

In addition to the adaptations already discussed, the most significant departure from the Latin source is the entire omission of the twenty-line laudatory verse to Mary at the end of the homily, poetry clearly not being one of the English homilist's stylistic desiderata. The English text instead contains the addition of the *Trinubium Annae*, a useful semi-exegetical text in this context. This latter short text appears to be integral to the D'Escures homily, only divided from the main homily by an enlarged initial *A*. This explication of the holy kinship narration, ultimately derived from the second-century *Proto-Evangelium* of James, adds considerably to the understanding of the homily inasmuch as the respective relationships of the various Marys, among others, are fully explained. This appendage is the earliest vernacular rendition of the *Trinubium Annae*, the first Anglo-Latin version of which comes from Bury St. Edmunds in the late eleventh century.[42] Here, though, the *Trinubium Annae* is used in an altogether different context: what the provision of the family history as an appendix to the Ralph D'Escures homily illustrates is the recontextualization of the material to an explanatory function, bearing directly on the preceding text, and situating Mary in her most human context, a concern of increasing significance for all twelfth-century writers, and particularly so for homiletic and hagiographic writers impressing upon their audience the need for personal devotion to God and his saints, an embryonic affective piety in many respects.[43]

It is the case therefore, that although the English version of the D'Escures Assumption homily remains substantively true to its source, it seeks both to improve the clarity, as is absolutely typical of adaptors of Old English texts, and to incorporate minor rereadings at various points that encapsulate both the old and the new. The English text bears witness to the Ælfrician homiletic tradition, rhetoric and diction, while simultaneously fully participating in twelfth-century developments in Marian devotion. This homily alone testifies that many texts in the vernacular in the post-Conquest period were no less sophisticated, theologically informed, or learned than their Latin sources and analogues, despite a tendency on the part of modern critics to dismiss the body of English material in the period up to ca. 1170 merely as copies of pre-Conquest texts or unoriginal translations of Latin exemplars. The homily reflects the requirement of the Vespasian D. xiv compiler to offer theologically contemporary analysis of the Lucan pericope, and to provide not simply the homilies of Ælfric for the Assumption, but something more indicative of post-Conquest devotional developments. That the compiler had no concern about melding pre-Conquest homilies with post-Conquest vernacular material is witness to the vitality of the former well beyond its usually perceived sell-by date.

Furthermore, this mid-twelfth century homily is representative of a wider trend in the compilation of manuscripts written in English that counters scholarly misconceptions about the period: from these texts we witness the learned nature of the audience despite the tendency to downgrade English to a medium fit only for the *illiterati* [illiterate]; we witness the dissemination of contemporary theology, despite the desire to situate English texts as testimony only to archaism and retrospectivity; we witness the institutional requirement for the production of texts and manuscripts, despite a current unwillingness to accept the potential of the native vernacular for literary expression; and we witness an adaptive creativity in English which parallels that preceding the Conquest, despite critical suggestions that copying such texts in the twelfth century simply illustrates the backward-looking imitation of scribes and manuscript compilers.

Notes

1. As Mary Swan has amply demonstrated in the preceding essay.
2. All the texts are edited by R. N. Warner, *Early English Homilies from the Twelfth-Century MS. Vesp. D. XIV*, EETS OS 152 (London: Oxford University Press, 1917 for 1915). For the contents and description, see N. R. Ker, *Catalogue of Manuscripts Containing Anglo-Saxon* (Oxford: Clarendon Press, 1957; repr. with supplement 1990), item 209; and Jonathan Wilcox, *Wulfstan Texts and Other Homiletic Materials*, Anglo-Saxon Manuscripts in Microfiche Facsimile 8 (Medieval and Renaissance Texts and Studies. Tempe: Arizona, 2000), pp. 53–64. For the *Dicts of Cato*, see E. M. Treharne, "The Form and Function of the Old English *Dicts of Cato*," *Journal of English and Germanic Philology* 102.4 (September 2003): 65–85. On the possible origins and purposes of the manuscript, see Mary P. Richards, "On the Date and Provenance of the MS Cotton Vespasian D.XIV, ff. 4–169," *Manuscripta* 17 (1973): 31–35, which argues for a Rochester origin; Rima Handley, "British Museum MS. Cotton Vespasian D. xiv," *Notes and Queries* 219 (1974): 243–50, which argues for a Christ Church, Canterbury origin; and Elaine Treharne, "The Dates and Origins of Three Twelfth-Century Manuscripts," in *Anglo-Saxon Manuscripts and Their Heritage: Tenth to Twelfth Centuries*, ed. P. Pulsiano and E. M. Treharne (Ashgate, 1998), pp. 227–52.
3. Cited in Margaret Laing's *Catalogue of Sources for a Linguistic Atlas of Early Middle English* (Cambridge: D. S. Brewer, 1993), at p. 83, is Cecily Clark's comment from *The Peterborough Chronicle 1070–1154* (Oxford: Clarendon Press, 1970) that the Ralph D'Escures piece is "usually classed as the earliest M[iddle] E[nglish]." See, more recently, Thomas Hahn, "Early Middle English," chap. 3 in *The Cambridge History of Medieval English Literature*, ed. David Wallace (Cambridge: Cambridge University Press, 1999), pp. 61–91.
4. Hahn, "Early Middle English," pp. 82–3. It should be observed that Hahn gives no evidence for naming this manuscript the *Rochester Anthology* other than the inclusion of the piece by Ralph D'Escures, who, as he points out, was Bishop of Rochester (p. 82, n. 41). D'Escures was also Archbishop of Canterbury. Moreover, as noted below, D'Escures's homily was copied into Worcester Cathedral Library MS F. 94 in the early twelfth century, a manuscript whose origin is Worcester. D'Escures's own institutional affiliations have little, necessarily, to do with the origin of those manuscripts in which his works appear.
5. James Milroy, "Middle English Dialectology," p. 193, states: "Variability in Middle English [equally well applied to the twelfth century] has sometimes been perceived as an obstacle rather than a resource. . .In editorial and descriptive commentary, it is very easy to find comments about chaotic or 'lawless' spelling and even editorial judgements to the effect that a given scribe could not have been a native English speaker—so variable is his orthography. . .However, judgements of this kind can effectively block further investigation of variable constraints in the texts in question: they can be dismissed as 'corrupt' or 'unreliable' specimens of language."

6. See, for example, Susan Irvine, "The Persistence of Old English in the Twelfth Century" and E. M. Treharne, "The Production of Manuscripts Containing English Religious Texts in the First Half of the Twelfth Century," in Swan and Treharne, *Rewriting Old English*, pp. 41–61 and 11–40 respectively. See also Mary P. Richards, *Texts and Their Traditions in the Medieval Library of Rochester Cathedral Priory*, Transactions of the American Philosophical Association, 78.3 (Philadelphia: American Philosophical Society, 1988).

7. Hans Sauer, "Knowledge of Old English in the Middle English Period?," in *Language History and Linguistic Modelling: A Festschrift for Jacek Fisiak on his 60 Birthday*, ed. Raymond Hickey and Stanislaw Puppel, Trends in Linguistics, Studies and Monographs 101 (Berlin: Mouton de Gruyter, 1997), pp. 791–814, at 796.

8. *Old English Homilies from Bodley 343*, ed. Susan Irvine, EETS OS 302 (Oxford: Oxford University Press, 1993), p. liii.

9. As Irvine suggests in relation to preaching in her *Old English Homilies*, pp. lii-liii (where she states of Bodley 343) "[it] shows no sign of having played any direct role in preaching. . .It shows none of the omission marks, changes in punctuation, and marginal additions that appear in eleventh-century manuscripts like D and F, and which would be usual in a manuscript intended or used for preaching. Moreover the material is not uniformly suitable for preaching purposes."

10. See Treharne, "Production of Manuscripts."

11. This evidence of monastic manuscript production in English problematizes the theory that French was the spoken language of the monastery proposed by Susan Crane in her essay, "Anglo-Norman Cultures in England, 1066–1460," chap. 2 in *Cambridge History of Medieval Literature*, ed. David Wallace, pp. 35–60, at 44. Ian Short likewise comments that "Anglo-Norman was a language of law and of record, an acceptable alternative to Latin in the cloister. . .," in "Language and Literature," in *A Companion to the Anglo-Norman World*, ed. Christopher Harper-Bill and Elisabeth Van Houts (Woodbridge, Suffolk: Boydell and Brewer, 2003), pp. 191–213, at 205. Neither Short nor Crane cite the source for this use of French in the cloister, with the exception of Dominica Legge's work, referenced in Short, "Language and Literature," p. 199, n. 4.

12. And it is to *The Eadwine Psalter*, Cambridge, Trinity College MS R. 17. 1, that I believe we should look for paleographical and linguistic *comparanda* with Vespasian D. xiv. Brief analyses in this direction have proven interesting and worthy of further examination.

13. These institutions are chiefly those monastic cathedrals involved in the tenth-century Benedictine Reform. This rather suggests a deliberate program of copying by a networked group of English manuscript compilers and scribes.

14. For which, see, for example, Michael Clanchy, *From Memory to Written Record* (Oxford: Blackwell, 2d ed., 1993), pp. 212; Seth Lerer, "Old English and its afterlife," chap. 1 in Wallace, *Cambridge History of Medieval Literature*, pp. 7–34

15. Beverley Mayne Kienzle, "Exegesis on Luke 10:38 around 1100: Worcester MS F. 94, ff. 1r-2r, a Tribute to James E. Cross," in *Medieval Sermon Studies* 40 (1997): 22–28; A. Wilmart, "Les homélies attribuées à S. Anselme," *Archives d'histoire doctrinale et littéraire de moyen âge* 2 (1927): 5–29, 339–41.

16. On the devotion of some monastic establishments to the Virgin in this period, see Thomas N. Hall, "The Earliest Anglo-Latin Text of the *Trinubium Annae* (BHL 505zl)," in *Via Crucis: Essays on Early Medieval Sources and Ideas in Memory of J. E. Cross*, ed. Thomas N. Hall with Thomas D. Hill and Charles D. Wright (Morgantown, Va.: West Virginia University Press, 2002), pp. 104–37.

17. Items xvi, xvii, and xviii in Warner, *Early English Homilies*. Item xvi and xviii are two separated parts of Ælfric's *Catholic Homilies I* text on the Assumption, while the intervening item, xvii, is from Ælfric's *Catholic Homilies II* text on the Assumption.

18. R. C. Love, states that: "The relics [of St. Neot] were inspected in the late eleventh century, and certified to be authentic by Anselm, archbishop of Canterbury;" see R. C. Love, "St. Neot," in *Blackwell Encyclopaedia of Anglo-Saxon England*, ed. Michael Lapidge, et al. (Oxford: Blackwell, 1999), p. 331. Tentatively, this might assist in the attribution of Cotton Vespasian D. xiv to Christ Church.

19. Kienzle explains this process. In the homily, we read that: "Quid ad gloriosam virginem Dei Genitricem lectio ista pertineat, ut in ejus festivitate legatur, plerique solent quaerere: unde quid ego sentirem, in conventu fratrum prout potui, vulgariter iam plusquam semel exposui;" see Kienzle, "Exegesis on Luke 10:38," p. 22.

20. See the discussion in Mary Clayton, "Homiliaries and Preaching in Anglo-Saxon England," *Peritia* 4 (1985): 207–42; repr. in *Old English Prose: Basic Readings*, ed. Paul E. Szarmach, Basic Readings in Anglo-Saxon England 5 (New York: Garland Publishing, 2000), pp. 151–98, where the use of the vernacular in homiletic writing is consistently associated with the laity, and Latin texts with the educated monastic environment.

21. Clayton, "Homiliaries and Preaching," 151–98; for a description of this manuscript, and Plate 26 for a portion of the text, see Rodney M. Thompson, *Catalogue of Manuscripts of Worcester Cathedral Library* (Woodbridge: Boydell and Brewer, 1999).

22. For the cult of the Virgin Mary generally in Anglo-Saxon England, and the Feast of the Assumption particularly, see Mary Clayton, *The Cult of the Virgin Mary in Anglo-Saxon England*, Cambridge Studies in Anglo-Saxon England 2 (Cambridge: Cambridge University Press, 1990), pp. 232–44.

23. See Giles Constable, *Three Studies in Medieval Religious Thought: The Interpretation of Mary and Martha, The Ideal of the Imitation of Christ, The Orders of Society* (Cambridge: Cambridge University Press, 1995), pp. 3–141, esp. 8–10, 45.

24. Kienzle, "Exegesis on Luke 10:38," lines 28–40.

25. This effective, visual image is significantly developed in later medieval literature including Robert Grosseteste's *Chasteau d'Amour* and its derivative,

the *Cursor Mundi*, as well as shorter texts, like Thomas Hales' *Love-Ron*: "Wyþ þeoves, wiþ reveres, wiþ lechers / Þu most beo waker and snel; / Þu art swetture þane eny flur / Hwile þu witest þene kastel."

26. There is only one "modern" loanword: "cæstel." Much of the vocabulary is Ælfrician in nature, so that relatively rare words like "wiðmeten," "bearneacinde," and "earplættigen" appear to be based on a thorough knowledge of Ælfrician prose. This predominance of "Old" English lexemes in the text undermines any attempt to label the text as "early Middle English."

27. A full study of which is in preparation, and which will appear in my forthcoming book, *Living Through Conquest: The Politics of Early English*.

28. "Quia enim credidit, perfecta sunt ei a Domino quae ab angelo dicta sunt, sicut ait ad eam Elizabeth" (Kienzle, "Exegesis on Luke 10:38," 25, lines 82–3).

29. Kienzle, "Exegesis on Luke 10:38," p. 24, lines 50–6.

30. It is conceivable, perhaps, that this insistence on Mary's continence can be regarded as an allusion to the twelfth-century conciliar canons enforcing clerical celibacy. See Jaroslav Pelikan, *The Christian Tradition: A History of the Development of Doctrine*, vol. 3: *The Growth of Medieval Theology (600–1300)* (Chicago: Chicago University Press, 1978), pp. 163–64.

31. Kienzle, "Exegesis on Luke 10:38," p. 25, lines 95–8.

32. Pelikan, *Growth of Medieval Theology*, pp. 160–74.

33. See, for example, Denis Renevey, "Enclosed Desires: A Study of the Wooing Group," in *Mysticism and Spirituality in Medieval England*, ed. William F. Pollard and Robert Boenig (Cambridge: D. S. Brewer, 1997), pp. 40–62, at 50–52.

34. See Constable, *Three Studies*, pp. 3–92.

35. For a general discussion of these issues, see n34, esp. pp. 44–92.

36. Kienzle, "Exegesis on Luke 10:38," p. 25, lines 88–93.

37. Or "which we now lead," if "one" is taken as a variant of "heonu."

38. Augustine, *Sermons*, pp. 103–4, cited in Constable, *Three Studies*, p. 18, n75.

39. Malcolm Godden, ed., *Ælfric's Catholic Homilies, Second Series*, EETS ss 5 (Oxford: Oxford University Press, 1979), Homily p. xxix, 256, lines 38–40: "On ðisum twam geswustrum wæron getacnode twa lif. þis geswincfulle ðe we on wuniað. and þæt ece ðe we gewilniað." For the commentary and sources of this homily, see Malcolm Godden, *Ælfric's Catholic Homilies, Series I and II: Commentary*, EETS ss 18 (Oxford: Oxford University Press, 2000), pp. 588–92.

40. Both homilies are written by the main scribe of Cotton Vespasian D. xiv.

41. Warner, *Early English Homilies*, pp. 48–9.

42. See Thomas N. Hall's comprehensive discussion of this text, together with an edition of the English version in Cotton Vespasian D. xiv, in his "The Earliest Anglo-Latin Text of the *Trinubium Annae* (BHL 505zl)," in Hall, Hill and Wright, *Via Crucis*, pp. 104–37.

43. For this thematic focus in twelfth-century hagiography, see E. M. Treharne, ed., *The Old English Life of St Nicholas with the Old English Life of St Giles*, Leeds Texts and Studies 15 (Leeds: University of Leeds, 1997). On these

emerging trends, and on theological and scholastic emphases in general in this period, see M.-D. Chenu, *Nature, Man and Society in the Twelfth Century*, ed. and trans. Jerome Taylor and Lester K. Little, Medieval Academy Reprints for Teaching 37 (Toronto: University of Toronto Press, 1997).

CHAPTER 8

ENGLISH POETRY OF THE REIGN OF HENRY II

Elizabeth Solopova

According to R. M. Wilson, "It is clear enough that there must have been a flourishing lyrical literature in English during the twelfth century, though almost nothing now remains of it. . .Many of the poems that were composed were probably never written down, and many that are still extant have been preserved only by the merest chance."[1] As evidence for the reality of a flourishing lyrical tradition, Wilson quotes the "Canute Song," St. Godric's hymns, a story told by Giraldus Cambrensis about a parish priest kept awake all night by singing, a few lines surviving as quotations in prose works, and references to poems that are no longer extant.

Considering the existence of such evidence, perhaps the most noticeable fact about English twelfth-century poetry is its poor survival. Since so few texts are extant from the period and none can be dated precisely, the present discussion will include texts that are found in manuscripts, or can be dated on historical grounds to the second half of the twelfth century and the beginning of the thirteenth century (see the appendix for full details). The issues of transmission and survival are crucial for understanding the nature of English poetry of the period, and how the small extant corpus may relate to what originally existed. In the first part of this paper an attempt is made to generalize about manuscript transmission of twelfth-century poetry, including reasons for the meager survival of lyrical verse referred to by Wilson.

Another much-discussed feature of early Middle English poetry is its complex relationship to the Old English poetic tradition. Several poems from the period demonstrate that their authors were familiar with alliterative technique, yet no poetry in Old English meter composed or copied during the period survives. This has given rise to an ongoing discussion among scholars on the nature of the continuity between Old English and Middle English alliterative poetry and prose. The second part of this paper provides an overview of poetry surviving from the period and concentrates on the discussion of its ties with the Old English alliterative tradition. The cosmopolitan character of the late twelfth-century English poetic corpus does highlight some differences with the Old English tradition, and the diversity of poetic styles and forms, and the poets' attitude to their choice possibly illustrate something of the nature of cultural contact in this period.

Manuscript Transmission and Survival

What becomes obvious when the small surviving corpus is examined is that the shorter works are largely fugitive and preserved in single copies. Examples of these include "The Grave" (Oxford, Bodleian Library MS Bodl. 343, dated to the third quarter of the twelfth century), a four-line exhortation to liberality, "Eueriche freman hath to ben hende / for to be large . . ." (preserved in Oxford, Bodleian Library MS Rawl. C. 22 and dated to the beginning of the thirteenth century), as well as poetry transmitted by the Tremulous Hand of Worcester, including the "First Worcester Fragment," the *Soul's Address to the Body* and a piece in London, British Library MS Royal 8.D.xiii, possibly also by the Tremulous Hand: "Ic an witles ful iwis."[2] The few exceptions are texts transmitted as part of longer works of prose, such as hymns of St. Godric to Burgwine, St. Mary, and St. Nicholas appearing in the context of his Latin *Life* written by Reginald of Durham, in a Latin chronicle by Roger of Wendover and other works in diverse manuscripts dating from the end of the twelfth century and later. Similarly the "Canute Song," quoted by Thomas of Ely writing in the second half of the twelfth century, is preserved in two copies of *Liber Eliensis* (Oxford, Bodleian Library MS Laud Misc. 647 and Cambridge, Trinity College MS O.2.1).[3]

Much of this, shorter lyrical verse, appears to have existed both literally and figuratively in the margins of the written tradition. "Ic an witles ful iwis" [I am completely without sense] is pencilled in a top margin, and "The Grave" is added at the foot of a folio after the end of an Old English sermon. At this period there is yet no evidence for the existence of multilingual codices of prose, poetry, and nonliterary items, such as we find later in, for example, London, British Library MS Harley 2253, Oxford, Bodleian Library MS Digby 86, or Oxford, Jesus College MS 29, collections which had such crucial roles in preservation of English poetry in the late thirteenth and fourteenth centuries.

In contrast, surviving longer works, , including Laȝamon's *Brut* and the *Poema Morale*, are preserved in more than one copy.[4] An exception is the *Ormulum* which survives as an author's holograph in a single manuscript as Oxford, Bodleian Library MS Junius 1. This pattern of transmittal, similarly, seems to have been present in the distribution of Old English poetry, in which texts surviving in multiple copies, such as "Cædmon's Hymn" or "Bede's Death Song" are short pieces preserved as part of prose works. Such a pattern may point to persistent differences in the transmission and survival of poetic genres. Lesser genres, including devotional and secular lyrical verse, appear to have had ephemeral and largely oral existence, and by the second half of the twelfth century their only established written context appears to have been that of prose works, including chronicles, treatises, and sermons in which a poetic form was used for a variety of reasons, such as historical and devotional interest, mnemonic, rhetorical, structural and other.[5]

It is also worth noting that two of the longer texts surviving from the period are by self-conscious authors, whose names, Laȝamon and Orm, are known from their compositions. Each tells of himself in his work and comments directly on the events and situations described. In contrast, we know the names of the authors of lyrical verse, including Cædmon, Bede and St. Godric only from prose narratives in which they are preserved. The literary historical phenomenon of continued anonymity and probably largely oral life of the "lesser" genres is a possible reason for their scanty preservation just as much or even more than the political and linguistic situation in England in the first two centuries after the Conquest.

Literary Context

English verse in the second half of the twelfth century and the beginning of the thirteenth century, remarkably diverse in its content, language and form, was subject to two major literary influences: contemporary Latin and French poetry and the Old English alliterative tradition. It was a product of a multilingual environment and written by multilingual authors for largely multilingual audiences. Laȝamon's English *Brut* is a free adaptation, considerably expanded with new material, of Wace's *Roman de Brut* written during the reign of Henry II and, according to Laȝamon, presented to Eleanor of Aquitaine. As other essays in this volume show, it shares cultural and political concerns with the *Roman de Brut* and other Latin and Anglo-Norman literature cultivated at court, including interest in the poetic recreation of the national past from Celtic and Anglo-Saxon legends and history.

Peter Lucas observes that literary patronage has its roots in a literacy that was largely clerical before 1066 and that until the twelfth century books were written, copied, read and preserved mainly in monasteries.[6] He points to Auerbach's comment that it was at the beginning of the twelfth century that the situation began to change, and that French and Provençal princes and other members of the Anglo-Norman aristocracy began to commission and receive poems in the vernacular, with most patrons of vernacular poetry at this early period being ladies of Anglo-Norman nobility.[7] Lucas draws attention to passages from twelfth-century poetry which point to the culture of literary patronage, particularly those which show high regard for poets in their role as "arbiters of fame," statements such as Wace's assertion that only a writer can confer immortality, or Chrétien de Troyes' belief that his art was destined for eternal fame.[8] It is likely that the composition of *Brut* was inspired by similar attitudes and is linked, like that of other vernacular poetry of the period, to the growth of lay literacy and royal literary patronage that existed in England in the second half of the twelfth century.[9] Arthurian legends became popular during the reign of Henry II and his successors as a way of celebrating the national past and the ideal of kingship. Laȝamon follows this tradition, even though, as has been repeatedly pointed out, as a poem in English, *Brut* deepens the paradox inherent in the glorification of king Arthur as an enemy of Saxons by writing about the defeats of Saxons in a style approximating that of Old English poetry, and translating a French text while avoiding French vocabulary.[10]

Literary culture of the royal court may have influenced not only Laȝamon's choice of subject matter, but also his perception of his role as author. His willingness to tell about himself in his work anticipates similar willingness on the part of Chaucer and Langland, but is virtually unknown in earlier English poetry. Royal and lay patronage, driven by political motives, supported culture where literary authorship could bring rewards and enjoy considerable prestige. Wace's and Chrétien de Troyes's views on the role of poets, referred to above, were likely to discourage anonymous transmission of literature and to motivate poets to assert ownership of their works.

Two other longer texts surviving from the period have diverse connections with Latin and French didactic poetry. The *Ormulum*, a series of sermons and a synopsis of Gospel history, is an adaptation of Latin sources and employs a highly regular fifteen-syllable verse imitating Latin seven-stressed meters. The *Poema Morale* is metrically similar to the *Ormulum*, though much less strict, and includes striking resemblances to a late twelfth-century Anglo-Norman verse-sermon in Alexandrines, the sermon of Guischart of Beaulieu.[11] This is extant in four manuscripts all of English provenance, including Oxford, Bodleian Library MS Digby 86 in which it has a heading "Ci comence le romaunz de temtacioun de secle." In London, British Library MS Harley 4388, which is the earliest extant copy of the sermon, it appears with a name "Guischart de beauliu" who is regarded by some scholars as the author of the original late twelfth-century work. It was suggested that Guischart took his name from the Benedictine priory of Beaulieu in Bedfordshire, in which case he lived not far from the author of the *Poema Morale*, a South-East Midland composition.[12]

In spite of its dependence on French and Latin poetry for subject matter and literary forms, English verse of the period shows that Old English literary heritage continued to be deeply and appreciatively received. Concern with Old English literacy, cultural, and political legacy and interest in Old English poetic technique is strongly present in "The Grave," the Worcester fragments, and Laȝamon's *Brut*. These poems employ the unrhymed alliterative line, either throughout as in "The Grave," or in conjunction with rhyming lines as in the Worcester fragments and *Brut*. Even texts in predominantly syllabic verse, such as the *Poema Morale*, use alliteration occasionally and include passages of stress-counting verse. In spite of an apparently wide acceptance of Old English poetic models by the twelfth-century poets, it is largely unknown what exactly these models were, how they were transmitted, or how they were perceived. Though scholars generally agree that in the second half of the twelfth century and the beginning of the thirteenth century the Germanic alliterative tradition continued to be influential, the details and routes of this influence are unclear because of the absence of contemporary manuscripts of Old English verse.[13] The relationship between early Middle English poetry and Old English poetry and prose is further discussed below.

Early Middle English Poetry and Old English Verse and Prose

The latest examples of verse in classical Old English meter belong to the first half of the eleventh century. The last metrical insertion in the C and D versions of the Anglo-Saxon Chronicle is verses on the death of Edward the Confessor in 1065, composed in a loose approximation of classical Old English meter. Several poems from the twelfth and thirteenth centuries use an unrhymed alliterative line, but few of the other metrical, syntactic, lexical, or stylistic constraints of Old English poetry. As pointed out by Derek Pearsall, this is followed by an almost complete disappearance of unrhymed alliterative verse from written records after the end of the thirteenth century: *Brut* and the late-thirteenth-century *Bestiary* appear to be the last examples of unrhymed alliterative line for over a hundred years. Though alliteration continues to be used in rhymed poetry, between the second recension of *Brut* in Cotton Otho C.xiii and the earliest poems of the Revival (1275–1350) there are now extant a mere twenty-eight lines of unrhymed alliterative poetry.[14]

Understanding the nature of continuity between the Old English alliterative tradition and later alliterative poetry has always presented considerable difficulties. Such continuity has been interpreted as either the poet's modeling his prosody to some degree on the style of Old English alliterative prose—which demonstrably continues to be copied and read in the twelfth century,[15] or as imitation of Old English meter and style learned from the study of surviving manuscripts of Old English poetry, as Chatterton might have done. Other interpretations include the use of alliterative style preserved in a contemporary living poetic tradition, oral or possibly recorded in lost manuscripts, going back to classical Old English verse, or, finally, to its "popular" variety which existed already during the Old English period.[16]

Laȝamon's *Brut* is a good illustration of early Middle English adaptation of alliterative techniques. Laȝamon's alliteration has sure structural purpose and appears to highlight metrical stress with some regularity, but its rules are not as strict as in Old English: about one in every three lines deviates from the classic pattern and stress position is not always predictable. The majority of Laȝamon's lines are four-stressed with a metrical break in the middle, and alliteration can fall on any stress including the last beat in the line. Although the majority of half-lines have two stresses, some may have three or four, with a rhythm that is not entirely clear or predictable.[17] Laȝamon has a strong preference for traditional use of clusters /sp, st, sk/ in alliteration, but this practice is no longer strict: he expands the use of cluster alliteration in ways similar to other Middle English poets.[18] Rhyme is often used to link half-lines, in conjunction with alliteration or on its own: slightly less than half the lines in *Brut* have rhyme or assonance. Laȝamon uses compound nouns and adjectives more extensively than any other poet of the period, but still does not come anywhere near the frequency of their occurrence in *Beowulf*.[19] Many of these compounds are common in Old and Middle English, whereas some are unique to his poem as far as our incomplete knowledge of the vocabulary of the period allows us to judge.[20] Laȝamon appears to be the only twelfth-century/early-thirteenth-century poet who builds himself a poetic vocabulary, partly Old English in origin.[21] This includes the use of Old English synonyms for "man, warrior" such as *beorn, guma, hæleð, rinc, secg*, and *wer*. There is evidence for Laȝamon's continued use of some words according to the "metrical rank" they had in Old English poetry, or a tendency to employ some synonyms in positions of alliteration, whereas others outside such positions. Thus the word *cniht*, very frequently used in *Brut*, alliterates only in a tiny proportion of its occurrences.[22] Laȝamon uses recurring collocations, reminiscent of formulas of the traditional poetry. In *Brut* such "formulas" are numerous but not trivial, and are probably Laȝamon's invention intended to give an epic flavor to his style.[23]

Several scholars have argued that Laȝamon's verse reads like a learned imitation of Old English alliterative poetry, rather than a product of a living tradition.[24] According to E. G. Stanley's convincing account, Laȝamon is deliberately archaistic in his meter, vocabulary, the choice of grammatical forms, and orthography out of a desire to "augment antiquity of his subject."[25] Commenting on Laȝamon's use of compounds, partly new and partly Old English in origin, Stanley remarks that they are coined as "tokens of a past" in an attempt to reanimate an "extinct art form." Stanley believes that many linguistic forms in Cotton Caligula A.ix, the language of which is dated for its time, are archaistic, rather than genuinely archaic: "antiquarian sentiments" preserved by the Caligula scribe were not shared by the Cotton Otho C.xiii reviser who, working at approximately the same time as the Caligula scribe, attempted to modernize Laȝamon's orthography and style. Laȝamon's apparent interest in the stylistic possibilities of archaistic orthography indicates a learned, literary context of his work. The same is suggested by the presentation of *Brut* in the Caligula manuscript with the illuminated first letter *A* showing a Benedictine monk writing.[26] All this seems to suggest that Laȝamon's stylistic and metrical models were literary and bookish, rather than popular or oral.[27] Though there is no evidence that Laȝamon read Old English poetry, his imperfect but often impressively detailed knowledge of Old English poetic technique and conventions suggests familiarity with manuscripts of Old English poetry. Daniel Donoghue argues that such manuscripts were available to Laȝamon: he lived only about ten miles away from the monastery at Worcester the library of which contained manuscripts with at least ten Old English poems, including six Chronicle poems.[28]

Laȝamon's verse seems to support the view that at least some Middle English alliterative poetry was a result of a learned imitation of Old English verse (the second of the four possible ways described above in which Middle English authors could continue the tradition of pre-Conquest poetry). It also highlights some of the reasons why poets turned to alliterative meter. Laȝamon's choice of alliterative verse for his work indicates how the strong-stress alliterative technique was perceived by a learned twelfth-century poet. Considering his epic and noble subject matter, and seriousness of purpose as a historian, Laȝamon's choice of form almost certainly reflects his perception of alliterative verse as prestigious and aristocratic, and an appropriate literary medium to tell of the deeds of heroes and kings. Unlike Old English poets, early Middle English writers had a variety of widely different metrical forms and styles available to them, and were interested in matching these metrical forms to their subject matter: thus verse derived from Latin fifteen-syllable meters was used for sermons (as in *Poema Morale* and *Ormulum*), whereas alliteration was used in a piece concerned with the achievements of the Anglo-Saxon Church (as in the "First Worcester Fragment") and in a historical narrative such as Laȝamon's *Brut*.

The poets' acceptance of widely different literary forms, used according to their stylistic associations, points to a larger difference between the late-twelfth-century and Old English poetic traditions. It reflects a major shift in authorial mentality which can be seen developing already at the end of the Old English period. This shift, further discussed below, can be described as the loss of traditional ties between the language, including meter, and the subject matter of poetry.[29] This loss was ultimately responsible for the disappearance of the classical Old English poetic tradition which was dependent on these traditional ties. It also resulted in the development of an international and cosmopolitan poetic culture in England in the second half of the twelfth century, with literary forms and meters easily migrating between different languages and used by individual poets as a stylistic choice.

Laȝamon's adaptation of Old English poetic technique is described as "scholarly" and "antiquarian" because it is highly unlikely that he had access to a living tradition of classical Old English verse. Though a sense of continuity with Old English is very strong in several late-twelfth-century/ early-thirteenth-century English poems the authors of which seem to be deliberately reproducing the old alliterative style, it is important to recognize that the lack of poetry in the classic Old English meter surviving from the period is not an accident of its survival and transmission. Continuous use of this form in the twelfth century is unlikely because the reasons for its decline appear to have been cultural and internal, rather than linguistic or political, such as the change from syntactic to analytical structure in language, or the lack of interest in preservation of such poetry. The development of analytical structure in language and the necessity for poets to cope with the abundance of unstressed syllables is often blamed for the loss of the classic Old English verse. But during centuries of its existence this verse managed to survive various linguistic changes that were sufficient to obliterate the whole corpus of poetry.[30] Tom Shippey describes the decline of Old English poetic tradition as a disappearance not of a verse form or a style, but "of a whole state of mind,"[31] and recent research has demonstrated the existence of close ties between Old English metrical form and its language, including grammar, vocabulary, and phraseology, as well as the existence of a further connection between the language and traditional themes.[32] Attempts to expand the language and meter, developed originally for heroic subject matter, to cover new subjects could have had destructive consequences even during the Old English period. Thus M. S. Griffith describes as "one of the most striking" features of the *Paris Psalter* the reluctance of the poet to use heroic poetic vocabulary although still composing in traditional alliterative meter. Griffith demonstrated that the poet's attempt to preserve the prosodic makeup of alliterative verse, while distancing himself from the poetic language, was highly abortive and resulted in the "disintegration of the Old English poetic mode," including the destruction of the system of rank and the disappearance of morphological constraints characteristic of alliterative verse.[33] Tom Shippey observes that the stability of Old English poetic tradition depended on the suitability of material to the demands of inherited style, though up to a certain point it responded well to new material. In late Old English poetry he observes "the beginnings of a 'divorce' between subject-matter and its expression."[34] According to Shippey the poet of the *Battle of Maldon* writes in classic Old English verse form when composing familiar scenes or speeches, but falls back to prosaic usage when he loses support of his models in trying to include less-traditional material.[35]

When formulaic usage, syntax, and special vocabulary with their complex prosodic and distributional rules were abandoned, Old English meter was replaced with loose alliterative verse which can be seen already in the less traditional of the Chronicle poems, such as the entry for 1036 describing the arrest of Prince Alfred, son of King Ethelred. According to Turville-Petre the entry is very unlike classic Old English verse: alliterative and stress patterns do not necessarily correspond to those of regular verse, alliteration is supplemented or replaced by rhyme or assonance, syntax is less-tightly organized, and the language is no longer characterized by use of poetic vocabulary and phraseology "which by their associations bring with them certain traditional attitudes to life and death."[36] Such verse with loose rhythm, irregular rhyme, and alliteration predates the Conquest and may have continued to exist throughout the early Middle English period, providing a form of continuity between Old English and Middle English alliterative traditions. It could have been familiar to Laȝamon, though the evidence for his learned antiquarianism, and apparent familiarity with such features of alliterative poetry as the use of formulas and special vocabulary, suggest the possible familiarity with manuscripts of the pre-Conquest poetry.

As pointed out earlier, Laȝamon's and other Middle English alliterative verse have also been explained as a result of influence from Old English rhythmical prose. The problem of the relationship between prose and verse is important for understanding the genesis of early Middle English poetry, and its position in the spectrum of literary forms. According to the view put forward by N. F. Blake and accepted by a number of scholars, alliterative meter was recreated by the twelfth- and thirteenth-century poets from works such as homilies of Ælfric and Wulfstan.[37] Blake argued that the relationship between "prose" and "verse" was much closer during the Old and Middle English period, and suggested a category of "rhythmical alliteration" that covers works in ornate, elevated style without invoking a modern distinction of prose and verse.[38] It is true that Old English and early Middle English alliterative prose and poetry use similar prosodic, stylistic, and rhetorical devices that obscure the difference between them and create grounds for mutual influence. The "First Worcester Fragment" has been described as both prose and verse,[39] whereas the highly ornamental prose of the Katherine group of texts has often been seen as one of the possible influences on the fourteenth-century Revival of alliterative poetry. There is evidence, however, that both Old and early Middle English writers were aware of the distinction between prose and verse and identified their work using these categories.[40] Roberta Frank observes that Ælfric used different terms to refer to the prose and verse *Life* of St. Cuthbert, and that different words were used in the preface to Alfred's *Boethius* to describe metrical and prosaic parts of the translation.[41] Laȝamon refers to *Brut* as "loft-songe" and clearly thinks of it as poetry.[42] However, as Roberta Frank remarks about Old English writers, we are "not quite certain where they drew the boundary."[43] Though this boundary almost certainly existed, it was obscured by the common prosodic and stylistic features that characterized not just the poetic register, but the literary register in general. This situation appears to have persisted in early Middle English, though the adoption by English writers in the twelfth century and later of Continental verse forms (which used prosodic structures uncharacteristic of elevated English prose) must have increased the distance between prose and verse. It must have contributed to the stylistic and genre differentiation of prose and verse, and eventually to the development of differences in their written presentation. All verse discussed in this chapter, apart from the *Poema Morale*, appears in manuscripts written as prose, following the Old English tradition. However, only one out of seven copies of the *Poema Morale* is laid out as prose). This again points to differences between genres of poetry: short texts preserved either as part of prose works or in their margins were written as prose, as they were in Old English manuscripts. Among longer texts there is a distinction according to metrical form: *Brut* with its alliterative verse is laid out as prose, whereas the *Poema Morale* with its syllabic meter is laid out as verse.[44] This shows emerging differences in the manuscript delivery of English prose and poetry, but also demonstrates once again that shorter vernacular verse was slow to establish itself in the written medium: it appears that it was less likely to be recorded in the second half of the twelfth century than other types of poetry, and that the development of its written presentation also largely happened at a later period.

Some Brief Conclusions

Surviving English poetry of the second half of the twelfth century and the beginning of the thirteenth century is learned and literary in nature, written by self-conscious poets interested in experimenting with genres, subject matter, style, and meter. The achievements of these poets include the adaptation of Arthurian material in the form of a verse chronicle, the development of a style intended to recall Old English poetry, adaptation of strict syllabic meter, and even experimentation with orthography, such as the phonologically aware spelling of Orm or possibly archaistic spelling used by Laȝamon.

Early Middle English poets had a choice of different metrical forms available to them and seem to have employed them according to their thematic and stylistic associations: seven-stress syllabic verse was used for sermons, whereas alliterative verse for a chronicle. In spite of the existence of such thematic connections, as well as further associations between metrical form and stylistic and lexical resources, as can be seen in Laȝamon's decision to avoid French vocabulary and to use formulas and compounds in alliterative verse, these connections and associations were a stylistic choice of individual poets, rather than an intrinsic, necessary part of the language of poetry. Unlike Old English poets, early Middle English authors no longer had "absolute language," integrated with a single metrical form and developed to express the traditional subject matter, originally largely historical and aristocratic.

Verse preserved from the second half of the twelfth century, particularly Laȝamon's *Brut* and poems recorded by the Tremulous Hand of Worcester, suggests that Old English poetry continued to be authoritative but as a stylistic influence among several others, and an object of scholarly interest, rather than as a living tradition. Though able to survive centuries of linguistic change and the emergence of the new Christian subjects and literary genres, it could not cope with the expansion of its role at the end of the Old English and the beginning of the Middle English period. This expansion was partly a result of European cultural influences, but in particular a result of the introduction of the new subject-matter due to the poets' portrayal of contemporary reality as can be seen already in the Chronicle poems. Whereas Old English poetry changed little over several centuries of its existence (which makes the dating of texts and the study of influences notoriously difficult) and used style, language, and meter that depended on continuity and were inseparable from the traditional subject-matter, the poetry of the second half of the twelfth century and the beginning of the thirteenth century was characterized by diversity and experiment—as a result and achievement of a different "state of mind," reflecting profound historical and cultural change.

Appendix: Texts Cited

1. "The Grave" (IMEV 3497) Oxford, Bodleian Library MS Bodl. 343, fol. 170 dated to the third quarter of the twelfth century. Twenty-five lines of unrhymed alliterative verse. Added at the bottom of a folio after the end of an Old English sermon. Written as prose.

2. Hymns of St. Godric to Burgwine (IMEV 589), St. Mary (IMEV 2988), and St. Nicholas (IMEV 3031) preserved in several manuscripts dating from the end of the twelfth century and later: the hymn to Burgwine survives in four copies, the hymn to St. Mary in thirteen copies, and the hymn to St. Nicholas in two copies. The hymns are composed in rhyming couplets and appear in the context of several prose works including the Latin *Life* of St. Godric written by Reginald of Durham, and a Latin chronicle by Roger of Wendover.

3. "Eueriche freman hath to ben hende / for to be large." (IMEV 740). An exhortation to liberality preserved in Oxford, Bodleian Library MS Rawl. C. 22: 298, dated to the beginning of the thirteenth century. Four monorhyming lines. Written as prose.

4. "Canute song" ("Merie sungen ðe muneches binnen Ely") (IMEV 2164) Quoted by Thomas of Ely in *Liber Eliensis* (ca. 1166). Preserved in three copies: Oxford, Bodleian Library MS Laud Misc. 647, fol. 44v, dating from the early fourteenth century; Cambridge, Trinity College MS O.2.1, fols. 73v–74, dating from the late twelfth century; and Ely, Dean and Chapter MS 1, fol. 72, dating from the early thirteenth century.[45] Four lines rhyming in couplets. Written as prose.

5. *Ormulum* (IMEV 2305) preserved as author's holograph in Oxford, Bodleian Library MS Junius 1. According to Malcolm Parkes there are two twelfth-century hands in the manuscript: the first responsible for the text and most of the corrections, and the second responsible for the added Latin cues and some corrections and additions to the English text.[46] The date for the completion of the manuscript is believed to be early in the last quarter of the twelfth century.[47] Composed in regular unrhymed verse of fifteen syllables. Written as prose.

6. *Poema Morale* (IMEV 1272) preserved in seven manuscripts from the third quarter of the twelfth century to ca. 1300, written in the following order: Cambridge, Trinity College MS B. 14. 52, fols. 2r–9v and London, Lambeth Palace Library MS 487, fols. 59v–65r, probably dating back to the second half of the twelfth century; Oxford, Bodleian Library MS Digby 4, fols. 97r–110v, London, British Library MS Egerton 613, fols. 7r–12v and

London, British Library MS Egerton 613, fols. 64r–70v, dating back to the first half of the thirteenth century, with Egerton, fols. 64r–70v being the earliest; Oxford, Jesus College MS 29 and Cambridge, Fitzwilliam Museum MS McClean 123 belonging to the last quarter of the thirteenth century. London, British Library MS Egerton 613 has two copies of the poem in different hands. The original of the *Poema Morale* is thought to have been composed ca. 1170–1190 or earlier.[48] The poem has around 398 mostly seven-stressed long lines in rhyming couplets and is laid out in long lines as verse in all manuscripts apart from Oxford, Bodleian Library MS Digby 4 in which it is written in half-lines arranged in quatrains, and London, Lambeth Palace Library MS 487 in which it is written as prose.

7. Laȝamon's *Brut* (IMEV 295) preserved in two copies in London, British Library, MS Cotton Caligula A.ix, fols. 3r–194v and London, British Library, MS Cotton Otho C.xiii, fols. 1r–146v, dated to the last quarter of the thirteenth century, independently derived from a common version that cannot have been the author's original.[49] The poem is believed to have been composed either late in the twelfth century, after the death of Henry II in 1189, or early in the thirteenth century. It is made up of 16,095 lines with alliteration and internal rhyme. Written as prose.

8. "First Worcester Fragment" (IMEV 3074.3) preserved in Worcester Cathedral Library MS F. 174, fol. 63, dated to the beginning of the thirteenth century. Consists of 18 lines with alliteration and rhyme. Written as prose.

9. *Soul's Address to the Body* (IMEV 2684.5) preserved in Worcester Cathedral MS F. 174, fols. 63v–66v, dated to the beginning of the thirteenth century. Contains of 349 lines with alliteration and rhyme. Written as prose.

10. "Ic an witles ful iwis" (IMEV 3512) A love lyric preserved in London, British Library MS Royal 8.D.xiii, fol. 25. Written in the top margin, as prose. Peter Dronke argues that the lyric is older than its early-thirteenth-century copy and that it goes back to the twelfth century.[50] Thirteen lines rhyming *ababacacddfdf.*

Notes

1. R. M. Wilson, *The Lost Literature of Medieval England*, 2d rev. ed. (London: Methuen, 1970), p. 163.

2. Christine Franzen, *The Tremulous Hand of Worcester: A Study of Old English in the Thirteenth Century* (Oxford: Clarendon Press, 1991), pp. 72–73.

3. The same applies to verses occurring in *Ancrene Wisse* and the Katherine Group of texts, including "Þenchen hu swart þing & suti is þe sunne" (IMEV 3570.5)—a moral warning inserted into the *Life of St. Margaret*, preserved in Oxford, Bodleian Library MS Bodl. 34, fol. 29v, and London,

British Library MS Royal 17.A.xxvii, fol. 49, and "Þench ofte mid sor of heorte o þine sunnen" (IMEV 3568)—a warning, inserted in *Ancrene Wisse*, and also found separately in thirteenth-century and later manuscripts.

4. *Brut* is preserved in manuscripts from the second half of the thirteenth century and its dating to an earlier period is conjectural. The date of *The Owl and the Nightingale*, traditionally believed to have been composed ca. 1189–1216, is disputed by Neil Cartlidge in "The Date of *The Owl and the Nightingale*," *Medium Aevum* 65 (1996): 230–47.

5. The use of vernacular verse in prose texts, particularly sermons and preaching aids, is discussed by Siegfried Wenzel, *Verses in Sermons. Fasciculus Morum and its Middle English Poems* (Cambridge, Mass.: Medieval Academy of America, 1978). He observes that the tradition of using verses in sermons dies out during the fifteenth century (pp. 98–100). See also Siegfried Wenzel, *Preachers, Poets, and the Early English Lyric* (Princeton, New Jersey: Princeton University Press, 1986), particularly the discussion of preservation of early lyrics in manuscripts connected with preaching in chap. 1, "Preachers and Poets."

6. Peter Lucas, *From Author to Audience: John Capgrave and Medieval Publication* (Dublin: University College Dublin Press, 1997), p. 250.

7. Erich Auerbach, "The Western Public and its Language," chap. 4 in *Literary Language and its Public in Late Latin Antiquity and in the Middle Ages*, tr. R. Manheim, Bollingen series 74 (New York: Pantheon Books, 1965), pp. 289–92.

8. Lucas, *Author to Audience*, pp. 259–60. See also J. Lough, *Writer and Public in France* (Oxford: Clarendon Press, 1978), p. 12.

9. That Arthurian material was addressed particularly to royal patrons has been argued by Rosalind Field in her "Romance in England," chap. 6 in *The Cambridge History of Medieval English Literature*, ed. David Wallace (Cambridge: Cambridge University Press, 1999), pp. 152–76. See also Christopher Dean, "Arthur and Chivalry," chap. 2 in *Arthur of England: English Attitudes to King Arthur and the Knights of the Round Table in the Middle Ages and the Renaissance* (Toronto: University of Toronto Press, 1987).

10. Laȝamon's concept of history is discussed, among others by E. G. Stanley, in "Laȝamon's Antiquarian Sentiments," *Medium Aevum* 38 (1969): 23–37 and Daniel Donoghue, "Laȝamon's Ambivalence," *Speculum* 65 (1990): 537–63. See also *Brut, or, Hystoria Brutonum*, ed. W. R. J. Barron and S. C. Weinberg (London: Longman, 1995), Introduction, pp. ix–xx. Donoghue points out that although the vocabulary of *Brut* largely consists of words of Germanic origin, this is almost certainly an artificial limitation: the vocabulary of *Ancrene Wisse* written approximately at the same time and in the same area includes 8–10 percent of French and Latin loan words (540).

11. A. Gabrielson, ed., *Le Sermon de Guischart de Beauliu*, Humanistiska Vetenskaps-Samfundet; Uppsala, Skrifter, 12:5 (Uppsala: Lundström, 1909).

12. For a discussion of the poem's language, provenance and authorship, see Betty Hill, "The twelfth-century *Conduct of Life*, formerly the *Poema Morale* or *A*

Moral Ode," *Leeds Studies in English* n.s. 9 (1977): 97–144. Hill doubts that the name which appears in British Library MS Harley 4388 is that of the author and argues that it may have been the name of the scribe (1977), pp. 123–26.

13. I have examined the *Metrical prayer, dialogue between Adrian and Ritheus, miscellaneous notes and Distichs of Cato,* 18. London, British Library MS Cotton Julius A. ii: s.xii; provenance unknown.

14. Derek Pearsall, "The Origins of the Alliterative Revival," in *The Alliterative Tradition in the Fourteenth Century,* ed. Bernard S. Levy and Paul Szarmach (Kent: Kent State University Press, 1981), pp. 1–24.

15. See essays by Swan and Treharne in this volume.

16. The use of "popular" form of Old English verse orally transmitted is suggested by Dorothy Everett in "Laȝamon and the Earliest Middle English Alliterative Verse," in *Essays on Middle English Literature,* ed. Patricia Kean (Oxford: Clarendon Press, 1955), pp. 25–8 and 37–38. R. W. Wilson, *Early Middle English Literature,* 3d ed. (London: Methuen, 1968), pp. 13–15, argues for oral transmission of "popular" alliterative poetry after the Conquest throughout the Middle English period until the Alliterative Revival.

17. See Herbert Pilch, "Versbau und Rhythmus," in *Layamon's Brut: Eine literarische Studie* (Heidelberg: C. Winter, 1960), pp. 135–56 and S. K. Brehe, "Rhyme and the Alliterative Standard," in *Medieval English Measures: Studies in Metre and Versification,* ed. Ruth Kennedy, *Parergon* n.s.18:1 Special Issue (2000): 11–26.

18. Donka Minkova, *Alliteration and Sound Change in Early English* (Cambridge: Cambridge University Press, 2003), pp. 245–61.

19. Comparison of the frequency of compounds in *Beowulf* and *Brut* can be found in J. P. Oakden, *Alliterative Poetry in Middle English,* 2 vols. (Manchester: Manchester University Press, 1930, 1935), 2:130 and Hans Sauer, "Compounds and Compounding in Early Middle English: Problems, Patterns, Productivity," in *Historical English: On the Occasion of Karl Brunner's 100th Birthday,* ed. Manfred Markus (Innsbruck: Institut für Anglistik, Universität Innsbruck, 1988), p. 167.

20. Oakden, *Alliterative Poetry,* 2:130–65; E. G. Stanley, "Laȝamon's Antiquarian Sentiments," pp. 23–37 and H. Sauer, "Laȝamon's Compound Nouns and their Morphology," in *Historical Semantics: Historical Word-Formation,* ed. J. Fisiak (Berlin: Mouton, 1985), pp. 438–532.

21. Thorlac Turville-Petre, *The Alliterative Revival* (Cambridge: D. S. Brewer, 1977), 12–13, and Henry Cecil Wyld, "Studies in the Diction of Layamon's *Brut,*" *Language* 6 (1930): 1–24; 9 (1933), 47–71 and 171–91; 10 (1934), 149–201; 13 (1937), 29–59.

22. Minkova, *Alliteration and Sound Change,* p. 313.

23. J. S. P. Tatlock, "Laȝamon's Poetic Style and its Relations," in *The Manly Anniversary Studies in Language and Literature* (Chicago: University of Chicago Press, 1923), pp. 3–11. According to Pilch, "Formeltechnik und Stilfiguren" and "Formeltechnik und Szenenbau," in *Layamon's Brut: Eine literarische Studie,* pp. 97–122, Laȝamon's use of formulas is stylistic, rather

than "epic;" they are a stylistic device available to him among many others, and used to recall Old English poetry.

24. Donoghue, "Laȝamon's Ambivalence," p. 545; Derek Pearsall, *Old and Middle English Poetry*, The Routledge History of English Poetry, vol. 1 (London: Routledge & Kegan Paul, 1977), pp. 80–81.

25. Stanley, "Laȝamon's Antiquarian Sentiments," pp. 23–37.

26. Lesley Johnson and Jocelyn Wogan-Browne, "National, World and Women's History: Writers and Readers of English in Post-Conquest England," chap. 4 in *The Cambridge History of Medieval English Literature*, ed. David Wallace (Cambridge: Cambridge University Press, 1999), pp. 92–121.

27. N. F. Blake, "Rhythmical alliteration," *Modern Philology* 67 (1969), pp. 118–24, discusses the notion of "popular" alliterative poetry, and points out that both Old and Early Middle English poetry was literary, and that Laȝamon's verse reads as particularly literary when he uses alliterative style.

28. Donoghue, "Laȝamon's Ambivalence," 541.

29. This is discussed in O. A. Smirnitskaia, "Stikh i iazyk drevnegermanskoi poezii," Filologiia 2 (1994): 423–34.

30. R. W. Chambers draws attention to the fact that there is a point beyond which, if we put language in its older form, the metrical structure of Old English alliterative lines will be destroyed (R. W. Chambers, with a Supplement by C. L. Wrenn, *Beowulf: An Introduction to the Study of the Poem with a Discussion of the Stories of Offa and Finn*, 3d ed. (Cambridge: Cambridge University Press, 1963), pp. 108–9). Thus the restoration of endings lost after long syllables will turn the half-line *fifelcynnes eard* into a metrically impossible form *fifelcynnes eardu*. Chambers observes that though such loss of a syllable would make a large number of formulaic half-lines in Old English unmetrical, it does not mean that at some point "the whole of O.E. poetry was at once scrapped, and entirely new poems composed to fit in the new sound laws."

31. Tom Shippey, *Old English Verse* (London: Hutchinson, 1972), p. 190.

32. The association between the subject-matter and language of traditional poetry is described in a number of studies concerned with the composition and poetic technique of formulaic epic and folk poetry, including A. B. Lord, *The Singer of Tales*, 2d ed., ed. S. Mitchell and G. Nagy (Cambridge, MA: Harvard University Press, 2000); M. Parry, *The Making of Homeric Verse: the Collected Papers of Milman Parry*, ed. A. Parry (Oxford: Clarendon Press, 1971, repr. Oxford: Oxford University Press, 1987); M. M. Bakhtin "Epic and Novel," in *The Dialogic Imagination: Four Essays*, ed. and trans. M. Holquist and C. Emerson (Austin: University of Texas Press, 1981).

33. M. S. Griffith, "Poetic Language and the Paris Psalter: the decay of the Old English Tradition," *Anglo-Saxon England* 20 (1991), pp. 167–86. According to Griffith the non-formulaic alliterative verse of the Paris Psalter "exemplifies a poetics in which rhythm and meaning have come to stand in an oblique, divergent relationship, where, for the *Beowulf* poet, these were

harmonious and mutually enriching. This could be construed as a symptom of a poetic mode in its death throes" (at p. 175).

34. Shippey, *Old English Verse*, p. 189.

35. Shippey, *Old English Verse*, pp. 188–9.

36. Turville-Petre, *The Alliterative Revival*, p. 8.

37. N. F. Blake, "Rhythmical Alliteration," *Modern Philology*, pp. 112–24; Angus McIntosh, "Early Middle English Alliterative Verse," in Lawton, *Middle English Alliterative Poetry*, pp. 20–33; S. K. Brehe, "Ælfric's Prose and the Origins of Laȝamon's Metre," in *The Text and Tradition of Layamon's Brut*, ed. Françoise Le Saux (Cambridge: D. Brewer, 1994), pp. 65–87; P. J. Frankis, "Laȝamon's English Sources," in *J. R. R. Tolkien, Scholar and Storyteller: Essays in Memoriam*, ed. Mary Salu and Robert T. Farrell (Ithaca: Cornell University Press, 1979), pp. 64–75. A recent refutation of Blake's views on the genesis of Middle English alliterative verse is found in R. D. Fulk, "Old English Poetry and the Alliterative Revival: On Geoffrey Russom's "The Evolution of Middle English Alliterative Metre," in *Studies in the History of the English Language II: Unfolding Conversations* (Topics in English Linguistics 45), ed. Anne Curzan and Kimberly Emmons (Berlin, New York: Mouton de Gruyter, 2004), pp. 305–12.

38. According to Blake, "Rhythmical Alliteration," p. 120 "The writers in the twelfth century would not have thought of some lines as verse and others as prose; they would have regarded different passages as being in a high or a low style." See also Angus McIntosh, "Wulfstan's Prose," *Proceedings of the British Academy* 35 (1949), pp. 109–42.

39. S. K. Brehe, "Reassembling the *First Worcester Fragment*," *Speculum* 65 (1990): 521–36.

40. See a discussion in Donoghue, "Laȝamon's Ambivalence," p. 539

41. Roberta Frank, "Poetic Words in Late Old English Prose," in *From Anglo-Saxon to Early Middle English. Studies Presented to E. G. Stanley*, ed. Malcolm Godden, Douglas Gray, and Terry Hoad (Oxford: Clarendon Press, 1994), p. 88.

42. Donoghue, "Laȝamon's Ambivalence," p. 539.

43. Frank "Poetic Words in Late Old English Prose," p. 88. From a linguistic and metrical point of view there is no impenetrable borderline between prose and verse: they are best seen as points in a continuum with intermediate and borderline forms in between. True borderline forms can be classified only conventionally through editorial or authorial will reflected in the layout. Classifying texts as prose or verse is further complicated by the fact that audiences react to different rhythm creating and stylistic factors subjectively and with different intensity: texts prosodically irregular can be classified as verse on the grounds of their style and vocabulary.

44. The *Ormulum* is written as prose, but is different from other texts as the author's draft and possibly an unfinished work.

45. E. O. Blake, ed., *Liber Eliensis* Royal Historical Society (London: Camden 3d ser. 92, 1962), Introduction, pp. xxiii–lx.

46. M. B. Parkes, *Scribes, Scripts and Readers* (London: Hambledon, 1991), p. 188, n. 10.

47. Parkes, *Scribes, Scripts and Readers*, p. 197.

48. Parkes, *Scribes, Scripts and Readers*, p. 196.

49. Barron and Weinberg, *Brut*, Introduction, pp. ix–xx.

50. Peter Dronke, *The Medieval Lyric*, 2d ed. (London: Hutchinson, 1978), p. 281.

CHAPTER 9

"GLOSER LA LETTRE": IDENTITY AND POWER IN THE POETRY OF MARIE DE FRANCE

Françoise Le Saux

Readings of Marie de France's literary works have long recognized the centrality of the issues raised by the exercise of power at the heart of much of her oeuvre. Her *Fables* is noteworthy for the importance it gives to feudal values and has been read as a form of *Mirror of Princes*,[1] while the *Lais* give numerous examples of abuse of power by authority figures in general and kings in particular, from the overprotective father of the young princess in "Deus Amanz" to murderous King Equitan. Marie's use of the conventions of the fable and *lai* to address contemporary problems of cultural identity has been less rigorously addressed. Nonetheless, I argue that Marie de France was acutely aware of the temptation to misrepresent people and facts to suit the whim or interests of the holder of power, thus undermining the personal and social integrity of all involved, and that her chosen poetic forms enabled her to comment acutely, if obliquely, on the obvious and inescapable plaiting together of ideas of identity and entitlement in the actions of the mighty.

Cultural identity would have been (at the very least potentially) a problematic concept for many nobles at the time of Henry II. The king himself was a cultural hybrid. He was essentially Angevin, through his father, but also Norman, through his mother, thus uniting in his person two hereditary enemies. The Norman legacy was responsible for his claim to the throne of England, yet Henry appears to have viewed it with some ambivalence, and the Normans themselves had to be subdued by force of

arms during a ten-year campaign before they would accept the young
Henry as their duke. The marriage to Eleanor of Aquitaine brought
Occitan culture within his immediate circle, while after his accession to the
throne the people of Britain further contributed to the admixture with languages and traditions with which Henry was (and would apparently
remain) unfamiliar. Within a feudal system, this in itself was not a cause for
concern: for the king, as for his nobility, rank and function in society
would have provided sufficient foundation for the construction of personal
identity. However, the politically hybrid status of Henry was both more
delicate and more liable to foster strife. As king of England, he was at the
top of the feudal hierarchy, answerable to no other secular ruler; but as
duke of Normandy and Anjou, he was a vassal of the king of France. And
in turn, the members of the nobility holding cross-Channel estates were
potentially in a situation of split loyalties toward the king of England and
the king of France, raising the question of their own perceived identity.

The problem of dual overlordship, as we know, reached crisis under
Henry's son King John and eventually resulted in his loss of Normandy; but
in her *Fables*, Marie de France repeatedly gives voice to fears of disloyalty
and treachery to one's overlord, suggesting that this was a matter for some
concern in the aristocratic audience she was targeting. The most striking
fable on this theme hints at the difficulty of identifying one's "real" overlord. Fable 23 of the collection tells the story of a bat.[2] The lion and the
eagle decide to wage war against each other; the lion sends a summons to
all animals that walk on four paws, while the eagle gathers all the birds that
have wings. Having surveyed the situation, the bat decides that the lion has
the best chance of winning and joins his side, but belatedly realizes that the
birds are going to win:

> des bestes est dunc departie.
> Ses piez musça, si fist folie:
> mes, quant les eles entreovri,
> par devant tuz les descovri.[3]

All the animals then realize that the bat is a traitor and as punishment it is
condemned to lose its plumage and much of its flesh, and never to see day-
light again. Marie's moral is that turncoats similarly lose their rank and
wealth and are a subject of opprobrium to their heirs. While there is no
question that the bat was guilty of seriously wavering loyalty, it is also clear
from the way the bat is described that it does not really have a "natural"
overlord. It has "piez" [feet] like the followers of the lion, and the Middle
Ages knew as we do that the bat is a mammal, and therefore a beast rather
than a bird. Yet the bat flies, it has wings, and according to the fable, it even

had feathers: it should therefore have joined the ranks of the birds, not the beasts. Both sides had legitimate claims on the bat, and the difficulty of making the "right" choice is at the heart of the double act of treachery that results in humiliation and a hereditary loss of social standing. Belonging to both sides, the bat identifies fully with neither.

Marie's advice in the epimythium is essentially that vassals should choose one lord and resist the temptation of crossing sides, because of the heavy price to pay:

> si honur en pert e sun aveir
> e repruver en unt si heir
> a tuz jurs en est si huniz
> cum fu dunc la chalve suriz,
> que ne deit mes par jur voler,
> në il ne deit en curt parler.[4]

The unsuccessful traitor faces the destruction of his social identity, through the loss of his substance, both material and moral; but perhaps more importantly, he loses his voice. "Il ne deit en curt parler" [he cannot speak in tribunal], indicates a further-reaching form of disenfranchisement than anything suggested in the body of the fable: he not only has to hide and live in poverty and obscurity, he is not even allowed to defend himself any more. His version of events, any mitigating circumstances, must remain unsaid. Once discovered, the traitor and his descendants are doomed to silence, and therefore vulnerability.[5]

The theme of (deprivation of) speech appears at its starkest in Fable 94. A peasant and his wife go out for a walk in a field. The peasant enthuses about how neatly the grass had been cut, but his wife disagrees: she thinks the grass looks as if it had been hacked with shears. The peasant argues with her, grows angry, and cuts out her tongue; then he repeats his question: was the grass cut with a scythe or with shears? Whereupon the woman, with her fingers, makes the cutting motion of shears. It is not immediately clear who is in the right in this quarrel. The woman is described as "une femmë espuse / que mut esteit cuntrarïuse" [a wife who was very contrary], yet the epimythium suggests that, in fact, she was the more reliable witness:

> Par cest essample veut mustrer
> —bien le peot hum suvent pruver—
> si fols parole une folie
> e autre vient que sens li die,
> ne l'[en] creit pas, einz s'en aïre;
> la u il set que l'en est pire,

> veut sa mençunge mettre avant;
> nul nel fereit de ceo taisant.[6]

This description of the obstinate person who will attempt to force people
to accept a lie rather than acknowledge that he might have been in the
wrong clearly corresponds to the peasant rather than to his wife; he in his
anger goes as far as to try to deprive her of speech altogether so that she can
no longer contradict him, and both spouses seem to be evenly matched
when it comes to obstinacy. This introduces an element of humor in a
particularly nasty tale and allows the reader(s)/audience not to dwell on the
more unsettling aspects of the fable. The actual quarrel scene, though
placed in a field between two peasants, carries overtones of accusations
of lese-majesty on the husband's part, hinting at a rather more weighty
message:

> "Tu es," fet il, "fole pruvee:
> ceste herbe fu od falcs copee.
> Mes tu iés si engresse e fole
> que avant veus mettre ta parole;
> la meie veus fere remeindre,
> par engresté me vols ateindre."
> Li vileins l'ad aval getee,
> si li ad la lange copee.[7]

In the mouth of a peasant, these words sound like paranoia and are slightly
ridiculous; but the use of the verb "ateindre" (line 18), which may also be
translated as "to trap" and belongs to the semantic field of treachery, points
to the true nature of the offence of the wife. In refusing to condone the
mistaken belief of her husband, she has challenged his authority, and he
cannot countenance this. He feels humiliated, interprets her lucidity as
betrayal, and makes her feel the full force of his power over her, making
her pay for her perceived transgression in a similar way to that suffered by
the bat: through mutilation, resulting in the loss of her voice.

   In contrast to the bat, the wife is not entirely disempowered; she cannot
speak but she can show, and she remains unwavering in her refusal to
undermine her integrity by pandering to her husband's desire to see things
other than they are. The Latin analogues of Fable 94 present the tale as an
exemplum of injustice;[8] Marie's version is more subversive, describing the
temptation to pervert the order of things by imposing a lie, and the inability of even the most violent show of strength to suppress witnesses to the
truth. This message would have taken on particular resonance set against
the backdrop of Henry II's conflict with Thomas Becket, and if the *Fables*
were written after 1171, the tale of the two peasants could well have been

meant as a veiled reproach to the king himself. In more general terms, the fable illustrates the dangers that come from being too close to those who wield enough power to feel entitled to unquestioning submission and suggests that grandees should be wary of a form of hubris that could weaken their grasp on reality. Fable 34, in which two men visit the court of the king of monkeys, gives a glimpse of the ridiculous image given by a monarch out of touch with facts, as well as the danger run by the honest man in a court of sycophants; like the peasant's wife, the man who describes things as they are to the monkey-king ends up "desiré e maumis" [tortured and ill-used].[9] Kings can willfully deceive themselves and may attempt to destroy those who resist the drive to misrepresent the world they live in.

The themes of identity, appearances, abuse of power, and loss of speech take on special resonance in Marie's *lai* of "Bisclavret," which also has in common with the fable of the bat the fact that its central character, Bisclavret, is torn between two mutually incompatible identities. The story line is well-known. A wife discovers that her husband's strange habits are due to the fact that, for three days in the week, he is a werewolf. She wheedles out of him where he puts his clothes when he changes shape, and, with the complicity of an old suitor, hides them away, thus trapping her husband in his animal form; she then gets remarried, to her accomplice. A year or so later, during a hunt in the forest, the king comes across the wolf and takes him under his protection. Bisclavret then lives at court with his overlord in animal form, until he encounters his former wife; to everyone's horror, he bites off her nose. But the king's advisor refuses to believe that such a tame wolf could do anything gratuitously vicious, and the king extracts a full confession from the lady, who is tortured and then exiled. Bisclavret is reunited with his clothes and regains human form, while his faithless wife gives birth to female descendants who are born without noses, thus perpetuating her shame. This *lai* is unusual in that the readers'/audience's sympathies are directed towards the werewolf, whereas wolves in general had an especially bad image in the Middle Ages.[10] The benign nature of Bisclavret is confirmed by the words of the king and the wise man who champions his cause, and by the end of the lay the werewolf is perceived by many critics as more human than his wife, whose act of treachery turns her, according to Kathryn Holten, into a "voluntary werewolf" as opposed to Bisclavret's involuntary metamorphosis.[11] This reading of the tale construes the werewolf as a man of truthfulness and honor, while his wife is a treacherous hussy who richly deserves her mutilation and silencing through exile. However, the extent of the discrepancy between medieval attitudes toward wolves and the positive depiction of Bisclavret may also be an invitation to look at the narrative from a different, less-trusting angle, to reveal a level of subversion in the tale that goes far beyond a simple inversion of received values regarding werewolves.

Marie's preface to her *Lais* openly advocates scholarly exegesis of written texts, placing her work within a tradition of aggregative authority and interpretation. The Ancients, she says, used to express themselves "assez oscurement" [quite obscurely] (line 120), so that later readers applying new interpretative grids to their work could reveal new meanings:

> K'i peüssent gloser la lettre
> E de lur sen le surplus mettre.[12]

In looking behind the voice of her narrator to identify hidden tensions, we are therefore responding to Marie's implicit injunction: "gloser la lettre," which—as pointed out by Michelle A. Freeman—involves the decoding of the silent message underlying the "fissures in the body of evidence" that makes up the various *lais*.[13] In the case of "Bisclavret," these fissures run throughout the narrative. An alternative way of decoding the *lai* of "Bisclavret" results in a "surplus" in which the tale is about the wolf and the king, rather than predominantly about the two spouses, and could be summarized as follows: a king has as his retainer a knight, Bisclavret, who turns into a ravening beast for three days in the week. The wife of the knight, confronted with her husband's apparently willing acceptance of this metamorphosis, rejects him and the evil he represents. She seeks out a new consort who frees her from the werewolf by banishing him from society. During a hunt, the king recognizes the qualities of the werewolf, protects it and keeps it with him at court, where Bisclavret resumes his duties as retainer. The werewolf attacks its wife's new husband, but this is overlooked, and when the werewolf bites off the nose of its former wife in a fit of rage, the king, encouraged by one of his advisors, refuses to punish it and tortures the wife instead. He secures the means to restore the wolf to human form, thus reestablishing Bisclavret's social identity, and the wife is punished and exiled, effectively silencing her and denying the bestial nature of her husband. Such a reading admittedly runs counter to the cues given to the reader in the body of the *lai*, but it is soundly based on the text, which evidences real tensions between what is offered to us as fact, and the interpretation the narrator or his/her perceived mouthpieces draw from these facts.

A fundamental issue in studies of "Bisclavret" is the essentially human nature of the werewolf, which justifies our condemnation of his wife's rejection of him. Yet in her prologue to the lay, Marie makes is abundantly clear that werewolves, when metamorphosed in animal form, forfeited all humanity:

> Jadis le poeit hum oïr
> E sovent suleit avenir,
> Hume plusur garval devindrent
> E es boscages meisun tindrent.
> Garvalf, ceo est beste salvage;
> Tant cum il est en cele rage,
> Hummes devure, grant mal fait,
> Es granz forez converse e vait.
> Cest afere les ore ester:
> Del Bisclavret vus voil conter.[14]

The prologue, one may notice, allows for no ambiguity: werewolves in their animal shape are evil creatures who are completely taken over by their "rage," in other words, they have totally lost all human reason. They are also cannibals—"hummes devure"—making their bestiality especially fearsome and repulsive. No suggestion is made that the werewolf of which we are going to hear is an exception to this gruesome rule; Marie's "cest afere les ore ester" [but I will not dwell on that] hints that more could be said about the condition that afflicts Bisclavret—not that it does not apply to him. It has been noted that Marie is careful not to claim personal experience of lycanthropy; Emanuel Mickel Jr. sees this as a distancing device intended to facilitate suspension of disbelief in her audience.[15] On the other hand, the appeal to the authority of age-old tradition enhances the credibility of the information provided in the prologue, whereas, as this chapter reveals, the body of the tale is undermined by inner contradiction. The last two lines of the prologue have been read as signaling the fact that, contrary to the "authoritative" accounts of lycanthropy, this is not going to be a horror story;[16] they also indicate that the point of view of the narrator in the body of the *lai* is not going to be that of the scholars or of the victims of the werewolves. "I want to tell you the story of the Bisclavret" could be interpreted as a warning that the tale that follows is not just about the werewolf, but is based on his own version of events. In other words, we should expect it to be biased in his favor, and be prepared to take some distance from it.

Part of the sympathy felt for Bisclavret by modern readers (in particular, Holten) is the assumption that the "hero" is the victim of forces beyond his control; and indeed, the term used by Marie ("rage," line 10) suggests a form of violent madness, which happens to be exactly what mainstream medieval science thought lycanthropy was.[17] But one of the more disturbing features of the exchange between Bisclavret and his wife is that it is by no means clear that his metamorphosis is entirely involuntary or in any way unwelcome. He does not lament his misfortune when he tells his wife of it, neither does he ask for her help or support. He has no desire to be trapped in his wolf's skin and forfeit entirely the comforts of a noble lifestyle—hence his reluctance to entrust his spouse with the secret of the hiding-place of his clothes—but he equally seems untroubled by any qualm of conscience or any craving for a normal Christian life. The fact that his shape-shifting takes place in an old chapel may be even interpreted as an act of religious irreverence, and the hiding-place of his clothes, in a large hollow stone that could be understood as a baptismal font, has overtones of blasphemy.[18]

It may be significant that Bisclavret's wife appears to accept his confession with relative equanimity until he mentions where he hides his clothes, at which point, we are told, she was overcome with repulsion and fear (lines 97–99). It is at this stage that, according to certain readings,[19] the werewolf's curse is transferred to his wife, who through Bisclavret's confession becomes contaminated by her husband's bestiality and urge to devour men. This is altogether excessive; in fact, the lady appears to have settled down happily and respectably with the suitor who rid her of her unnatural husband, and her act of treachery towards Bisclavret, though represented as cruel, involves neither physical violence nor literal destruction, and arguably has some justification. She is the ultimate "malmariée." The key reason for why we perceive the wife to be an evil character lies in the open and almost immediate affection felt by the king for the werewolf, who is described in terms that modern readers (along with the king) see as distinctly human.[20] Bisclavret, about to be torn apart by hounds, recognizes the king and seeks sanctuary with him: "Il l'aveit pris par sun estrié, / La jambe li baise e li pié" [He seized him by the stirrup / He kisses his leg and foot] (lines 147–8). This is interpreted by the king in totally anthropomorphic terms:

Cest merveillë esgardez,
Cum ceste beste d'humilie!
Ele ad sen d'hume, merci crie.[21]

The conclusion drawn by the king, however, would not necessarily have been perceived as correct by medieval audiences. Quite apart from the fact that animals in fables (a genre where anthropomorphism is commonplace) are not meant to be thought of as actually human, this passage bears a number of similarities with the grateful animal of romance, or with the taming of dangerous beasts by saints in hagiographical narratives. Yvain's lion, in Chrétien's *Chevalier au lion*, is also credited with human-like behavior; but at no time is the reader led to understand that the beast—however noble—has "sen d'hume" [human understanding]. It remains an animal.

There is a bond between the king and the wolf, as there is between Yvain and the lion, and this bond is described in both cases as quasi-vassalic in nature. However, while the lion has the benefit of highly positive symbolical connotations, the same cannot be said of the wolf (and even less so of the werewolf). In taking the wolf to his bosom, the king could be construed as being foolish, possibly even perverse. In his *Roman de Rou*, Wace quotes what appears to be a common proverb in twelfth-century Normandy (and therefore also, one assumes, in Anglo-Angevin England): "L'en ne prant mie lou ne goupil souz son banc," literally, "You don't invite a wolf or a fox under your bench";[22] yet that is exactly what the king does. Bisclavret is treated like a favorite pet: he is pampered and even sleeps with the king, a detail that makes Faure and others detect homoerotic undertones in the relationship between the man-wolf and his master.[23]

The narrator of the *lai* makes a point of stressing that Bisclavret's behavior at court was exemplary and that he was loved by all;[24] yet this love seems to have been in response to the king's direct order rather than a spontaneous and heartfelt emotion. The king has to intervene twice to prevent his wolf getting killed by his courtiers: when Bisclavret is first taken to court and the king warns his retainers that "ne li mesfacent de rien" [refrain from harming him [i.e., the wolf] in any way] (line 172), and when the wolf attacks his wife, prompting an immediate threatening response ("De tutes parz l'unt manacié / Ja l'eüssent tut depescié" [They have threatened him from all sides and would have completely flayed him] lines 237–8). The only reason they not do so is due to the intervention of "un sages hum" [a wise man] (line 239)—though not, one may note, a priest or a cleric—who voices an opinion suspiciously in accord with what the king presumably wishes to hear:

> Unke mes humme ne tucha
> Ne felunie de mustra,
> Fors a la dame qu'ici vei.
> Par cele fei ke jeo vus dei,
> Aukun curuz ad il vers li
> E vers sun seignur autresi.
>
> . . .
>
> Kar metez la dame en destreit,
> S'aucune chose vus direit
> Pur quei ceste beste la heit.[25]

This "wise" man is misrepresenting the situation. This is not the first case in which the wolf has tried to harm someone: he attacked the lady's husband and had to be restrained by the king himself, whose view on the matter is pandered to by his courtiers—that the beast must have had a reason to avenge himself on the man.[26] The second time round, the courtiers want to act on their common sense and outrage, but the "official version" is imposed by the king's "wise man" whose reasoning is openly unjust. His main reason for suspecting the lady, it would appear, is the fact that she was once married to that nice knight who disappeared. The under-lying logic is misogynistic (perhaps even gynophobic) in nature and appears to be founded on resentment at the woman who married not just one but two knights from the royal pack, and who is enjoying greater material pros-perity than more "deserving" members of the male military brotherhood. It is significant that the lady is bearing "riche present" [rich gifts] (line 230) for the king when the assault takes place. Despite the fact that events seem to prove him right, the wisdom of the "wise" man consists of an instinctive desire to protect a member of the male, military inner circle against a female outsider, combined with the shrewdness of the sycophant who knows exactly what his king wishes to hear. The injustice of the situation is patent: the woman has just been the victim of a vicious attack by a dan-gerous wild beast, yet it is she who is tortured, on the off-chance that she might have done something to provoke it.

The end of the lay raises the question of what exactly the lady is punished for. Treachery to her husband seems to be the obvious answer, but one may notice that her accomplice seems to be let off very lightly in comparison. He apparently follows his lady in exile of his own free will. Faure suggests that the true transgression of the lady was against the king himself, in that she took it upon herself to "punish" her werewolf husband, thus usurping the king's prerogative of administering justice:

> N'avait-elle pas tenté de se substituer à la justice royale en prenant une décision individuelle qui devait aboutir au crime, et en utilisant les services d'un ancien amant? Détournement de l'amour conjugal, détournement de l'amour courtois, et usurpation du pouvoir, mâle et royal. C'est le dernier chef d'accusation qui paraît le plus important.[27]

According to Faure, the main issue is feudal in nature, and the real crime of the lady is to have taken into her own hands a matter to which, as a woman, she was not entitled to respond otherwise than as a victim.

On the other hand, what would the king have done if the wife had approached him with her concerns? From what can be gathered from the text, probably nothing. The relationship between the monarch and his wolf-knight is that of a king and his favorite; in human form, the knight had been highly appreciated, as a wolf he had been loved and protected, and once the werewolf regained his human form, the king embraced him on his own bed with what (to modern eyes at least) seems suspicious warmth: "Li reis le corut enbracier; / Plus de cent feiz l'acole e baise" [the king ran to clasp him in his arms; more than one hundred times he embraced and kissed him] (lines 300–301). There is a troubling affinity between the king and the man-wolf that brings to mind those fables of Marie dealing with predatory overlords who devour their subjects.[28] Through her mutilation and silencing, Bisclavret's wife is reminiscent of the peasant's wife whose tongue is cut out so that she can no longer undermine male authority; but like the peasant's wife, one may argue that her defiance continues. The loss of her nose, often read as indicative of her moral turpitude and the lupine nature she has taken over from her husband, is explicitly unaccompanied by the vices one would expect. She appears to be a good and faithful wife to her second husband, and the bond of affection between them is such that he follows her in exile and gives her many children (something the werewolf had been incapable of doing). The absence of a nose that afflicts many of her female descendants from birth could be read as the hereditary taint of treachery (the parallel with Ganelon's lineage has been noted),[29] but from a different perspective it could be seen as a paradoxical badge of honor, comparable to the iconography of martyrs whose wounds are emblematic of their superior moral and spiritual stature, as compared to their corrupt and godless torturers.

Faure argues that "la figure du roi sort grandie de l'histoire,"[30] while Gros credits Bisclavret's return to humanity to "la fine fleur de la charité: l'amitié d'un roi" [the fine flower of charity: the friendship of a king].[31] This is debatable. The king in "Bisclavret" is worryingly close to King Equitan in the *lai* of the same name. Both are prone to listening to voices that flatter their own desires, and are prepared to suppress their innate sense of truthfulness and respect for their subjects in order to achieve their aims. King Equitan allows himself to be manipulated by his mistress into a coarsening of his moral sense that eventually leads him to plot the death of his most faithful retainer in order to secure the sexual favors of his wife; Bisclavret's king seems to value the brute strength of (male) bestiality over and above his duty as maintainer of social justice. Faure sees the king in "Bisclavret" as a good feudal monarch who is successful in harnessing the anarchic tendencies of a potentially vicious class of professional warriors; the successful integration of the werewolf is emblematic of a wider policy of appeasement that allows the overlord to channel the bellicose urges of his men to further his own means and ensure that society remains in a state of relative peace and stability:

> Ainsi sera désamorcé le danger que peuvent représenter les chevaliers ou les vassaux, devenus loups-garous apprivoisés. Ainsi seront imposés des devoirs et des dévouments qui assureront au roi sécurité et puissance.[32]

This is true, but it is only part of the picture. The king, like the werewolf, seems singularly detached from Christian values and practices. No priests are mentioned at his court, while the only chapel we see him enter is abandoned and in ruins. His compassion seems to be directed exclusively toward those who can strengthen his power. This king is arguably a morally and spiritually flawed person. Marie's ambiguous moments of silence and her strategically placed hints of inner contradiction reveal the price to pay for the maintenance of a strong political power. For each tamed werewolf, a lie has to be sustained, and for each lie uncovered, a new scapegoat has to be found. Bisclavret's wife lost her looks, her possessions, and her social identity in order to allow her husband to maintain his status; yet she is the one who proves to be fruitful and bear children, albeit muti-lated, with the man of her choice. The true future lies with her, not with her bestial first spouse, and her exile ultimately weakens the kingdom rather than strengthening it.

Perhaps the most worrying aspect of the *lai* of "Bisclavret" is that we do not really know how it ends. The knight regains human shape, but is this permanent? Will he be shape-shifting again—a real possibility, since we do not know the cause for his fits of blood-lust—and if he does, what gruesome crimes will he commit? Will the emotional support of the king be sufficient to enable him to overcome his addiction to bloodshed? Or will the king cyn-ically make use of his knight's moral weakness? The very fact that we are not told that Bisclavret went on to live a decent human life makes one suspect that his wife's drastic action, forcing him to face his personal responsibility for what he had become, might not have been as callous as it seems. In bringing him back into the military fold, on the other hand, the king might have jeopardized the wolf-man's chance to reflect on his sins and repent. The story, insists Marie in the epilogue, is "veraie" [true] (line 316); but it is the truth as told by the powerful, who are able to control the accounts of events and ensure that identities, both private and public, conform to their political agenda. The gaps and silences in their narrative, however, speak more loudly than they think. And eventually, like the fingers of the peasant woman deprived of her tongue, silence reveals a suppressed counter-narrative.

Notes

1. See Hans Robert Jauss, *Untersuchungen zur Mittelalterlichen Tierdichtung* (Tübingen: Niemeyer, 1959), pp. 24–55; and, more recently, Karen K. Jambeck, "The *Fables* of Marie de France: A Mirror of Princes," in *In Quest of Marie de France A Twelfth-Century Poet*, ed. Chantal A. Maréchal (Lewiston, Queenston, Lampeter: Edwin Mellen Press, 1992), pp. 59–95.

2. All further references to and quotes from the *Fables* are from Charles Brucker, ed., *Marie de France. Les Fables. Edition critique accompagnée d'une introduction, d'une traduction, de notes et d'un glossaire*, 2d ed. (Paris, Louvain: Peeters, 1998). Fable 23 is to be found at pp. 124–31; it is sixty-six lines long.

3. Fable 23, 27–30 "So it left the other animals. It hid its feet (that was a foolish thing to do), but when it opened its wings, they were revealed for all to see." All translations of the *Fables* are my own.

4. Fable 23, lines 61–66. "Thus he loses his honor and his wealth, and his descendants are reproached for it; he is forever shamed like the bat that is no longer allowed to fly by day, and he is not allowed to speak at the court of law."

5. This loss of voice is particularly apt if it is considered that within a feudal context, the bat was not only guilty of desertion, but probably also of breaking his oath of allegiance. See Jambeck, "The *Fables*," pp. 88–91.

6. Fable 94, lines 29–36, pp. 342–45. "This example aims to show (you can experience it very often) that if a foolish person says a foolish thing and then someone else turns up who speaks sensibly, he will not believe him but get angry; when he knows he is losing the argument, he wants to enforce his lie; nobody could make him keep quiet."

7. Fable 94, lines 13–20. " 'You are,' he said, 'completely mad. This grass was cut with a scythe. But you are so nasty and foolish that you want to have the last word; you want to discredit me, you want to trap me out of cruelty.' The peasant threw her on the ground and cut out her tongue."

8. See Brucker, *Marie de France*, p. 345. The exact sources used by Marie for her *Fables* are mainly unknown, and the Latin analogues that have come down to us postdate Marie.

9. Fable 34, line 54; pp. 162–67.

10. See Kirby F. Smith, "An Historical Study of the Werewolf in Literature," *PMLA* 9 (1894): 1–42; also M. Faure, "Le *Bisclavret* de Marie de France: une histoire suspecte de loup-garou," *Revue des langues romanes* 83.2 (1978): 344–56.

11. Kathryn I. Holten, "Metamorphosis and Language in the Lay of *Bisclavret*," 193–211, in Maréchal, *Quest*, p. 204. This view is also shared by Milena Mikhaïlova, *Le Présent de Marie* (Paris, New York, Amsterdam: Diderot, 1996), pp. 178–98.

12. Mary's prologue to her *Lais*, lines 14–15. "So that they may comment on the text and enrich it with their own interpretation." The *Lais* are quoted from Jean Rychner, ed., *Les Lais de Marie de France* (Paris: Honoré Champion, 1973); translations are my own.

13. Michelle A. Freeman, "Marie de France's Poetics of Silence: the implications for a feminine *translatio*," *PMLA* 99 (1984): 860–83; esp. 861–62.

14. Marie de France, "Bisclavret," lines 5–14. "In the olden days it was said, and it often happened, that many men became werewolves and lived in the woods. A werewolf is a savage beast; as long as he is in this rabid state, he devours men, he does great evil, he lives and goes about in the big forests. But I will not dwell on that: I want to tell you the tale of the Bisclavret."

15. Emanuel J. Mickel, Jr., "Antiquities in Marie's *Lais*," in Maréchal, *Quest*, pp. 123–137, esp. 126.

16. See for example Philippe Ménard, "Histoires de loups-garous," *Travaux de littérature* XVII (2004): 97–118.

17. See Laurence Harf-Lancner, "La métamorphose illusoire: des théories chrétiennes de la métamorphose aux images médiévales du loup-garou," *Annales: economie, societe, civilizations* 40 (1985): 208–226.

18. The implications of the location of the werewolf's metamorphosis is analyzed by Gérard Gros, "Où l'on devient Bisclavret. Étude sur le site de la métamorphose (Marie de France, 'Bisclavret,' lines 89–96)," in J. Claude Faucon, Alain Labbé, and Danielle Quéruel, eds., *Miscellanea Mediaevalia. Mélanges offerts à Philippe Ménard*, 2 vols. (Paris: Honoré Champion, 1998), pp. 1, 573–83. Gros also suggests that the hollow stone could have been the hermit's desecrated grave (p. 579). Whether it is a grave or a baptismal font, stresses Gros (580–2), Bisclavret's metamorphosis is a regression to bestiality that is a direct inversion of Christian spirituality and leads to the loss of his soul.

19. See Milena Mikhaïlova, *Le Présent de Marie* (Paris, New York, Amsterdam: Diderot, 1996), pp. 178–98; also François Suard, "Bisclauret et les Contes du Loup-Garou: essai d'interprétation," *Marche romane* 30 (1980): 267–76, esp. 274–5.

20. See for example Jeanne-Marie Boivin who notes that the werewolf experiences his animal shape "comme une souffrance"; "Bisclavret et Muldumarec: la part de l'ombre dans les *Lais*," in *Amour et merveille. Les Lais de Marie de France*, ed. Jean Dufournet (Paris: Honoré Champion, 1995), pp. 147–68, at 160.

21. Marie de France, "Bisclavret," lines 152–55. "Look at this marvel, how this beast is humiliating itself! It has human understanding, it is appealing for mercy."

22. A. J. Holden, ed., Wace, *Roman de Rou*, 2 vols. (Paris: Société des Anciens Textes Français, 1970–1973), "Deuxième Partie," line 520.

23. Faure, "Le *Bisclavret*," 349–51. Faure also notes that Bisclavret's return to human form takes place in the king's chamber, on the king's very bed, and that moreover, the tale ends with the werewolf's definitive loss of his wife, and therefore of licit heterosexual activity. On homosexuality in "Bisclavret" and other medieval texts, see William E. Burgwinckle, *Sodomy, Masculinity and Law in Medieval Literature: France and England 1050–1230* (Cambridge: Cambridge University Press, 2004).

24. Marie de France, "Bisclavret," line 178: "N'i ad celui ki ne l'ad chier" (there was none who did not cherish him).

25. Marie de France, "Bisclavret," lines 245–50 and 255–7. "He has never touched a human being or behaved in a treacherous way, except towards the lady I see here. By the faith I owe you, he has some cause for anger toward her, and toward her husband too. Subject the lady to torture, she would tell you the reason why this animal hates her."

26. Marie de France, "Bisclavret," lines 204–10.

27. Faure, "Le *Bisclavret*," p. 350. "Did she not attempt to substitute herself to the royal justice by taking an individual decision that was to result in crime, and by making use of the services of an old lover? She was guilty of a subversion of conjugal love, of a subversion of courtly love, and of usurping male and royal power. This last accusation is the one that appears to be most serious."

28. For example, Marie's Fables 2 (The Wolf and the Lamb) and 6 (The Marriage of the Sun), or especially 19 (The King of the Doves) and 29 (The Wolf-King).

29. Faure, "Le *Bisclavret*," p. 355, n16.

30. Faure, "Le *Bisclavret*," p. 352. "The figure of the king emerges heightened from the story."

31. Gros, "Où l'on devient Bisclavret," p. 583.

32. Faure, "Le *Bisclavret*," p. 352. "Thus will be defused the danger potentially represented by knights and vassals, as they have become tame werewolves. Thus are imposed the duties and sacrifices that will ensure the king's security and might."

CHAPTER 10

THE MEANING OF SUFFERING:
SYMBOLISM AND ANTISYMBOLISM IN
THE DEATH OF TRISTAN

Laura Ashe

The twelfth century saw the reinvention of fiction, in western Europe, as a mode of expression and exploration. But from its inception, fiction begins a slide into ideology; its methods are appropriated by the proponents of political, nationalistic, racial, cultural, and behavioral ideals. This is evidently because, despite the ostensible lack of external referentiality which characterizes fiction, language is itself organized according to cultural patterns, as Paul Ricoeur suggests:

> Discourse cannot fail to be about something. . .In one manner or another, poetic texts speak about the world. But not in a descriptive way. . .The reference here is not abolished, but divided or split. The effacement of the ostensive and descriptive reference liberates a power of reference to aspects of our being in the world that cannot be said in a direct descriptive way, but only alluded to, thanks to the referential values of metaphoric and, in general, symbolic expression.[1]

The key is pattern. Texts of all sorts are understood by the reader by means of their accord with accepted patterns—of cause and effect; of behavior and perception of behavior; of motivation and action. Thus it is that the shared tropes of a genre are developed, as Rosalind Field elaborates in this book, in her discussion of the insular romance. But the implication of this is that the individuality of the fictional text is continually effaced, supplanted by its appropriation into a system of universal relevance and shared meaning.

Thus emerges ideology—which can be defined, for my purposes, as a contextually valuable moral code—from fiction. Such appropriations are not always conscious on the part of the author, and indeed develop naturally from the cultural utility of the text: a term by which I mean the cultural functions performed by the text for its author and audience, the justifications and rationalizations it offers of the cultural master narrative. Indeed, it may seem that fiction and ideology are inseparable; that, in fact, the former exists in order to serve the latter, while the latter is engendered and promoted by the former.

But I would like to argue that Thomas of Britain's *Tristran*, known at the court of Henry II,[2] stands alone both in the larger corpus of Anglo-Norman romance and within its own sub-genre of Tristan stories, in its response to the ideology of the Tristan legend.[3] Thomas's text embodies the other, opposing impulse inherent in fictional literature: to break free of ideology, which offers universality and generality, offering instead an inscription of specificity and particularity. In sum, while fiction often embodies its society's most valued ideologies, it can also fight free of them, and in so doing encode its own inherent value as derived directly from that freedom. I suggest that this is the key to Thomas's version of the Tristan story.

I seek to argue that the intense and problematic audacity at the heart of this text is Thomas's refusal to make the lovers' death symbolic. Where critics have read Tristran's tragedy as either a secular martyrdom, or contrarily as a negative exemplum, an alternative reading may be an exploration of genuine, psychological, and above all *particular* suffering: a human suffering which will not offer itself up to the creative symbolism of the death for a "faith," a suffering the nobility of which comes directly from its futility. I argue that Thomas's *Tristran* is one of the very few pure "tragedies" of the Middle Ages, depicting pain without sublimation, without reward, even reward on a metaphysical level, such as the triumph of the Wagnerian *liebestod*, the love crowned with death. Tristran and Yseut do not suffer and die with any symbolic purpose or meaning: their pain is simply laid bare as a psychological fact. The resultant difficulty of the text for its audience, and its uncomfortable, a-religious resonances of meaninglessness, has seen the engendering of a tradition that does not uphold Thomas's bleak vision: turning to other renderings of the tale, the familiar tropes of symbolic creativity reemerge and flourish. In this sense the text of the *Tristran* cuts against the literary tradition of the Tristan legend. Although the very existence of that legend is indicative of the lovers' availability as symbolic archetypes of love, Thomas instead systematically acknowledges and then rejects this textuality, carving out his own story (under the standard trope of the probably invented authority).

Seignurs, cest cunte est mult divers. . .
Oï en ai de plusur gent.
Asez sai que chescun en dit
E ço qu'il unt mis en escrit
Mé selun ço que j'ai oy
Nel dient pas sulun Breri,
Ky solt lé gestes e lé cuntes
De tuz lé reis, de tuz lé cuntes
Ki orent esté en Bretaingne. . . .
Thomas iço granter ne volt. . .

[My lords, this tale comes with so many variants. . .I have heard many tell the tale. I am well acquainted with the story each has told and with those consigned to writing, but, from my experience of the telling of these tales, they do not follow the version told by Breri, who knew the tales, epic and romance, of all the kings and all the counts ever to have lived in Brittany. . .Thomas will accept none of this [alternative version].[4]

Later redactions treat the tale differently; Béroul's version is a highly socialized study of permissible courtly adultery, as Stephen Nichols has persuasively argued,[5] and the lovers' anguish is hardly in focus. Other texts, and chiefly Gottfried von Strassburg's magisterial work, freely impose—or reimpose—a symbolic significance upon the lovers and their suffering. Thus Thomas's text stands apart from the Tristan legend, much as it stands apart from its contemporary literature, in its astonishing—and it is very difficult not to say *modern*—quality of psychological depth.

The twelfth-century understanding of death as justification and salvation, apparent in the figure of the martyr-saint, was during Henry II's reign most decisively and influentially embodied in the person of Archbishop Thomas Becket. The response to his killing in 1170, and his unprecedentedly rapid canonization three years later, illustrates the extreme cultural vitality of such allegorization of suffering, by which death becomes the guarantor of value. This interpretation of death has emerged in modern criticism of Thomas's *Tristran*. Scholars have frequently attempted to equate Tristran's death for love with the martyr's death for the faith, and thereby to draw similarly creative, eternal truths from its presumed ideology—or even religion—of love.[6]

la mort qui transfigure, est au coeur même de cet amour. Seule la mort peut sauver les amants de l'impitoyable usure de quotidien et consacrer à jamais leur amour.[7]

[Death, which transfigures, is at the very heart of this love. Only death can save the lovers from the pitiless wear and tear of daily life, and consecrate their love to eternity].

In the context of the vernacular romance of adultery, however, this is potentially problematic: is a death for love to be equated with a death for the faith, in either a twelfth-century or a modern mind? Some recent critics have argued instead for the text's being a negative exemplum of the "bankruptcy of a love linked to death";[8] Matilda Bruckner concludes that Thomas leaves the text open to either interpretation. In this respect I concur most closely with her and wish further to explore the implications of such ambiguity. If it is not clear what meaning should be drawn from the tale of the lovers' affair and death—not even at any superficial level—then this text is strikingly unusual. Although critics frequently question the assumptions of the narratorial voice in twelfth-century texts, they are usually clear on the position being taken by that voice, even if that position is then regarded as ironic.

Thomas's text can, in fact, be read as antisymbolic, and hence rejective of "meaning." As Tracy Adams has astutely noted, it is not governed by any "psychology or ideology of love. . .[whether] ennobling or degrading . . . passionate love simply existed."[9] It can be seen that the text repeatedly tackles and rejects the notion of its characters as symbol or paradigm, and seeks to exist in some alternative sphere: the sphere of individual experience, which cannot be made generic. One might note that the main action of the poem takes place in the minds of the characters, while locations and minor players fade into obscurity. The self-aggrandizing, idealized courtliness of the romance, filled with "graceful manners and pompous ceremonies"—in Auerbach's formulation "an absolute aesthetic configuration" designed solely to elevate itself and its practitioners—is absent from this deep study of loss and paranoia.[10] Tristran's love is explored in all its *ig*nobility, riven with doubt, and as such it is a truthful exposition of emotion, rather than an idealized depiction of beauty.

> Hicest penser errer le fait
> Errur son corage debote;
> Del biau Cariados se dote
> Qu'envers lui ne torne s'amor. . .
> Tristran d'amor si se contient:
> Sovent s'en vait, sovent revent,
> Sovent li mostre bel semblant,
> E sovent lait, com diz devant.
>   (lines 955–95)

[This brooding induced false beliefs, and those false beliefs assailed his heart; he had his fears about the handsome Cariado, that the queen might switch her affection to him. . .This was the way Tristran was because of love: often he would leave [the statue], then return, often treating her kindly, and often badly, as I have said before.]

In this characteristic, Thomas's *Tristran* stands against the prevailing tone of the legend as it was known during the twelfth and thirteenth centuries. Peter Dembowski has written of the twelfth-century "symbiosis of the sacred and profane," under the "powerful. . .influence of hagiography."[11] Whether clerical writers approved of the genre or not, it was an easy transference for the ideals of martyrdom to be applied to the romances, if only in structural terms. The result is the creation of symbolic paradigms underlain by the motifs of suffering and struggle. This reinterprets the Tristan story as one of the ultimate apotheosis of love, and indeed for many writers the tale was no more than an easy touchstone of ideal love. Bernart de Ventadorn declares that he endures more pain than "the lover Tristan, who suffered many sorrows for the love of fair Isolde"; Chrétien de Troyes that "I never drank of the philter that poisoned Tristan; yet I love more than he."[12] In this way the structure of the tale was instantly available as a frame of reference, within which the author could be confident of the audience's understanding. It is this freedom which gave rise to the short narrative poems such as Marie de France's "Chevrefoil," the German *Tristan als Mönch*, and the two *Folies Tristan*. These single episodes accrete around the legend in the understanding that the lovers' death has become a symbolic guarantor of the height of their passion. Marie declares that she writes

De Tristram e de la reïne,
De lur amur que tant fu fine
Dunt il eurent meinte dolur,
Puis mururent en un jur.

[Of Tristan and of the queen, whose love was so pure that it caused them great suffering, until they died on the same day.][13]

Mary's *lai* is an exquisite piece of unfulfilment, devoted to the beauty of its imagery and the poignancy of the stolen time in the forest. It is structured around a symbol for the lovers—that of the hazel and the honeysuckle—and draws upon the lovers as symbols themselves, for its tableau of pure and impossible love. Thus the poem is fully textualized and intertextualized, relying upon an interpretative and engaged reading, and a prior knowledge of—and commitment to—given tropes and structures. Marie employs her audience's understanding of the symbolic tragic lovers, whose irresistible love will lead them to death, as the necessary weight and heft behind the commemoration of the lovers' meeting. The stolen time in the forest carries the burden of the audience's knowledge that for these lovers, time is both eternal and short. It is their fate, and hence their symbolic martyrdom to love, which makes this timeless episode worthy of remembrance and heavy with poignancy. In contrast, I would argue that it is Thomas's feat of characterization that allows him to suggest that Tristran's suffering might be worthy of witness merely because it exists.

The two *Folies Tristan* enfold the episodes of the tale into miniature emblematic reminiscences, and embody most strongly the power of physical symbolism: in the *Berne*, Yseut is incapable of recognizing her lover until he shows her the gold ring she gave him.

> Ele cuide que je me faigne:
> Ele verra la destre enseigne
> Q'ele me dona en baisant . . .
> Cet enelet petit d'or fin.[14]

[She thinks that I am pretending: I'll show her the very sign she gave me with her kisses. . .this little ring of solid gold.]

In the *Oxford*, " 'Les ensegnez crei,' "[15] [" 'I believe the signs' "] declares Yseut: she will believe in a symbol. When the ring is produced, she immediately assumes it must connote Tristan's death, because in her eyes the symbol has been detached from its signified reality—the ring is not in the hand of her lover. Yseut cannot see beyond the fool's appearance, " 'kar cist est laiz / E hidus e mult cunterfaiz; / E Tristran est tant aliniez, / Bels hom, ben fait, mult ensenez' " [" 'because he is ugly and gross and all deformed; Tristan is slender and well-built, an elegant, well-bred man' "] (lines 577–80). His status as signifier and signified has been compromised: the ring cannot "mean" him, because in this guise he does not "mean" himself. With the revelation of his identity, not only is the proper direction of her love restored, but it is mediated through the symbol, from ring to Tristan, and the integrity of both the ring and Tristan himself as symbols of unbreakable love is recreated. In the familiar disguise/mistaken identity narrative, the world is understood as a complex web of potentially dangerously obscure signs, necessarily subjected to hermeneutic reading. This habit of thought extends to the characters of the text, who become signs themselves, temporarily thrown out of their correct significatory positions in order to provide the dynamic of the tale.

In contrast, Thomas has little time for this. When Yseut, and indeed Brengain, look upon a disguised Tristran, they see Tristran in disguise; these characters look through superficial signs to particular truth: "Regarde Tristran, sil cunut" ["She looked at Tristran, recognized him"] (line 1832). The closest moment of correspondence with the *Folie*'s story occurs when Yseut recognizes the disguised Tristran's begging bowl before the man; but the effect is merely to cause her properly to look at the leper whose eyes she had been avoiding:

> Veit le hanap qu'ele cunuit;
> Que Tristran ert ben s'aparçut

Par sun gent cors, par sa faiture,
Par la furme de s'estature.
                    (lines 1820–23)

[Then she saw the bowl and recognized it. Now she well perceived that
it was Tristran, because of his handsome body, his shape, the height of the
man.]

This moment of recognition is also notable for its concentration upon
individuality: what she sees is not a set of stock characteristics, as the Yseut
of the *Folie Oxford* reels off, but the distinctive build and height of her
lover. Later, when Thomas has his character engage in the romance trope
of the disguised joust, the poet breaks the rules of the cliché: "Tristran i fud
reconeüz, / D'un sun ami aparceüs" ["Tristran was recognized there,
spotted by one of his friends"] (lines 2078–79). Similarly, Thomas disre-
gards an alternative version of the story's end on the grounds that a character well-known to the king could hardly pass for a merchant from abroad:
"Quë humë issi coneüz / N'i fust mult tost aparceüz?" ["How could a man
so well known fail to have been detected immediately?"] (lines 2144–45).
Thomas's work is not populated by symbolic carriers of the plot, but by
individuals, who will be recognized by other individuals.

In effect, Thomas's text repeatedly rejects the symbolization of the lovers,
to the extent that Tristran is destroyed by his momentary reference to his
own textuality. In encountering Tristran the Dwarf ("le Naim"), there is
established a juxtaposition which suddenly writes Thomas's hero as "Tristran
the Lover," where he had been simply Tristran the character. This is imposed
upon him immediately by the strange knight's address, asking for " 'Le castel
Tristran l'Amerus' " [" 'the castle of Tristran the Lover' "] (line 2196) and in
his very existence as an alternative Tristran: there being two, individuality is
replaced by the need to distinguish, which results in a symbolic identification.
Most importantly, the Dwarf does not know Tristran the man, does not recognize him: is seeking the Lover. Yet Tristran rejects this naming, implicitly,
in his reply: he states merely " 'jo sui Tristran apellez.' " [" 'I am called
Tristran.' "] (line 2202). As Tristran "le Naim" introduces himself, it is in
terms of dangerous generality, accessing familiar tropes of knightly endeavor
without any of the individuality characteristic of Thomas's poem:

Castel i oi e bele amie.
Altretant l'aim cum faz ma vie,
Mais par grant peiché l'ai perdue:
Avant er nuit me fud tollue . . .
Humage vus frai e lijance
Si vus m'aidez a la fesance.
                    (lines 2208–39)

[I had a castle and a beautiful maid, whom I love as much as my own life, but to my great sorrow, I have lost her: she was taken away from me two nights ago. . . . If you give me your help with this, I shall pay you homage as my liege.]

The knight summons up an intertextual, not to say clichéd, world relatively foreign to the rest of the poem, which, rather than resting in a network of reference, embodies a definitive account of the travails of the lovers. In response to this plea, Tristran absently suggests that they first rest for the night: this is not, after all, his Yseut. And that is exactly the point which Thomas is tacitly making, as Tristran the Dwarf showers Tristran with invective and challenges his identity.

> Vus n'estes cil que tant a pris!
> Jo sai que, si Tristran fuissét,
> La dolur quë ai sentissét,
> Car Tristran si ad amé tant
> Qu'il set ben quel mal unt amant. . . .
> Qui que vus seiét, baus amis,
> Unques n'amastes, ço m'est vis.
>   (lines 2247–57)

[You are not he who is so renowned! I know that, if you were Tristran, you would feel the pain I feel, for Tristran has loved so deeply that he knows full well the hurt that lovers feel. . .Whoever you might be, my fair friend, you have never loved, it seems to me.]

The dwarf is searching for the symbolic Tristran, "Tristran the Lover," champion and archetype of ideal love. But the Tristran of Thomas's text is a dynamic, individual character, whose love is intensely personal. There is no transference for this character—Tristran the Dwarf's lady is not Yseut. Tristran is not capable of embodying the symbolic force the dwarf hopes for, because he is a man, and not a symbol. But as a character, he is moved by the other knight's "grant reisun," his impassioned argument, and takes up the mantle required of him: " 'jo sui Tristran l'Amerus' " (" 'I am Tristran the Lover' ") (line 2283). Disaster results. Thomas's lack of interest in the quest itself is evident in its brief treatment: within thirty lines "Tristran li Naim fud mort ruez, / E li altre Tristran navrez / Parmi la luingne d'un espé, / Ki de venim fut entusché." ["Tristran the Dwarf was struck down dead, and the other Tristran wounded in the loin by a spear which had been tipped with poison."] (lines 2314–17). Suddenly the hero has become "the other Tristran," and for his brief presumption of the role of "the Lover" he receives the wound that traditionally signifies loss of sexual function.[16] It is fittingly the wound which kills him.

The episode is yet more significant for, as noted above, Thomas takes some time to refute the alternative versions of the events that lead to

Tristran's death. "Seignurs, cest cunte est mult divers," ["My lords, this tale comes with so many variants,"] (line 2104), he comments, viewing the scatterings of the legend: and there is one story, apparently the usual one, that he cannot admit:

Ensurquetut de cest ovraingne
Plusurs de noz granter ne volent
Ço que del naim dire ci solent
Ki Kaherdin dut femme amer;
Li naim redut Tristran navrer
E entusche[r] par grant engin
Quant ot afolé Kaherdin;
Pur ceste plaie e pur cest mal
Enveiad Tristran Guvernal
En Engleterre pur Ysolt.
Thomas iço granter ne volt
                    (lines 2121–31)

[Above all else, what myself and many of my contemporaries will not accept in the tales told is the usual episode about the dwarf whose wife Kaherdin loved, and the dwarf's subsequent wounding of Tristran with a cunningly contrived poisoned weapon, following his slaying of Kaherdin. [According to this version] it was because of this wound and the resulting sickness that Tristran sent Guvernal to England to bring Yseut. Thomas will accept none of this.]

The story that Thomas then does tell appears to be of his own invention, and it serves more than one purpose. In the composition of his own tale, Thomas asserts the rights of his Tristran as a character drawn out of, and distinguished from, the morass of surrounding stories bearing his name. The quest he lights upon is also rather less ignoble than that of pursuing another man's wife for his friend, by which Thomas indicates his sense of what is and is not consistent with the character of Tristran. And finally, it directly permits that juxtaposition of character with symbol which I consider so essential to the text.

Thomas's condemnation of the obsession with symbolism is present throughout the poem. It is evident in his psychological analysis of Tristran's action in marrying Yseut of the White Hands. Lacking Yseut, Tristran seeks to recreate her experience by replicating it, thus obtaining some symbolic correspondence with her. Alongside this only partly subconscious doubling, Thomas explains, lie a series of impossibly contradictory desires:

Tristran quida Ysolt gurpir
E l'amur de sun cuer tolir;
Par espuser l'altrë Ysolt

D'icestë delivrer se volt.
E si cestë Ysolt ne fust,
L'altre itant amé ne oüst,
Mais par iço qu'Isol amat
D'Ysol amer grant corage ad.
                    (lines 358–65)

[Tristran thought to abandon Yseut and wipe out the love from his heart; by
marrying this new Yseut he hoped to escape from the first. And if it had not
been for the first Yseut, he would never have desired the new, but, because
he loved the first Yseut, so this Yseut was the object of his strong desire.]

He only wants the new Yseut because she in some way symbolizes his
love Yseut; but in doing so, she also symbolizes the loss and lack of his love
Yseut, which is in turn signified by his very desire for the new Yseut. The
attempted transference of love, and of meaning, only reiterates his hopeless,
individual, antisymbolic love of Yseut, as he discovers in the marital bed.
What he loves is not a lady named Yseut, or love itself, or beauty, or
physical satisfaction: no representation of a generic "beloved" can suffice.
He loves Yseut, who is an individual and dynamic character under
Thomas's hands, just as Tristran is. Astonishingly (though perhaps more of
note for scholars of deconstruction than for scholars of *Tristran*), Tristran is
engaged in the deconstructionist project, which in Gabrielle Spiegel's
words "strives to liberate itself from a lingering nostalgia for *presence*, a presence that it simultaneously acknowledges is always already absent and,
thus,. . .an unattainable object of desire." Here Yseut is the "always already
absent" object the existence and absence of which are both symbolized in
the new Yseut, whose own presence cannot therefore eradicate Tristran's
interminable desire for the original.[17]
    Only suffering results from this attempted misuse of a person as a
symbol: "Espus est a icele Ysodt / Qu'amer ne puet n'amer ne volt. . .Il ha
dolur de ce qu'il a," ["He is married to an Yseut whom he cannot love, and
does not want to love. . .He is pained by what he has,"] while his wife "De
lui desire avoir deduit / E rien n'en a ne li enuit" ["Longs to have her pleasure with him, and obtains from him nothing but pain"] (lines 1052–80).
The failure of the symbolic ritual of marriage actually to join Tristran with
this second Yseut is complemented by the memorable account of her revelation of the truth, when her horse stumbles into water (lines 1154–96).
The meaningless splash of water on her thigh seems the ironic counterpart
of her meaningless marriage, which brings no touch so near:

"Ceste aigue, que ci esclata,
Sor mes cuisses plus haut monta

Quë unques main d'ome ne fist,
Ne que Tristran onques me quist."
                  (lines 1193–96)

["that water which splashed up and touched me here came higher up my thighs
than ever did a man's hand or than where Tristran ever sought to touch me."]

The touch at her thigh calls to her mind all the touches she has never
experienced, in an immediately convincing psychological detail. Touch for
her symbolizes lack of touch, just as to touch her would only symbolize the
not-touching of Yseut the Blonde for Tristran. He cannot do it; it is better
not to touch than to not-touch.

Thomas's exploration of his characters' suffering is vastly more
expansive than in other Tristan texts, in that he devotes time to the pain of
King Mark and the second Yseut, alongside the lovers:

Entre aus quatre ot estrange amor:
Tut en ourent painne e dolur,
E un e autre en tristur vit,
E nuls d'aus nen i a deduit . . .
Hici ne sai que dire puisse
Quel d'aus quatre a greignor angoisse.
                  (lines 1012–86)

[The love these four experienced was strange: all suffered pain and grief, each
one of them lived a life of sorrow, not one of them had any pleasure.. . .I do
not think I can say here which one of the four had the greatest torment.]

This lengthy discussion, in which Thomas considers the nature and the
quality of each character's experience, definitively abstracts his Tristran and
Yseut from the cultural code of martyred suffering. Their pain cannot act
as a symbolic justification of the purity of their love, for it is matched by
the pain of other, guiltless, protagonists. This willingness on the part of
the author to give his lesser characters individuality and agency of their
own actually brings them into conflict with the lovers in a manner that
compromises their love, as when Brengain's justified anger over Yseut's
treatment of her leads Yseut, in despair, to curse her lover:

"Vus m'avez, dame, fait hunir
Pur vostre maveisté plaisir . . ."
"Tristran, vostre cors maldit seit!
Par vus sui jo en cest destreit!"
                  (lines 1306–55)

["Lady, you have shamed me in order to gratify your own wickedness . . ."
"Tristran, a curse be upon you! It is you who have put me in such straits!"]

The importance of other characters as not merely obstacles to the lovers, but rather as individuals permitted to express their own emotional experience, functions as a repeated condemnation of the attempt to use people as symbols in one's own narrative. Ultimately, the impotently suffering Yseut of the White Hands, in a final indictment of reductionist symbolism, becomes an agent whose actions lead to the death of the lovers.

In contrast, the episode of the statues illustrates the benignity of a closed symbol. The making of the statues of Yseut and Brengain provides a harmless outlet for Tristran's unstable feelings:

> Por iço fist il ceste image
> Que dire li volt son corage,
> Son bon penser, sa fole errur,
> Sa paigne, sa joie d'amor,
> Car ne sot vers cui descovrir
> Ne son voler ne son desir.
>   (lines 986–91)

[He made that statue because he wanted to tell it what was in his heart, his good thoughts, his wild misconceptions, the pain he felt, and the joy of love, since he knew not to whom to disclose his longing and his heart's desire.]

The statue is not a symbol in any true sense: it does not partake of the nature of Yseut, or provide a spiritual access to her. It is an *aide memoire*, just as the ring is: it provides Tristran with access to himself, and to the nature of his own love. This mirroring symbol, accessing the true nature of the observer rather than that of the apparent signified, is a representation of the possibilities of Thomas's text as a whole. The tale of Tristran and Yseut does not supply some ideology of love: it displays the sufferings of one couple, which may perhaps allow the reader greater knowledge of, and access to, his or her own experience of love. Their death is rendered not as a glorious apotheosis of eternal love, but a tragic coincidence of events, such as might compose reality.

> Tristrant murut pur sun desir,
> Ysolt qu'a tens n'i pout venir
>   (lines 3120–21)

[Tristran died out of longing, Yseut because she could not come in time]

Their death, like their love, is "meaningless" because it points to nothing other than itself: it is irreducible, untransformed suffering. Hence it may have some claim to be called tragic: which is to say that it shares with the great tragedies some quality that calls for witness, and perhaps for wonder, but never for emulation.

As the earlier discussion of the shorter narratives has suggested, this "antisymbolic" quality of Thomas's text is unsustained by other versions of the legend, most of which make some creative accommodation with death. One of the most popular versions of the entire legend, surviving in more than eighty manuscripts and providing the source for several later renditions, is the thirteenth-century French *Prose Tristan*.[18] This lengthy text fully inaugurates the tale as a component of Arthurian legend, thus placing it within a more extended and well-established frame of reference, and reiterating Tristan's symbolic identity by denoting him the lover-knight of the Round Table. More importantly, its handling of the lovers' death is a clear production of symbolic significance employed as a creative and binding force: "All who hear the news come to Dinas's castle, and when they see the two lovers lying dead in each other's arms, they declare that this is the greatest marvel that ever happened, and that as long as the world lasted people would talk about the extraordinary love of Tristan and Iseut." (p. 324). In an independent and comparable development, the thirteenth-century Norse *Tristrams saga ok Ísöndar* has the lovers symbolically united in death: "an oak or other large tree sprouted from each of their graves and grew so tall that their limbs intertwined above the gable of the church":[19] a union that, it will be noted, overtops the structures of religion.

The *Prose Tristan* is the source of the fourteenth-century Italian *Tavola Ritonda*, and of Malory's "Book of Tristram de Lyones" of his *Morte Darthur*. The former contains a disquisition on the qualities of their ideal love— "they had in themselves the seven qualities that make the perfect lover," and their bodies are embalmed and displayed, and commemorated with "two golden images . . . exactly like them . . . The image of the queen held a flower in its hand, to show that this was Isotta, flower of all others in the land, and Tristano's statue held a sword to show that he, through his prowess, had set the kingdom free."[20] This multiple layering of symbolism, in the lovers themselves, the statues, and the objects held by the statues, is indicative of the erasure of individuality in a network of significance, the cultural paradigm of love and courtly conduct. Malory does not trouble with the transformation of the lovers' death at all: he leaves the tale to turn to other matters of the Round Table. As such, the tragedy has come full circle: bleakly and terribly rendered by Thomas, it is progressively ameliorated by the symbolic habit of thought of the Middle Ages, transferring an individual's destruction into an idea's creation, to the extent that the fifteenth-century writer need not attend to its inception. When Tristram's death comes, it is as one component of the losses at the close of the "Book of Sir Launcelot and Queen Guinevere,"[21] in which is the beginning of the destruction of the entire court.

It is Gottfried who, in his thirteenth-century rendering of Thomas's romance, addresses both its uniqueness and the implications of its transference into a cultural symbol: a transference which, he acknowledges, is performed by the production of his own text. Critics have spoken of Gottfried's triumphal symbolic creation: "for him love is not just sorrow and pain; it becomes an almost religious experience, and the story is a kind of Eucharist offered to all noble lovers . . . Gottfried sets up a religion of love which borrows its imagery and its basic structure from Christianity."[22] However, I would argue that Gottfried is aware of what he does; that he is both the supreme exponent of the apotheosis of the legend of Tristan, and the finest reader of Thomas's own refusal to engage in that legend. He asserts the primacy of Thomas's version, in a revealing choice of phrase, deriding those who "niht rehte haben gelesen" ["have not read correctly"].[23] For Gottfried, the question is a hermeneutic one; those who offer a different version of the legend have misinterpreted its meaning, which is to say that Thomas's romance does not rest as a component of the intertextual web of the legend, but is rather a truth located anterior to interpretation. Gottfried sets out to add to this vision with a finely turned use of symbolism which yet acknowledges the individual quality of the lovers' experience:

> uns ist noch hiute liep vernomen,
> süeze und iemer niuwe
> ir inneclîchiu triuwe
> ir liep, ir leit, ir wunne, ir nôt;
> al eine und sîn si lange tôt,
> ir süezer name der lebet iedoch
> und sol ir tôt der werlde noch
> ze guote lange und iemer leben,
> den triuwe gernden triuwe geben,
> den êre gernden êre . . .
> wan swâ man noch hoeret lesen
> ir triuwe, ir triuwen reinekeit,
> ir herzeliep, ir herzeleit,
> Deist aller edelen herzen brôt.
> hie mite sô lebet ir beider tôt.
> wir lesen ir leben, wir lesen ir tôt
> und ist uns daz süeze alse brôt.
>   (lines 218–36)

[Today we still love to hear of their tender devotion, sweet and ever fresh, their joy, their sorrow, their anguish, and their ecstasy. And although they are long dead, their sweet name lives on and their death will endure for ever to the profit of well-bred people, giving loyalty to those who seek loyalty, honor to those who seek honor . . . For wherever still today one hears the recital of their devotion, their perfect loyalty, their hearts' joy, their hearts' sorrow—this is bread to all noble hearts. With this their death lives on. We read their life, we read their death, and to us it is sweet as bread.][24]

Gottfried has become an accurate reader of Thomas's *Tristran*—a reader, above all things. He recognizes that the work of endowing the tale with meaning takes place in the mind of the reader, not in the persons of the lovers. As all reading is allegorical, as readers translate the story in the terms of their own experience, so the text is recognized as the analogue of Tristran's statue of Yseut—as an object that provides access to one's own spirit, "den triuwe gernden triuwe geben, / den êre gernden êre." ["loyalty to those who seek loyalty, honor to those who seek honor."] What Gottfried offers is not a pair of symbolic lovers, but a text which, in the action of reading, provides an allegory of the reader's own capacity for love: this document itself is the nexus wherein may be found not the translucence of an ideal symbol, but the reflection of the reader's soul, laid bare in the process of his "right reading," his understanding, of the text— and hence available only to "edelen herzen" [noble hearts]. A symbolic transformation has been performed upon Thomas's text, but it is aware of itself, and at least in part it is an exterior one:

> There is a time and place in Gottfried where love endures. It is not a metaphysical realm of death, but very much in this life. It is the time and place of Gottfried's own writing. The love of Tristan and Isolde lives for as long as it is commemorated in literature.[25]

Gottfried's focus upon the text itself as a reflective symbol is a triumphal extrapolation of Thomas's more modest and intentionally limited purposes. In contrast with Gottfried's confident location of value within the document, Thomas's presentation of his own text is paradoxically antitextual in its commitment to the truth of temporality: he effaces the role of his writing, and the value of that writing, in a truth-claim that asserts instead the precisely mimetic, and hence particular, qualities of the work. This elision of the understanding of language as itself a system of signs is Thomas's final, powerful rejection of symbolism.

> Tumas fine ci sun escrit. . .
> Si dit n'ai a tuz lor voleir,
> Le milz ai dit a mun poeir,
> E dit ai tute la verur
>   (lines 3124–32)

[Here Thomas ends his book. . .I might not have pleased all with my tale, but I have told it to the best of my ability, and I have told the whole truth]

This is a text which rests in ambiguity, rejects interpretation, and refuses to ameliorate the suffering of his lovers, or to make of it a symbolic triumph. Tristran's death is a real death, filled with the genuine suffering that does not make history, or provide access to the sublime, but rather makes humanity, futile and fleeting as it may be. The "grant confort" that Thomas hopes to offer is, in effect, and anachronistic as that might seem, the catharsis of tragedy: something "se recorder"—matter to remember, to reflect upon, to feel with, and perhaps, as Bédier tentatively suggested of the reflexive verb, from which to "reprendre coeur" (take heart).[26] The work to be done with the story is not within the tale itself, but in the listener; the suffering of Tristran and Yseut is not to be sublimated to a triumph, but to be meditated upon in a manner that might alter one's own understanding of the possibilities of love. The tale is to be remembered not because it offers access to some higher truth, but because it encompasses the shocking scope of individual suffering as it may be experienced in love. Beyond that, there is the escape offered the audience to a tragedy: that it is not theirs. *Tristran* stands as a stark negation of the claims of martyrdom to have recuperated suffering; pain, for Thomas, is not primarily an historical force, but rather an irreducible burden of being human. We might find meaning in its being shared—grief is known to all—but that meaning is recast in pathos with the understanding that grief is essentially an isolating emotion. The lovers suffer, and die, separately from one another: indeed, *because* they are apart; in turn, the reader cannot grieve "with" them because the emotion is not, and cannot be, shared—a particular grief in another merely reminds one of one's own, equally individual, sorrows. Yseut dons her leather corselet in an urge to feel pain, knowing that her lover is suffering: a touching attempt to "partir . . . ove Tristran / A la dolur e a l'ahan" ["share with Tristran in the pain and the suffering"] (lines 2020–21) which seems to emphasize, rather than reduce, the untransferable nature of grief. This facet of sorrow is most strikingly represented, if the temporal leap can be forgiven, in the *Iliad*'s scene of Achilles's and Priam's simultaneous, but unshared, and indeed contrary, grieving.[27] The sharing of emotional outpourings is seen to amount to no more than weeping in the same room. However, when Achilles has been moved to feel his own sorrows, he becomes capable of pity for those of another, and honors Hector's body in response to his new awareness of the ubiquity of pain. Thus, when Thomas expresses his hope that his tale might serve "pur essamplë" (line 3135), I believe that he means not, as has been implied, as an *exemplar*, but rather no more than an *example*, an instance, of the sufferings of love. Like Achilles watching Priam weep, lovers may derive "plaisir" (pleasure) (line 3137) from an indulgence in their own mirroring experience of "change . . . tort . . . painë e dolur" ["change . . . wrong . . . pain and suffering"] (lines 3141–42), as they understand the limitless possibilities of hurt. But while the legendary Tristan has his suffering sublimated to the triumph of love, Thomas's Tristran is no such vehicle, and retains the paradoxical grandeur of his individuality in the particularity and non-significance of his pain. Thus Thomas's *Tristran* displays most incisively one of the deep potentialities of fiction. This possibility is that the experience of the individual—the particular, specific, and unallegorized experience—might itself be a worthy object of remembrance. Thomas does not permit us the escape of transcendence; the result is mesmerizing, and perhaps, one might argue, modern.

Notes

1. Paul Ricoeur, *Interpretation Theory: Discourse and the Surplus of Meaning* (Fort Worth Texas: Texas Christian University Press, 1976), at pp. 36–37.

2. Walter Haug, "Reinterpreting the Tristan Romances of Thomas and Gotfrid: Implications of a Recent Discovery," *Arthuriana* 7 (1997): 45–59, at 45; Haug estimates composition c. 1160. See also Tony Hunt, "The Significance of Thomas's *Tristan*," in *Reading Medieval Studies* 7 (1981): 41–61, at 53; Hunt believes it "likely that Thomas was writing at the court of Henry II in the 1170s." Ian Short notes that dating of the text is necessarily unreliable, but suggests either c. 1170, or "within the last third of the twelfth century"; see Thomas, "*Le Roman de Tristan*" suivi de "*La Folie Tristan*" de Berne et de "*La Folie Tristan*" d'Oxford, ed. Félix Lecoy, trans. Ian Short and Emmanuèle Baumgartner (Paris: H. Champion: 2003), pp. 11, 38.

3. The legendary character typically known as "Tristan" is named "Tristran" in the version of Thomas of Britain, a useful (although not in itself meaningful) distinction which I preserve throughout.

4. Thomas of Britain, *Tristran*, ed. and trans. Stewart Gregory, Garland Library of Medieval Literature, A: 78 (New York: Garland, 1991), lines 2104–31.

5. Stephen G. Nichols, Jr., "Ethical Criticism and Medieval Literature: *Le roman de Tristan*," in *Medieval Secular Literature*, ed. William Matthews (Berkeley Calif., University of California Press, 1965), pp. 68–89.

6. This is a particularly popular interpretation with French critics; one is tempted to speculate about the effect on the mind of the collocation *l'amour/la mort*. See for example Jean-Charles Payen, *Le motif du Repentir dans la littérature française médiévale* (Geneva: Droz, 1968); Pierre Jonin, *Les personnages féminins dans les romans français de Tristan au XIIe siècle: Etude des influences contemporaines, Publication des Annales de la Faculte des Lettres, Aix-en-Provence, n.s.* 22 (Aix-en-Provence: Ophrys, 1958); Jean Frappier, "Le Concept de l'amour dans les romans arthuriens," *Bulletin Bibliographique de la Société Internationale Arthurienne* 22 (1970): 119–36.

7. Jacques Ribard, "Quelques réflexions sur l'amour tristanien," in *La legende de Tristan au Moyen Age: Actes du Colloque des 16 et 17 janvier 1982: Göppinger Arbeiten zur Germanistik 355*, ed. Ulrich Müller, Franz Hundsnurscher and Cornelius Sommer (Göppingen: Kummerle Verlag, 1982), pp. 69–79, at 71.

8. Matilda Tomaryn Bruckner, "The Representation of the Lovers' Death: Thomas's *Tristan* as Open Text," in *Tristan and Isolde: A Casebook*, ed. Joan Tasker Grimbert, *Garland Reference Library of the Humanities* 1514 (New York: Garland, 1995), pp. 95–109, at 95. See also Tony Hunt, "The Significance of Thomas's *Tristan*," *Reading Medieval Studies* 7 (1981): 41–61; Neil Thomas, "The *Minnegrotte*: Shrine of Love or Fools' Paradise? Thomas, Gottfried and the European Development of the Tristan Legend," *Trivium* 23 (1988): 89–106.

9. Tracy Adams, " 'Pur vostre cor su jo em paine': The Augustinian Subtext of Thomas's *Tristan*," *Medium Aevum* 68 (1999): 278–91, at 278–79.

10. Erich Auerbach, *Mimesis*, trans. Willard R. Trask (Princeton N.J.: Princeton University Press, 1953), p. 138.

11. Peter Dembowski, "Literary Problems of Hagiography in Old French," *Medievalia et Humanistica* 7 (1975): 117–30, at 121.

12. Both quoted in Mark Chinca, *Gottfried von Strassburg: Tristan* (Cambridge: Cambridge University Press, 1997), p. 18.

13. Marie de France, "Chevrefoil," in *Marie de France: Lais*, ed. and trans. Glyn S. Burgess and Keith Busby, 2d ed. (London: Penguin, 1999), lines 7–10.

14. *La Folie Tristan (Berne)*, ed. and trans. Samuel N. Rosenberg, in *Early French Tristan Poems: Volume I*, ed. Norris J. Lacy (Cambridge: D. S. Brewer, 1998), lines 526–30.

15. *La Folie Tristan (Oxford)*, in Lacy, *Early French Tristan Poems*, line 957.

16. See for example Marie de France's *lai* "Chaitivel," in Burgess and Busby, *Lais*, pp. 181–89.

17. Gabrielle M. Spiegel, "Orations of the Dead / Silences of the Living: The Sociology of the Linguistic Turn," in Speigel, *The Past as Text: The Theory and Practice of Medieval Historiography* (Baltimore: John Hopkins University Press, 1997), pp. 29–43, at 42.

18. See *The Romance of Tristan: The Thirteenth Century Old French "Prose Tristan,"* trans. Renée L. Curtis (Oxford: Oxford University Press, 1994), p. xvi.

19. Marianne E. Kalinke, *Norse Romance Volume I: The Tristan Legend* (Cambridge: D. S. Brewer, 1999), p. 223.

20. *Tristan and the Round Table: A Translation of La Tavola Ritonda*, Anne Shaver (Binghamton N.Y.: Medieval & Renaissance Texts & Studies, State University of New York at Binghamton, 1983), p. 323.

21. Malory, *Works*, ed. Eugène Vinaver, 2d ed. (Oxford: Oxford University Press, 1971), p. 666.

22. Joan M. Ferrante, *The Conflict of Love and Honor: The Medieval Tristan Legend in France, Germany and Italy* (The Hague, Paris: Mouton, 1973), pp. 19–20.

23. Gottfried von Strassburg, *Tristan und Isold*, ed. Friedrich Ranke, 4th ed. (Berlin: Weidmannsche Verlagsbuchhandlung, 1959), line 147.

24. Gottfried von Strassburg, *Tristan*, trans. A. T. Hatto, 2nd ed. (Harmondsworth: Penguin, 1967), p. 44.

25. Chinca, *Gottfried: Tristan*, p. 1.

26. Thomas of Britain, *Tristran*, ed. Gregory, lines 3139–40, 171. n.

27. Homer, *The Iliad*, trans. Robert Fagles, introduction by Bernard Knox (Harmondsworth: Penguin, 1991), Book 24, lines 592–99.

CHAPTER 11

ARTHUR, EMPERORS, AND ANTICHRISTS:
THE FORMATION OF THE ARTHURIAN
BIOGRAPHY

Judith Weiss

The Arthurian "biography" was concocted by Geoffrey of Monmouth
in his *Historia Regum Britanniae* in the late 1130s. For the first time,
some of the scattered legends about Arthur, which we nowadays encounter
in Welsh histories, literature and saints' lives, were used and embroidered
into a coherent whole, which recast the king as an international figure
when he moves beyond the bounds of his own land to confront and defeat
the emperor of Rome and appropriate his empire. This and other elements
of the biography invented by Geoffrey can, I believe, be significantly
linked to certain historical and cultural attitudes and beliefs current in the
twelfth century: views on empire and imperial pretensions on the one
hand, and beliefs conditioned by prophetic and eschatological writing on
the other. Such attitudes and beliefs are, of course, not confined to the
twelfth century: they continue well beyond it and so also influence
Geoffrey's chronicler successors. I describe these in this chapter after a brief
recall of some of the most striking elements Geoffrey added to the
Arthurian legend.[1]

It is the *Historia Regum Britanniae* that first supplies us with Arthur's
parentage—Uther Pendragon and the wife of Gorlois of Cornwall,
Ygerna—and a birth story, which, in its portrayal of regal lust and coer-
cion, and supernatural interference, is a dubious start to the tale of a great
king, and, though it has distinct similarities to earlier pagan stories about
the birth of heroes such as Perseus and Alexander, might even be seen

faintly parodic of the origins of Christ.[2] Geoffrey may also have been influenced by the story of Merlin's supernatural conception in the ninth-century *Historia Britonum*.

He depicts Arthur, and indeed his whole line, as appearing at a time of national crisis. The British are in turmoil again, as they so often are in Geoffrey's *Historia*: Britain is depleted of young men; the Romans have withdrawn their legions; there is no one on the throne and the country is under attack from Picts, Scots, Norwegians, and Danes. Armorica sends Constantine and his children to the rescue. But this provides only a temporary respite: along comes Vortigern, the Saxon invaders and settlers, and the Pictish poisoners of Aurelius and Uther. It is only after Arthur is born that peace and prosperity gradually arrive. Geoffrey may have remembered Gildas's sixth-century account of a general collapse of the kingdom after the retreat of the Romans: vice flourishes, the land is devastated by fire, and the Saxon invaders pollute sanctuaries and altars. In inventing the dynasty that produces Arthur, he certainly would have been aware of the resonances attached to the name of Constantine.

Arthur defeats the Saxons, the Scots, the Picts, and the Irish and conquers Iceland, securing a state of peace for twelve years, during which he marries Guinevere. Then he extends his conquests to Norway, Denmark, and Gaul. This last provokes the might of Rome, which sends him a demand for tribute, which in turn provokes Arthur's invasion of the Continent and the ultimate defeat of the Roman Empire. Geoffrey, earlier in the *Historia*, had invented the British brothers Belinus and Brennius who triumph over the Romans; Brennius for a time rules Rome. Arthur can then invoke such predecessors when he defeats the emperor Lucius and appropriates his empire. One of his vassals also refers to a Sibylline prophecy (actually invented by Geoffrey) that for the third time a Briton will seize the Roman empire. Arthur proceeds to defeat the Burgundians and, having earlier had ideas of conquering all of Europe, wants to go on to Rome; he is only checked by news of trouble at home and returns to fight his last battle. Here, in all probability using Welsh prophecies of the return of heroes like Cynan and Cadwallader, Geoffrey famously invents the story of the wounded Arthur's retreat to Avalon and his probable return.[3]

In investigating these elements added to Arthur's career, I was first struck by Arthur's confrontation with, and victory over, a Roman emperor, nominally Christian but with heathen allies. He seemed an unexpected adversary by comparison with, say, Charlemagne's Saracens: the emperor Baligant in *La Chanson de Roland* unequivocally represents the forces of evil.[4] It seems certain that this unexpected development of Arthur's career must, in part, reflect the contradictory and ambivalent insular views of Holy Roman emperors in the twelfth (and thirteenth) centuries.[5] Western emperors were inextricably associated with German kings by the 1130s, when Geoffrey was writing, and had been so ever since Otto the Great had in the tenth century revived the empire of Charlemagne. Insular attitudes to these emperors, both of the dominant Hohenstaufen dynasty (1137–1250), and their predecessors, were, despite important Anglo-German alliances,[6] cool or outright hostile, mirroring continental resentment at German arrogance and political dominance. In particular, insular chroniclers commented unfavorably on the emperor Henry V, husband of Matilda, daughter of Henry I: Orderic Vitalis in his *Ecclesiastical History* remarks that Henry V revolted against his father, Henry IV—also depicted in a hostile light and said to have committed incest with his sister—but was a tyrant like him, laying siege to Rome and arresting the pope and inevitably being excommunicated.[7] On account of Henry's sins, observes Orderic, he failed to have an heir. William of Malmesbury paints a similar disparaging picture.[8]

Tatlock has suggested that Geoffrey drew on what he had read about conditions in the reigns of two fifth- and sixth-century emperors of the Eastern Empire, Leo I (457–74) and Justinian (527–65).[9] But he would also have been able to incorporate tyrannical aspects of the emperors of his day. Arthur, as the opponent of emperor and empire, seems the virtuous British curber of a tyranny that aims at domination of the Western world and beyond. However, in his own territorial ambitions and assumption, however briefly, of the imperial mantle, might he not also be regarded as a tyrant himself?

A much more obviously mixed attitude to successful conquerors of the past is to be found in representations of Alexander in this period, who in many ways, as has often been observed, was a pagan model for Geoffrey's Arthur.[10] In the 1130s, insular portrayals of the classical hero by Walter of Châtillon and Thomas of Kent were still to come, but already accounts of him from before the Conquest mingled admiration and reproach.[11] Josephus's widely known account of Alexander, confining the hosts of Gog and Magog behind iron gates, allowed Christian historians to interpret him as a secular forerunner of Christ, although his insatiable curiosity to discover the secrets of the universe and enlarge his dominions was condemned.[12] His reign, like Arthur's, was said to last only twelve years.[13]

But Geoffrey's creation of the Arthurian biography may well also have been influenced by apocalyptic and prophetic writing, as in the Sibylline Oracles and the Revelations of Pseudo-Methodius, which envisioned two figures of power appearing in the last days of the world. The first of these, the Last World Emperor, is a positive, messianic figure,[14] a last great king representing Christ in his fight against the forces of evil who travels to

Jerusalem before he finally yields Christendom up to God and dies. The Tiburtine Oracle calls him Constans, and sees him as returning from the dead to unite the Western and Eastern halves of the empire in a reign of, in one variant, twelve years. Such ideas were as popular in Britain as in other European countries: an Anglo-Norman verse version of the Tiburtine Sibylline Prophecies was composed around 1139 (its emperor-figure appropriating Alexander's defeat of the tribes of Gog and Magog),[15] and forms of the Prophecies circulated in Wales.[16] Both Germany and France closely linked rulers like Henry IV and Charlemagne with aspects of the Last-World-Emperor legend, such as journeys to Jerusalem and a "death" that is only a sleep before a triumphant return.[17]

The second figure of power at the end of the world was the blackest possible: Antichrist, the antitype and mirror image to the Last World Emperor, who brings the emperor's rule to an end and succeeds him. A way of depicting pagan Roman emperors for Jews and early Christians, Antichrist was derived in part from a conflation of the two beasts in Revelation, the many-headed red dragon and the horned monster from the pit. Numerous types of Antichrist, such as Antiochus IV of Syria, Herod, and Nero, were supposed to anticipate his arrival. The events of his "life" parodied Christ's.[18]

Antichrist is a Jew, engendered either naturally, from sinful, often adulterous, parents, a hypocritical monk, or an evil nun; or unnaturally, from an evil spirit and a whore or, in other stories, a virgin.[19] Universal moral and religious decay and a great increase in evil are signs of his imminent birth: Lactantius (ca. 240–320) predicted that confusion, disorder, civil discords, and war resulting from the decline of Roman power[20] would show the moment when Antichrist would appear.

Antichrist is a master magician who works "wonders." He hypocritically imitates Christ; at first he wears religious garments, but underneath there is a military breastplate. He becomes a powerful king through clever alliances, and pretends to support Christianity against paganism, but in reality he is a horrible tyrant. He claims resurrection: he pretends to die and come to life again after three days. He is killed when he commits the ultimate act of hubris: climbing the Mount of Olives to ascend into heaven. The dragon is his main and constant figural representation.[21]

Twelfth century (and later) emperors were happy to be compared to the saintly Last World Emperor,[22] but were just as likely to be depicted as Antichrist by their opponents, especially those supporting the papal cause.[23] Imperial "Roman" greed was especially singled out for attack. The words of Joachim of Fiore towards the end of the twelfth century as quoted by Marjorie Reeves seem apposite here: he "shared the common view that the Roman Empire had been ordained to keep the peoples of this world within their prescribed limits. When it lusted after illicit conquest itself, it ceased to fulfil this function."[24]

If we return to Geoffrey's biography of Arthur, we can see that features of it remind us of these antithetical views of empire. Arthur is a great king—but dubiously engendered, with the aid of a still more dubiously engendered magician. He appears at a time of great national crisis, from a lineage including Constantine and Constans. He reigns for twelve years of peace and plenty. His death is apparent rather than real and he will possibly return from the dead. He checks the aggression of a greedy Roman emperor. Yet his standard is the dragon, an originally Roman ensign and not an unequivocally "good" one,[25] the sign of Antichrist in Revelation. He defeats Lucius but then is set to "become" Lucius: the Roman mantle is a potentially corrupting one.[26] "As so often in the *Historia*, Geoffrey creates a story which...invites development by later authors," wrote Rosemary Morris[27]; he gave later writers the possibility of depicting Arthur as either black or white, and his text left a space into which more critical views could be inserted.

Later writers quickly seized this opportunity. Gaimar was one of the earliest: his *Estoire des Engleis* (1135–40) shows Arthur invading Denmark, killing Guntier, father of Haveloc, and handing the land over to whomever he pleased.[28] In his version of Arthur's conquests beyond Britain, Wace's *Roman de Brut* (ca. 1155) inserts a number of details suggesting a more tyrannical, less justified career. While Arthur's first victory, over Norway, is characterized in both Geoffrey and Wace by burning and plundering, Wace extends his chronicle by describing a narrowly averted campaign against Denmark, in which the Danish king Aschil, anxious that he should not be "harmed or his good land despoiled...his gold and silver spent or his people killed or his towers surrendered," wisely decides to come to terms. Arthur is pleased with his conquests but, Wace remarks, "it was not yet enough for him."[29] As he invades France, its commander under the Romans, Frollo, is presented more sympathetically than in the *Historia*. He notes Arthur's "saisines e damages" [seizures and damages] which "as Romains lur dreit toleient" [rob Romans of their rights]. This mention of *dreit* recurs many times in the ensuing narrative in a way that implicitly challenges the king's view of his actions. Arthur himself, in a speech to his vassals after the arrival of the Roman ambassadors, says that "force n'est mie dreiture / Ainz est orguil e desmesure" [force isn't justice, but overweening pride] and "l'um ne tient mie ço par dreit / Que l'um ad a force toleit" [What is taken by force is not justly held], but he contradicts his own words by then supporting the argument for force majeure: "Or ait tut ki aver le puet; / Altre dreiture n'i estuet!" [may he who can get it, have it; there's no need for any other right!] No wonder his vassal Angusel is encouraged to claim: "Tut prendrum a dreit e a tort" [We shall seize everything [after Rome] rightly or wrongly].[30] Arthur has placed himself on the same level as his Roman adversary. Interesting, too, that Wace gives us the new information that Arthur and Guinevere are childless (9657–58), reminding us of Orderic Vitalis's comment on the connection between the emperor Henry V's political hubris and his lack of an heir.

Wace's *Brut* was, according to Laȝamon, presented to Eleanor, not Henry, but there is no reason to suppose that he intended any comparison to be made between Henry and Arthur.[31] A later twelfth-century "chronicle," *Draco Normannicus* (1167–69), by Stephen of Rouen, a monk at Bec, in fact draws a sharp contrast between the two monarchs that is distinctly unflattering to Arthur. In the midst of a eulogy of Henry, Stephen inserts an exchange of letters between him and Arthur, now a ruler over the fairy world of the Antipodes and a boastful tyrant who challenges Henry to withdraw from Brittany. Henry maintains his "right" and "law" to what he holds; the implication is that Arthur—who compares himself to Alexander, though Henry thinks he is more like Darius—has not been so scrupulous.[32]

Two Latin romances featuring Arthur, from the last quarter of the twelfth century, are not kind to him either. In *De Ortu Waluuanii*, he is arrogant, boastful, and humiliated by Gawain, in disadvantageous contrast with the good emperor of Rome, and in *Historia Meriadoci*, though the emperor of the Germans here is bad, Arthur is not much better, since he has illegally appropriated the lands of three knights and has to be forced to return them.[33]

One of the many reasons for the immense popularity of the *Historia Regum Britanniae* was the scope it allowed later writers to freely adapt its material and in particular to follow up the ambiguities in the presentation of its most famous figure. Increasingly polarized views of empire in the twelfth century, influenced alike by reactions to "Roman" emperors, especially the Hohenstaufen dynasty, and by prophetic ideas about those dominant rulers at the end of time, the Last World Emperor and Antichrist, certainly seem likely to have contributed to Geoffrey's picture of Arthur; they would also seem to have fed into a progressively more critical portrayal of the king by Geoffrey's successors in the reign of Henry II. Ideals seldom remain untarnished for long, but it is tempting to read the speed with which the Arthurian one is undermined as a reflection of the age's equivocal attitudes to the exercise of supreme power.

Notes

A precursor to this paper, focusing on Anglo-Norman romance rather than exclusively on Arthurian material, can be found in "Emperors and Antichrists: Reflections of Empire in Insular Narrative, 1130–1250," in

The Matter of Identity in Medieval Romance ed. Phillipa Hardman (Cambridge: D. S. Brewer, 2002), pp. 87–102.

1. Geoffrey of Monmouth, *Historia Regum Britanniae*, trans. Lewis Thorpe (Harmondsworth: Penguin, 1966).
2. The stories of Perseus and Alexander each show a god having his way with a closely guarded young woman. On the Alexander story influencing Geoffrey's account of Arthur's birth, see Rosemary Morris, "Uther and Igerne: a study in uncourtly love," *Arthurian Literature* 4 (1984): 70–92, at 71. The First Variant Version of the *Historia* compared Ygerna and Uther to David and Bathsheba whose child, Solomon, was considered a type of Christ.
3. Merlin is the child of a nun who has "never known a man"; Nennius, *British History and the Welsh Annals*, ed. and trans. John Morris (London: Phillimore with Rowan and Littlefield, 1980), chap. 41. Geoffrey makes the father an incubus.
4. For Geoffrey's prophecy, see *Historia* 9: 17; on "genuine" Sibylline prophecies, see Bernard McGinn, *Visions of the End: Apocalyptic Traditions in the Middle Ages*, Records of Civilization, Sources and Studies 96 (New York: Columbia University Press, 1937; repr. 1979); on the Welsh prophecies, see Weiss, "Emperors and Antichrists," p. 93, n. 23. The belief in the return of Arthur, though not Avalon, was, of course, already attested to in 1115. By the time Geoffrey writes the *Vita Merlini* (1148) he makes Morgen promise Arthur will recover; see *Geoffrey of Monmouth: The Vita Merlini*, ed. John Jay Parry, Illinois Studies in Language and Literature 10: 3 (Urbana, Ill.: The University of Illinois, 1925).
5. The creation of the Arthurian biography is certainly in part a response to the growing cult of the figure of Charlemagne for national and political purposes. See Dominique Boutet, *Charlemagne et Arthur, ou, Le roi imaginaire*, Nouvelle bibliothèque du Moyen Age 20 (Paris: Honoré Champion, 1992); Lucie Polak, "Charlemagne and the Marvels of Constantinople," in *The Medieval Alexander Legend and Romance Epic: Essays in Honour of David J. A. Ross*, ed. Peter Noble, Lucie Polak and Claire Isoz (Millwood, N.Y.: Kraus International Publications, 1982), pp. 159–71, at 167; Gaston Paris, *Histoire Poétique de Charlemagne* (Paris: Emile Bouillon, 1905), p. 55.
6. See Weiss, "Emperors and Antichrists," pp. 87–102.
7. For example, the emperor Henry V married the English Matilda, and Henry the Lion, duke of Saxony, was son-in-law of Henry II; see *The Ecclesiastical History of Orderic Vitalis*, ed. and trans. Marjorie Chibnall, Volume 5 (Oxford: Clarendon Press, 1975), Books 9 and 10: 197, 201.
8. Orderic Vitalis, *Ecclesiastical History*, 10, pp. 197, 201; *William of Malmesbury, Gesta Regum Anglorum*, ed. and trans. R. A. B. Mynors, completed R. M. Thomson and M. Winterbottom, Oxford Medieval Texts, 2 vols. (Oxford: Clarendon Press, 1998–99), Book 3: 266, 288; Book 5: 420. The fourteenth-century Anglo-Norman Mohun Chronicle even depicts Henry V as poisoning his father. I am grateful to John Spence for this information from his transcript of the manuscript.

9. J. S. P. Tatlock, "Certain Contemporaneous Matters in Geoffrey of Monmouth," *Speculum* 6 (1931): 206–24, 213–17. William Matthews, *The Tragedy of Arthur: a study of the alliterative 'Morte Arthure'* (Berkeley, Calif.: University of California Press, 1960), pp. 69–73; Betty Hill, "Alexanderromance: the Egyptian connection," *Leeds Studies in English*, n.s. 12 (1981): 186–94, 191; Julia C. Crick, *The "Historia Regum Britanniae" of Geoffrey of Monmouth IV: Dissemination and Reception in the later Middle Ages* (Cambridge: D. S. Brewer, 1991), pp. 220–21.

10. For example, the Old English translation of Orosius gives a negative picture of Alexander, begotten by the magician Nectanebus, while another Anglo-Saxon writer translates the *Epistola Alexandri Magni ad Aristotelem*, Alexander's encounters with monsters and marvels (see *Three Old English Prose Texts*, ed. Stanley Rypins, EETS OS 161 (London: Oxford University Press, 1924)); Alcuin sent Charlemagne a copy of the *Collatio cum Dindimo*, Alexander's supposed correspondence with the king of the Brahmins: see Gerrit H. V. Bunt, *Alexander the Great in the Literature of Medieval Britain* (Groningen: Egbert Forsten, 1994), pp. 14–16.

11. Ian Michael, "Typological Problems in Medieval Alexander Literature: the Enclosure of Gog and Magog," in Noble, et al, *Medieval Alexander Legend*, pp. 133–34.

12. Otto of Freising, *Chronica sive Historia de Duabus Civitatibus*, ed. A. Hofmeister (Darmstadt: W. Lammers 1961), Book 2: 154. The work draws on Orosius for this: see Orose, *Histoires Contre les Paiens*, ed. and trans. Marie-Pierre Arnaud-Lindet, 3 vols. (Paris: Les Belles Lettres, 1990), 3, chap. 23: 6. f the MS.

13. Otto was writing for his nephew, Frederick Barbarossa, who, like several other European monarchs, was compared with Alexander. See Xenja von Ertzdorff, "Alexander der Grosse und Friedrich Barbarossa: zu zwei Königsbiographie der Stauferzeit," in Noble, et al, *Medieval Alexander Legend*, pp. 57–70, at 57.

14. See Weiss, "Emperors and Antichrists," pp. 91–94.

15. *Livre de Sibile by Philippe de Thaon*, ed. Hugh Shields, Anglo-Norman Text Society 37 (London: Westfield College, 1979); it was addressed to the Empress Matilda.

16. One of the oldest is preserved in the White Book of Rhydderch: see Margaret Enid Griffiths, *Early Vaticination in Welsh*, ed. T. G. Jones (Cardiff: University of Wales Press, 1937), p. 41.

17. Weiss, "Emperors and Antichrists," pp. 92–93.

18. One of the early and most influential lives of Antichrist was the tenth-century Abbot Adso's *De Ortu et Tempore Antichristi*, written for Queen Gerberga, wife of Louis IV; it has nine different versions and is found in MSS of the *Historia* along with its late tenth-century derivative by Alboin, *De Antichristo quomodo nasci debeat*: see Adso Dervensis, *De Ortu et Tempore Antichristi*, ed. D. Verhelst, Corpus Christianorum 45 (Turnhout: Brepols, 1976), pp. 1–5, 55, and Crick, *Historia: Dissemination and Reception*, pp. 24, 31.

19. "Adso's Essay on Antichrist," Appendix to *The Play of Antichrist*, translated with an introduction by John Wright (Toronto: Pontifical Institute of Mediaeval Studies, 1967), p. 102; R. K. Emmerson, *Antichrist in the Middle Ages* (Manchester, Manchester University Press, 1981), pp. 81–82.

20. Emmerson, *Antichrist*, p. 88.

21. Emmerson, *Antichrist*, pp. 20–22, 90–92.

22. The *Play of Antichrist (Ludus de Antichristo)* was composed for Frederick Barbarossa and cast the Holy Roman Emperor in the messianic role. After his death, his son Henry VI was announced as the monarch who would unite Greeks and Romans under his rule, destroy or convert the infidels and finally, in Jerusalem, place the empire in the hands of God. His grandson, Frederick II, was particularly adept at projecting himself as the king announced by the Sibyls who would save the world. Both Philippe Auguste of France and his son Louis were linked to the Last World Emperor by an early thirteenth-century prophecy. See Weiss, "Emperors and Antichrists," p. 93, n. 20, and Elizabeth A. R. Brown, "La notion de la Légitimité et la Prophétie à la cour de Philippe Auguste," in *La France de Philippe Auguste*, ed. Robert-Henri Bautier, *Colloques internationaux du Centre national de la recherche scientifique* 602 (Paris: Editions du Centre national de la recherche scientifique, 1982), pp. 77–111, at 88.

23. Henry IV was equated with Antichrist by Gerloh of Reichersberg and Rupert of Deutz. By the thirteenth century, the rumor spread that the "miraculous" birth of Frederick II to a mother of nearly forty was due to a demon impregnating her: see Thomas Curtis Van Cleve, *The Emperor Frederick II of Hohenstaufen* (Oxford: Clarendon Press, 1972), p. 15.

24. Marjorie Reeves, *The Influence of Prophecy in the Later Middle Ages: a study in Joachimism* (Oxford: Clarendon Press, 1969), p. 304.

25. J. S. P. Tatlock, "The Dragons of Wessex and Wales," *Speculum* 8 (1933): 223–25 (Tatlock points out that the Welsh use of the dragon is late), and Michael Curley, "Animal Symbolism in the Prophecies of Merlin," *Beasts and Birds of the Middle Age*s, ed. W. B. Clark and M. T. McMun (Philadelphia: University of Pennsylvania Press, 1989), pp. 151–62, at 156, 158–59: Gildas, playing on the Welsh *draig* (= dragon, warleader), reproaches the tyrant Maelgwyn of Gwynedd with the terms *insularis draco*; Ammnianus explicitly identifies the dragon as imperial *signum* when describing Julianus Caesar's campaign against the Alamanni in 357. Curley points out that the two dragons in the Prophecies of Merlin in the *Historia* are used to suggest rancor and divisiveness within the Anglo-Norman ruling aristocracy (Michael J. Curley, *Geoffrey of Monmouth* (Twayne, N.Y.: Maxwell Macmillan International, 1994), p. 63).

26. The distinctions made by St Augustine between just and unjust wars are of value here: see Boutet, *Charlemagne et Arthur*, pp. 74–75.

27. Morris, "Uther and Igerne," p. 76.

28. Geffrei Gaimar, *L'Estoire des Engleis*, ed. Alexander Bell, Anglo-Norman Text Society (Oxford: Blackwell, 1960), lines 408–15. The later *Lai d'Haveloc* makes the picture still bleaker.

29. *Wace's Roman de Brut: a History of the British*, text and translation by Judith Weiss (Exeter, University of Exeter Press, 1999; repr. 2002), lines 9873–89.
30. Wace, *Roman*, lines 9918, 9920, 10829–30, 10831–32, 10893–94, 11035.
31. Note, however that Schmolke-Hasselmann thought the Round Table, introduced by Wace into the chronicle, symbolized Henry's policy of divesting his barons of much of their power by showing them they were all equals in his eyes: Beate Schmolke-Hasselmann, "The Round Table: Ideal, Fiction, Reality," *Arthurian Literature* 2 (1982): 41–75, at 66.
32. H. Omont, *Le Dragon Normand et autres poèmes d'Etienne de Rouen* (Rouen: Ch. Métérie, 884), pp. 105–16. See J. S. P. Tatlock, "Geoffrey and King Arthur in *Normannicus Draco*," *Modern Philology* 31 (1933): 1–18, 113–25; Mildred Leake Day, "The Letter from King Arthur to Henry II: Political Use of the Arthurian Legend in *Draco Normannicus*," *The Spirit of the Court*, 4th Congress of the International Courtly Literature Society, ed. Glyn S. Burgess and Robert A. Taylor (Woodbridge, Suffolk: Boydell and Brewer, 1985), pp. 153–57; Siân Echard, *Arthurian Narrative in the Latin Tradition* (Woodbridge, Suffolk: Boydell and Brewer, 1998), pp. 85–92.
33. *De ortu Waluuanii nepotis Arturi*, ed. and trans. Mildred Leake Day, Garland Library of Medieval Literature 15 (New York and London: Garland Pub., 1984); *Historia Meriadoci regis Cambrie*, ed. and trans. Mildred Leake Day, Garland Library of Medieval Literature 50 (New York and London: Garland Pub., 1988).

CHAPTER 12

CHILDREN OF ANARCHY: ANGLO-NORMAN
ROMANCE IN THE TWELFTH CENTURY

Rosalind Field

"A warning for future ages and to instruct our readers"

In *Piers Plowman*, Passus V, the figure of Sloth confesses that he would rather recite the stories of Robin Hood or Ranulph, earl of Chester than his prayers.[1] This remark is famous for casually providing the earliest evidence of the Robin Hood tradition, but it also indicates that the twelfth century provided a source and a subject matter for long-lasting and popular fiction.

We are concerned here with those Anglo-Norman romances, dating from the mid–twelfth century to the early thirteenth, that have been seen as definitive of insular narrative of the Anglo-Norman period.[2] These so-called ancestral or historical romances provide the earliest extant versions of several familiar romances—those dealing with Haveloc, Horn, Guy, Bevis, Ipomedon—as well as some less well-known figures—Waldef, Protheselaus, Fouke Fitzwarin.[3]

While the fashionable chronicles of Wace and Benoit and possibly the *Tristans* of Thomas and Beroul can be associated with the royal court,[4] the majority of the Anglo-Norman romances seem to owe little to the international and peripatetic court of Henry and Eleanor. They are, in short, baronial, local, and insular. They are also ambitious in scope and inter-textual with a marked preference for English settings and "history." What is of particular interest here is their concern with good rule and evident anxiety about disorder, tyranny, and the mundane realities of warfare. The primary characteristic of the Anglo-Norman romances is length—from 5,000 to over 20,000 lines of verse, either the *laisse* [assonanced verse paragraph] verse of the *chanson de geste* [Old French Epic] tradition or the more fashionable octosyllabic couplet. Such length betokens leisure on the part of both audience and author, with the accompanying socioeconomic implications. This is borne out by the fact that many of the authors are named and that the allusiveness and often humor of their narratives suggests a known and particular coterie audience. To recognize this is just to find an internal, narrative logic to support the researches of Dominica Legge and others into the likely historical contexts of patrons and audiences.[5] The evident intertextuality and traceable influences between the romances also argue a socially coherent background and even a network of like-minded authors. All these characteristics distinguish the Anglo-Norman romance from the anonymous Middle English romances that followed them.

Romance is a genre in which questions of identity, self-image, and historicity are fundamental and it is typical of the genre that it is, at one and the same time, nostalgic and prescriptive. Nostalgia for an imagined past—whether the stability of an ideal reign or the chivalric splendors of Camelot—combines with instruction for the present in new values, codes of law, marriage, or chivalry. The romances of Anglo-Norman England are no longer seen as attempts to emulate the chivalric romances of Chrétien and his followers on the continent, but rather as a deliberate and precocious insular narrative,[6] closely rooted in the experiences and concerns of its authors and audiences. This chapter aims to consider such historicity and purpose, not just in the terms of its immediate contemporary context, but also as a response to formative earlier events.

It has long been recognized that the literary antecedents of these romances are to be found in the historiography of the 1130s. The appearance of Geoffrey of Monmouth's *Historia* was followed by the imitative, or competitive, vernacular chronicle of Gaimar, the *Estoire des Engleis*. The relation between the two is well known: Gaimar's patrons, the FitzGilberts, borrowed a copy of the *Historia* from Walter Espec of Helmsley.[7] This early evidence of book-lending between Anglo-Norman aristocratic households suggests that both works were responding to as well as creating demand amongst a new audience that included the masculine and clerical, the feminine and lay. Between them these two works established the choices for later historic fiction—British or English, Latin or vernacular, prose or verse—and the urge to explore, invent, and communicate the history of the British Isles may be seen as expressive of a desire to use the past to illuminate the present. Wace's translation of Geoffrey in the early years of the reign of Henry II made the British material available to a lay public and opened the way for vernacular romances of the *matière de Bretagne* [Matter of Britain] by Chrétien and others. The material gathered and dramatically presented by Gaimar a generation earlier seems to have inspired a more localized movement of Anglo-Norman romance writing, one that offered tales set in familiar surroundings—Southampton, Grimsby, Warwick, Atleborough, the Welsh marches. Gaimar provides a starting point for Anglo-Norman romance, but he still operates within the restrictions of his, perhaps ill-defined, discipline, the vernacular chronicle.[8] The romance, still a very fluid genre in the later twelfth century, offered greater opportunities for invention and the romance writers were to take considerable freedom in constructing myths of origin for their Francophone public. The move away from chronicle enabled authors to adopt the "fictional contract"[9] and produce narratives that invite interpretation, not belief. So the depiction of events is not intended to be taken as literal history (although it may have been) but to be interpreted as guidance for the readers' present times and a way of handling the memories of the immediate past.

The plausible historicity of romance is very evident in the Anglo-Norman corpus. A significant majority are concerned with the rewriting or invention of local history or legend, using localities from Grimsby to Southampton. The main exception to this are the two romances by Hue de Rotelande, *Ipomedon* and *Protheselaus*, which are set in the Norman kingdoms of Sicily and Apulia, but in the past of the *romans d'antiquité* [romances of the ancient world]. Although the Anglo-Norman romances of English heroes are firmly localized in recognizable places, they are set in a romance past, which is evocative of Anglo-Saxon England but not recognizably authentic; it relates to pre-Conquest England with something of the imaginative freedom with which Chrétien's Britain relates to the kingdom of the Celts. The legendary England of Horn, Haveloc, Gui, Waldef, and the rest is the invention of the Anglo-Norman writers. But there were powerful precedents for this interest in the pre-Conquest past; as Christopher Hill points out, Henry I, in claiming to restore the laws of Edward the Confessor, "helped to build up a mythology of a golden Saxon past which played its part in the struggles that won Magna Carta."[10] "The reign of Henry I," as Ian Short says in his account of the genesis of Gaimar's *Estoire*, "is precisely the time when the second generation descendants of the Francophone incomers would have sought to begin integrating themselves historically as well as socially into the indigenous Anglo-Saxon culture of their adoptive homeland."[11]

So here it is the *English* past; one of the curious features of Anglo-Norman romance (with the partial exception of *Fouke Fitzwarin*) is the avoidance of Gaufredian material, including the account of the reign of Arthur. The more we understand the place of Arthurian propaganda in the construction of Plantagenet monarchy the clearer it seems that authors writing for the Anglo-Norman aristocracy and distanced from the interests of the royal

court recognized the agenda behind the development of Arthurian material and avoided it—not only in the larger picture by means of an alternative, English past, but even on the microcosmic scale of nomenclature.[12]
The romances of Hue de Rotelande are interesting here: burlesques of
chivalric *matière de Bretagne* romances, they offer a witty displacement of
Angevin propaganda, moving the setting to an alternative Norman kingdom, that of southern Italy, and thus freeing the strong didactic message of
his romances from association with royal rule in England.

In order to examine further the relationship between the period in
which Geoffrey and Gaimar were active and that of the Anglo-Norman
romances, it is first necessary to survey briefly the corpus of material
presented by these romances. They are long, complex, repetitive texts and
a full summary is not possible here—what follows selects the political
concerns and patterns discernible in these works at the expense of the more
personal and chivalric elements.

The story of Haveloc, in its two Anglo-Norman versions, as an episode
in Gaimar's *Estoire* and as a freestanding *Lai*, is the quintessential lost-heir
tale, a pattern doubled by the similar status of the heroine, Argentille. In
the Lai (dated late twelfth century) the machinations of the two villains,
Edelsi in England and Adulf in Denmark, are developed and set against the
increased status of the hero who is given a four-year rule in Denmark
before invading England to reclaim his wife's heritage. In both versions, a
good king is by definition one who consults his barons while a bad one,
such as Edelsi, cows them with a show of force. In both versions, it is
Argentille's battle strategy which brings victory over the usurper of her
lands. In the end, Haveloc, the simpleton king, claims his double kingdom,
continental and insular, by combining his inheritance with that of his wife
and he rules "par le cunseil de ses barons" [by the counsel of his barons].[13]

The *Romance of Horn* adds to the basic exile-and-return pattern a depiction of the hero's unease at losing the quest to regain his own lands amid
the easier acquisition of lands through marriage; he is chosen by the heiress,
Rigmel, but refuses to settle into marriage until he has regained his patrimony. At the court of Hunlaf of Brittany and again at the Irish court of
Gudreche, Horn proves himself the youthful supporter of a king sinking
into decrepitude and weak judgment. He is accused of unseemly ambition
through the treachery of a false friend. By the time he finally regains his
own lands and his wife, in that order, Horn has developed into the only
strong and effective king in the romance, excelling his own father. He
quells his barons, decides the fate of three countries, and attains lands and
influence beyond those originally lost. The ostensible foes here are the
"Saracens" who seize his kingdom and threaten Ireland, but the more
difficult challenge is the political mastery of those he ultimately rules. If, as

has been persuasively argued, the poem was written for Henry II's entertainment in Ireland in 1171–72, this may go some way to account for the positive portrayal of decisive kingship, unusual elsewhere in Anglo-Norman romance.[14]

Boeve is much more critical of kings and particularly of kings ruling from London. The crusading element in the plot is straightforward in its dilemmas and difficulties compared with the way the second half of this bi-partite work deals with the problems Boeve encounters as the powerful vassal of a weak and untrustworthy king.[15] Boeve himself gains a foreign crown through marriage with a converted Saracen princess. As far as his English lands are concerned, he not only reclaims his patrimony twice lost through the actions of evil rulers, but also establishes a royal dynasty through the marriage of his son to the king's daughter and heiress. Evidence from the longer Middle English redaction indicates that the anti-London feeling in the romance was at some intermediate stage increased in both content and acrimony.

There is not room here to summarize the 22,000 lines of *Waldef*, except to note that it is set in an imagined pre-Conquest England of warring petty kingdoms, and the warfare is both localized and vicious. The dangers of civil war are clearly exemplified in the enmity between friends and allies and even between fathers and sons. It adapts the "Sohrab and Rustem" theme of father-and-son battle that Malory was later to use as a synecdoche for the tragedy of civil war. The drama of the divided family, familiar to narrative since at least the Greek romances, is here used to explore the political processes of the gaining and claiming of lands through birth and marriage. The high king ruling from London is a villainous concoction of injustice, tyranny, and personal spite. As I have argued elsewhere,[16] the final effect of this long and unswerving study of a land at war is unrelentingly pessimistic.

Perhaps unexpectedly, the two romances of Hue de Rotelande, the *romans courtois*, well-informed burleques of the French courtly romance, set in the distant kingdoms of Southern Italy and peopled with characters with names derived from *romans antiques* [the romances of antiquity], provide some of the most direct political comments, often making explicit what other romances convey implicitly through their fictions. The marriage of the heiress of Calabria is the center of the plot of *Ipomedon*, and Hue is impatient with romance solutions to the serious political problems it poses—a woman is unfit to rule, because unable to bear arms, but she is allowed the choice of a husband, and her refusal to make this choice responsibly is as much the trigger for burlesque parody of romance themes as is the stubborn refusal of the hero, Ipomedon, to declare his suitability as her suitor. The measured advice of the baronial council is both ignored, and in Hue's usual style, parodied. The potential for disruption all this causes is exemplified in the climactic duel between unrecognized brothers. Ipomedon establishes a dynasty by the end of the first romance, but it is the dynastic quarrels of his sons, stirred up by the ambitious and duplicitous baron, Pentalis, that are the subject of the sequel. Powerful women play a major role in the complex plot, and again it is the scene of brothers fighting in disguise which brings an end to the warfare, although it is not until the (natural) death of the elder brother, Daunus, that Protheselaus comes into possession of the double kingdom of Calabria and Apulia, and the romance ends.

Among the second generation of Anglo-Norman romances, written in the thirteenth century, we find *Gui de Warewic* echoing the feudal concerns of the earlier romances from which it derives. A new note of serious piety is introduced, with the relationship between the hero and God expressed in feudal terms, indeed in terms of the clash of conflicting feudal loyalties. The theme of enmity between the hero and the king of England has largely evaporated, but Gui is still the means by which the king defeats the Vikings and retains his own, Christian, rule over England. The implication remains that the king needs a champion and is totally dependent on the support of good men. One likely reason for the remarkable and long-lasting success of the story of Gui is that the complexities and painful compromises of the earlier Anglo-Norman narratives are here presented simply and unproblematically as evidence of the providential protection afforded to both the hero and to England.

If there is one romance which exemplifies the themes of baronial independence, of feudal custom, and of the struggle to regain a rightful inheritance from an unjust king, it is the latest and most historically factual, the thirteenth-century *Fouke Fitzwarin*. Here Henry II himself has a walk-on part and the tensions of John's tyrannical reign are seen as rooted in earlier formative events, some as trivial as boyish quarrels over the chessboard.[17] The combination of historical actuality and wild fantasy carries this material on into the traditions of outlaw-heroes and eventually the Robin Hood legend, itself decisive in forming later attitudes towards Plantagenet kingship. A departure from the outlaw tradition, however, is to be found in *Fouke*'s clear depiction of the horrors of baronial warfare over border territories.[18] The breakdown in firm royal rule and particularly in a just distribution of lands and inheritances is shown responsible for the sufferings of the innocent populace.

From our perspective of hindsight, such narrative patterns may seem familiar enough. But looking afresh at these romances as providing a selection from a wider range of narrative possibilities available to twelfth-century authors, we can see evident expression of anxieties about civil war, social disruption, and unjust or illegal rule.

Scholars have tended to contextualize these works in the immediate historical moment of their production in the reign of Henry II, from the 1170s through to the early years of the reign of John. This period does provide ample resources for narratives of royal and baronial conflict—the murder of Becket, the centralization of royal power, the rebellion of the Young King, the conquest of Ireland, the imprisonment of Eleanor. Yet the romances do not obviously respond to these events. Romance as a genre, of course, is not chronicle, it does not provide a careful account of current affairs; but the silences are noticeable. There is no "cycle of rebellious barons" material, no response to the Becket controversy, and, *pace* Legge, no evident partisanship over the royal marriage debacle.[19] Other than the quasi-chronicle account the late romance of *Fouke Fitzwarin*, the responses to current events that are evident are largely decorative, such as the interest in Sicily or the Dublin setting of the Irish episode in the *Romance of Horn*. The more fundamental concerns, I suggest, can be traced back to the civil wars between Stephen and Matilda in the middle of the century—a period that would have provided the formative years of those who later wrote and commissioned these romances. The dispute between two rivals, who were both claiming succession through the female line, raised issues of inheritance, of gender, of law, and of the use of violence, issues which occur throughout the narratives of the next generation.

The civil war of the reign of Stephen has traditionally been called the "Anarchy," although David Crouch challenges this persuasively, placing it as a Stubbesian perspective of history in which magnates are invariably disruptive of the stabilizing power of the monarch.[20] It was a civil war caused by a double blow to the process of automatic and smooth succession—the loss of one heir, William Atheling in the White Ship in 1120, and the fact that the remaining heir was female. Both Stephen and Matilda were William the Conqueror's grandchildren—Matilda his granddaughter through her father and Stephen his grandson through his mother, Adela of Blois—a neatly balanced gender triangle.

Reduced to simple terms, the events of the mid-twelfth century in England are resonant with traditional tale patterns: the strong king loses his only son and entrusts his heiress daughter to the loyalty of his vassals, bound by oath; the challenger deprives her of her inheritance; war and divided loyalties split the kingdom. It is left to the next generation to achieve a satisfactory outcome—an acknowledged heir arrives from across the water (the only other challenger having conveniently died a natural death) and establishes a strong rule.[21] It is a pattern that allows episodes of individual heroism, dilemmas of loyalty, and scenes of warfare. Support of loyal barons is essential to the claimant's success, whether expressed in rhetorical speeches or the dashing rescue of an imprisoned damsel. It has to be said that traditional patterns do not so easily allow for complicating factors such as the wide support for the claims of Stephen and the unappealing character of the displaced heiress, Matilda.

It was a civil war that threatened to destroy the well-run kingdom of Henry I, and this danger was recognized at the time: "The wars split the nation. By 1135 England had long been a stable nation with a well-defined idea of itself as an entity. It was an idea that the Norman Conquest had not troubled in the slightest. The collapse of the nation into warring factions caused a number of people to think hard about the reasons why they were suddenly fighting amongst themselves, and then to argue about them."[22]

The creation of the literature of a generation is rooted in that generation's past, in its formative experiences, as well as in its present. We recognize this with regard to more recent literature, but the foreshortening of historical distance can obscure this perspective when dealing with early literature. It was the children of that time who were to become the authors and the audiences of the reign of Henry II.[23] With this in mind, we can look again at the narrative patterns of the "ancestral" romances.

These are narratives of disruption—the initial crisis is the loss of the strong father/king and the exile (apparent loss) overseas of the heir, often accompanied by a loss of identity. Although the clear line of succession from father to son is seen as vital in maintaining social order, there is no sign of sacerdotal kingship (except perhaps for Haveloc's flame), but rather rulers are judged by their actions particularly in upholding the law. There are variations on the theme of a land suffering from anarchy or tyranny; Edelsi's Lindsey, Waldef's England, the littoral lands of Horn's travels. Each hero is deprived of his rightful heritage and the main concern of the narrative lies in his effort to regain and hold his lands in a world governed by injustice and treachery. The hero's motivation, character and actions are a conscious self-expression of the ideals of twelfth-century feudal society, responsive to but not dominated by the claims of romantic love and Christian piety.

Fear of the insecurity caused by female inheritance initiates action in *Ipomedon, Horn*, and *Haveloc*, but there is also fear of unchecked royal power, often centered in London (*Boeve, Waldef*). The exiled heir is dependent on the support of loyal nobles and often on the support of a strong woman, who is his equal in rank. Women may well be not only active wooers[24] but also active political figures, not the passive prizes of chivalric romance. In a century of figures such as Empress Matilda, Matilda of Boulogne, and Eleanor of Aquitaine, narrative will support heroines like Josiane, Argentille, La Fière, and Matilda Walter, although Medea, a powerful older woman supplying the love-interest in *Protheselaus* is comically testing generic limits.

Villains are of two types; powerful barons and courtiers who turn out to be plausible traitors capable of manipulating the system and attracting followers, or tyrannical rulers using fear and autocratic power to cow a nation. The fear of civil war, sometimes in its symbolic configuration of combat between brothers, provides a narrative concern stronger than love or individual chivalric achievement: brother fights brother in both of Hue's romances and father fights sons in *Waldef*. There is no shortage of violence, which is after all the romance medium for self-expression and achievement, but the violence is unexpectedly reflexive, its consequences and its victims are often acknowledged: *Waldef* presents a nightmare vision of England as a patchwork of warring mini-kingdoms, and the innocent are shown to suffer in *Fouke Fitzwarin* and *Romance of Horn*. It comes as something of a relief to encounter a genuinely external foe, as in the occasional appearance of the Saracens as adversaries. There is no material here to support an opposition along ethnic or language lines. Partly this is because there is an occluding of English-Norman differences: the English are invisible because they are *us*—or because they share the invisibility of all lower ranks in courtly romance. There is no sense of superiority, none of that expression of Norman identity we find in the chronicles of an earlier generation, such Ailred's Latin dramatization of the Battle of the Standard.[25] But there are political enemies and rivals, bad kings in plenty, true and false friends, corrupt courts of law, all of which encourage consideration of good rule, justice, and social cohesion.

The conclusion is usually optimistic with the restoration of the lost heir to his lands or kingdom. However, this achievement is not his alone but is shown to be dependent on essential support, from his followers, his lover, even, in the case of Boeve, his horse: the egocentric solitary romance hero is not appreciated in these narratives. The restoration is of the stability of the father's reign, often increased by linking with more lands through marriage to give a joint kingdom, a greater inheritance than that left by the father. However, in some cases the anxieties may be strong enough to carry a generically transgressive pessimistic conclusion—the death of the hero in *Waldef* and the abandoning of England in *Boeve*. We can therefore read the Anglo-Norman romances as responses to civil war, interrogating the insecurity of the kingdom and the individual heritage, often symbolically one and the same. They show life as surprisingly hard and insecure for a genre that is usually noted for its lifestyle and aspirational tone. Personal adventure, love, and exotic travel can be developed against this underlying concern—so personal development results in wise rulers, domestic happiness reflects or creates political harmony, travel brings the protagonists home.

These are not just romance commonplaces, but a selective and coherent pattern, indicative of inter-textuality and a sense of purpose: part celebration, part exemplary warning. In this respect the label "ancestral" seems unconvincing. As texts of self-aggrandizement for particular families they are remarkably ineffectual to the extent that there remains uncertainty as to which families are the recipients of this attention. With the obvious exception of the Fitzwarins we find nothing remotely comparable to Chrètien's clear identification of Marie de Champagne. It seems rather that they are a more generalized expression of the interests of the baronial and landowning classes.[26] The interest in patrons is symptomatic of a certain approach to history, that of "great men" and more recently, of their women, supported by the records of families and public affairs. I would suggest that it is the clerical authors, rather than the patrons and audiences, who were responsible for the cohesive nature of Anglo-Norman romance in a program of educating the leaders of the nation in public and self-governance. Although such men, and women, may well have been literate,[27] we are not looking at lay authorship but at the activities of clerks whose education equipped them to contribute to the debates of the time, and whose privileged position vis-à-vis their audience can be gauged from the tone of the romances. We should perhaps be asking, not so much what interest of the patron the work serves, but what the patron and the wider audience would learn from the work.

Clanchy has drawn attention to the statement in the cartulary of Romsey Abbey (situated in the worst area of the "Anarchy") that the Abbey had lost almost everything in the "dark and gloomy" days of King Stephen, and that the volume was to be "a warning for future ages and to instruct our readers."[28] Crouch has similarly identified the civil-war period as one engaged in debate in Latin. Within a generation this debate moves into the vernacular and engages wider attention through the medium of romance. These romances offer evidence that the anxieties of the audience about the state of the country are recognized and also that the audience is instructed in the qualities of good rule, of the importance of law, and the equal dangers of unbridled individual violence and unchecked royal rule.

Such works are the product of a vernacular literary movement. Although literary history has long been attentive to the struggle between the two vernaculars English and French, during the centuries between the Conquest and Chaucer, it has to some extent been at the expense of a clear sense of the purpose and achievements of writers working deliberately in the vernacular despite their personal capabilities in the more prestigious international and academic language of Latin. Clanchy makes the point that the Latinate clergy such as Master Nicholas of Guildford, Master Thomas of the *Romance of Horn*, Fantosme, Orm, Layamon, Benedeit, and the cleric Philip de Thaon, were also the pioneers of vernacular writing. "There is no real contradiction in this paradox. . .often perhaps it was the most sophisticated and not the most primitive authors who experimented with vernaculars."[29] So the choice of language is governed not by the capabilities of the author, but by the audience he wishes to address and the freedom of working outside Latin. In writing in the vernacular, these clerks are not simply popularizing or patronizing, but moving onto the territory of those whose actions and decisions are vital to the future of the realm— "the few dozen baronial families who constituted the powerful elite of medieval England."[30]

There is also evidence that the clerks made up a circle of professional, perhaps even personal, association; this would account for the inter-textuality of the Anglo-Norman romance corpus. Hue de Rotelande jokes about Walter Map's skill in the art of lying,[31] and his romances, like the *Romance of Horn* of "Mestre Thomas," engage in debate with fashionable Tristan material. The relationships between *Horn, Boeve, Waldef*, and *Gui* suggest activities ranging from engaged debate to wholesale borrowing.

We can appreciate what opportunities the fledgling genre of romance offered the Anglo-Norman clerical writers: a historical perspective on the present; a vernacular freedom with facts and styles; the chance to sugar the didactic pill with sex, violence, and humor and to hold up a mirror to their audience; to create narratives that could explore and even exorcise the anxieties concerning society and disorder; and to achieve the ambition of all writers at all times—to influence the course of public events through well-placed words in the right quarter. It may be that their efforts have borne fruit in the outcome of the next breakdown in regnal order, a crisis that resulted not in anarchy, but in Magna Carta.

Finally, to return to the evidence of Sloth, I would suggest that we are now able to recognize the context for his other reference to popular narrative. Ranulph II, "aux Gernons" [with the moustache], Earl of Chester (ca. 1100–53), experienced a dramatic war. Apparently motivated by the desire to regain lands seized by Stephen, he was engaged in the siege of Lincoln in which Stephen was captured, but later was imprisoned by the king.[32] The careers of his son and grandson, who makes an appearance in *Fouke Fitzwarin* and is the usual candidate for Langland's "rimes,"[33] suggest that the heroic figure here may be a composite of identically named lords, along the lines of the romance of the collective Fouke Fitzwarins. It is not surprising that such a figure should become a popular hero. The period of the "Anarchy" was one of those dramatic and uncomfortably interesting periods that produce colorful figures and significant narratives. The reign of Henry II saw these events transformed into memorable and long-lasting fiction that was to affect the development of English narrative throughout the middle ages and beyond. From Anglo-Norman the line is direct through translation to the Auchinlech Manuscript, with its narratives of the

"Knights of England,"[34] and the so-called Matter of England romances. The characteristics that have long been identified as distinguishing English romance from continental originate in the Anglo-Norman period, more precisely in the second half of the twelfth century. The literature of the reign of Henry II is seminal to the development of English fiction.

Notes

1. "I kan noght parfitly my Paternoster as the preest it syngeth, / But I kan rymes of Robyn Hood and Randolf Erl of Chestre" [I do not know my "Our Father" accurately, as the priest sings it, but I do know the rhymes about Robin Hood and Randolf Earl of Chester] (William Langland, *Piers Plowman*, ed. A. V. C. Schmidt (London: Dent, 1978), 5: 395–96).

2. Other twelfth-century romances are Thomas of Kent's *Roman de Toute Chevalerie* and *Amadas et Ydoine* as well as the various versions of the Tristan story. For details of all Anglo-Norman romances and their manuscripts, see Ruth J. Dean and Maureen B. M. Boulton, *Anglo-Norman Literature: a Guide to Texts and Manuscripts*, Anglo-Norman Text Society, Occasional Publications Series 3 (London: Birkbeck College, 1999): 88–102.

3. Geffrei Gaimar, *L'Estoire des Engleis*, ed. Alexander Bell, Anglo-Norman Text Society 14, 15, 16 (Oxford: Blackwell, 1960); *Le Lai d'Haveloc*, ed. Alexander Bell (Manchester: Manchester University Press, 1925), trans. Judith Weiss, *The Birth of Romance* (London: Dent, 1992); Thomas, *The Romance of Horn*, ed. Mildred Katharine Pope, Anglo-Norman Text Society 9, 10, 12, 13 (Oxford: Blackwell, 1955, 1964), trans. Judith Weiss in *The Birth of Romance* (London: Dent, 1992); *Der anglonormannische "Boeve de Haumtone,"* ed. A. Stimming (Halle: Niemeyer, 1899); *Le Roman de Waldef,* ed. A. J. Holden, Bibliotheca Bodmeriana Textes 5 (Cologny-Geneva: Fondation Martin Bodmer, 1984); *Gui de Warewic: Roman du XIIIe siecle*, ed. Alfred Ewert (Paris: Champion, 1932–3); *Hue de Roteland: Ipomedon*, ed. A. J. Holden (Paris: Klincksieck, 1989); *Protheselaus*, ed. A. J. Holden, Anglo-Norman Text Society 47, 48, 49 (London: Birkbeck College, 1993); *Fouke le Fitz Waryn*, ed. E. J. Hathaway, P. T. Ricketts, C. A. Robson, and A. D. Wilshere, Anglo-Norman Text Society 26, 27, 28 (Oxford: Blackwell, 1975–76), trans. Stephen Knight and Thomas H. Ohlgren, in *Robin Hood and Other Outlaw Tales* (Kalamazoo Mich.: TEAMS Medieval Texts, 1997). The romances have been recently discussed in M. Dominica Legge, *Anglo-Norman Literature and its Background* (Oxford: Clarendon Press, 1963); Susan Crane, *Insular Romance: Politics, Faith and Culture in Anglo-Norman and Middle English Literature* (Berkeley: University of California Press, 1986); William Calin, *The French Tradition and the Literature of Medieval England* (Toronto: University of Toronto Press, 1994); Rosalind Field, "Romance in England, 1066–1400," chap. 6 in *The Cambridge History of Medieval English Literature*, ed. David Wallace (Cambridge: Cambridge University Press, 1999), pp. 152–176.

4. See John Gillingham's paper in this volume and on Eleanor's putative patronage of Wace, Ian Short, "Patrons and Polyglots: French Literature in Twelfth-Century England," *Anglo-Norman Studies* 14, Proceedings of the Battle Conference, 1991 (Woodbridge, Suffolk: Boydell and Brewer): pp. 229–49, at 231, 237–38. However, the speculation is attractive enough to re-appear, with varying degrees of emphasis, in the recent *Cambridge History of Medieval English Literature*, ed. Wallace, pp. 42, 97, 267.

5. Legge, *Anglo-Norman Literature*; Crane, *Insular Romance*.

6. M. Dominica Legge, "La Précocité de la Litterature Anglo-normande," *Cahiers de Civilisation Medievale* 8 (1965): 327–349.

7. Ian Short, "Gaimar's Epilogue and Geoffrey of Monmouth's *Liber vetustissimus,*" *Speculum* 69 (1994): 223–43.

8. Peter Damian-Grint, *The New Historians of the Twelfth-Century Renaissance: Inventing Vernacular Authority* (Woodbridge, Suffolk: Boydell and Brewer, 1999).

9. D. H. Green *The Beginnings of Medieval Romance: Fact and Fiction 1150–1220* (Cambridge: Cambridge University Press, 2002), pp. 1–17.

10. Christopher Hill, "The Norman Yoke," chap. 3 in *Puritanism and Revolution: Studies in Interpretation of the English Revolution of the 17th Century* (London: Secker & Warburg, 1958), pp. 50–122, at 58.

11. Short, "Gaimar's epilogue," p. 323.

12. Rosalind Field, "What's in a Name?: Arthurian Name-Dropping in the *Roman de Waldef*," in *Arthurian Studies in Honour of P. J. C. Field*, ed. Bonnie Wheeler, Arthurian Studies 57 (Cambridge: D. S. Brewer, 2004), pp. 63–4.

13. *L'Estoire des Engleis*, ed. Bell, p. 750.

14. Judith Weiss, "Thomas and the Earl: Literary and Historical Contexts for the *Romance of Horn*," in *Tradition and Transformation in Medieval Romance*, ed. Rosalind Field (Cambridge: D. S. Brewer, 1999), pp. 1–14. The treatment of the kingship of Horn is discussed by David Burnley in "The *Roman de Horn*: Its Hero and Its Ethos," *French Studies* 32 (1978): 385–97.

15. For the bi-partite nature of *Boeve* see Judith Weiss, "The date of *Boeve de Haumtone,*" *Medium Aevum* 55 (1986): 238–41.

16. Rosalind Field, "*Waldef* and the Matter of/with England," in *Medieval Insular Romance: Translation and Innovation*, ed. Judith Weiss, Jennifer Fellows, and Morgan Dickson (Cambridge: D. S. Brewer, 2000), pp. 25–40.

17. For the youthful chessboard fight between Fouke and John and the parental response of Henry II, see *Fouke Fitzwarin* (ed. Hathaway et al., at pp. 22–23).

18. For further analysis of the treatment of warfare in *Fouke Fitzwarin* see Rosalind Field, "Romance as history, history as romance," in *Romance in Medieval England*, ed. Maldwyn Mills, Jennifer Fellows, and Carol Meale (Cambridge: D. S. Brewer, 1991), pp. 171–72, at 163–73.

19. Legge's suggestion that the use of the *laisse* in Anglo-Norman romance was a sign of the rejection of the fashionable couplet romances associated with Eleanor of Aquitaine at the time of her disgrace, has not gained wide acceptance: "The Influence of Patronage on Form in Medieval French

Literature," in *Stil-und Formprobleme in der Literatur*, ed. Paul Boekmann (Heidelberg: Carl Winter Universitätsverlag, 1959), pp. 136–41.

20. David Crouch, *The Reign of King Stephen, 1135–1154* (Harlow: Longman, 2000), pp. 2–7.

21. I have discussed this in more detail in "The King Over the Water: Exile and Return Revisited," in *Cultural Encounters in Medieval English Romance*, ed. Corinne Saunders (Cambridge: D. S. Brewer, 2005).

22. Crouch, *Reign of King Stephen*, p. 1.

23. This approach is taken by Pope in her introduction: "[Thomas's] formative period fell in the last years of the reign of Henry I and the turmoil of that of Stephen" (Pope, *Romance of Horn*, 2: 124), and also by Donald R. Howard in his biography of Chaucer: "Foremost of Chaucer's childhood memories as the one he shared with all his generation: the Black Death of 1348–1349"; *Chaucer and the Medieval World* (London: Weidenfeld & Nicholson, 1987), pp. 12–19.

24. A recurrent motif in Anglo-Norman romance; see Judith Weiss, "The Wooing Woman in Anglo-Norman Romance," in Mills et al., *Romance in Medieval England*, pp. 149–162.

25. Christopher Baswell, "Latinitas," chap. 5 in Wallace, *Cambridge History of Medieval English Literature*, p. 131.

26. See Crane, *Insular Romance*, pp. 16–17.

27. Crouch, *Reign of King Stephen*, p. 122.

28. M. T. Clanchy, *From Memory to Written Record: England 1066–1307* (Oxford: Blackwell, 1979, 2nd ed. 1993, repr. 2003), pp. 101–2.

29. Clanchy, *From Memory*, p. 215.

30. Danny Danzinger and John Gillingham, *1215: the Year of Magna Carta* (London: Hodder & Stoughton, 2003), p. 176.

31. *Ipomedon*, ed. Holden, line 7186.

32. See Crouch, *Reign of King Stephen*, pp. 137–42, 225–29; Henry of Huntingdon gives Ranulph some stirring speeches; see *Henry, Archdeacon of Huntingdon, Historia Anglorum*, ed. and trans. Diana E. Greenway, Oxford Medieval Texts (Oxford: Clarendon Press, 1996), pp. 724–38.

33. Since Skeat, editors of *Piers Plowman* have accepted Ritson's identification of Ranulph as Ranulph III (1170–1232). As this seems to rest solely on Ritson's obsession with minstrels (a group of whom came to the rescue of Ranulph II in a Welsh skirmish) it seems worth considering Wright's intervening opinion that the Earl referred to was Ranulph "des guernons."

34. Thorlac Turville-Petre, *England the Nation: Language, Literature and National Identity 1290–1340* (Oxford: Clarendon Press, 1996).

INDEX OF MANUSCRIPTS

INDEX